MOBILE APPLICATIONS

FOR STUDENTS AND PROGRAMMERS

iTSt@rt

Wojciech Jaśkowiec, Krzysztof Kułacz, Marta Kanafa-Suchan
Edited by: Marta Kanafa-Suchan, Krzysztof Kułacz

The book "Mobile Applications for Students and Programming Technicians" is intended for anyone who wants to learn about creating mobile applications for the Android system.
In the first part of the book, the reader is introduced to the intricacies of the Java language. They thoroughly learn about topics such as object - oriented and concurrent programming. Issues such as classes, objects, and threads are discussed.
In the second part, we learn about creating mobile applications in the Android Studio environment. The visual aspect of the application is created using XML markup language, while Java is responsible for controlling the application's operation. The book is a detailed guide for anyone interested in creating Mobile Applications.

Cover design: Daniel Pliszka
Editing and layout: Marek Smyczek, Marta Kanafa - Suchan
Translate: Joanna Margowniczy

IT publishing house

http://www.itstart.pl
email: itstart@itstart.pl

ISBN 978-83-67989-18-3

First edition – Piekary Śląskie 2025

Table of contents

CHAPTER 1

PREFACE

1. Preface

The book discusses the creation of Mobile Applications in the Android system. When creating such applications, developers currently have a wide range of tools and languages to choose from. The tool discussed in this book, the Android Studio SDK, allows the creation of applications in several programming languages, such as Kotlin, Java, and C++.

The choice of Java as the main language in this study is dictated by the fact that this book is primarily intended for technical school students specializing in programming. The curriculum for this subject includes creating mobile applications for the Android system using XML and programming in Java. Hence, the choice of technology was obvious.

If the reader is interested in expanding their knowledge of mobile application development and would like to compare the Java language presented in this book with Kotlin, I highly recommend reading the book titled "Modern Mobile Applications – Kotlin and Android JetPack Compose."

All source codes are available at: http://moapl.itstart.pl. To gain full access to the files, you need to log in using a username: **moapl** and password: **moapi!@mobVERen**

CHAPTER 2

INSTALLATION AND CONFIGURATION OF SOFTWARE

1 Installation and Configuration of Software

Java is one of the most popular programming languages. It is an object - oriented, high - level, and structured language based on classes. This language is quite portable because it is interpreted by the multi - platform Java Virtual Machine (JVM), which converts source code into bytecode.

This language is characterized by strong typing, meaning that expressions have a predetermined data type that cannot be changed during program execution. The basic concepts of Java were taken from the Smalltalk language and partially from C++, making Java's syntax similar to that of C++.

Java was designed to be user - friendly. It includes many built - in libraries that provide ready - made solutions, which is a significant convenience for programmers. It is a statically typed language, ensuring that syntactic and type correctness is checked before the program is executed, making it easier to find potential errors.

This language is platform - independent, so it can run on systems such as Windows, Linux, and MacOS. It is also worth mentioning that Java is a universal language. It is most commonly used for creating the backend of web applications, but it has many other applications. Java consists of three main components:

- **JDK (Java Development Kit):** A multi - platform development environment offering libraries and tools needed to create applications. It includes tools such as javac (for compiling), jdb (for debugging), jar (for archiving), and javadoc (for generating documentation).
- **JRE (Java Runtime Environment):** A set of components responsible for creating and running applications.
- **JVM (Java Virtual Machine):** A virtual machine that allows bytecode to be executed.

Java was created by a working group led by James Gosling, who was working for Sun Microsystems at the time, and the language first appeared in 1995.

Figure 2.1 Changing Java logos over the years. From the left, the oldest, and on the right, the current and widely used one.

Games such as Minecraft, Street Fighter II, and Wolfenstein RPG are just examples of projects written in this language. Some of the most well - known applications include Gmail, OpenOffice, NetBeans, and Eclipse. Knowledge of Java is also useful for creating mobile applications. As you can see, Java is used daily by the most popular corporations worldwide.

Figure 2.2 Minecraft is one of the most popular games in the world.

1.1 Installation of the Java Environment

Starting your journey with Java programming requires preparing your computer to work in this environment. The two basic elements you will need are the previously mentioned JDK and a development environment, known as an IDE (Integrated Development Environment). For our purposes, we will use IntelliJ IDEA by JetBrains. Of course, this is not the only program you can use. There are many other environments available on the market, and the choice is entirely up to the programmer.

1.1.1 Installation of JDK for Windows

The installation process begins with downloading the JDK itself. The link to the package can be found at https://www.oracle.com/java/technologies/downloads/.

Select the appropriate installation file for your system. By default, the download page will display the latest version of the JDK, but there are situations where an older version of Java is needed. Available versions can be found in the **Java archive** tab.

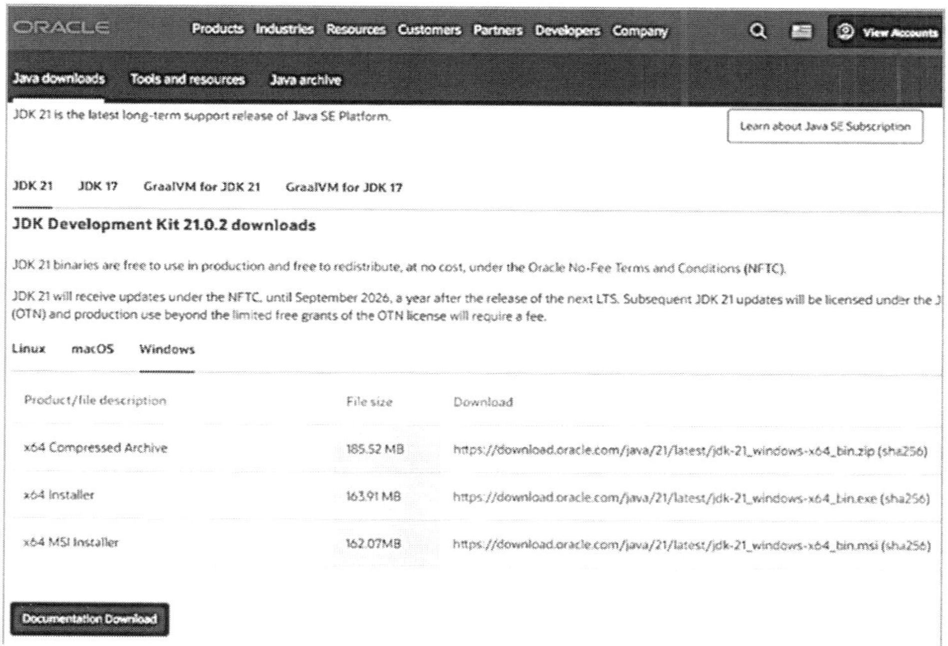

Figure 1.1 The JDK environment can be downloaded from the Oracle website.

Download and run the installation file. The system will display a message asking for permission to make changes to your computer. Select **Yes**. The welcome window of the installation program will open, where you click **Next**.

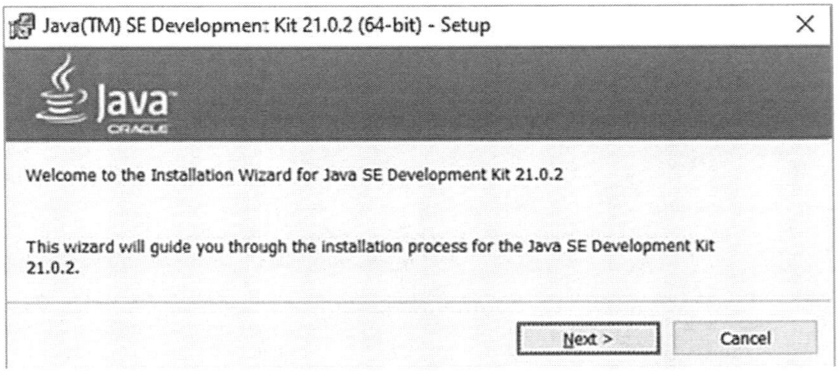

Figure 2.4 Welcome window of the installer.

Now, choose the location cn your computer where Java will be installed.

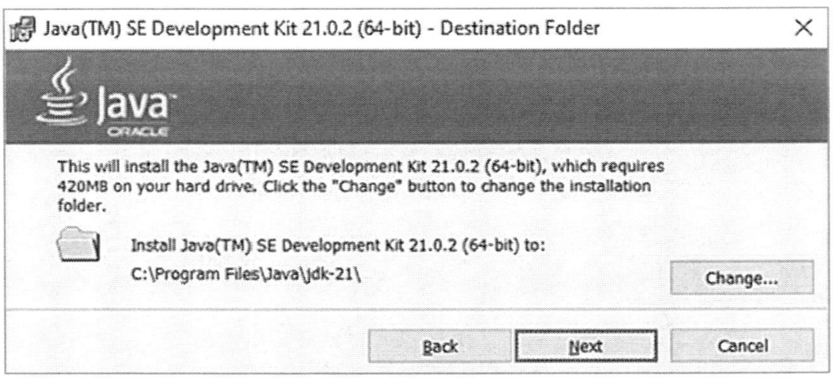

Figure 2.5 Specifying the location for JDK.

Change or keep the location and click "Next". The installation will begin shortly after.

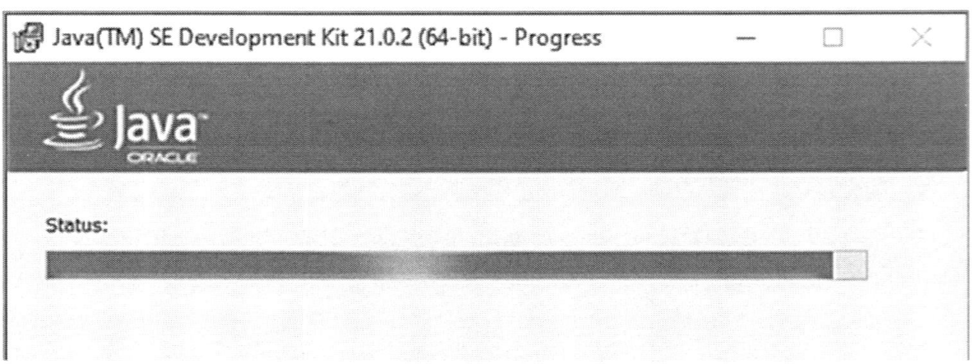

Figure 2.6 Installation progress

After completion, you will receive a message indicating that the JDK has been successfully installed. Click **Close** to exit the program.

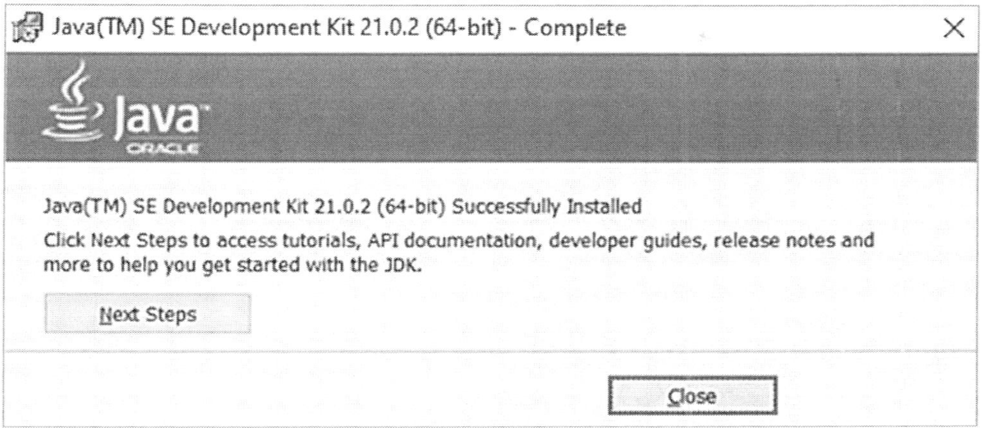

Figure 1.2 Successful installation.

However, this is not the end of our actions, as we now need to add the Java path to the environment variables. For this, we need the exact location where it was installed. If we did not change the default path during the installation process, it will look like the one below. It is important to enter the JDK folder and then the **bin** folder. Copy the path:

Figure 1.3" Path to the "bin" folder.

Now, click the Windows button and search for the phrase **"Edit system environment variables."**

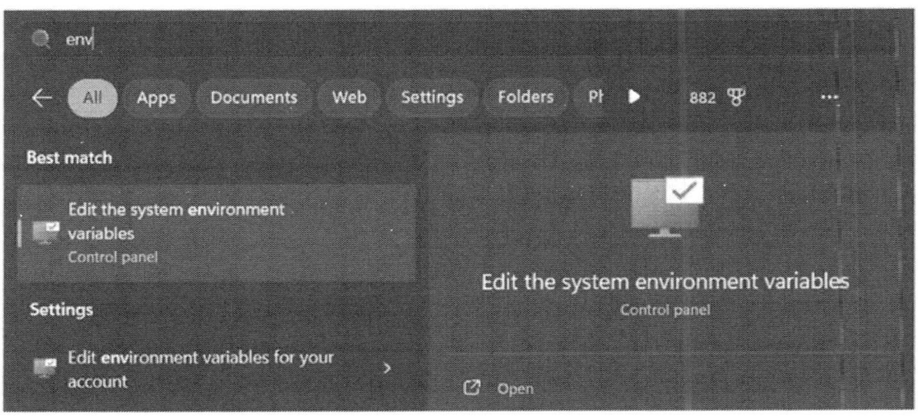

Figure 1.4 Searching for environment variables.

The system properties window will appear. Go to **"Environment Variables...".**

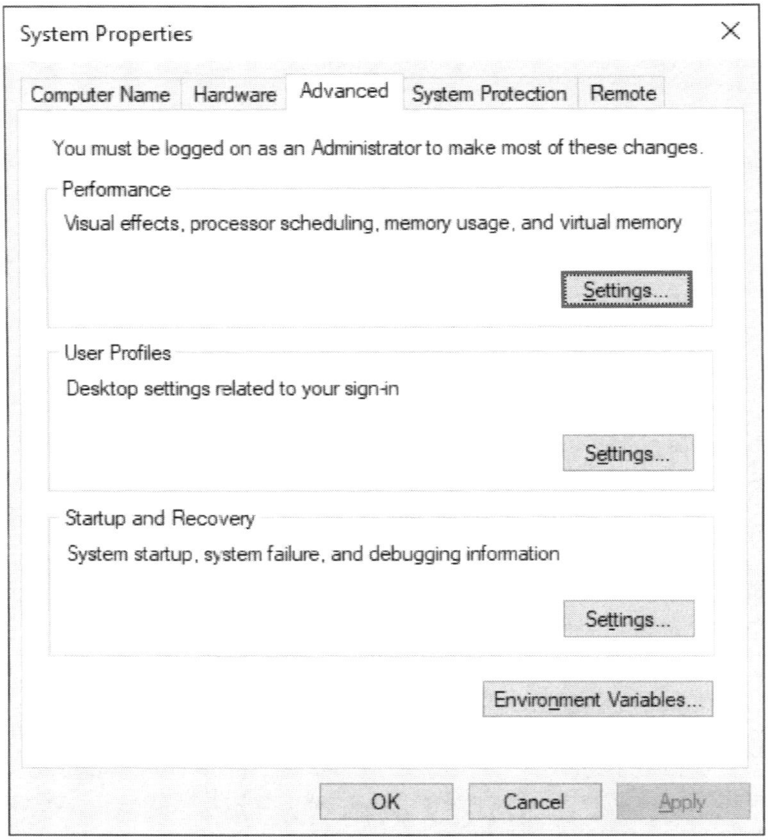

Figure 1.5 System properties window.

In the user variables table, select "**Path**" and click "**Edit**".

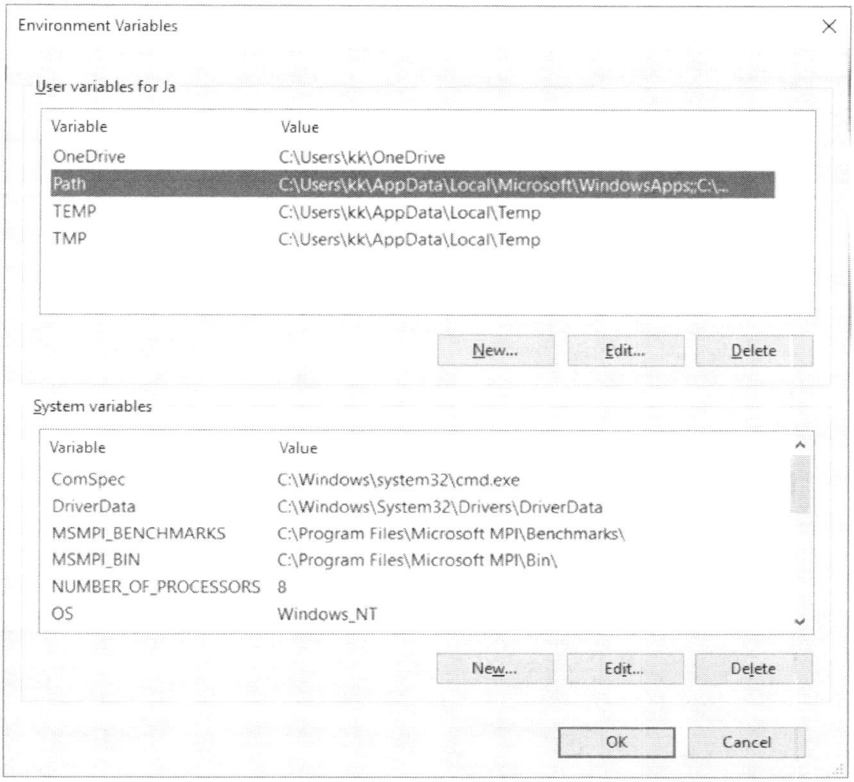

Figure 1.6 Environment variables window.

Now, we will add a new variable. Click "**New**" and paste our path.

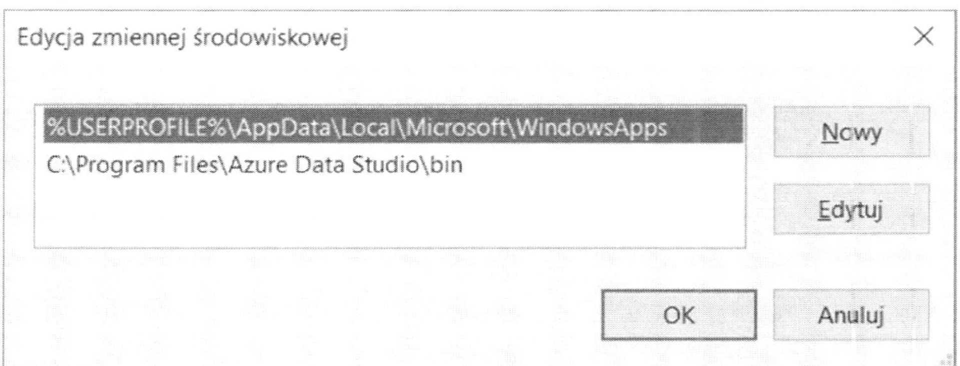

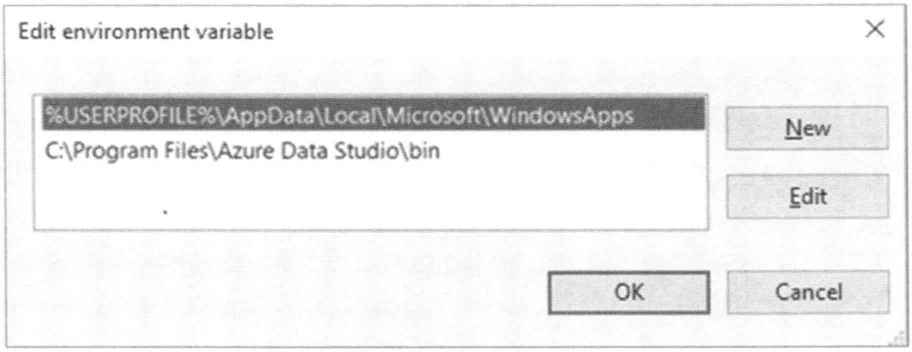

Figure 1.7 Adding a new variable.

Finally, confirm all the open windows by clicking "**OK**."

The last step we can take is to check if the JDK was successfully installed. To do this, open the command prompt (CMD) and type the command **java - version**. If everything went well, the installed version of Java will be displayed.

Figure 1.8 Displaying information about the installed Java version in the CMD console.

Now our system is ready to compile and run applications written in Java. We still need an editor to write the code. Theoretically, a simple notepad could be used for this purpose, but it is impractical, and programming in it would be tedious and time - consuming. A dedicated development environment will work much better.

1.2 Installation of IntelliJ IDEA for Windows

The installation process begins by downloading the environment from: **https://www.jetbrains.com/idea/download.**

You can choose between the **Ultimate** and **Community Edition**. The former requires a license. There are several ways to obtain it for free, such as having student status, but it is mainly intended for creating more complex and extensive projects. For our purposes, it is not needed. Therefore, we choose the **Community Edition.**

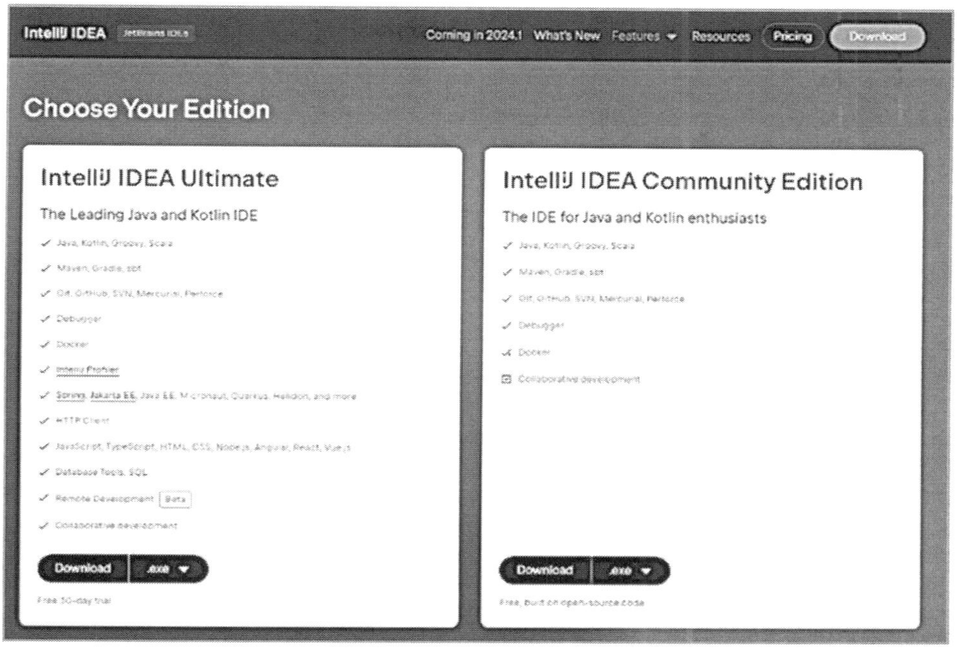

Figure 1.9 IntelliJ IDEA from the manufacturer's website.

Click "**Download**," and once the installer is downloaded, run it.

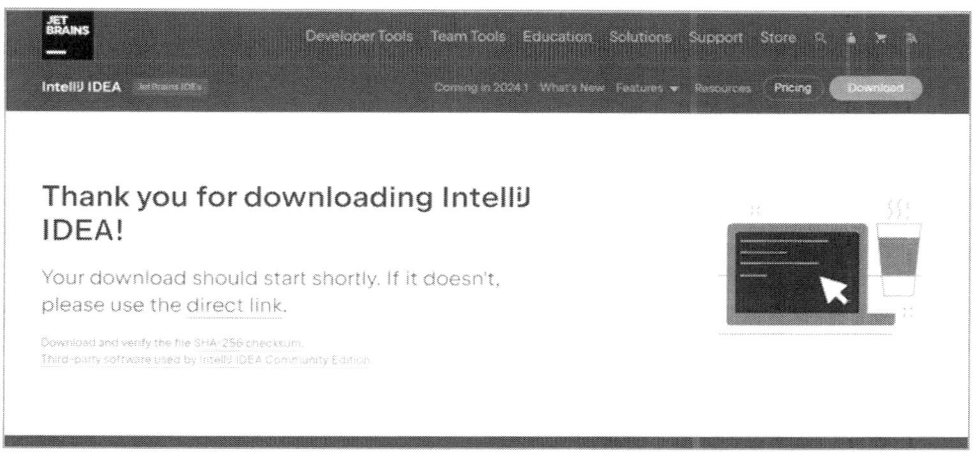

Figure 1.10 Download confirmation page.

In the welcome window, click "**Next**."

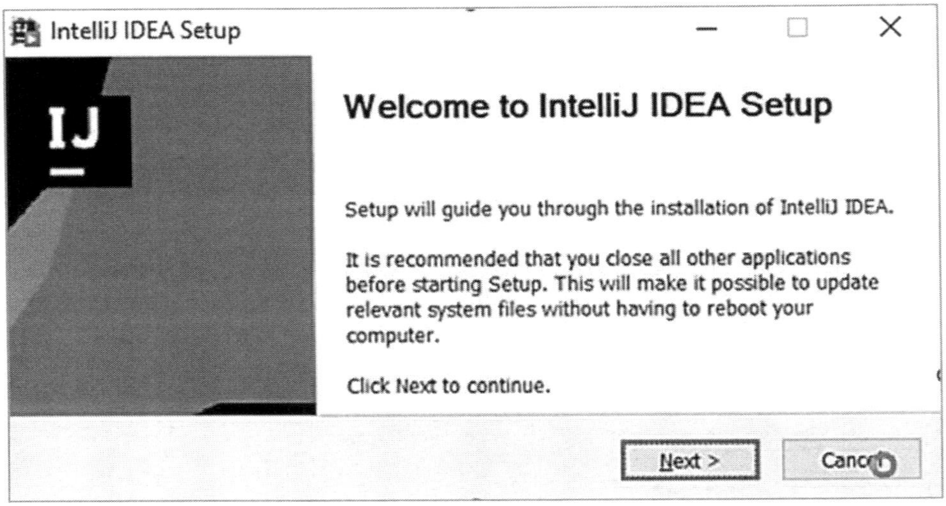

Figure 1.11 Welcome window of the IntelliJ installer.

Now, we can decide where the program will be installed. Then, proceed to the next step.

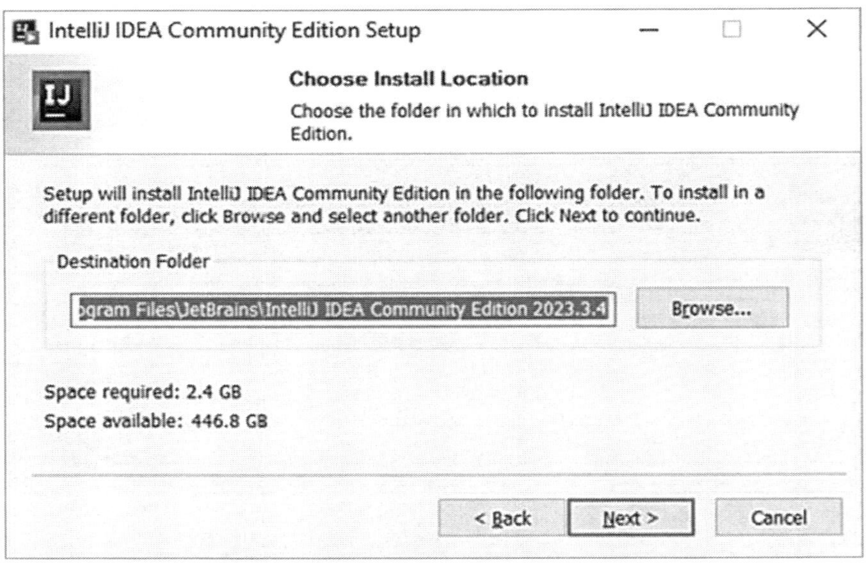

Figure 1.12 Choosing the installation location.

At this stage, we have several options that we can include in the installation. All these settings can be changed later, but it is worth checking the boxes now:

- **Add "Open Folder as Project";**
- **Add "bin" folder to the PATH;**
- **.java** and **.pom** in the **"Create Associations"** tab.

Then click "**Next**."

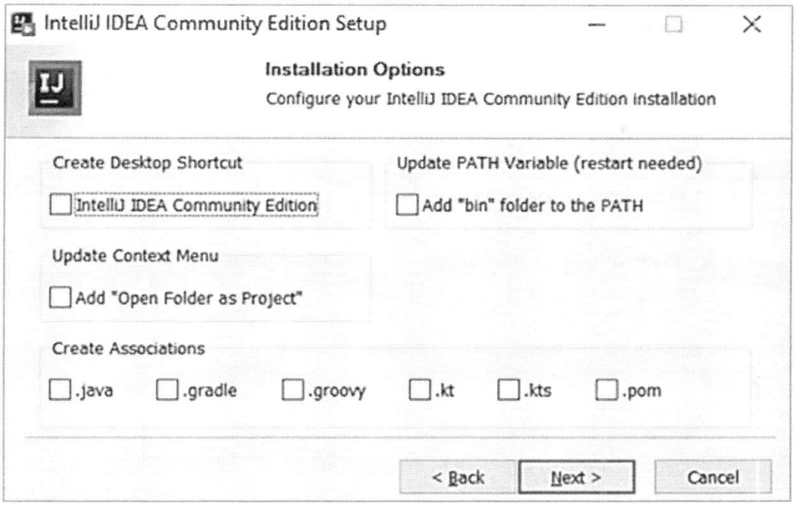

Figure 1.13 Configuration selection window for installation.

A window will appear asking for the location of application shortcuts. It is best to leave the default value. Click "**Install**" and wait for the program to complete the installation.

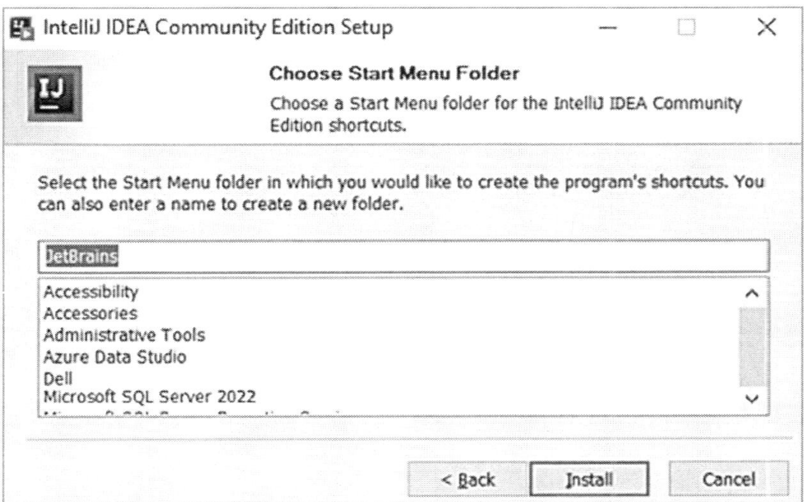

Figure 1.14 Start Menu folder selection window.

We can monitor its progress in real - time.

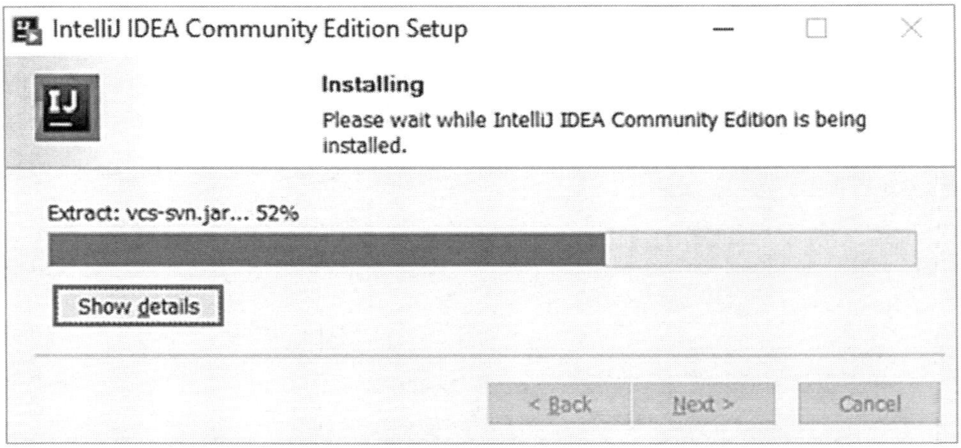

Figure 1.15 Installation progress bar.

The program has been installed. Now we can launch it.

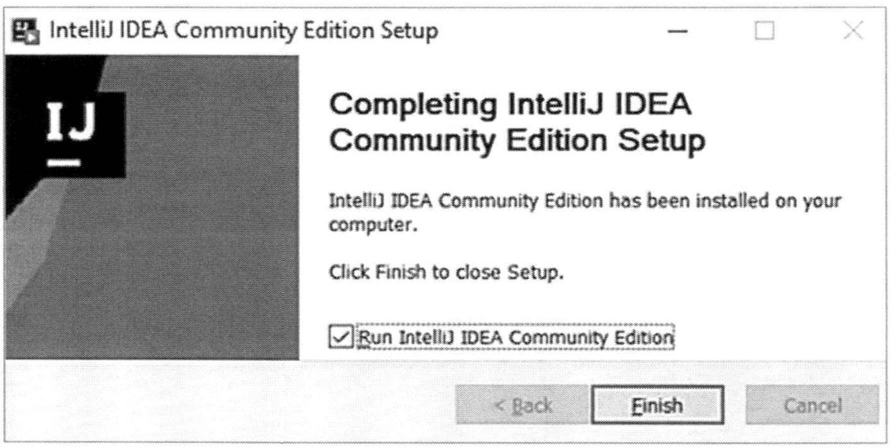

Figure 1.16 Installation completed successfully.

Upon the first start, a terms of use message will be displayed, which you need to read and accept.

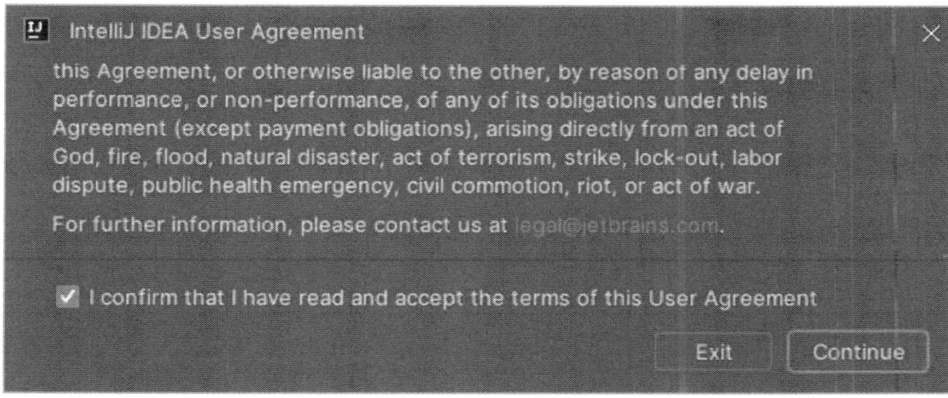

Figure 1.17 Terms of use.

From now on, we can freely use the program. Let's start by creating a new project.

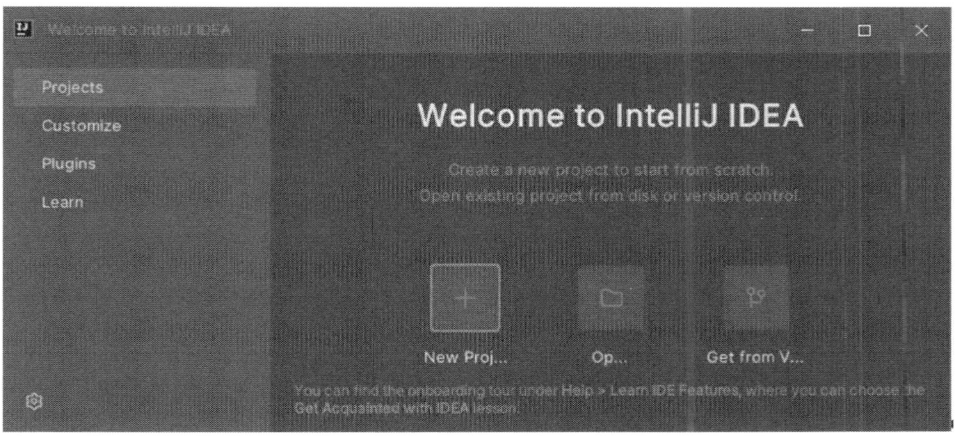

Figure 1.18 Welcome panel of IntelliJ IDEA.

After clicking "**New Project**," the project wizard will open. Here, we need to decide on its structure using several parameters:

- **Name**: Enter the name of our project.
- **Location**: Specify the path where the project will be located.
- We can also link it to a GitHub repository here, as IntelliJ has a special module for this.
- **Language**: Define the language in which we will write. This allows the compiler to recognize the syntax.
- **Build system**: Choose the type of system that will manage the build of our project.
- **JDK**: The default value that appears is the currently installed version of Java, but we can also download the JDK directly from this level.

Let's build a new project with the example name "**projekt1**." Choose the location according to your preference, set the language to "**Java**," leave the project structure as the default "**IntelliJ**," and do the same with the JDK. Then click "**Create**."

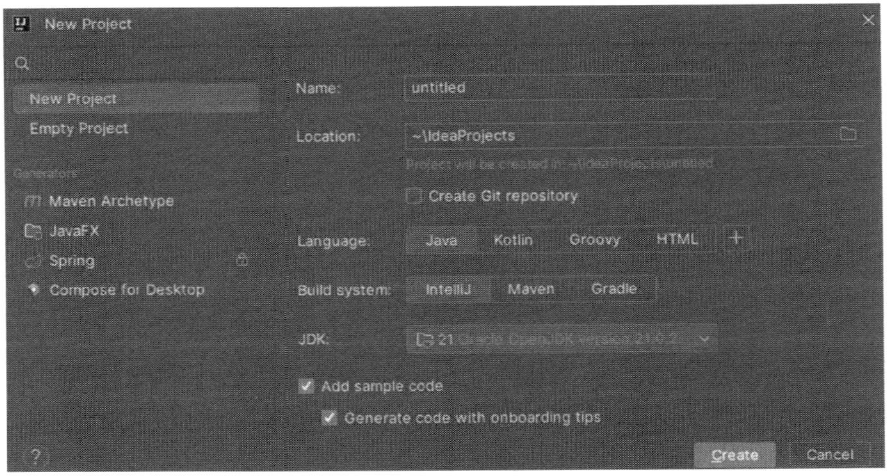

Figure 1.19 New project wizard.

A new project has been created. Most of the coding work will take place here. Useful tips on navigating the program will appear in the following chapters as new topics are introduced.

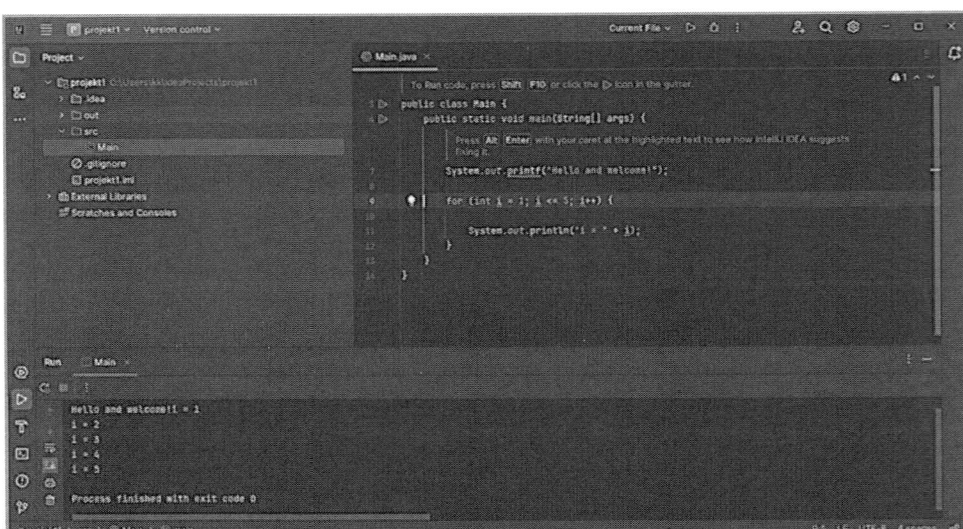

Figure 1.20 View of the Development Environment

The default view of the program has undergone minor changes in recent years. If we find it unintuitive, we can revert it to the classic look. To do this, expand the menu in the upper left corner, then select File and choose Settings. In the newly opened window, search for New UI and uncheck the Enable New UI box. The program will need to restart, and the appearance of our system will change.

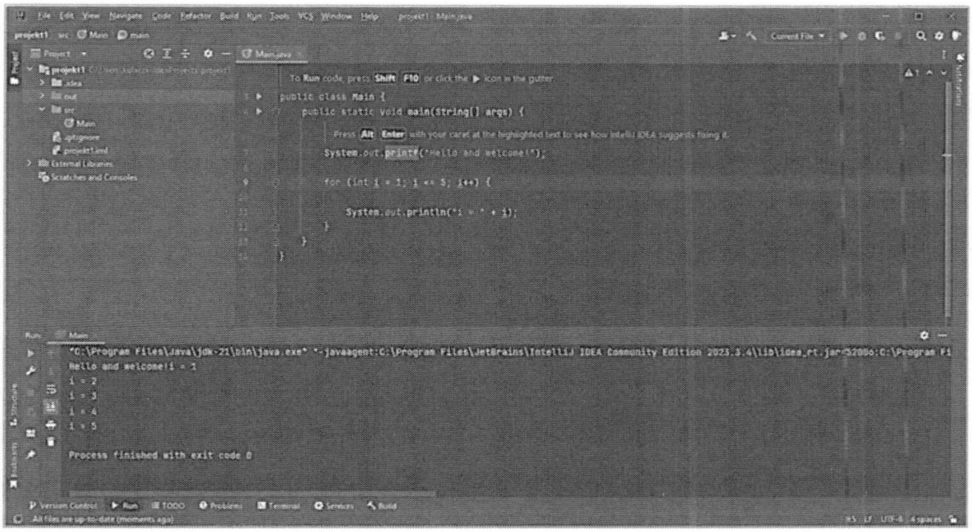

Figure 1.21 Classic Look of the Program

1.3 Installation of IntelliJ IDE for MacOS

The installation process of the IntelliJ IDEA environment on MacOS systems is simple and intuitive. We start by going to the website **https://www.jetbrains.com/idea/download**.

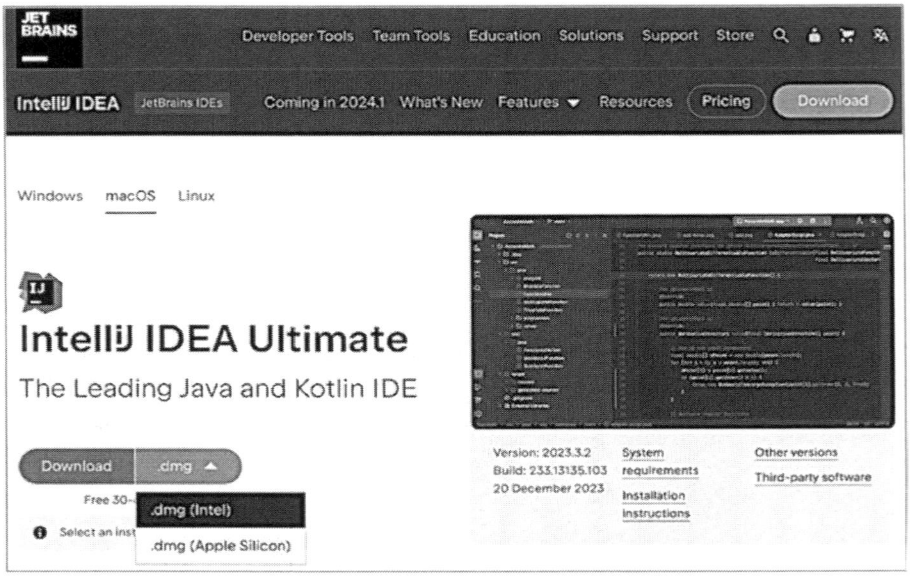

Figure 1.22 Downloading IntelliJ IDEA from the JetBrains Website

We select the installation file appropriate for our system and click "**Download**."

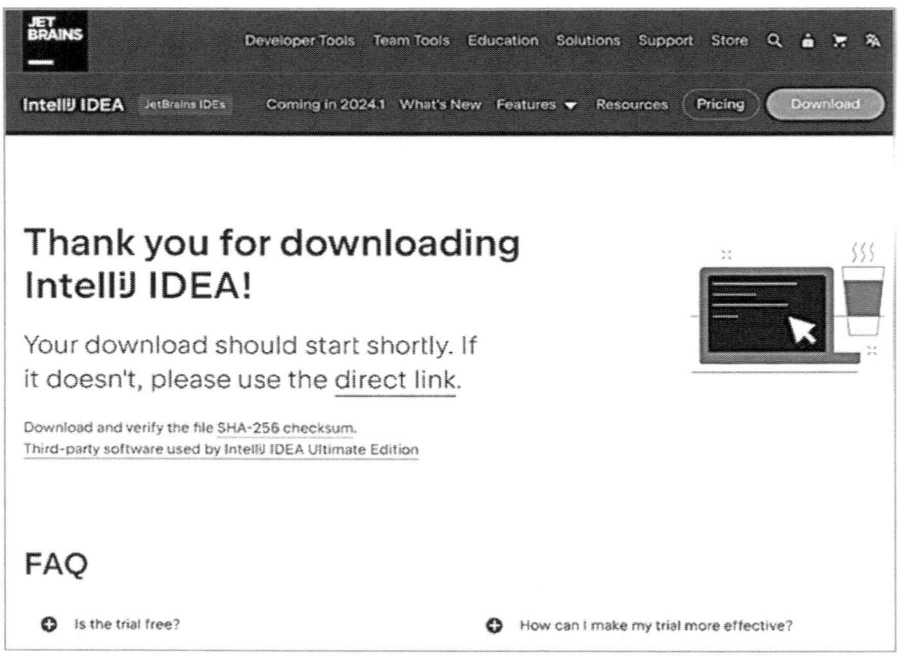

Figure 1.23 Message Indicating the Start of Program Download

When the installer finishes downloading, we launch it. A window will appear where we need to drag our program into the "**Applications**" folder.

Figure 1.24 Installation Process

That's it. Our program is ready to use. When we launch it, a user agreement will appear, which we need to read and accept. After these steps, the project management panel will open. We can immediately create a new project.

Let's select "**New Project**." In the "**Name**" and "**Location**" fields, enter an example name and a convenient location for us. Then, in the "**Language**" field, choose Java. This will help the compiler recognize the language syntax. We also need to choose which system will manage our project. This is necessary to ensure that all application files and directories are supervised.

Additionally, using such a system makes it easier for the developer to add new dependencies and configurations to the project. When first learning the language, it doesn't matter which system we choose, so we can leave the default. Finally, we need to select the JDK version. In the earlier subsection on installation for Windows, the installation via the Oracle website was presented. Here, we will do it from within the IDE. Expand the selection bar in the "**JDK**" field, and then click "**Download JDK...**".

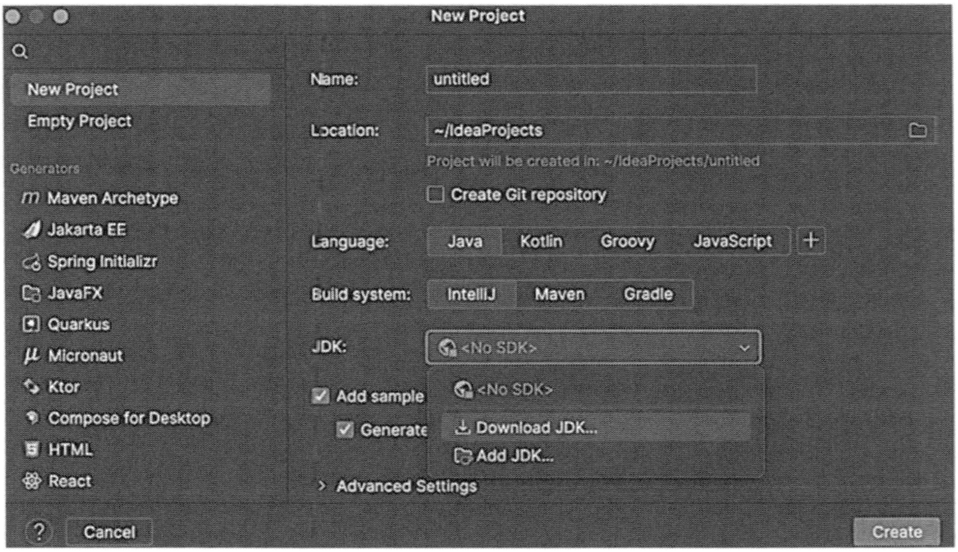

Figure 1.25 New Project Creation Wizard

A new window will appear. In this window, we select the version of Java we are interested in, then the provider and the location to save it. Finally, click "**Download**."

Figure 1.26 Selecting and Installing JDK from Within IntelliJ

IntelliJ will download the selected JDK and prepare it for use.

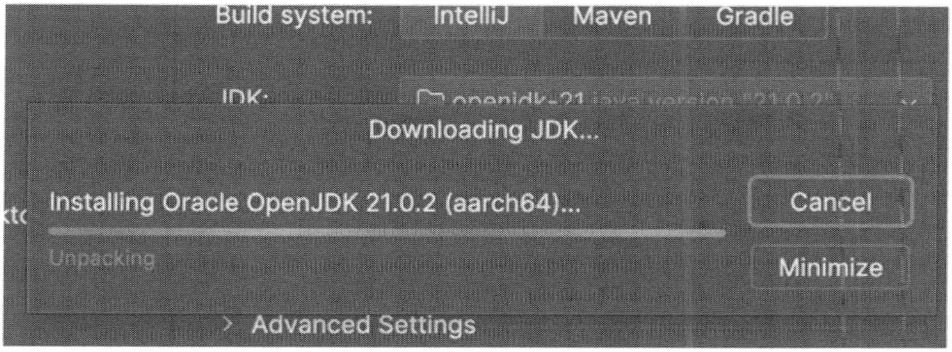

Figure 1.27 Download and Installation Progress Bar

After the download and installation are complete, the option to select the new JDK will appear in our wizard. We confirm it and click "Create" to create the project.

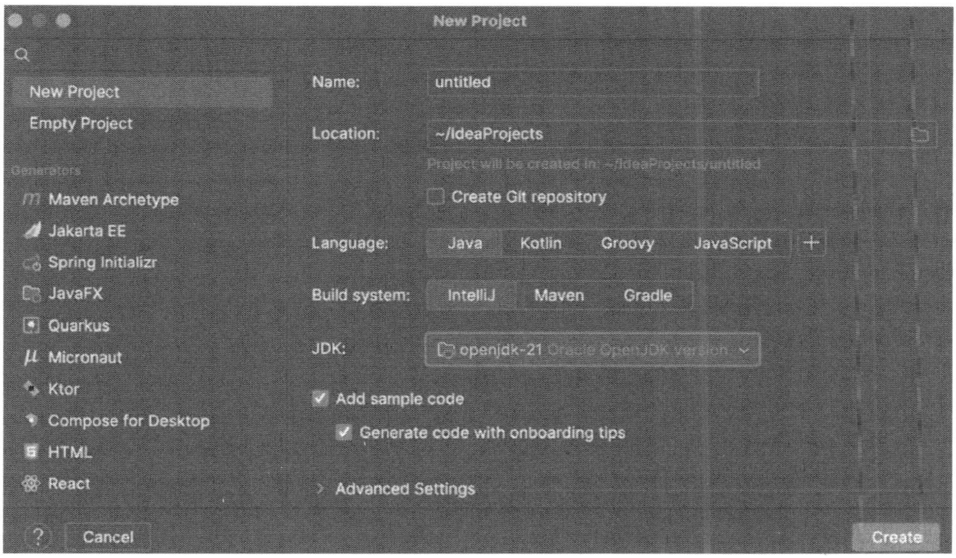

Figure 1.28 New Project Build Configuration

The new project will start automatically and load the necessary dependencies. From this point on, it is ready to begin work.

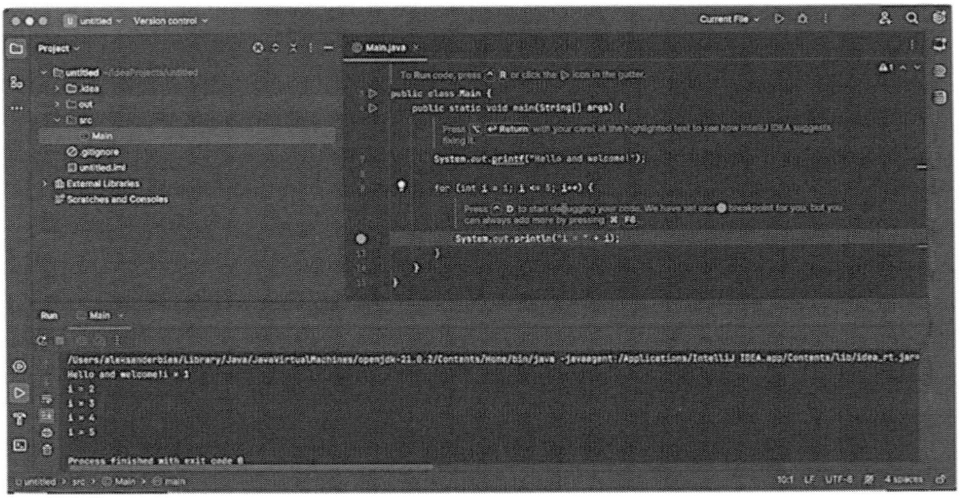

Figure 1.29 Editor View

CHAPTER 3

BASICS OF PROGRAMMING IN JAVA

2 Basics of Programming in Java

2.1 „Hello World"

We have successfully made it through the first chapter. We learned a bit about the language itself, understood why Java is so popular among developers, and prepared our environment for work. Now it comes the moment many of us have been eagerly awaiting – we will move on to practice and start writing our first lines of code in Java. The "Hello World" chapter is a symbolic starting point for this journey.

The "**Hello, World**!" program is a traditional way to start learning any new programming language. A simple program that prints "Hello, World!" on the screen allows us to quickly verify that the environment is correctly configured and that the compiler and interpreter are working without issues. It is also a great way to get acquainted with the basic syntax of the language. This chapter will be like the first step on the path to mastering the art of programming. There is nothing left but to dive into the code and start building our programming skills from scratch.

First, let's open our development environment and create a project, then a new class named "**HelloWorld**."

We can create it by right - clicking on the "**src**" of our project, then hovering over "**New**" and selecting the "**Java Class**" option.

Figure 2.1 Creating a New HelloWorld Class

A window will appear where we enter the name of our class and press the **Enter** key.

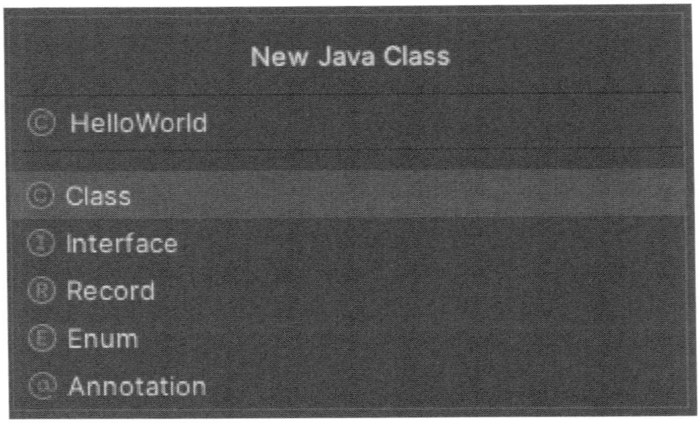

Figure 2.2 Creating a New HelloWorld Class - Continuation

For the purpose of the first program, we recommend the name "**HelloWorld**." After creating it, we should have the following code saved:

```
public class HelloWorld {
}
```

Listing 2.1 class HelloWorld

"**Public class HelloWorld**" defines a class named "HelloWorld." Between the braces, we write "**public static void main(String[] args).**" It should look like this:

```
public class HelloWorld {
    public static void main(String[] args) {
    }
}
```

Listing 2.2 Code of the HelloWorld class after adding the main method

In Java, the **main** method plays a crucial role and is the entry point of every program. This is where the code execution begins.

At this stage, we will not yet describe the words we have written in detail, but briefly explain what they mean. Namely:

- **public** – is an access modifier.
- **static** – means that the main method is directly associated with the class.
- **void** – indicates that the main method does not return any value.
- **main** – is the name of the method.
- **String[] args** – is a parameter of the main method. It allows passing command - line arguments to the program during its execution.

We will discuss more about the above elements later in this book. Ultimately, the line "**public static void main(String[] args)**" indicates that this particular method is the starting point for a program written in Java. When the program is run, the Java interpreter looks for this method to start executing the code.

Now, inside this line of code, let's write System.out.println("Hello, World!");. This command will display the text given in parentheses in the console. The entire program code should look like this:

```
public class HelloWorld {
    public static void main(String[] args) {
        System.out.println("Hello, World!");
    }
}
```

Listing 2.3 Adding System.out.println to the main method

Let's now run our first program. Locate the triangle - shaped icon on the top bar of the environment and click it. You can also do this by pressing the shortcut Shift+F10 on the keyboard.

Figure 2.3 First program run

If everything is saved correctly, the console should display:

```
Hello, World!

Process finished with exit code 0
```

Figure 2.4 Console output after running the program

At this moment, we have succeeded! The first program has run and printed "Hello, World!" in the console.

Understanding the above code is the first step to mastering Java. As we progress through the chapters, it will become more comprehensible. Now that we have completed the first program, we can look forward with joy, ready for the challenges that learning Java will bring us.

Let's get to work.

2.2 Communication with the User. Input - Output Operations

After writing your first program, it's time to get acquainted with input and output operations. In the previous program, we did not use any communication with the user. The program only displayed information in the console.

To make the program more interesting and, more importantly, more functional, we will need to help our program "**listen to us**," that is, establish communication with us.

In the next exercise, we will write a program that acts as a calculator. We will obtain the data for calculations from the user, so the application will have a broader scope of operation.

2.2.1 System.in and System.out Commands

To read data from the keyboard, we use the **System.in** function, and to display its actions, we use the **System.out** function. We use so - called streams to perform both tasks.

I/O streams (Input/Output) are used to communicate with the user in the program. In Java, we deal with three types of streams, namely:

- **System.in** – input operation,
- **System.out** – output operation,
- **System.err** – handling exceptions (or errors), a less commonly used type of output stream.

To create the simplest input stream, we can use a **Scanner**. It will be an object of a class that reads the entered data.

We will start by creating a class named **InputData** and placing the main method in it. Next, we need to create an object of type **Scanner**.

We will need an instance of this object. An instance is nothing more than a copy or occurrence of independent code that conforms to a pattern. In the **main** method, we place the following code:

```
Scanner sc = new Scanner(System.in);
```

Listing 2.4 Creating the variable sc1 of type Scanner

Let's take a closer look at this notation

- **Scanner** - the name of the class whose instances we want to create;

- **sc1** - the name of the object (instance);
- „=" - assignment operator;
- **słowo kluczowe new** - it allows us to create objects;
- again the name of the class.

As you can see, the parentheses contain the input operation **System.in**, which will be used to read data entered from the keyboard.

At the end, we place a semicolon – it is somewhat equivalent to a period in a sentence and indicates the end of the line. It is important to remember it, as its absence will generate an error.

The name **Scanner** will probably be highlighted in red. This happens because we have not imported the appropriate package that provides us with the Scanner object. At the very top (above the **InputData** class), you need to include:

```
import·java.util.
```

Listing 2.5 Importing the Scanner Package

The entire code should now look as follows:

```
import java.util.Scanner;
public class InputData {
public static void main(String[] args) {
Scanner sc = new Scanner(System.in);
    }
  }
```

Listing 2.6 Full code of the InputData class

The **Scanner** class is very versatile and allows scanning text for numbers, strings, and other objects.

In the exercise, objects of the Scanner class have been created, which will be used to call methods that allow reading different types of data.

This object creation pattern is worth remembering because it will be used when creating most objects.

So, we already have the element responsible for reading the data entered by the user. Now it's time to create a program that allows displaying the value in the console.

For this, the **System.out** method will be useful.

However, before we proceed, we need to add one very important instruction to the code. At the moment, the program will terminate immediately after starting without the possibility of entering any data. This happens because the declared object does nothing by itself. It simply exists.

The value we want to enter into the program must be stored somewhere.

Variables are used to store data in the program. To place data in a variable, it must be assigned to a location that will store its value.

Variables are used to store data. They will be described in detail in the next subsection, but for the sake of the example, we will use them now.

In the **main** function, we add the following code:

```
String text = sc.nextLine();
```

Listing 2.7 Adding a String variable and assigning it the value read from the next line

Now the code will lokk like this:

```
import java.util.Scanner;
public class InputData {
public static void main(String[] args){
Scanner sc = new Scanner(System.in);
String text = sc.nextLine();

      }
   }
```

Listing 2.8 Code of the InputData class after adding the text variable

After running the program, you need to enter text and then press **Enter**.

The program no longer closes immediately after starting, but only when we provide it with data and confirm with the **Enter** key

2.2.2 String Type

The String type is used to store sequences of characters, i.e., strings.

After the assignment operator =, we enter the value that the variable with the given name should store.

You may notice that the string is underlined with a green line. Do not worry about this, as it happens in **IntelliJ** when you provide a word that is not in the English dictionary.

In the next line, after the =, there is a reference to our **Scanner** named **sc** and a method that will be executed. The **sc.nextLine() method** pauses the program and waits for the user to enter something in the console. After entering and pressing the **Enter** key, the program resumes operation. This method reads the word entered from the keyboard and assigns its value to the text variable.

Now we will use the previously mentioned **System.out**. In a new line, we enter the following code:

```
System.out.println(word);
```

Listing 2.9 The System.out.println method printing the word

The entire code should look as follows:

```
import java.util.Scanner;
public class InputData {
public static void main(String[] args){
Scanner sc = new Scanner(System.in);
String text = sc.nextLine();
System.out.println(word);
     }
  }
```

Listing2.10 Full code of the InputData class after adding System.out.println

In the previous exercise, the **System.out.println() method** was introduced. At that time, the given text was entered in quotation marks. In this program, the value of the variable stored by "**word**" will be printed.

Now run the program and enter any text, then press **Enter**.

In the next line, the value of the variable, i.e., the text entered by the user from the keyboard, was printed. We will now modify the program to make it more functional. Change the name of the variable "**word**" to "**name**". Of course, don't forget to change it in the **System.out.println()** method as well. In the parentheses of this method, before the variable "name", add "**Hello** " in quotation marks and place a "+" sign.

It is important to leave a space after the word "**Hello**". If you don't, the text will merge with the given name, making the console output unreadable. The code should now look like this:

```
import java.util.Scanner;

public class InputData {
public static void main(String[] args){
Scanner sc = new Scanner(System.in);
String name = sc.nextLine();
System.out.println(„Hello „ + name);
     }
  }
```

Listing 2.11 Full code of the InputData class after updating the System.out.println method

Run the program, enter your name, and see the result.

The program greeted us!

There are endless combinations like this, and you can do it in any way you want. To avoid having to write System.out.println() every time, we can use one of **IntelliJ**'s additional functionalities.

2.2.3 Comments

Let's assume that for convenience, we want to note somewhere in the program what a given line of code does. It is also possible to make notes without interfering with the program's operation. This is what comments are for.

We will write in the comment what the last line of the program does, to make it easier for us to assimilate information at the beginning of our programming journey. Comments are also useful when we open the program after a long time. Thanks to them, we can understand what the various parts of the code or, for example, created functions, classes, variables are for.

To create a comment, we make a space between the last and second - to - last lines in the main function.

We enter the symbol // twice – two slashes. After them, we can write the content of the comment. The program will ignore these entries. They are information only for you. In the comment, you can write information, for example, in the following way.

```
import java.util.Scanner;

public class InputData {
public static void main(String[] args){
Scanner sc = new Scanner(System.in);
String name = sc.nextLine();
//method that greets the user
System.out.println(„Hello „ + name);
     }
  }
```

Listing 2.22 Using Comments in the Program

Comments are written in grey font by default.

But what if the comment is so long that it doesn't fit within the screen width? This is where **multi - line comments** come in handy. We write them using a slash and an asterisk at the beginning - /*, and end them in the opposite way - */. It looks like this:

```
import java.util.Scanner;

public class InputData {
public static void main(String[] args){
Scanner sc = new Scanner(System.in);
String name = sc.nextLine();

/*
method
that greets the user
*/

System.out.println(„Hello „ + name);
     }
  }
```

Listing 2.33 Using a multi - line comment in the program

When creating this type of comment, be careful not to accidentally enclose a line of correctly functioning code within them. In such a case, the program will not function properly.

There is also a third type of comment, called **documentation comments**.

It resembles a multi - line comment but has a different use. We create it in the same way as a multi - line comment, but we add one more asterisk at the opening.

```
import java.util.Scanner

public class InputData {

/**
* main - method
* @param args parameters
**/

public static void main(String[] args){
    Scanner sc = new Scanner(System.in);
    String name = sc.nextLine();
    System.out.println(„Hello „ + name);
    }
}
```

Listing 2.44 Using a Documentation Comment in the Program

In the first line, we provide a description and the operation of our method. Then, the text **"@param args"** will be automatically generated, after which we enter the parameters. To see the result of this comment, we need to click on the main method, and then from the top bar of **IntelliJ**, select **View** and **Quick Documentation,** or use the shortcut combination **CTRL + Q**.

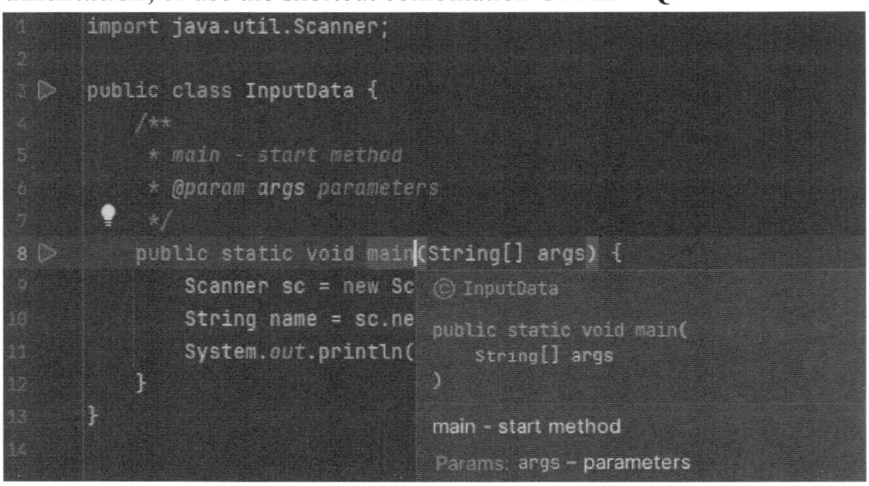

Figure 2.5 Result of Using a Documentation Comment in the Program

As we can see, the comment we provided is displayed in the window. It is worth noting that comments are primarily optional and their use is not required. We can use them when we feel the need to note something or temporarily disable a specific part of the code. However, we should not overuse comments, as excessive use can make the code less readable.

2.3 Data Types, Variables, and Constants

We have already written our first program in Java. We also know how input and output operations work and how to place comments.

Now, let's get acquainted with **variables**.

A **variable** is one of the fundamental elements of programming. Without them, it is difficult to create a more advanced and complex computer program. A variable is a memory area where values of a given type are stored during the execution of a program.

The basic characteristics of a variable are:

- **Type** - the kind of information that will be stored
- **Value** - the information that is stored in the variable
- **Name** - identifies the variable, allowing it to be distinguished from others

Simply put, a variable can be compared to a container used to store values. In almost all programming languages, variables should have a defined data type that they store.

The name of a variable should start with a letter and cannot contain any characters other than numbers, letters, and the underscore ("_").

In Java, there are also about 50 words that cannot be used as variable names. Here they are:

abstract	continue	for	new	switch
assert	default	goto	package	synchronized
boolean	do	if	private	this
break	double	implements	protecte	throw
byte	else	import	public	throws
case	enum	instanceof	return	transient
catch	extends	int	short	try
char	final	interface	static	void
class	finally	long	strictfp	volatile
const	float	native	super	while

Table 2.1 Expressions that cannot be used as variable names

These words are names of functions, events, or types. If they were used as variable names, the computer would have trouble distinguishing them, which is why they are prohibited. Below are the general rules for naming variables:

- A variable name can contain letters, numbers, underscores, and the dollar sign.
- A variable name must start with a letter.
- A variable name should start with a lowercase letter, dollar sign, or underscore.
- A variable name cannot start with a whitespace character.
- Variable names are case - sensitive, meaning "mojazmienna" and "mojaZmienna" are two completely different variables.
- Variable names cannot be the previously mentioned words (while, abstract, etc.).

All values in Java are objects of a given type.

In Java, we distinguish several data types. They are listed in the table below:

Type name	Number of bytes	Acceptable Values	Default Value	Description	Example
boole	1	true or false	false	Accepts boolean values true	true
byte	1	- 128 to 127	0	8 - bit signed integer value	1
char	2	0 to 65536	'x0'	Character code in 16 - bit Unicode	'a'
short	2	- 32 768 to 32 767	0	16 - bit signed integer value	2
int	4	- 2^31 to 2^31 - 1	0	32 - bit signed integer value	- 2
long	8	- 2^63 to 2^63 - 1	0	32 - bit signed integer value	1L
float	4	- 3.xE+38 to 3.xE+38	0.0f	32 - bit floating - point value	3.14f
doubl	8	- 1.xE+308 to 1.xE+308	0.0d	64 - bit floating - point value	1.23d

Table 2.2 Basic Data Types in Java

Based on their structure, data types in Java are divided into:

- **Primitive or simple types** – int, char, boolean, float, double;

- **Non - primitive types** – String, arrays, and classes;

Based on the type of data they store, they are divided into:

- **Whole numbers** – byte, short, int, and long;
- **Real numbers** – float and double;
- **Logical values** – boolean;
- **Unicode characters** – char.

Among the integer types, the most common ones are **long** and **int**. They are preferred and most frequently used. We rarely encounter the **short** and **byte** types.

As for real numbers (also known as floating - point numbers), they are mainly used in various scientific calculations and graphics processing.

The **float** type differs from the **double** type in the number of decimal digits stored. **Float** stores only six or seven, while **double** stores about fifteen.

Predefined types (also known as built - in types) are types that the compiler handles in a special way. One example of such a type is int, which is a predefined type for integer values that occupy 32 bits in memory.

```
String nazwa = „Minecraft";
Int rok_wydania = 2011;
```

Listing 2.55 Declaring a Variable and Saving the Operation as a Result

In the previous subchapter, we learned about the **System.out.print() function**, but it was not described in detail. This function is used to display text inside the console.

Within this function, we also have the ability to enter symbols or special characters. One such character is \n, which moves the text entered after it to the next line. We achieve the same effect by using the **System.out.println()** function. It differs from the previous one in that it contains the letters ln before the parentheses, indicating that the function will display the text in a new line. Below are examples of its operation:

```
System.out.print(„Hello");
System.out.print(„buddy");
```

Listing 2.66 Example of the System.out.print() function operation

Program output:

```
Hellobuddy
Process finished with exit code 0
```

Figure 2.6 Console output of the previous operation

If we use the **System.out.println()** method, we will get the following result:

```
Hello
buddy

Process finished with exit code 0
```

Figure 2.7 Console output of the previous operation using System.out.println

As you can see, the function used in the first example displays the text in one line, while the one from the second example displays each text separately. Besides the text enclosed in quotation marks, we can also provide the name of a variable or enter an expression whose result we want to obtain, for example:

```
int number = 4+2;
System.out.println(number);
System.out.println(„6");
System.out.println(4+2);
```

Listing 2.77 Printing the number 6 in different ways

After saving and running the above code, the value 6 will appear three times in the console.

Another example of a predefined type is **String**. It represents sequences of characters, for example, "**Java**".

```
String text = „Java";
System.out.println(text);
```

Listing 2.88 Declaring a variable of type String and printing its content

For the **String** type, Java has a number of methods for modifying text.

```
String text = „           Java";
System.out.println(text.toUpperCase());
System.out.println(text.toLowerCase());
System.out.println(text.trim());
System.out.println(text.replace('a','o'));
```

Listing 2.99 Operations on the String Type

```
    JAVA
    java
Java
    Jovo

Process finished with exit code 0
```

Figure 2.8 Console output of string operations

At the beginning, we declared a variable of type String named text, which stores the value " Java". We intentionally added extra spaces before the text.

The first method, **toUpperCase()**, makes the entire text display in uppercase letters.

The second method**, toLowerCase()**, works opposite to the previous one. The entire text will be written in lowercase letters.

The **trim()** method removes all spaces before and after the word, leaving only the text. This is useful, for example, when creating a program where we need to enter a login or password. If the user provides a login that contains a space at the beginning, we can use the trim method to remove all spaces and avoid issues.

The last method presented in the example is **replace()**. It replaces a selected letter with another. In the above example, we replaced the letter "**a**" with "**o**", so the console returned "**Jovo**" instead of "**Java**".

Strings, like other words, can be concatenated into a complete sentence using the "+" sign:

```
String name = „Adam”;
String surname = „Kowalski”;
System.out.println(„My name is: „ + name + „ „ +
surname);
```

Listing 2.20 Combining Two Strings into One Sentence in the System.out.println Method

As a result of the program's operation, we will get the following in the console:

```
My name is: Adam Kowalski

Process finished with exit code 0
```

Rysunek 2.9 Console output after printing with System.out.println

As we can see, we printed two strings in one sentence. We added an empty quotation mark between one variable and the other to separate them. They simply act as a space character. You can also combine other data types into one sentence, e.g., a **string** with an **int**:

```
String name = „Minecraft";
int publication_year = 2011;
System.out.println(„The game " + name + „ was created in " + publication_year + „.");
```

Listing 2.21 Using a string and an int in one sentence with System.out.println

The console will return:

```
The game Minecraft was created in 2011.

Process finished with exit code 0
```

Rysunek 2.10 Console output after printing System.out.println

In this example, we can combine two variables, "firstName" and "lastName", into one. One variable will then store both the first name and the last name. We combine two string variables in the following way:

```
String name = „Adam";
String surname = „Kowalski"
String fullName = name + „ " + surname;
System.out.println(„My name is „ + fullName);
```

Listing 2.102 Adding two string variables together and assigning the result to a variable.

In the console we will see:

```
My name is Adam Kowalski

Process finished with exit code 0
```

Figure 2.11 Console output after adding two variables together and printing their value.

Another predefined type is the **boolean** type. It only allows two values – **false** or **true**. The default value of a variable of this type is **false.**

Example of the boolean veriable type:

```
boolean text = true;
System.out.println(text);
```

Listing 2.113 Example of using the boolean type

The variable will return the value true, which we can observe in the console.

We can also check the **boolean** value when comparing two variables. Let's assume we have two variables storing numbers. Let's check which one has a greater value.

The **System.out.println()** method will help us in the solution. So:

```
float value1 = 3.4f;
float value2 = 7.3f;
System.out.println(value1 > value2);
```

Listing 2.124 of float values and printing the result in the console

As you can see, in this example, we used the **float** data type. After running the program, the console will display the value **true**. This notation allows us to shorten the code to one line.

We just need to provide the numbers and the greater - than sign within the parentheses.

The code will look as follows:

```
System.out.println(32 > 35);
```

Listing 2.135 Comparison of two values in System.out.println()

In this exercise, we will get the value **false**.

During the execution of the program, you can change the values of the variables that previously stored a value. For example:

```
float number1 = 2.3f;
System.out.println(number1);
number1 = 2.4f;
System.out.println(number1);
```

Listing 2.146 Changing the value of a variable during program execution and printing the value before and after the change

In this case, the console will first return the value **2.3**, and upon the next print, **2.4**.

You can also change the values of variables in the following way:

```
float number1 = 2.3f;
System.out.println(number1 + 2);
```

Listing 2.157 Another way to change the value of a variable during program execution

We added the number **2** to the variable, so its value will now be **4.3**, and this number will be displayed by the console after compilation.

Another data type is **char**. It stores a single character, which can be a number, letter, or symbol. The values stored by the char type are written in single quotes (not double quotes!).

The **char** type allows storing values in decimal or hexadecimal notation.

Thanks to the char type, we can also use values in decimal or hexadecimal form that correspond to characters in the **Unicode** table.

In Java, we also have special characters, whose description and operation are presented in the table below:

Symbol	Description
\t	Inserts a tab in the text
\b	Inserts a backspace in the text, which deletes
\n	Inserts a new line in the text
\r	Inserts a carriage return in the text
\f	Inserts a form feed in the text
\'	Inserts a single quote in the text
\"	Inserts a double quote in the text
\\	Inserts a backslash in the text

Table 2.3 Special characters in Java

```
System.out.println(„Fruits: \n -apple\n-pear\n");
System.out.println(„I quote: \"I wanted to go, but
I couldn't..\b\"");
```

Listing 2.168 Using special characters in a program

Let's see how some of these special characters look in practice:

```
Fruits:
-apple
-pear

I quote: "I wanted to go, but I couldn't."

Process finished with exit code 0
```

Figure 2.12 Console output of this program

In the first line of code in the **System.out.println()** method, we placed three newline characters. As a result, each text appeared on a separate line.
The **\n** character at the end of the string caused a space between the first and the next text.

In the second example, it was demonstrated how to print a special character, which is **"**. Directly before the symbol, there is a \ character, which changes the " from a string delimiter to a graphical symbol printed in the console.

The **\b** character removes the preceding character. Therefore, only one dot was printed in the console.

```
char symbol1 = 'a';
char symbol2 = '@';
char symbol3 = '2';
char symbol4 = '\u00A9';
char symbol5 = '©';
System.out.println(symbol1 + „ " + symbol2 + „ " +
symbol3 + „ " + symbol4 + „ " + symbol5);
```

Listing 2.29 Example usage of the char type

As we mentioned earlier, char values are enclosed in single quotes, and the length of the stored characters cannot be greater than one. In the variable named **char4**, one of the **Unicode** characters was used.

There are many **Unicode** characters. All of them are placed in special tables that can be easily found on the Internet. After running the program, we see that **char4** returns the same value as **char5**.

We can also create char variables using the **Character constructor**.

In Java, there is a declaration of a variable whose stored value will not change throughout the program's execution. In other words, it is a variable whose value will never change. It is called a **constant**. We use it when we are sure that our variable will store a final value. Such a variable is declared in the same way as a regular one, but we add the word final before the type name (e.g., **int**). In Polish, it is called a final variable, constant variable, or ultimate variable. Below is an example of its declaration:

```
final float pi = 3.14f;
System.out.println(pi);
```

Listing 2.30 Declaration of a final variable

What happens if we decide to change the value of a constant variable?

For instance:

```
final float pi = 3.14f;
pi = 3.5f;
System.out.println(pi);
```

Listing 2.17 Attempt to change the value of a final variable

Even before compiling the program, we will notice that our pi is underlined in red. When we run the program, the console will display a message saying:

```
java: cannot assign a value to final variable pi
```

Figure 2.13 Error message in the console when attempting to change the value of a final variable

Each primitive data type has specific values that it can store. But what if we want an **int** to store a floating - point value like **float** or **double**? We can achieve this by type casting or conversion. In Java, we distinguish between two types of conversions:

- Widening conversion (automatic) – involves converting a smaller data type to a larger one, e.g., - **byte → short → char → int → long → float → double**;
- Narrowing conversion (manual) – involves converting a larger data type to a smaller one, e.g., - **double → float → long → int → char → short → byte**;

Widening conversion is performed automatically when we provide a smaller data type as a value for a larger type.

```
int variableInt = 6;
float variableFloat = variableInt;
System.out.println(variableInt);
System.out.println(variableFloat);
```

Listing 2.18 Example of widening conversion

First, we declared an **int** variable storing the number **6**. Then, in the second line, we assigned the value of the **int** variable to a **float** variable. The conversion happened automatically.

Unfortunately, narrowing conversion must be done manually by placing parentheses with the variable type before its name. It looks like this:

```
float variableFloat = 3.64f;
int variableInt = (int) variableFloat;
System.out.println(variableInt);
System.out.println(variableFloat);
```

Listing 2.19 Example of narrowing conversion

Here, we started by declaring a **float** variable (since we are converting from a larger to a smaller data type). Then, we assigned the **int** value from the **float** variable to an **int** variable. After compiling the program, you will see the following result:

```
3.64
3

Process finished with exit code 0
```

Figure 2.14 Console output of narrowing conversion

Since **int** does not store floating - point values, from the **float** variable with the value **3.64**, we get the integer part with the value **3**.

2.3.1 Check yourself!

1) **What data type would you use to store integers in the range from - 2^31 to 2^31 - 1?**

   a) int
   b) short
   c) long

2) Which of the following data types is used to store logical values (true/false)?

a) boolean
b) char
c) double

3) Which of the following data types is used to store single characters?

d) int
e) char
f) String

4) Which of the following data types is used to store single - precision floating - point numbers?

g) double
h) float
i) long

5) Which of the following conversions is automatic in Java?

a) Variable of type double to type int
b) Variable of type int to type double
c) Variable of type String to type Boolean

6) Which of the following variable names is not allowed in Java?

j) "my - variable"
k) "2abc"
l) "_abc"
m) "abc_xyz"

Task 3.3.1

Write a program that will convert a numerical value given as a String to the floating - point data type **float**. Then, the program should display both values and the accuracy of the conversion.

2.4 Basic Arithmetic and Logical Operations

After learning about variables and data types, it's time to delve into another area that is crucial for creating more advanced programs. In this chapter, we will focus on arithmetic and logical operations, which form the foundation for many aspects of programming. We will start with arithmetic operations, also known as mathematical operations. Arithmetic operations are fundamental to every programming language, as they allow us to manipulate numerical data. In Java, we have access to standard operations that enable us to perform basic mathematical calculations. These include:

Operator	Name	Description	Example
+	addition	adds two values together	a + b
-	subtraction	subtracts one value from another	a - b
*	multiplication	multiplies two values	a * b
/	division	divides one value by another	a / b
%	modulo	returns the remainder of division	a % b

Table 2.4 Basic Arithmetic and Logical Operations

Now we will apply the above operations in practice. We will create a new **class** named "**BasicOperations**". In the "**main**" method, let's write:

```
int additionResult = 3+7;
System.out.println(additionResult);
```

Listing 2.20 A variable that takes the sum of two values as a result, and then prints its result

Addition in Java is intuitive and works on both integers and floating - point numbers. The values **3** and **7** are added, and the result is assigned to the variable **sumResult**. Then we print its value to the console. The number **10** should appear.

We can also simplify this notation a bit:

```
System.out.println(3 + 7);
```

Listing 2.21 Simplified version of the previous code

The result will be the same, but in the previous example, the sum was assigned to a variable, while here it is simply displayed.

Now we will subtract two numbers. In the same class, we will write:

```
double subtractionResult = 8.40d - 5.20d;
System.out.println(subtractionResult);
```

Listing 2.22 A variable that takes the difference of two values as a result, and then prints its result

The subtraction operation works in the same way as the addition operation. The above example illustrates a simple subtraction operation of two floating - point numbers of type **double**.

It is worth noting that at the end of the number, e.g., **8.40d**, we use the literal **'d'** to specify that these are double - type floating - point numbers. As a result, the variable **subtractionResult** stores the result of subtracting **5.20** from **8.40**, which will be **3.2**. This result should appear in the console.

The next operation is multiplication:

```
int multiplicationResult = 4*5;
System.out.println(multiplicationResult);
```

Listing 2.23 A variable that stores the product of two values, followed by printing its result.

This operation calculates the product of two numbers, in this case **4** and **5**. The result will be **20**. The final operation is division:

```
double divisionResult = 6d/4d;
System.out.println(divisionResult);
```

Listing 2.24 A variable that takes the quotient of two values as a result, and then prints its result

Division in Java can lead to floating - point values. It is advisable to use the double type to store the result of dividing two numbers. In this case, the result of the division will be **1.5**.

Attempting to divide a number by **0** will cause a program error. For the double type, the console will display 'Infinity'. However, if we divide int type numbers by **0**, we will see this error in the console:

```
Exception in thread "main" java.lang.ArithmeticException Create breakpoint : / by zero
    at BasicOperations.main(BasicOperations.java:42)
```

Figure 2.15 Error in the console when attempting to divide a number by zero

Java also has the modulo operator, which outputs the remainder of the division.

```
double moduloDivisionResult = 7d%3d;
System.out.println(moduloDivisionResult);
```

Listing 2.25 A variable that takes the remainder of the division of two values as a result, and then prints its result.

The value of the variable **moduloResult** will be **1**, because the number 3 fits into **7** only twice, leaving a remainder of **1**. These basic arithmetic operations are essential for performing all kinds of mathematical calculations in programming. In practice, they are often used in algorithms, mathematical equations, and numerical data manipulations in general. In previous chapters, we mentioned incrementing, e.g., **i++**. This is an example of unary operators, which operate on a single operand, i.e., one variable or one expression. In Java, there are several unary operators, such as increment and decrement operators. They play a very important role in programming. The first operator is used to increase the value of a variable, while the second is used to decrease it.

```
int number = 6;
number++;
System.out.println(number);
```

Listing 2.26 Increasing the value of a variable using the increment operator

In the above example, we used the **increment** operator on the **variable number**. After this operation, the value of the variable **number** will be 7.

```
int number = 6;
number--;
System.out.println(number);
```

Listing 2.27 Decreasing the value of a variable using the decrement operator

Now we have decreased the value of the variable by **one** using the **decrement** operator. These operators are particularly useful when we want to quickly increase or decrease the value of a variable by a constant value (in this case, by **one**). In practice, they are often used in **loops** and other situations where it is necessary to repeat operations on numerical variables. Besides these two, there is also the **negative** operator. Its operation is not complicated. It can be used to change a positive value to a negative one. For example:

```
int result = 20;
result = -result;
System.out.println(result);
```

Listing 2.28Changing the value of a variable to its opposite value, in this case negative

We declared a variable result with an initial value of **20**. In the next line, we assigned the value of the variable result but with a **minus** sign, which simultaneously changed this value to **negative**. As a result, the console will display the number - 20.

These operators are important in various programming contexts, and their use depends on the needs of the task at hand. Increment and decrement operators are useful in the context of manipulating numerical variables. **Unary** operators allow for more complex operations on single variables. We have already used value assignment to variables multiple times, so now let's take a closer look at **assignment** operators. They are a significant element of programming in Java, enabling the assignment of values to variables. The general format of the assignment operator is:

```
int value = 30;
int variable = value;
```

Listing 2.29 Assigning a variable as a value for another variable

The value on the right side must be of the same type as the variable on the left side to ensure correct data assignment. Of course, in this example, we could simply assign the value **30** to the variable named variable without creating an additional variable. The = operator is the basic and simplest **assignment** operator. However, there are also compound assignment operators. These include symbols like +, - , or / combined with the = sign. They are also known as assignment operators with arithmetic operations.

```
int x = 5;
x += 3; // x = x + 3
```

Listing 2.30 Increasing the value of a variable using the assignment operator with an arithmetic operation

The variable **x** initially holds the value **5**. Then we use the assignment operator with the addition operation of the number **3**, which means we add the value 3 to **5**. These operators allow us to shorten the notation, especially when we want to perform an operation on a variable and assign its result back to the same variable. The comment contains an alternative notation for this line.

```
int x = 5;
x *= 2; // x = x * 2
System.out.println(x);
```

Listing 2.31 Increasing the value of a variable by multiplying its value and printing the result

In the above example, we replaced addition with multiplication. We multiply the value of the variable x by two, which will give us the result **10** in the console.

In Java, it is possible to compare data, for example, the values of variables. We can check which variable is greater among two. For this, we use **relational** (comparison) operations. They are used to compare two values and return a boolean result **true/false** based on the fulfillment of certain conditions. Below is a table of example relational operations:

Operator	Description	Example
==	Equal	a == b
!=	Not equal	a != b
>	Greater than	a > b
<	Less than	a < b
>=	Greater than or equal to	a >= b
<=	Less than or equal to	a <= b

Tabela 2.5 Example relational operations

Below there is a sample code containing the equality operator:

```
int number1 = 5;
int number2 = 5;
boolean isEqual = number1 == number2;
```

Listing 2.32 Checking if variable values are equal using the equality operator

In this example, the boolean variable **isEqual** will store the value **true** or **false**, depending on whether **number1** is equal to **number2**. In this case, it will be **true** because both variables hold the value **5**. Now we will use a few selected comparison operations.

Here is the sample code:

```
int number3 = 5;
int number4 = 7;
boolean isNotEqual = number3 != number4;
boolean isGreater = number3 > number4;
boolean isLessThanOrEqual = number3 <= number4;
```

Listing 2.33 Example of using selected comparison operations

In the code, two integer variables **number3** and **number4** are defined. Then relational operators are used for comparisons. The boolean **isNotEqual** checks if **number3** is different from **number4**. In this case, the operation is true because **5** is not equal to **7**. In the next line, there is the variable **isGreater**, which checks if **number3** is greater than **number4**. As we know, it is not. Therefore, the variable **isGreater** will have the value **false**. In the last line, the variable **isLessOrEqual** is used. This will check if **number3** is less than or equal to **number4**. In this situation, **5** is less, so the result will be true.

Relational operations are crucial in logical conditions and loops, allowing the program to make decisions based on the relationship between different values.

Java also has logical operations. They are a key element of programming, enabling the program to make decisions based on specific conditions. A key aspect of this mechanism is the ability to control the flow of the program depending on whether certain logical conditions are met or not. The table below presents the most important information about these operations.

Operator	description	Example
&&	returns true when both conditions are met	a && b
||	returns true when one of the conditions is met	a || b
!	Returns the inverted values (e.g. false when the result is true)	a ! b

Table 2.6 Example logical operations

First, we will discuss the logical **AND** operation **("&&")**. The **AND** operation returns **true** only if both conditions are met. Below is an example of using this operator:

```
boolean condition1 = true;
boolean condition2 = false;
boolean resultCon = condition1 && condition2;
```

Listing 2.34 Example of using the logical "AND" operator

The value of the variable **resultCondition** will be false because the condition was not met. A good example of using the **AND** and **OR** variables would be checking if a number is even or odd and greater or smaller than the given number. We will use relational operations in it:

```
int number = 15;
boolean conditionAND = (number % 2 == 0)
&& (number > 10);
boolean conditionOR = (number % 2 != 0)
|| (number <= 5);
System.out.println(„Is number even and greater
than 10? " + conditionAND);
System.out.println(„Is number odd or less than
or equal to 5? " + conditionOR);
```

Listing 2.35 Example of using the logical "AND" and "OR" operators, and then printing the result

In this example, we have a variable number with a value of **15**. The variable **conditionAND** checks if this number is both **even** and greater than **10**. In this case, the result will be **false** because **15** is not an **even** number. The second boolean variable **conditionOR** will check if the number is either odd or less than or equal to **5**. In this situation, the result will be true because the number **15** is greater than **5**, thus meeting the condition.

In Java, there is also the **NOT** operator, denoted by an exclamation mark "**!**". It performs the negation of a boolean value, meaning it changes **true** to false and vice versa. Below is an example of using this operator:

```
boolean True = true;
boolean False = !true;
System.out.println(False);
```

Listing 2.36 Using the negation operator and printing this variable

We used **boolean** type logical variables. The value **true** represents the variable **truth**, while **false** takes the value negating the truth variable. As a result, the **false** variable will be equal to false.

The **NOT** operator is often used in conditional expressions where we want to reverse the logical value. Logical operations are useful in conditional structures, loops, and controlling the flow of the program. In practice, they are used to make decisions based on various conditions.

In this chapter, we learned about operations on variables and operators and explored various aspects of data manipulation and program flow control. Arithmetic operations provide basic tools for performing numerical calculations. We applied them in the context of various problems, which allowed us to better understand their practical application.

We analysed unary operators and noticed how they can be used to manipulate variable values, making changes to their values concisely. We also know that assignment operations allow updating variable values during program execution, which can contribute to more readable code. We also focused on relational operations that enable value comparison. Logical conditions created using these operators determine the course of the program.

Finally, we used logical operations to create logical conditions that affect the program's operation depending on the fulfillment of specific criteria. In summary, we understood how these operations integrate into the syntax of the Java language, enabling programmers to perform various tasks, from simple calculations to more advanced control decisions.

2.4.1 Check yourself!

1. Which of the following operators is used for logical "or" in Java?

a) &&

b) ||

c) !

d) ==

2. Which of the following operators is used for incrementing in Java?

a) +

b) -

c) ++

d) - -

3. Which of the following operators is used for comparing objects by reference in Java?

a) ==

b) ===

c) equals()

d) compare()

Task 3.4.1

Write a Java program that will calculate basic arithmetic operations on two numbers and display the results. Use the following input data:

- number1: 25;
- number2: 7;

The program should calculate and display the following operations: **Sum, Difference, Product, Quotient, Remainder** (modulo).

2.5 Conditional Statements

Now it is time to turn our attention to conditional statements, which are very important in programming. They rely on decision - making and allow the program to adapt its behavior depending on changing situations.

In this chapter, we will learn how to use conditional statements to check logical conditions, choose between different execution paths, and how these elements can make our programs more intelligent and responsive.

At this point, we already know that Java supports the use of relational operators, which allow us to check, for example, whether a given variable is greater than or equal to the value of another variable. We can use them to perform various actions when different conditions are met. In practice, they often work in tandem with conditional statements.

2.5.1 If and Else Statements

In Java, the main mechanism for implementing conditional statements are the **if, else if**, and **else** constructs. We will start by discussing the first one mentioned, which is the most commonly used.

The **if** conditional statement allows certain instructions to be executed only when a specified condition is met.

Let's now create a new class named **ConditionalInstructions,** and then write the **main** method in it.

```
int number = 10;

if(number > 0){
    System.out.println(„The number is positive");
}
```

Listing 2.37 Example of an "if" conditional statement

We declared a variable **number** that holds the value **10**. We will analyze this number in the context of a conditional statement.

In the next line of code, we used an **if** conditional statement with the condition number > **0**.

The statement **System.out.println("The number is positive")** will be executed only if this condition is true, meaning the **number** is greater than zero.

If the value of the variable **number** is less than **0**, this statement will not be executed, and the program will continue its execution.

But what if we want our program to inform us that the number is negative if it is not greater than zero?

In this case, the **else** statement comes. This statement is used in conjunction with the **if** statement and allows us to define a block of code that will be executed when the condition of the **if** statement is not true. Below is an example of using the **else** statement in practice:

```
int number = -5;

if(number > 0){
    System.out.println(„The number is positive");
}else{
    System.out.println(„The number is not positive");
}
```

Listing 2.38 Conditional statement with "else" displaying a specific message

This time we changed the value of the variable to **- 5**. First, the program checks if the **number** is greater than **zero**. In this case, the condition is not met, so the program will move to the **else** block. The code inside the **else** will be executed. As a result, we will see the message "**The number is not positive**" in the console.

In short, if the **if** condition is met, the code inside the **if** is executed; if not, the code inside the **else** is executed. In Java, we also find nested else if statements.

In the context of a conditional statement, this means introducing another condition to consider if the first condition in the **if** statement is not met. This solution is a way to account for different cases in the program. An example of using else if:

```
int number = 0;

if(number > 0){
    System.out.println(„The number is positive");
}else if(number < 0){
    System.out.println(„The number is not positive");
}else{
    System.out.println(„The number is zero");
}
```

Listing 2.39 Conditional statement with "else if" displaying a specific message

This time the variable **number** holds the value **0**. The first conditional statement checks if the number is greater than zero. If so, the given message is printed, but in the current program, this condition is not met. Next, we use the **else if** construction. If the condition associated with the first **if** is not met, the program moves to the next conditional statement. This checks if the number is less than **zero**. If the condition is met, the program will also display an appropriate message.

With the given data, the condition will not be met. Therefore, the program moves to the block of code inside the **else** statement. This is the message that will be shown in the console because our **number** is zero. The **else** and **else if** statements are optional and can follow an if statement. They make the code more flexible and adaptable to different cases.

Conditional statements in Java can be nested, allowing for even more complex decision - making scenarios. Below is an example:

```
int a = 5;
int b = 8;
int c = 10;

if(b > a){
   if(b > c){
      System.out.println("Number b is
the largest of the three variables");
   }else{
      System.out.println("Number b is
the second largest number among the three
variables");
   }
}else{
   System.out.println("Number b is the
smallest of the three variables");
}
```

Listing 2.40 Nested "if else" conditional statement displaying specific messages

This code analyses three integer variables: **a, b**, and **c**. We will focus on the variable **b**. Let's assume that the program knows that the value of **c** is greater than **a**. This allows us to immediately determine the hierarchy of the given numbers.

First, the **if** conditional statement checks if the value of variable **b** is greater than the value of variable **a**. If this condition is met, the program proceeds to the block of code inside this statement. However, within this block, there is another conditional statement that checks if the number **b** is greater than **c**. This is an example of nesting conditional statements. If the condition **b** > **c** is not met, the program then proceeds to the block of code inside the **else**. In our case, this will happen, and the program will output the message "**The number b is the second largest number among the three variables**" in the console. Finally, we have an else that will execute if the number **b** turns out to be less than **a** at the very beginning.

In summary, this code is an example of nested conditional statements that allow us to determine the relationships between three variables and print appropriate messages depending on their values. There is a shorter way to write conditional statements. We can do this using ternary expressions. Unlike full **if - else** statements, ternary expressions allow us to shorten the code, especially when we want to assign a value to a variable depending on the condition being met. Their general structure looks like this:

```
condition ? value_if_true : value_if_false;
```

Figure 2.16 Structure of a ternary expression

Below is the practical application of this expression:

```
int number = 15;
String result = (number % 2 == 0) ? „even" :
„odd";
System.out.println(„The number is " + result);
```

Listing 2.41 Example of using a ternary expression

The variable **number** holds the value **15**. In the next line, there is a **string** variable **result** that takes the value of the ternary expression. This expression checks if the remainder of dividing **number** by **2** is equal to **0**. If the condition is met, **meaning the number is even**, the text "**even**" is assigned to the variable **result**; otherwise, "**odd**" is assigned. Finally, the program will print the message "The number is odd." Below is how this example relates to the general structure:

- **expression:** (number % 2 == 0)
- **value_if_true:** "even"
- **value_if_false:** "odd"

This code demonstrates how to use a ternary expression to determine whether a number is even or odd and print the appropriate message to the console. Using this expression is a good way to shorten the code for simple conditional statements. However, if we wanted to write this code in the traditional way, as at the beginning of this chapter, we could do it like this:

```
int number = 15;
String result;

if(number % 2 == 0){
    result = „even";
}else{
    result = „odd";
}
System.out.println(„The number is " + result);
```

Listing 2.42 Previous code without using a ternary expression

As you can see, there are a few more lines of code, but the program's functionality remains unchanged. Ternary expressions have many benefits. They offer a shorter syntax, making the code more concise, especially in simple cases. These expressions are also ideal for use in single - line situations where a full **if - else** structure is unnecessary.

However, ternary expressions have their drawbacks. Primarily, they are limited to two possible outcomes, which means they cannot be used for more complex problems. Additionally, in the case of more complicated conditions, they may not be entirely readable. In such cases, the if - else structure is more suitable.

2.5.2 Switch - case

In the previous chapter, conditional statements were introduced, which allow the program to take different actions depending on whether certain conditions are met. Now, we will focus on more advanced control structures, specifically the **switch** statement.

The switch statement allows for more readable management of multiple cases treated equally. In Java, the switch statement is used to select one of many possible execution paths based on the value of an expression. It is an alternative to long chains of if - else statements. Let's now proceed to demonstrate the switch statement in practice. So, let's create a new class named SwitchCase and add the main method to it. Then, write the following code:

```
int dayOfTheWeek = 3;
switch(dayOfTheWeek){
    case 1:
        System.out.println(„Monday”);
        break;
    case 2:
        System.out.println(„Tuesday”);
        break;
    case 3:
        System.out.println(„Wednesday”);
        break;
    case 4:
        System.out.println(„Thursday”);
        break;
    case 5:
        System.out.println(„Friday”);
        break;
    case 6:
        System.out.println(„Saturday”);
        break;
    case 7:
        System.out.println(„Sunday”);
        break;
    default:
        System.out.println(„Weekend”);
        break;
}
```

Listing 2.43 Example of a "switch - case" statement

A program with the days of the week is one of the best examples to illustrate the **switch** statement.

Initially, we created an integer variable **dayOfWeek**. It is initialized with the value **3**, which corresponds to Wednesday.

The **switch** statement specifies the value to be compared with different **cases**. Within the braces, we write the case values. These are the possible cases that may occur. They specify the value to be compared with the expression. If the expression matches the case, the code for that **case** is executed.

In the example, each **case** will print the day of the week corresponding to the number of the expression in the console.

The **break** statement interrupts the execution of the **switch - case** statement. The last option in the structure is **default**, which is an optional block that executes when no case matches the value of the expression. It is equivalent to **else** in conditional statements.

In our program, if the variable **dayOfWeek** had a value other than **1** to **7**, the console would display the message **"Weekend"**.

In summary, the program will look for the case that matches the value of the variable **dayOfWeek** and execute the code block of the corresponding **case**. If it encounters the word **break**, it ends the execution. Using **break** is usually required to stop the execution of the **switch - case** after the condition is met. Its absence can lead to the execution of code for subsequent **cases**, even if the condition for them is not met. Therefore, it is important to remember it.

For **dayOfWeek** equal to **3** (as in our program), the program will display **"Wednesday"** in the console. The remaining cases will not be checked after finding the matching **case**, thus efficiently managing the program's execution paths.

```
int dayOfTheWeek = 3;
switch(dayOfTheWeek){
    case 1 -> System.out.println(„Monday");
    case 2 -> System.out.println(„Tuesday");
    case 3 -> System.out.println(„Wednesday");
    case 4 -> System.out.println(„Thursday");
    case 5 -> System.out.println(„Friday");
    case 6 -> System.out.println(„Saturday");
    case 7 -> System.out.println(„Sunday");
    default -> System.out.println(„Weekend");
}
```

In **switch - case** statements, you can also use an alternative syntax with the arrow operator. We can transform the above example in the following way:

Listing 2.44 Example of a "switch - case" statement with the arrow operator

The arrow operator (→) in Java is a shorthand for simple code blocks. As you can see, it is also useful in the **switch - case** statement. It is worth noting that there is no need to use **break** because the arrow operator automatically ends the execution of the current **case**.

The **switch - case** statement is useful when dealing with multiple cases treated equally, such as days of the week. For variables or more complex comparisons, it may be better to use the **if - else** statement.

Thus, we have expanded our knowledge of statements. We have understood how to effectively compare expression values and how to easily manage multiple scenarios depending on the input variable.

We have learned the syntax of the **switch** statement and the use of the arrow operator for more concise code.

We also know why break is necessary for this statement and how to avoid potential errors related to it.

This statement is concise and readable, especially when dealing with multiple equal options. However, it is important to remember that **switch** is not always the best choice, and sometimes it is better to use the **if - else** statement.

2.5.3 Check yourself!

1. **Which logical operator combines two conditions in a conditional statement in Java, checking if both are true?**

a) &&

b) ||

c) !

d) ==

2. **Which of the following instructions checks if two values are different from each other?**

   a) !=

   b) ==

   c) >

   d) <

3. **Which conditional statement in Java allows choosing one of many options based on the value of a single variable?**

   a) if

   b) else

   c) else if

   d) switch

4. **How many times can the if, else, and else if statements appear within a single block of conditional statements in Java?**

   a) Each of them can appear any number of times

   b) if can appear only once, else can appear only once, else if can appear any number of times

   c) if can appear any number of times, else can appear only once, else if can appear any number of times

   d) if can appear only once, else can appear only once, else if can appear only once

Task 3.5.1

Write a program in Java that will check whether a given number is **even** or **odd.** Then, the program should display an appropriate message informing about the result of the check.

Task 3.5.2

Write a program in Java that, based on the given student's **grade** in the form of a **number**, displays the corresponding grade in the form of a word according to the Polish grading system. Use the **switch - case** statement. For example, for the number **5**, it returns "**very good**".

2.6 Arrays , lists, maps

2.6.1 Arrays

In previous chapters, we dealt with variables whose task was to store data.

Imagine a situation where we need to store, for example, **100** values of the same type in a program. Creating **100** separate variables would be very time - consuming, troublesome, and above all, impractical.

This is where **arrays** come to our aid. Arrays are structures that gather a specified amount of data in an orderly manner. We can assign a name and size to arrays.

In Java, there are several different types of arrays. We will start with the simplest one – the one - dimensional array.

Arrays are declared as follows:

```
int[] array = new int[10];
```

Listing 2.45 Array Declaration

First, we specify the type of the **array**, followed by **square brackets**, which indicate that this part of the program is an array.

Next, we give the array a **name** and use the **equals sign** to create a new empty array. Finally, in the square brackets, we specify the **size** of the array. In this case, it is **10**.

There is also a second way to create a one - dimensional array.

It looks as follows:

```
int array[] = new int[10];
```

Listing 2.46 Another way to declare an array

It differs from the previous one only in the placement of the **square** brackets. The next method creates an array along with its **values**. It looks like this:

```
int array[] = new int[]{1,2,3,4};
```

Listing 2.47 Array declaration with values

As you can see, the concept of creating an array changes a bit. After the keyword **new int[],** the elements of the array are provided. We place them in curly braces.

When creating an array with values, we no longer need to specify its **size**.

We refer to the elements of the array using **indices**. Every array starts indexing from **0**. In this case, the number **1** will be at index **0**. To refer to this number, we will need to write **array[0]**. This means we are retrieving the element at index **0** from the array, which is the number **1**. If we want to refer to the last index of the array, we will need to write **array[3]**. An array can be of any type, including **String**. It will look like this:

```
String[] array = new
String[]{„first", „second", „third");
```

Listing 2.48 Declaration of a String array with values

An **array variable** can also be declared just like a **regular variable** without immediately creating it. In that case, we make the following notation:

```
int array[]
array = new int[]{1,2,3,4};
```

Listing 2.49 Declaration of an array without immediately creating it

To print the elements contained in the array, we can of course use the previously learned function **System.out.println().** In the parentheses, we provide the **name** of the array and its **index**. Such notation:

```
String[] array = new
String[]{„first", „second", „third", „fourth");
System.out.println(array[0]);
System.out.println(array[2]);
```

Listing 2.50 Printing array elements using System.out.println

It will return the following output in the console:

Figure 2.17 Console output of printed array indices

You already know how to print selected indices from an array. What if you want to create an array of a given size without knowing what values to put in it yet? Let's assume your array is supposed to hold **5** elements, but at the moment you want to enter only **3** and fill in the rest in the future. This is possible and relatively simple. We do it this way:

```
float[] array = new float[5];
array[4] = 3.14f;
System.out.println(array[4]);
```

Listing 2.51 Assigning a selected value to a chosen index in the array and then printing it using System.out.println

In the console, we will then get:

Figure 2.18 Console output of array index values

If we exceed the size of the array, the program will simply return an error. If we do not assign a **value** to an index, it will be automatically filled with the **default value** of the given type. For example, for a **float** array, the default value will be **0.0f**, and for a **boolean** array, it will be **false**.

Now let's move on to **multidimensional arrays**. As the name suggests, they have more than one dimension. Such an array can consist, for example, of **3 rows** and **4 columns**. They are declared in a similar way to one - dimensional arrays, but in these we use two square brackets:

```
int[][] array = new int[3][4];
```

Listing 2.52 Declaration of a multidimensional array consisting of 3 rows and 4 columns

We can imagine that a multidimensional array is simply a square with the given dimensions. An array can also have **three** dimensions. We create it by adding additional square brackets.

Now we will focus on two - dimensional arrays. Multidimensional arrays can be initialized with values just like one - dimensional arrays. We can do it this way:

```
int[][] array = { {1,2} , {3,5} };
```

Listing 2.53 Declaration of a multidimensional array with values

In these types of arrays, we store data in **curly braces** and separate the data with **commas**. As for printing values from specific indices in the array, we do it in a very similar way to one - dimensional arrays:

```
int[][] array = { {1,2} , {3,5} };
System.out.println(array[0][0]);
System.out.println(array[1][1]);
```

Listing 2.54 Declaration of a multidimensional array along with printing specific values

The given notation will display the following numbers:

```
1
5

Process finished with exit code 0
```

Figure 2.19 Printing selected indices of a multidimensional array in the console

In the first case, we received the number **1** because under the first index **[0]** there are two numbers – **1** and **2**. The next index is also **[0]**, which indicates the number **1**. Similarly, the same happens with the second result.

Java allows us to check the length of our array using the **length** function. This method will be useful in loops, which we will discuss in the later stages of this book. We print the length of the array in the following way:

```
float[] array = new float[3];
int[][] array_w = { {1,2} , {3,5} };
System.out.println(array.length);
System.out.println(array_w.length);
```

Listing 2.55 Checking and printing the length of an array in the console

```
3
2

Process finished with exit code 0
```

Figure 2.20 Printing the length of arrays in the console

In the first array, we can read the length already during initialization, whereas the second does not have a defined size, so this method is useful here. Arrays can be limiting in some respects. A particular disadvantage is the size, which cannot be changed and must be set during declaration.

2.6.2 Lists

In Java, there are also **lists**, which are a type used for storing data. A **list** is a flexible version of an **array**.

Regarding lists, we have two types of implementations:

- **ArrayList** – array - based implementation
- **LinkedList** – linked implementation

We typically use the **array - based** implementation when we care about the access time to data, and the **linked** implementation when we will frequently perform operations of adding and removing elements.

Lists are declared just like other objects. If we declare them as **List**, our code will be more universal, and we can change the implementation at any time without altering the rest of the code. It looks like this:

```
List list1 = new ArrayList();
List list2 = new LinkedList();
```

Listing 2.56 Declaration of lists

When you enter the following code in the main function, the words List, ArrayList, and LinkedList will certainly be underlined in red. This is because we need to import the appropriate libraries. Add at the very top:

```
import java.util.ArrayList;
import java.util.LinkedList;
import java.util.List;
```

Listing 2.57 Importing libraries for handling lists

There is also another way to create lists:

```
ArrayList<Integer> list1 = new ArrayList<Integer>();
LinkedList<String> list2 = new LinkedList<String>();
```

Listing 2.58 Another way to declare lists

First, we choose one of the two implementations – **Array** or **Linked**. Then, between the "< >" symbols, we write the type of the list. Next, we place the **name** of the list and the **equals sign**, and finally the word **new**. In Java, we have several basic methods for handling lists, regardless of which implementation we choose. These are:

- **add(Object)** – adding an element to the list;
- **remove(Object/int)** – removing an element or a specific index from the list;
- **size()** – checking the size of the list (works the same as length() for arrays);
- **get(int)** – retrieving a specific index from the list;

Now let's demonstrate the operation of these methods in practice. Enter the following code:

```
ArrayList<String> list = new ArrayList<String>();
//adding elements to the list, then printing the
list contents
list.add(„element1”);
list.add(„element2”);
list.add(„element3”);
System.out.println(list);

//removing an element from the list by its
name, then printing the list contents
list.remove(„element2”);
System.out.println(list);

//removing an element from the list by its
index, then printing the list contents
list.remove(1);
System.out.println(list);

//printing the size of the list after adding
and removing elements
System.out.println(list.size());

//retrieving the element from the list at
index 0, then printing it
System.out.println(list.get(0));
```

Listing 2.59 Operations on lists

The comments describe the exact operation of all methods. This is exactly what should be displayed in the console:

```
[element1, element2, element3]
[element1, element3]
[element1]
1
element1

Process finished with exit code 0
```

Figure 2.21 Result of list operations in the console

At first, we see all the elements of the list – just as we added them. Then, only two elements are displayed.

After removing **two** of the **three** elements, the **size** of the list is displayed, and at the very end, we print the element at index **0** – **element1**.

2.6.3 Maps

In Java, a **Map** is a data structure that consists of keys **and** their corresponding values. It can be considered as a pair: **key - value**. Each key is **unique** and corresponds to **one** value.

Maps are very useful when we need to store data in memory and later quickly search for **values** based on **keys**.

In Java, there are many implementations of the **Map** interface, but the most commonly used are:

- HashMap
- TreeMap
- LinkedHashMap

HashMap is most commonly used because it provides constant time access to elements.

TreeMap sorts elements by key, and LinkedHashMap maintains the order of insertion of elements.

For example, we can create a HashMap that stores the names of countries in Europe as keys and their population as values:

```
import java.util.HashMap;
import java.util.Map;
public class InputData {
   public static void main(String[] args){
Map<String, Integer> countriesPopulation = new
HashMap<>();
   countriesPopulation.put("Germany", 82370000);
   countriesPopulation.put("France", 62151000);
   countriesPopulation.put("Ukraine", 45994000);
   countriesPopulation.put("Spain", 40491000);
   countriesPopulation.put("Poland", 38501000);
   }
}
```

Listing 2.60 Creating a map and adding values and keys to it

In the above example, we create a **HashMap populacjaPanstw**, where the **keys** are of type **String** (country name) and the **values** are of type **Integer** (population).

Next, we add **five** elements to it using the **put()** method. To get the value for a given key, we use the **get()** method. We also need to import the appropriate libraries for maps, **Map** and **HashMap**.

```
System.out.println(„Population in Poland: " +
countriesPopulation.get(„Poland"));
System.out.println(„Number of provided countries: "
+ countriesPopulation.size());

countriesPopulation.remove(„Germany");
System.out.println(„Number of provided countries: „
+ countriesPopulation.size());
```

Listing 2.61 Examples of using methods on maps

In the example, we print the **population** of Poland and the total number of **countries** in the map.

We can remove elements from the map using the **remove()** method. In the example, we remove **Germany** and then print the updated number of countries in the map.

```
Population in Poland: 38501000
Number of provided countries: 5
Number of provided countries: 4

Process finished with exit code 0
```

Figure 2.22 Result of using methods on maps

The **get()** method used on the map will return the population of Poland. Next, we will get the number of countries we have in our map. In the first case, the returned value is **5**, and in the next case, it is **4**, because we removed **Germany** using the **remove()** method. Manually printing all elements of the map using the **get()** method would be too time - consuming. We will use a **foreach** loop to display them.

```
for(Map.Entry<String, Integer> x :
countriesPopulation.entrySet()){
    String country = x.getKey();
    int population = x.getValue();
    System.out.println(„The population of ″
+ country + „ is: „ + population);
}
```

Listing 2.62 Printing map elements using the "foreach" loop

In this code snippet, a foreach loop is used. It serves to iterate through all **key - value** pairs in the **populationofcountries** map. In each iteration of the loop, the variable x has the type **Map.Entry<String, Integer>,** which means it stores **one key - value** pair in the map.

The variable **country** is initialized with the key in the given **key - value** pair, representing the country name, and the variable **population** is initialized with the value in the given **key - value** pair, representing the population of the country. Then, information about the country's population is displayed using **System.out.println(),** which prints the country name and its population. In the console, it should look like this:

```
The population of Ukraine is: 45994000
The population of Poland is: 38501000
The population of France is: 62151000
The population of Spain is: 40491000

Process finished with exit code 0
```

Figure 2.23 Console output after printing map elements

A map does not allow having two identical keys, but values can be repeated. In **HashMap** and **LinkedHashMap**, null keys and values are allowed, whereas **TreeMap** does not allow them. Below is a list of selected methods from the map interface:

- **get()** - returns the value assigned to the given key or null if the key does not exist in the map.
- **size()** - returns the number of key - value pairs in the map.
- **keySet()** - returns a set of keys in the map.

- **entrySet()** - returns a set of Map.Entry objects representing key - value pairs in the map.
- **put()** - adds a key - value pair to the map or updates the value if the key already exists.
- **clear()** - removes all key - value pairs from the map.
- **containsKey()** - returns true if the map contains the given key.
- **containsValue()** - returns true if the map contains the given value.
- **equals()** - returns true if the map is equal to the given object.
- **hashCode()** - returns the hash code for the map.
- **isEmpty()** - returns true if the map does not contain any key - value pairs.
- **putAll()** - adds all key - value pairs from the given map to this map
- **remove()** - removes the key - value pair with the given key.
- **values()** - returns a collection of values in the map.

2.6.4 Check yourself!

1. **Which type of collection can the following methods be used for: put(key, value), get(key), containsKey(key), containsValue(value), and keySet()?**

   a) Only for arrays;

   b) Only for lists;

   c) Only for maps;

   d) Only for sets;

   e) Both for lists and maps;

   f) Both for maps and sets;

2. **How to get the length of an array in Java?**

   a) array.length();

   b) array.size();

   c) array.length;

3. **How to add a key - value pair to a map in Java?**

   a) map.add(key, value);

b) map.put(key, value);

c) map.insert(key, value;

Task 3.6.1

Write a program that calculates the average grade of a student based on a predefined array of grades.

2.7 Loops

In previous chapters, we got acquainted with arrays and lists. Both structures are commonly used in programming. Using appropriate methods, we can edit them. We can add, remove elements, and change their values.

However, let's consider the case where we have a **100 - element** array and want to make modifications to a larger number of elements.

We would have to repeatedly use the same method. Such a number of operations would take us a lot of time. What if the number of elements in the array is **1000 or more**? The solution to this problem is to use loops.

It is one of the basic constructs found in all programming languages. They are used in almost every program. Thanks to them, we can perform a specific method, function, or action as many times as we determine or until a certain condition is met. In Java, we have several types of loops, which are:

- While;
- to... while;
- for;
- foreach;

2.7.1 While loop

We use the **while** loop in situations where we do not know the exact number of operations to be performed. In short, the loop will run **as long** as the condition is **true**.

However, if the condition is **not met at all** (right at the start of its execution), it will not **run** at all. The flowchart along with the general scheme of the while loop are shown below:

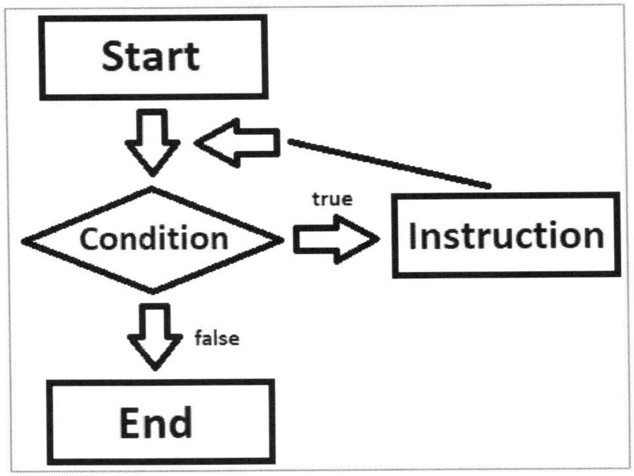

Figure 2.24 While loop diagram

```
while(true){
    //execution instruction
}
```

Listing 2.63 General scheme of while loop

First, the keyword **while**, then in parentheses is the **condition**, and inside the loop are the **instructions** that will be executed during the loop.

Now let's see how the while loop works in practice:

```
int i = 0;
while(i<10){
    i++;
    System.out.println(„The loop has
executed " + i + „ times");
}
```

Listing 2.64 Using the "while" loop

At the beginning, we declared a variable of type **int.** It stores a specific value – in this case, the **number 0**.

Next, the **while loop** appears. The condition for its execution is the logical comparison **i < 10**. This means that the loop will execute as long as the value of the variable i is less than **10**. Thanks to the incrementation **i++** within the loop body, we increase the value of the variable **i by one**. The **System.out.println** instruction will print the text that informs us **how many times** the loop has executed. Let's look at the program's operation:

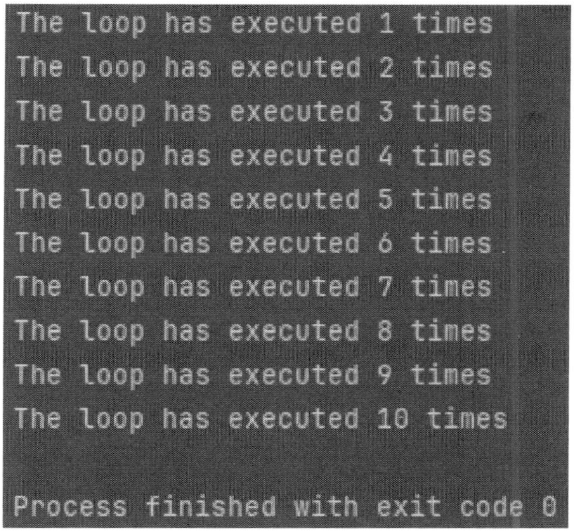

Figure 2.25 Result of the while loop program

As you can see, the loop executed exactly **10** times before it stopped. At the beginning, our variable i was equal to **0**. After the loop executed for the first time, its value increased to **1**. After the tenth execution of the loop, the value increased to **10**, and then the program stopped the loop because the condition was no longer true.

2.7.2 The do - while loop

Now it's time for the **do - while** loop. At first glance, it looks similar to the **while** loop. It differs mainly in that, regardless of the condition, the loop will execute at least once. This happens because the **condition** is checked only after the loop's **instructions** are executed, so at the beginning, it is not considered at all. The general scheme of the do - while loop looks like this:

```
do{
    //execution instruction
}while(true);
```

Listing 2.65 General scheme of the "do - while" loop

The construction of this loop differs from the regular **while** loop. This time, we start with the keyword **do**, then place the **instructions** to be executed inside, and finally, we place the loop **condition** preceded by the keyword **while**. A semicolon should also be placed here.

Let's see how the **do - while** loop works:

```
int i = 10;
do{
    i++;
    System.out.println(„The value of variable i is: ″ + i);
}while(i<10);
```

Listing 2.66 Using the "do - while" loop

And here is the result:

```
The value of variable i is: 11

Process finished with exit code 0
```

Figure 2.26 Result of the program using the "do - while" loop

If we used a regular **while** loop with the variable **i=10**, it would not execute at all. In the case of the **do - while** loop, the instruction will execute once regardless of the **condition**.

2.7.3 The for loop

It's time for the **for loop** – one of the most commonly used and simplest loops in Java. We use it when we know the exact number of iterations our loop should perform. For example, if we wanted to increase the value of a variable **100** times.

The general scheme of the for loop is as follows:

```
for(int i=0; i<10; i++){
    //execution instruction
}
```

Listing 2.67 General scheme of the "for" loop

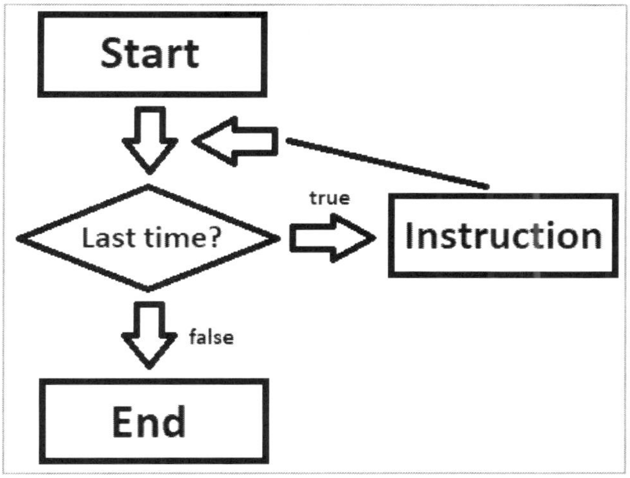

Figure 2.27 General scheme of the "for" loop

Let's move on to the for loop in practice:

```
int number = 100;
for(int i=0; i<10; i++){
    number--;
}
System.out.println(number);
```

Listing 2.68 Using the "for" loop

At the beginning of the program, we declared a variable of type **int** named **number**, whose initial value is **100**.

The **for** loop consists of three instructions separated by semicolons:

- The first is the **initial expression**;
- In the middle, we find the **condition** (similar to the while loop);
- The last is the counter modifier.

Inside the **loop** (between the curly braces), we place the **instruction to be executed**. In the above example, the **variable i**, which we start with, has an **initial value** of **0**.

Considering that the value is **0** and we increase it by **one** with each loop iteration, the loop will execute exactly **ten** times, as the condition will no longer be true after exceeding the value of **10**.

The operation of the program is illustrated by the following diagram:

```
90

Process finished with exit code 0
```

Figure 2.28 Result of the program using the "for" loop

Let's write a program that prints consecutive even numbers starting from 2.

```
for(int i=0; i<20; i+=2){
    System.out.print(i + ",");
}
```

Listing 2.69 Printing even numbers using the "for" loop

In this example, the variable **i** initially has a value of **0**.

Then its value increases by **2** each time until it exceeds **20**. The program prints the content of the variable and a comma in each loop iteration.

The result of the operation can be seen in the diagram below:

```
0,2,4,6,8,10,12,14,16,18,
Process finished with exit code 0
```

Figure 2.29 Even numbers printed by the "for" loop

In the next example, we will calculate the sum of numbers in the range from **0** to **100** that are divisible by **5**.

The loop will execute **one hundred** times – from the declared **i = 0** to the end of the condition, which is **100**. During the loop's execution, it will check if the current number is divisible **by 5**. A conditional statement is used here. It checks if the remainder of dividing the number by **5** is equal to **0**. If it is, the selected number will be added to the variable **sum.**

After the loop completes, the program will print the content of the variable **sum**.

```
int sum = 0;
for(int i=0; i<=100; i++){
    if(i % 5 == 0){
        sum+=i;
    }
}
System.out.println(„The sum is: "
+ sum);
```

Listing 2.70 Using the "for" loop to calculate the sum of numbers divisible by 5 within a specified range

```
The sum is: 1050

Process finished with exit code 0
```

Figure2.30 Printing the sum of the variable in the console

2.7.4 Loops in handling arrays and lists

Loops are very useful when handling **arrays** and **lists**.

They are helpful, for example, when we want to iterate through each element of a given **structure** and perform a specific operation on it.

First, we will declare a simple array and then fill it with numbers from 1 to 5.

```
int[] array = new int[5];
for(int i=0; i<array.length; i++){
    array[i] = i;
}
```

Listing 2.71 Array of type int filled with numbers using the "for" loop

Before using the **loop**, an **array** was initialized. To determine the **condition**, the **length** method was used, which counts the number of elements in the array. This value will be compared with **i**.

Next, in the **loop**, we used the **array.length** function, which tells us the number of elements, i.e., the length of the **array**. This means that the loop will run as long as the array is. Inside the **for** loop, we assign the value of the variable **i** to the individual elements of the array.

In the next example, we will use the for loop to print the contents of the array:

```
int[] array = new int[5];
for(int i=0; i<array.length; i++){
    array[i] = i;
}
for(int i=0; i<array.length; i++){
    System.out.println(„array[„+i+„] =
„ + array[i]);
}
```

Listing 2.72 Printing values from an array using a "for" loop

To the previous code snippet, we add a new "**for**" loop in which we print the values inside the array. The result in the console will be as follows:

```
array[0] = 0
array[1] = 1
array[2] = 2
array[3] = 3
array[4] = 4

Process finished with exit code 0
```

Figure 2.31 Console output of printing array contents

As you can see, each element of the array has a value equal to its index.

Sometimes, when using loops, we want them to execute a certain number of times but break at some point when a condition is met. In such cases, we can use the well - known break statement.

In the next example, we will demonstrate its use in a loop. The program will break the loop when it finds the number **3**.

This time, we will use a list. We will fill the list with selected numbers from the range **1 - 7**. If the loop encounters the number **3**, it will simply break its execution.

First, we will start by creating the list, filling it, and printing all the numbers that are in it. We do it this way:

```
ArrayList<Integer> list = new ArrayList<Integer>();

list.add(6);
list.add(4);
list.add(1);
list.add(3);
list.add(7);

for(int i=0; i<list.size(); i++){
    System.out.print(list.get(i) + „, ");
}
```

Listing 2.73 Declaring a list, filling it with numbers, and printing using a "for" loop

First, we declare a simple list of type **int**, and then we add **five** elements to it using the **add** method. The **for** loop's task is to print the contents of the list to the screen. In this exercise, we replaced the **length** method with the **size** method. It works similarly and returns the exact same value – the **size of the list**.

The **get()** method retrieves the index number of each element in the list. The console should return exactly this:

```
6, 4, 1, 3, 7,
Process finished with exit code 0
```

Figure 2.32 Console output after printing the list numbers

We complete the above code as follows:

First, we create a **loop** in which we use the **break** statement. It will be triggered when the program retrieves the value **3** from the index. To check the retrieved **index**, we use a **conditional statement**.

The program code will look like this:

```
ArrayList<Integer> list = new ArrayList<Integer>();

list.add(6);
list.add(4);
list.add(1);
list.add(3);
list.add(7);

for(int i=0; i<list.size(); i++){
    if(list.get(i) == 3){
        break;
    }else{
        System.out.println(list.get(i) + „, ");
        continue;
    }
}
```

Listing 2.74 Printing values from a list using a loop until it encounters the number 3

```
6,4,1,
Process finished with exit code 0
```

Figure 2.33 Console output of this program

2.7.5 Check yourself!

1. **Explain when to use a do - while loop instead of a while loop in Java. Provide examples of situations where a do - while loop is more appropriate.**

2. **How many times will the for loop execute in the following code?**

```
int sum = 0;
for(int i = 0; i<=10; i++){
    sum += i;
}
```

a) 10 times

b) 11 times

c) 9 times

d) 100 times

3. What happens if no condition is provided in the declaration of a while loop?

a) The compiler will display an error and the code will not compile.

b) The while loop will execute unconditionally until it is interrupted by a break statement..

c) The while loop will not execute at all, and the program will proceed to the next statement outside the loop.

d) The while loop will continue indefinitely, causing the program to hang.

4. How to execute a do - while loop in Java?

a) do { } while (condition);

b) while (condition) { } do;

c) while (condition) { } until;

Task 2.7.1

Write a Java program that calculates the **factorial** of a given integer using a **loop**. The factorial of a number n, denoted by **n!**, is the product of all **positive** integers less than or **equal** to **n**. For example, **5! = 5 * 4 * 3 * 2 * 1 = 120**.

Task 2.7.2

Write a program that displays integers in the range **<100, 1>** in descending order with a step of **2**.

2.8 Variable Scope

In the previous chapters, we expanded our knowledge on creating variables, using conditional statements, and loops. Now, we will address another important topic in Java programming – **variable scope**.

Variable scope simply refers to the area where our variables can operate and be understood. This is important because it affects how secure and organized our code is.

Let's consider a simple example with a **class** where the scope of a variable in the class is publicly accessible. Let's proceed to create a class named **ScopeClass**, and then declare an **int variable** named **visibleVariable** in it:

```
class ScopeClass {
    int visibleVariable = 5; //publicly accessible
variable
}
```

Listing 2.75 Class with a Public Variable

Now that we have this **variable**, let's check if we can actually use it, for example, in **methods**. To do this, let's add two new methods with arbitrary names inside the **class**. In both of them, we will try to print the **value** of our variable. We can do it this way:

```
class ScopeClass {
    int visibleVariable = 5; //publicly accessible
variable
    public void printValue(){
        //we can use it within this method
        System.out.println(„The value of the
variable: „ + visibleVariable);
    }
    public void doubleValue(){
        visibleVariable*=2;
        //we can use it within this method
        System.out.println(„The value of the
variable: „ + visibleVariable);
    }
}
```

Listing 2.76 Class with Two Methods Printing the Variable

In this case, the **sharedVariable** is accessible to both **methods** in the **class**. You can think of it as a tool available to everyone.

Now, let's consider what happens if we create a new variable in one of the methods and try to use it outside its scope. To see this, let's add another arbitrary method similar to the previous ones and declare a variable named **localVariable** in it:

```
public void thirdMethod(){
    int localVariable = 6; // local variable
available only within thirdMethod
    System.out.println("The value of the
variable: " + localVariable);
}
```

Listing 2.77 Method Containing a Local Variable and Printing Its Value

If we run our program by calling this method, the result will appear in the console without any issues. However, now let's place this variable in one of the other methods and see what happens when we try to compile the code. For example:

```
public void printValue(){
        //we can use it within this method
        System.out.println("The value of the
variable: " + visibleVariable);
        //attempting to use localVariable
outside its scope (will not compile)
        System.out.println("The value of the
variable: " + localVariable);
}
```

Listing 2.78 Placing a Local Variable in Another Method

Unfortunately, we won't be able to compile this code due to the lack of visibility of the **localVariable** by the **printValue** method. In other words, **localVariable** is a private variable only for the **thirdMethod**, which means it is accessible only within its scope and cannot be used in other parts of the code.

We have already understood how to control variables in **classes** and **methods**. Now, let's deal with **loops**, where we most often use variables for a short time. Let's create a new **method** in the **class**, and within it, a **loop**. For example:

```
public void loop(){
    for(int i=0; i<3; i++){
        //variable i is available only inside
the loop
        System.out.println(„Loop iteration
number ″ + i);
    }
    //outside the loop, variable i no longer exist
    System.out.println(i);
}
```

Listing 2.79 Method containing a "for" loop and the variable "i" accessible only within the loop

The values of variables in loops are available only inside the loop, which means they are used in a specific situation and do not exist outside of it. In the above example, such a variable is i. Just like in the previous case with **thirdMethod**, our method **loopMethod** will not compile.

Finally, let's look at a local variable for a specific block. Moving from **loops** to the **scope of variables** in **blocks**, it is worth noting that local variables can exist only in specific parts of the code. To illustrate this better, we will create a new method that includes a **conditional statement** along with a **variable.** Here is an example:

```
public void blockLogic(boolean condition){
    int externalVariable = 10; //variable accesible
throughout the method
    if(condition){
        int blockVariable = 5; //variable accesible
only within this block
        System.out.println(„Condition met. The value
of the variable: „ + blockVariable);

    //we can use external variables inside the block
    System.out.println(„Sum: ″ + (blockVariable +
externalVariable));
    }else{
        //at this point, blockVariable is no longer
accessible
        System.out.println(„Condition not met″);
    }
    //at this point, blockVariable is no longer
accessible
}
```

Listing 2.80 Method containing a conditional statement with a local variable

In the above example, the variable **blockVariable** is visible only within the if block. If the condition is met, we have access to this variable inside the block as well as to the variable **outerVariable**. If the condition is not met, then inside the else block we only have access to **outerVariable**. Using **blockVariable** outside the if block will cause an error. Understanding the scope of variables is crucial for maintaining order in the code and avoiding errors. It allows us to control the availability of variables in different parts of the program.

Knowing where a variable is accessible makes it easier to track and understand what values it can take and how it is used. With proper management of variable scope, our programs become more readable and transparent.

2.9 Memory Management – Garbage Collector

When we write a program, we mainly focus on designing and implementing specific elements of business logic and solving encountered problems. As much as possible, we improve the quality of the code itself by applying good programming practices. In short, we strive to build a functional application that meets our requirements.

Every project, regardless of its complexity, has its own memory where it stores variable values, classes, and their objects. However, this memory is not infinite. Often, we do not pay attention to what happens to the created objects when we stop using them. If they remained in memory permanently, they could quickly lead to its exhaustion. Fortunately, there is a mechanism that locates and removes unused objects. This is the **Garbage Collector**.

In general terms, the **Garbage Collector (GC)** is a mechanism responsible for automatic memory management in computer programs. Its main task is to reclaim memory occupied by objects that are no longer used by the program, which helps avoid memory leaks and maintain system stability and performance. In Java, the GC is an integral part of the Java Virtual Machine (JVM), but it can also be found in other programming languages, such as C# and Python.

To better illustrate what cleaning up memory from unused objects involves, let's look at the following code snippet.

```
public class GarbageCollectorExample {
    public static void main(String[] args) {

        String name1 = "Alexander";
        String name2 = "John";

        name1 = name2;
    }
}
```

Listing 2.81 Example of Losing Reference to the Value "Adam"

As you can see, the initial value of the variable **name1** was overwritten. Now both variables store the name "**Bartek**". So, what happened to the value "Adam"? It is no longer accessible, it lost its reference, yet it still occupies space in the application's memory. When the Garbage Collector starts the cleanup process, this value will be removed. Now, imagine similar overwriting of values in a loop that executes several thousand times. From the complexity perspective of this program, we are dealing with a trivial example, yet it generates unnecessary garbage. We often make similar mistakes in much larger projects, producing a lot of unnecessary objects.

Not so long ago, when the Garbage Collector did not exist, programmers had to manage memory manually in their programs. Every memory allocation had to be precisely tracked, and every released memory had to be manually freed. This practice was not only inconvenient and time - consuming but also very error - prone.

The **Garbage Collector** is an automatic mechanism. We do not need to call it to start working. It also does not require any configuration from our side. However, it is possible to manually call it using the **system.gc()** method, which indicates where it is worth carrying out the memory cleaning procedure. The second available method is **finalize()**, which allows the implementation of instructions that will be executed as the last action before the object is removed. However, it is not popular to use these methods because their operation is not always predictable and in certain situations can impair the **GC's** work. They are used in exceptional situations and rather only as a last resort or during application testing. Knowledge of their existence and application should be treated more as a curiosity, nevertheless worth remembering.

In summary, the **Garbage Collector** is an extremely useful tool that can save a lot of work for the programmer. By controlling the use of memory resources, it has a real impact on the performance and stability of the application. However, it should be remembered that no mechanism will replace optimized code. Therefore, let's focus on creating thoughtful programs instead of relying on the system to think for us.

2.10 Try - Catch Blocks

In previous chapters, we have already discussed conditional statements that helped our programs make various decisions. Now it's time to look at something more advanced – the **try - catch** statement.

This tool allows us to handle errors that may occur during the execution of our program, but it also allows us to anticipate them. We can imagine that **try - catch** is like a set of repair tools. It helps us first identify the problem and then solve it.

One of the better examples to illustrate this statement is the attempt to divide a number by zero. So let's move on to the practical application of try - catch:

```
public class TryCatchInstruction {
    public static void main(String[] args){
        int dividend = 6;
        int divisor = 0;
        int result = dividend/divisor;
    }
}
```

Listing 2.82 Attempt to Divide the Dividend by 0

First, we create a new class named **TryCatchInstruction**, and within it, the **main** method. Then, we declare three variables – **dividend, divisor**, and **result**. Each of these is of type int. The **dividend** takes any value greater than zero. In this example, it is the **number 6**. The **divisor** takes the value **0**.

The result is the quotient of the **dividend** divided by the **divisor**. When attempting to run the program, the following error will be displayed:

```
Exception in thread "main" java.lang.ArithmeticException Create breakpoint : / by zero
    at TryCatchInstruction.main(TryCatchInstruction.java:5)
```

Figure 2.34 Error Caused by Attempting to Divide by 0

As you can see, it is impossible to divide a number by **zero**. Now, let's try to include the previously mentioned **try - catch** statement in the above code. In the **main** method, let's write:

```
int dividend = 6;
int divisor = 0;

try{
    int result = dividend/divisor;
    System.out.println(„Division result: " +
result);
}catch(ArithmeticException e){
    System.err.println(„Arithmetic error with
message: " + e.getMessage());
}
```

Listing 2.83 Attempt to Divide a Variable by 0 in a "try - catch" Block

Below the variables **dividend** and **divisor**, we use the **try** statement, inside which is the code that could potentially cause an exception. In our program, this is the attempt to divide by zero and then assign the **result** to the variable result.

Next, we print the result using the **System.out.println()** statement. If an error occurs while executing the code in the **try** block (for example, division by zero), the program moves to the **catch** block.

In parentheses, we place the name of the exception that **catch** will handle and the name of the object (most commonly, the letter **e** is used in catch). In this case, the **catch** block handles the **ArithmeticException**, which is displayed in the event of an arithmetic error. This error message was already displayed during the first attempt to compile our program.

Inside the catch block is the code that handles the error. We display an error message on the standard error output System.err. Information about the error is obtained from the object **e**, which is an instance of the **ArithmeticException** class. **getMessage()** allows the object e to retrieve the message about this exception. The following message should appear in the console:

```
Arithmetic error with message: / by zero
```

Figure 2.35 Displaying an Error Message in the Console

This example demonstrates how, using the **try - catch** statement, we can control situations where errors occur (such as division by zero) and handle them in a controlled manner, instead of leaving the program with a visible error. Now, we will show the handling of another exception related to arrays. Let's create a new array of type int with three elements:

```
int[] numbers = {1,2,3};
```

Listing 2.84 Creating a Three - Element Array

The array contains three numbers. Let's see what happens if we try to access the fourth index of the array.

For example:

```
System.out.println(numbers[4]);
```

Listing 2.85 Attempt to Access a Non - Existent Array Index

When we run the program, it will return an error:

```
Exception in thread "main" java.lang
 .ArrayIndexOutOfBoundsException Create breakpoint : Index 4 out of bounds
 for length 3
    at TryCatchInstruction.main(TryCatchInstruction.java:16)
```

Figure 2.36 Error Accessing a Non - Existent Array Index

We cannot access an index that does not exist in a given array. Now, let's handle the given exception using the **try - catch** statement. The complete code should look like this:

```
int[] numbers = {1,2,3};
try{
    System.out.println(numbers[4]);
}catch(ArrayIndexOutOfBoundsException e){
    System.err.println(„Array index error: ” +
e.getMessage());
}
```

Listing 2.86 Handling Array Index Exception Using "try - catch"

We placed our **System.out.println()** in the **try** block, while **System.err.println()** is in the catch block. If we run the program, we will get the following in the console:

```
Array index error: Index 4 out of bounds for length 3
```

Figure 2.37 Array Index Error Displayed in the Console

We can also use general **exception** handling. Replace **ArrayIndexOutOfBoundsException** with the word **Exception**. The result will be the same, but using this is not recommended because it can make diagnosing and fixing errors more difficult. Additionally, it can hide details of the specific type of exception.

The **try - catch** statement in Java allows handling various types of exceptions. Those used in the examples above are among the most popular. Besides them, other common exceptions include:

- **NullPointerException** – when we try to access a method or field of an object that has a null value.
- **NumberFormatException** – when we try to convert a string to a number, and it is not possible.
- **IllegalArgumentException** – when we try to pass invalid arguments to a method.

These are just a few of the available exceptions. There are many more in Java.

2.11 Check yourself!

1) What are the advantages of a garbage collector?

a) Manual memory management, which allows for more precise control over resources.

b) Automatic memory release, eliminating the need for manual memory management and preventing memory leaks

c) Forcing memory cleanup with each operation, ensuring immediate release of unused resources.

2) What is the main role of the try - catch block in Java?

a) Protects the code from errors and provides an alternative execution path in case an exception occurs.
b) Provides a mechanism to execute code repeatedly until a certain condition is met.
c) Allows creating sections of code that will only be executed if nc exception is thrown.

CHAPTER 4

OBJECT – ORIENTED PROGRAMMING

3 Object – Oriented programming

3.1 Classes, Methods, Objects

Classes are the fundamental elements of programs in Java. Everything we create in Java is related to **classes** and **objects**. A class is a structure that defines objects called **fields**, and their behaviour in the program is managed by the class methods.

A **class** is a template or blueprint from which **objects** are created. We define it in a separate file that has the same name as the class. Its name usually starts with a capital letter.

A special **method** of each **class** is called a **constructor**. It is invoked when the **class** is created and defines how **objects** are instantiated.

Let's move on to practice, which involves creating **classes**. In Java, objects are created based on a **class**.

We create a new file named **Class**. Then, we define a class named **Class** within it, where we will place one **variable** and then call it in the **main** method.

So:

```
class Class {
    int number = 10;

    public static void main(String[] args){
        Class kl = new Class();
        System.out.println(kl.number);
    }
}
```

Listing 3.1 Creating a class containing a variable and then its object

First, we create a class named **Class** by preceding the entered name with the word **class**. Inside it, we place a variable **number,** which we assign a numeric value of **10**. Then, the main method appears.

As a reminder, **main** is the startup method of the program. It allows us to execute various instructions. To make the task easier and save some time, you can create it by typing **psvm** in the program and then pressing **Enter**. It will be automatically added to the code.

We create the **class object** inside the **main** method. First, we provide the **name** of the **class** for which we are creating the **object** (in this case Class), then the name of our object (here **kl**). Later, using the keyword new, we create a new instance of the class with the name provided at the end of the code.

In this way, we have created an object of our class named **kl**.

In the next line, we call the **variable** located in the **class**. To do this, we first need to provide the name of the **object** of the appropriate **class**, followed by the dot symbol "**.**" and the name of the **variable** or **method** that is in the **class.** We will call the whole thing using the **System.out.println()** method.

After running the program, the number **10** will appear in the console – the value of the **variable number**. In the **main** method, we can create an infinite number of objects.

For example:

```
class Class {
    int number = 10;
    String text = "New object";

    public static void main(String[] args){
        Class kl1 = new Class();
        Class kl2 = new Class();
        System.out.println(kl1.number);
        System.out.println(kl2.text);
    }
}
```

Listing 3.2 Creating two objects of the class and printing their values in the main method

In the class, we additionally placed a new **string** variable named **text**, which stores **text**. In the main method, we changed the name of the object **kl** to **kl1** and added a new object named **kl2**. In this way, we have two objects of one class.

The **System.out.println()** method will print the text assigned to the object kl2.

In the console, we will see the following result:

```
10
New object


Process finished with exit code 0
```

Figure 3.1 Console output of the previous program

We can, of course, swap these objects so that the object **kl1** calls the variable **text**, and the object **kl2** calls the variable **number**, or call both **variables** using only one **object**. Thanks to class objects, we have the ability to change the values of variables.

For example:

```
class Class {
    int number = 10;
    String text = "New object";

    public static void main(String[] args){
        Class kl1 = new Class();
        Class kl2 = new Class();
        kl1.number = 50;
        kl2.text = "Changed object";
        System.out.println(kl1.number);
        System.out.println(kl2.text);
    }
}
```

Listing 3.3 Changing the values of variables through a class object

We added two new lines to the previous program. In these lines, we assigned new **values** to two **variables**.

After running the program, these new values will be printed in the console instead of the ones declared in the **class**. Such a change in values cannot be made if the **variable** is of the **final** type.

3.1.1 Class Method

You've already learned a lot about **methods** while reading this book, but now it's time to get to know them a bit closer and more in detail. In Java, a **method** is a **block** of code that performs a specific operation or computation.

A **method** can be called from anywhere in the program, and the result of the method's operation can be returned to the place from which it was executed.

A method can be used to perform specific operations repeatedly without the need to repeat the code. It usually consists of three elements: the **name**, the **parameter list** (optional), and the **body**, which contains the **instructions** to be executed when the method is called. Now, let's discuss some important methods in Java that you will definitely use in the future.

First, we'll look at **non - static methods**, which are methods called on an **object** of a given **class**. They are useful for performing operations on the **state** of an **object**. An example of the simplest such method, which everyone encounters at the beginning of their programming journey, is a method that returns "**Hello World**."

Here's the code for this method:

```
class Class {
   public static void helloWorld(){
      System.out.println("Hello World");
   }

   public static void main(String[] args){
      helloWorld();
   }
}
```

Listing 3.4 Example Method "helloWorld"

In the code above, the word **public** means that the method is accessible from anywhere in the program. **Static** means that the **method** belongs to the **class**, not to its instance. **Void** means that the **method** does not return any **value**, and **helloWorld** is the name of the **method**.

We call this method inside the **main** method, which is the entry point of the program. When the program is run, the text "**Hello World**" will be displayed on the screen. The method can be called an infinite number of times.

```
class Class {
   static void addNumbers(int number){
      System.out.println(number + 5);
   }

   public static void main(String[] args){
      addNumbers(3);
   }
```

As mentioned above, the **method** can accept information as **parameters** and **arguments**. Parameters behave like variables inside the method. They are specified after the method name in **parentheses**.

Listing 3.5 Example Method with a Parameter

First, we created a new static variable named **addingNumbers**, whose parameter is an **int** type variable named **number**. Next, in the **main** method, we call our method. Since our parameter is an **int** type variable, we need to provide an **integer** in parentheses (in this case, the **number 3**). The operation of the method is very simple: it adds the **number 5** to the number we provided when calling the method. The console will display the **number 8**, which is the **sum** of the given numbers.

A method can have more than one parameter, and they can be of different types.

For example:

```
class Class {
   static void subjectGrade(int grade,
String subject){
      System.out.println("The student received
a grade of " + grade + " in the subject " +
subject);
   }
   public static void main(String[] args){
      subjectGrade(5,"computer science");
   }
}
```

Listing 3.6 Example of Using a Method with Two Parameters

Another parameter of type **String** is separated by a **comma** from the previous one. Each subsequent **parameter** will also be written after a comma.

The next methods to be discussed are **static** methods. These are methods that are called without **creating** an **object** of the **class**. They are useful for performing operations that do not require the **state of an object**.

The keyword **void** in the above examples informs us that the method does not return any value.

To make a method return a value, we need to replace **void** with a primitive data type (e.g., **int, char**, etc.). Additionally, we need to include the keyword **return** in our method. Thus:

```
class Class {
    static int addNumbers(int number){
        return number + 5;
    }

    public static void main(String[] args){
        System.out.println(addNumbers(3));
    }
}
```

Listing 3.7 Example of a Method Returning a Value

This is the same program we wrote previously (a method with one parameter), but it has been updated to return a value. In the program, the keyword **int** replaces **void**, which means that our method returns a value of type **int**.

Inside the **method**, there is the keyword **return**, which indicates the **value** to be returned. After return, we write exactly what the method should return. In the **main** method, our method is called. To display the result in the console, it must be written in **System.out.println().**

Now, let's write a program with a method that returns a value and has two parameters. Below, there is an example program:

```
class Class {
    static int subtractNumbers(int x, int y){
        return x-y;
    }

    public static void main(String[] args){
        int result = subtractNumbers(5,3);
        System.out.println(result);
    }
}
```

Listing 3.8 P Example of a Method Returning a Value with Two Parameters

Our **method** will involve **subtracting** two **integers** from each other. The structure of the method is the same as in the previous program, but we add another parameter, separated by a **comma** from the previous one. In the **main** method, we added a variable **result** of type **int**, which will store the value returned by the **method**. Then, in **System.out.println(),** we place this **result**. This is a different, more organized way of printing the value to the console because the **result of the method** is stored by the **variable**.

3.1.2 Method Overloading

Let's take a look at the following example:

```
class Class {
    static int addNumbers(int x, int y, int z){
        return x+y+z;
    }

    static int subtractNumbers(int x, int y, int z){
        return x-y-z;
    }

    public static void main(String[] args){
        int additionResult = addNumbers(7,4,2);
        int subtractionResult = subtractNumbers(5,3,1);
        int finalResult =
additionResult-subtractionResult;
        System.out.println(finalResult);
    }
}
```

Listing 3.9 Example of Methods Returning a Value with Three Parameters

The program contains two methods – **addingNumbers** and **substractingNumbers**. In the first method, the returned value will be the sum of all three numbers, while in the second method, it will be their difference.

The results of calling these methods are stored in variables – **resultofAdding** and **resultofSubstraction**. Then, the difference between these two variables is stored in the variable **finalResult**, and this is what is printed by **System.out.println().**

What if we wanted to add more or fewer than **three** numbers? Or maybe we would prefer them to be of type **double** instead of **int**?

In such a situation, we would have to create numerous methods with different names to know which one corresponds to the given types and quantities. This is certainly not the best solution. This is where overloaded methods come to our aid. **Method overloading** is a mechanism in the Java programming language that allows defining multiple methods with the same name but differing in **types** and/or numbers of parameters. This allows for more flexible use of the method depending on the needs. For example, if we have a class **Mathematics**, we can define an overloaded addition method that accepts different numbers of arguments, such as:

```
public class Mathematics {
   public int add(int a, int b){
       return a + b;
   }
   public int add(double a, double b){
       return a + b;
   }
   public int add(int a, int b, int c){
       return a + b + c;
   }
}
```

Listing 3.10 Example of Method Overloading "add"

In the example above, we have three methods named **add**, but they differ in the **number** and/or **types of parameters**. The first method accepts two parameters of type **int**, the second – two parameters of type **double**, and the third – three parameters of type **int**. When calling the method, the Java compiler automatically matches the arguments to the appropriate method based on their types and numbers. For example, when we call the **add** method with two **int** arguments, the **first method** is called; when with two **double** arguments – the **second method**; and when with **three int arguments** – the **third** method.

Thanks to **method overloading**, we can avoid excessive creation of methods with different names, which increases code readability and makes it easier to maintain. Below is an example of using these three **add** methods:

```
public class Main {
   public static void main(String[] args){
      Mathematics calculator = new Mathematics();

      int result1 = calculator.add(3,4);
      double result2 = calculator.add(4.2, 5.3)
      int result3 = calculator.add(2,4,7);

      System.out.println(result1);
      System.out.println(result2);
      System.out.println(result3);
   }
}
```

Listing 3.11 Example of Using the Overloaded "add" Method

The results of the add methods are assigned to the variables **result1** (for adding two **int** variables), **result2** (for adding two **double** variables), and **result3** (for adding three **int** variables). **System.out.println()** will display three different results in the console, corresponding to the respective methods.

3.1.3 Accessor Methods (Getters and Setters)

The next methods we will discuss are accessor methods (**getters and setters).** These are **methods** that allow **reading** and **writing the values** of private fields (attributes) of a class. This way, we avoid direct access to the class fields from other classes, which increases control over the data.

A **getter** returns the value of a private field, and a **setter** sets the value for that field.

Here is an example:

```
class Class{
   private String name;

   //Getter
   public String getName(){
      return name;
   }

   //Setter
   public void setName(String newName){
      this.name = newName;
   }
}
```

Listing 3.12 Example of Setter and Getter in a Class

This code defines a private field of the **class** named **Name**. It is of type **String.** The **field** is private, which means it is not directly accessible from other classes.

Next, the class defines two public methods: **getName** and **setName**. These are called **getters** and **setters**. They are used to get and **set** the value of the **name** field.

The **setName** method sets the value of the **name** field to the value passed as the parameter **newName**. This is an example of a **setter** method, which allows setting the value of the field from outside.

The method is also marked with the **public** access modifier to be accessible from other **classes**. In the body of the **setName method**, the keyword **this** is used, which refers to the current object, i.e., the instance of the class in which this method is called. Using this indicates that we want to set the value of the **name** field for the current object, not for another one. The **getName method** returns the value of the **name** field, allowing the current value of this field to be read from other **classes**. This **method** is also marked with the **public** access modifier.

Here is an example of using these methods:

```
class Class{
   private String name;

   //Getter
   public String getName(){
      return name;
   }

   //Setter
   public void setName(String newName){
      this.name = newName;
   }

   public static void main(String[] args){
      Class person = new Class();
      person.setName("Anna");
      System.out.println("The person's
name is: " + person.getName());
   }
}
```

Listing 3.13 Example of Using Setter and Getter

In this example, we create a new object of the class and set its name using the **setName** method. Then, using the **getName** method, we retrieve the value of the **name** field and display it in the console. This way, we accessed the private variable **name** and used it.

Another important method in Java is the **toString()** method. It returns a textual representation of an object of the class. This **method** is useful for displaying information about the **object**. Here is an example:

```
class Class{
   private String name;

   //Getter
   public String getName(){
      return name;
   }

   //Setter
   public void setName(String newName){
      this.name = newName;
   }

   @Override
   public String toString(){
      return "Person's name is " + name;
   }
}
```

Listing 3.14 Example of Using the "toString" Method

In this program, the **class** has one private field **name**, and its value is set using the **setName method**. In the **toString()** method, a text representing the object of the class **Class** is returned.

Now, create a new **class** named **Main** and write the following code in it:

```
public class Main {
   public static void main(String[] args){
      Class person = new Class();
      person.setName("Arthur");
      System.out.println(person.toString());
   }
}
```

Listing 3.15 Code of the New Class

In the **main()** method, a new object of the class **Class** is created. The name of this person is set using **setName()** and the result of the **toString()** method for this object is displayed. The console will return:

```
The person's name is: Arthur

Process finished with exit code 0
```

Figure 3.2 Displaying Object Information Using the "toString" Method

A useful feature in the **IntelliJ** environment is the automatic generation of the above methods, i.e., **getter, setter**, and **toString().** To do this, simply right - click anywhere in your code, then select **Generate**... and choose one of the options: **Getter, Setter, Getter and Setter, toString().** A window will appear where you select the variables that will be elements of your chosen methods. In this case, it is **name**.

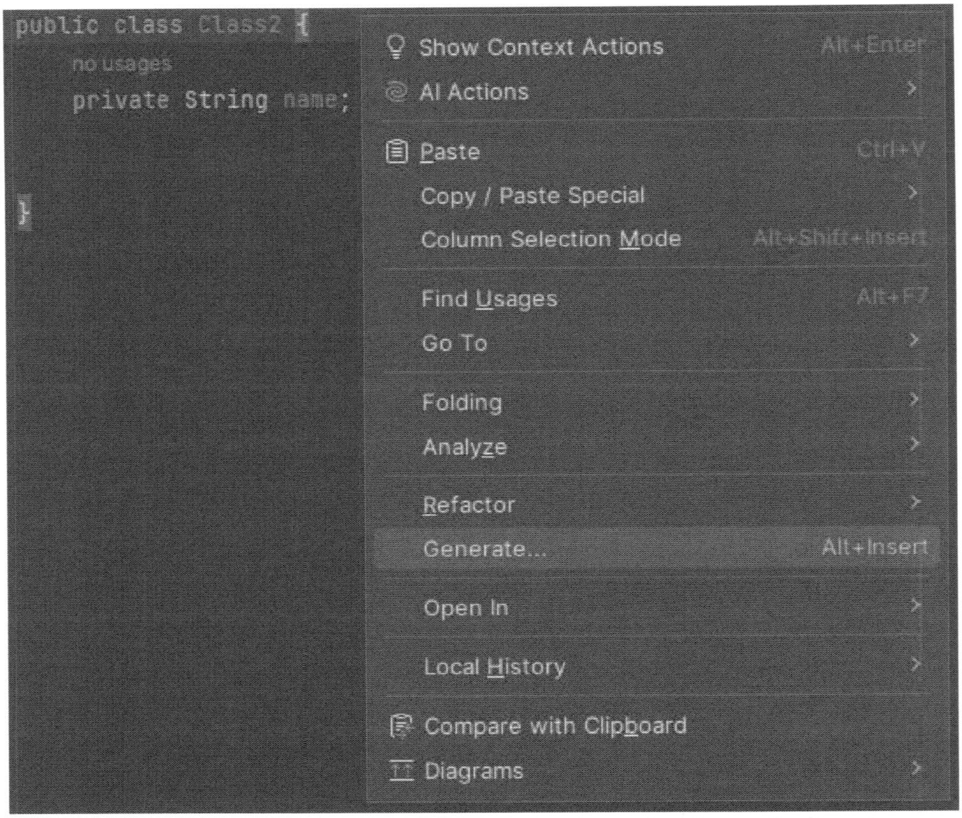

Figure 3.3 Right - clicking on a free area of the code, then selecting the "Generate..." option.

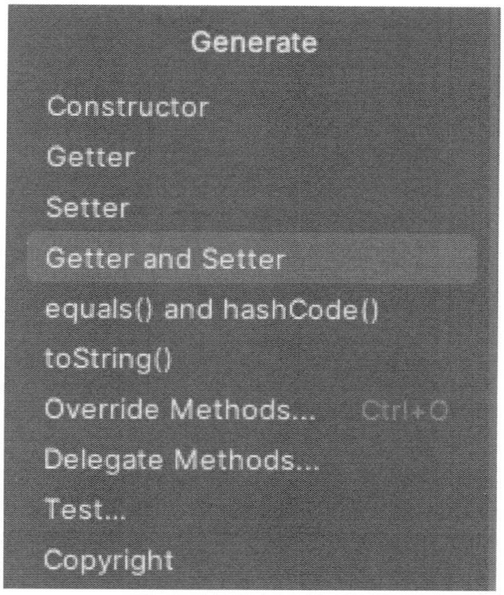

Figure 3.4 Selecting the methods we are interested in – "Getter and Setter", to generate them in the program.

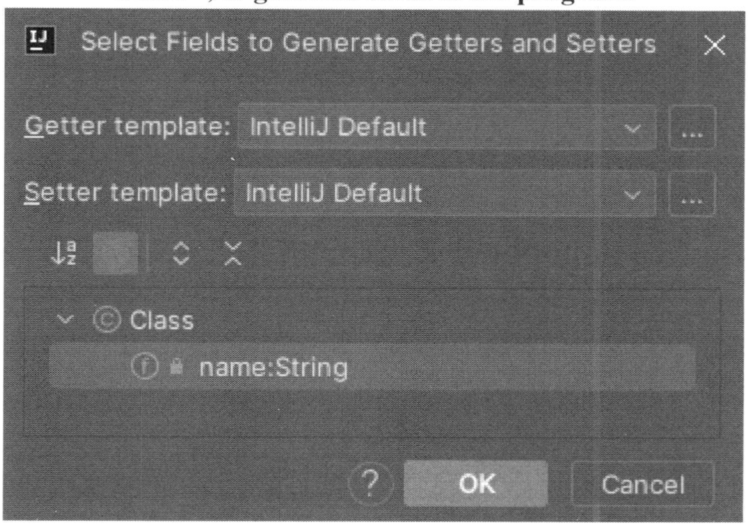

Figure 3.5 Choosing the variable that will be an element of our generated method.

```
class Class {
    2 usages
    private String name;
    no usages
    public String getName() {
        return name;
    }

    no usages
    public void setName(String name) {
        this.name = name;
    }

}
```

Figure 3.6 Generated "Getter and Setter" Methods

As you can see, the program has automatically generated both the **Getter** and **Setter** methods for us. You can now do the same with the **toString()** method. The result will be as follows:

```
class Class {
   private String name;

   //Getter
   public String getName(){
      return name;
   }

   //Setter
   public void setName(String newName){
      this.name = newName;
   }

   @Override
   public String toString(){
      return "Class{" + "name='" + name + '\'' + '}';
   }
}
```

Listing 3.16 Generated "toString()" Method

3.2 Access Modifiers and Encapsulation

3.2.1 Access Modifiers

In Java, we have two types of modifiers: **access modifiers** and **other types of modifiers**.

The latter includes modifiers like **static** and **abstract**, but in this chapter, we will focus only on access modifiers. These modifiers define which fields, methods, or classes are accessible within what scope. We can regulate the access levels of these fields by using the appropriate modifiers. In Java, there are four different access modifiers:

- **default (no modifier)** – This is the default access modifier (when none of the others are declared). It provides access control within a specific package, protecting against unwanted access from outside the package.
- **private** – Restricts access to fields and methods to the class in which they are declared. It protects data from direct access from outside the class, allowing controlled access through public methods.
- **protected** – Allows access to fields and methods within the package and by inheriting classes, maintaining access control.
- **public** – Allows access to fields and methods from anywhere in the program.

Below there is a table presenting the visibility of access modifiers in different contexts:

Access Modifier	Within the same class	Within the same package	Outside the package only through	Outside the package, from any
Private	Yes	No	No	No
Default	Yes	Yes	No	No
Protected	Yes	Yes	Yes	No
Public	Yes	Yes	Yes	Yes

Table 3.7 Visibility of Access Modifiers in Different Contexts

Now let's move on to practice, where we will demonstrate the application of each of the above modifiers in code. First, let's create a class named **VariableScope**. It's important to remove the word **public** from the class name in this example.

Above the class, we define the package by writing **package myPackage**;. Packages in Java help organize code, allowing the grouping of classes with similar functionality.

At this point, the program should look like this:

```
package myPackage;
class VariableScope{}
```

Listing 3.17 Package Definition and Class Creation

The name'**myPackage**'is likely underlined in red. This happens because the **class** should belong to a **package**. To fix this, simply right - click on the name '**myPackage**' (or use the **Alt+Enter** combination).

Here's how you can define the package and create the class:

Figure 3.7 Showing Context Actions for the Package

A menu with various options will appear. We select **Show Context Actions**, which will display possible solutions. We then choose the option **Move to package 'myPackage'**, which will move our class to the package.

Figure 3.8 Moving the Class to the Package

You will notice that a new package with the name you previously provided has appeared on the right side in the **src** directory. Our **VariableScope** class has been moved to this package.

Figure 3.9 Creating a New Package in the "src" Directory

Inside the existing package, we will create another class. This will be a test class where we will check the accessibility of selected fields. We create the class in the standard way, but this time we right - click on **myPackage** instead of **src**, as we did previously. Then, we go to the **New** option and select **Java Class**.

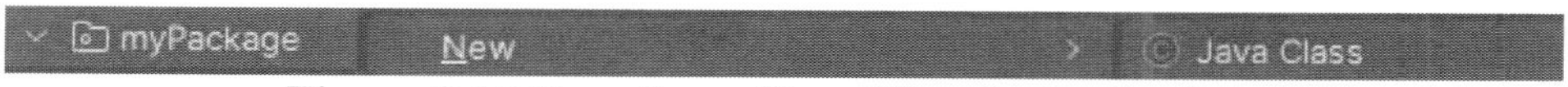

Figure 3.10 Creating a New Class in the Package

We name the new class **TestClass**. Now, both classes are inside the **myPackage** package. When we open **TestClass**, we will notice that the package for this class has been created automatically.

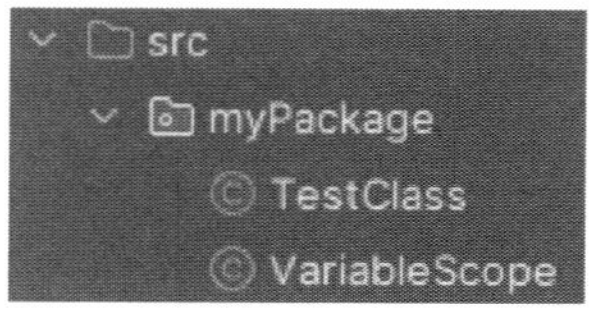

Figure 3.11 A New Class in the Package

Let's go back to the **VariableScope** class and add a new **static variable** named **number** of type **int**, which stores the value 7. It should look like this:

```
package myPackage;
class VariableScope{
   static int number = 7;
}
```

Listing 3.18 Class with a Static Variable

In this example, the variable **number** is declared as static, which allows access to it from another class without needing to create an object. Since we haven't yet dealt with object - oriented programming, we need to do it this way.

Now, let's go to **TestClass** and create a **main** method. Within this method, we will try to access the **number** variable from the **VariableScope** class. Inside the main method, we use the **System.out.println** command to display the value of the static variable **number**. To access this **number** variable from the **VariableScope** class in **TestClass,** we use the syntax **VariableScope.number**, which is possible because both classes are in the same package. The code should look like this:

```
package myPackage;
public class TestClass{
   public static void main(String[] args){
      System.out.println("Value of the
variable: " + VariableScope.number);
   }
}
```

Listing 3.19 Creating the main Method in a Class and Displaying the Value of a Variable from Another Class

When you run the program, the console should display the message'**Variable value7'.** If we refer back to the table showing the visibility of access modifiers in different contexts, we notice that variables with the **default** modifier are accessible within the same package. If we now add the word private before the name of the static variable in the **VariableScope** class, we would lose access to it in the **TestClass** class, and the program would display an error when trying to run it.

Speaking of the **private** modifier, we know that it is only accessible within the same class. However, it is possible to use these variables in other classes, but for this purpose, **getters** and **setters** must be used. These object - oriented programming concepts will be discussed in more detail later in the book. Now, let's create a new class named **ZZ_private**. It is important not to place it in the **myPackage** package. Then, declare a new private variable of type int named **number**, and below it, add the **main** method. Inside the main method, try to print the value of the private variable using **System.out.println().** The entire code should look like this:

```
public class SV_private {
    private int number = 6;

    public static void main(String[] args){
        System.out.println(number);
    }

}
```

Listing 3.20 Attempting to Print a Private Variable from Another Class

The variable **number** will be highlighted in red because the **main** method does not have access to it. Essentially, we can't do much with a private variable because it has very limited accessibility. To display it in the **main** method, we need to add the word **static** between **private** and **int** for our variable **number**. This will allow the program to run and print the value **6**. As mentioned, without **getters** and **setters**, we cannot access private variables in other classes.

Now, let's move on to the **protected** access modifier. This modifier plays an important role in the accessibility of fields and methods, especially in the context of inheritance. We will learn more about this in the chapters on object - oriented programming, but for now, let's show a simple example of using **protected**.

Let's create a new package named **myPackage2**, and within it, create two classes named **ZZ_protected** and **TestClass**. In the first class, declare a new protected static variable of type int named **number**, with a value of **10**. In the **TestClass** class, write the main method, and inside it, try to print the value of the **number** variable. The code for the **ZZ_protected** class should look like this:

```
package myPackage2;
public class SV_protected {
   protected static int number = 10;
}
```

Listing 3.21 Class with a Protected Variable

Below there is the example code for the **TestClass** class:

```
package myPackage2;
public class TestClass {
   public static void main(String[] args){
      System.out.println(SV_protected.number);
   }
}
```

Listing 3.22 Displaying a Variable from Another Class in the Same Package

In this case, the **TestClass** class can directly use the **protected** variable from the **ZZ_protected** class without utilizing inheritance. The **protected** modifier allows access to class elements from other classes within the same package or even from different packages.

The last access modifier is **public**.

To demonstrate its functionality, let's create another class named **ZZ_public**, and within it, declare a public static variable named **number**, which holds the value **15**. Here is the example code for this class:

```
public class SV_public {
   public static int number = 15;
}
```

Listing 3.23 Class with a Static Varaible

Now, let's create a new class named **PublicTest**. This class will attempt to access the **number** variable from the **ZZ_public** class. We will declare the main method in it. Inside this method, we use **System.out.println()** to display the value of the **number** variable.

Here is the code for the **PublicTest** class:

```
public class PublicTest {
    public static void main(String[] args){
        System.out.println(SV_public.number);
    }
}
```

Listing 3.24 Printing a Public Variale from Another Class

When you run this program, the console will display our number. The public modifier is the least restrictive and thus the most accessible from other classes.

Using appropriate access modifiers helps maintain the security and integrity of the code. By restricting access to variables and methods (e.g., using private), you can prevent accidental changes. There is a principle called the '**least privilege**' principle, which suggests assigning the minimum permissions necessary. Avoid using **public** where **protected** or **default** would suffice.

The scope of variable visibility and access modifiers are key elements in managing code in Java. Proper use of them also affects the readability and maintainability of the project. We will learn more about their use in future chapters.

3.2.2 Encapsulation

Encapsulation is one of the fundamental concepts of object - oriented programming, aimed at hiding the implementation details of an object and restricting access to its fields and methods.

In Java, **encapsulation** is achieved by defining **private** fields within a class, meaning they can only be modified within that class. To access these fields from outside, we use public methods known as **getters** and **setters**, which allow us to read the value of a field or set a new value. This approach protects our code from uncontrolled access and modification of field values, leading to improved security, easier code maintenance, and data consistency. Here's an example:

```
public class Person {
   private String name;
   private String surname;

   public Person(){}

   public Person(String name, String surname){
      this.name = name;
      this.surname = surname;
   }

   public String getName(){
      return name;
   }

   public void setName(String name){
      this.name = name;
   }
}
```

Listing 3.25 Example of Encapsulation

In the example below, we define a **class Person** that has private fields **firstName** and **lastName**. To access these fields from outside, we define **getters** and **setters**. These methods are public, meaning they can be called from anywhere in the program. If we try to modify the value of a field directly from outside, for example:

```
public class Main {
   public static void main(String[] args){
      Person man = new Person();
      man.name = "Jack";
   }
}
```

Listing 3.26 Attempting to Modify a Field Value Directly from Outside

The name **firstName** will be highlighted in red, and when trying to compile, an error will be generated because the field is private and inaccessible from outside the **Person** class. Thanks to encapsulation, we can be sure that our code works correctly and ensures data security. The ability to generate **getters** and **setters** in **IntelliJ** further simplifies the use of encapsulation.

3.3 Constructors

In this chapter, we will discuss objects in more detail. Objects are the fundamental units of object - oriented programming in Java and represent instances of classes. They are data structures containing variables and methods that can be invoked within that instance. An object is created based on a class that defines its structure and behaviour.

We can say that an object has the following characteristics:

- **State** (represented by the object's attributes),
- **Behavior** (represented by the object's methods),
- **Identity** (gives the object a unique name).

A good example to illustrate this concept is a **Car** object:

- **Identity:** the name of the car,
- **State or attributes:** e.g., the color of the car, model, or year of manufacture,
- **Behavior:** e.g., driving, braking, or parking.

When creating an object in Java, we need to specify which class of the object we want to create. To create a **new** object, we call the class constructor using the new keyword. For example, if we want to create an object of the Car class, we can do it as follows:

```
class Car {
    Car auto = new Car();
}
```

Listing 3.27 Creating a New Object of the Car Class

In this example, **car** is a variable that refers to the newly created object of the **Car** class. We call the constructor of the **Car** class.

A constructor is a special method that is called when a new instance of a class is created. It is used to initialize the object's variables, set initial values, and perform other tasks required when creating a new object. The constructor has the same name as the class and does not return any value or have any return type. The constructor is called using the **new** keyword, and its name must be the same as the class name.

Constructors can have different access modifiers (**public, private, protected, or no modifier**). This means we can decide whether the constructor will be accessible to other classes and objects or not. They do not return any value, but they are not of type **void** either. Their purpose is solely to create new objects and initialize their fields.

If we do not define any constructor in the class, a default no - argument (empty) constructor will be automatically created. An empty constructor does not take any parameters. Its task is to initialize the object's fields with default values.

Here is an example of an empty constructor in the **Person** class:

```
public class Person {
    private String name;
    private int age;

    public Person(){}
}
```

Listing 3.28 Example of an Empty Constructor

Now, let's create a default constructor that includes arguments. Here is an example of using such a constructor:

```
public class Person {
    private String name;
    private int age;

    public Person(String name, int age){
        this.name = name;
        this.age = age;
    }
}
```

Listing 3.29 Creating a Class Constructor

Above, we created a constructor for the **Person** class that takes two arguments - **firstName** and **age**. Inside the constructor, these values are assigned to the corresponding fields using the **this** keyword. Now, you can create a new object of the **Person** class using the constructor:

```
public class Main {
    public static void main(String[] args){
        Person adult = new Person("Adam",40);
    }
}
```

Listing 3.30 Creating an Object of a Class Using a Constructor

In the example above, a new object of the **Person** class named **Adam with an age of 40** is created. The constructor initializes the values of the **firstName** and **age** fields.

Constructors in **IntelliJ** can be generated automatically, just like the methods discussed earlier, such as **getters, setters**, or **toString().** If we want to create more than one variable, we can hold down the **Ctrl** key to select multiple variables.

Let's now try to print the name of our person. How we do this depends on whether our variable is public. In our case, the variable is private, so simply writing a new line to print the variable will not work. The **firstName** will be highlighted in red, as shown in the illustration below:

```
public class Main {
    public static void main(String[] args) {
        Person1 adult = new Person1( name: "Adam", age: 40);
        System.out.println(adult.name);
```

Figure 3.12 Error when trying to print the Person's Name

If you change **private** to **public**, the problem will be resolved. Here is the example:

```
public class Person {
   public String name;
   public int age;

   public Person(String name, int age){
      this.name = name;
      this.age = age;
   }
}
```

Listing 3.31 Changing the Visibility of the private Variable to public

By changing the visibility of the **firstName** variable from private to public, it becomes possible to print the person's name directly in the console. However, if we decide to keep the variables private, we will need to use **getters** and **setters**.

Let's correct the **Person** class:

```
public class Person {
    private String name;
    private int age;

    public String getName(){
        return name;
    }

    public void setName(String name){
        this.name = name;
    }

    public int getAge(){
        return age;
    }

    public void setAge(int age){
        this.age = age;
    }

    public Person(String name, int age){
        this.name = name;
        this.age = age;
    }
}
```

Listing 3.32 'Getter' and 'Setter' methods to the class

Meanwhile, the **Main** class will look as follows:

```
public class Main {
    public static void main(String[] args){
        Person person = new Person("Adam",40);
        System.out.println("The person is named "
+ person.getName() + " and is " + person.getAge()
+ " years old");
    }
}
```

Listing 3.33 Printing the name and age of a person using methods

Here we have an example of encapsulation. To make the **Person** class clearer and the program more useful, we will introduce new methods to it.

The first will retrieve and print the person's name, the second their surname, and the third their age. Let's move on to the **Person** class and add these methods and variable to the code:

```
public class Person {
    String name;
    String surname;
    int age;

    public Person(String name, String surname,
int age){
        this.name = name;
        this.surname = surname;
        this.age = age;
    }

    public void printName(){
        System.out.println("The person's name is "
+ this.name);
    }

    public void printSurname(){
        System.out.println("The person's surname is "
+ this.surname);
    }

    public void printAge(){
        System.out.println("The person is " + this.age
+ " years old");
    }
}
```

Listing 3.34 Dodanie nowych metod i zmiennej Adding new methods and variable

Three new methods have appeared: **printFirstName, printName**, and **printAge.** The program has also been slightly modified because our variables are no longer private, so the **Getters** and **Setters** have been removed. Now we will move on to the Main class. In it, we will add two new **person** objects and use our methods. The program will look as follows:

```
public class Main {
   public static void main(String[] args){
      Person human1 = new Person("Adam",
"Morris",40);
      Person human2 = new Person("Alicia",
"Palmer",30);
      Person human3 = new Person("Jude",
"Smith",20);
      human1.printName();
      human2.printSurname();
      human3.printAge();
   }
}
```

Listing 3.35 Adding Two New Objects and Using Methods from Another Class

When we run the program, the console will return the **first person's name**, which is **Adam**, the second person's surname – **Kowalska**, and the third person's age – **20.**

Now, let's imagine there is a person whose first name and surname are known, but unfortunately, we do not know their age. We want to add this person to our program as a new object.

In the current situation, it is not possible to create a person object without providing their age. In such a case, we can use overloaded constructors. You have already learned about overloading with methods. Constructor overloading involves defining more than one constructor in a class, but with different input parameters. This way, depending on the needs, we can create objects in different ways using the appropriate constructors. Here is an example of constructor overloading in the **Person** class.

```
public class Person {
    String name;
    String surname;
    int age;

    public Person(){}

    public Person(String name){
        this.name = name;
    }

    public Person(String name, String surname){
        this.name = name;
        this.surname = surname;
    }

    public Person(String name, String surname,
int age){
        this.name = name;
        this.surname = surname;
        this.age = age;
    }
```

Listing 3.36 Example of Constructor Overloading

In the **Person** class, we have written four different **constructors**. The first one is empty, the second one contains only one argument – **name**, the third one has two arguments – **name** and **surname**, while the fourth one has three arguments – **name, surname**, and **age**. Thanks to these, we now have the ability to create objects in four different ways.

Let's move on to the **Main** class and create a few objects in it.

```
public class Main {
   public static void main(String[] args){
      Person individual1 = new Person();
      Person individual2 = new Person("Matthew");
      Person individual3 = new Person("Sadie",
"Davies");
      Person individual4 = new Person("Steven",
"Jones",25);
   }
}
```

Listing 3.37 Example of Creating Objects with Different Constructors

The first object is **person1**, which does not have any arguments. The second person has only the **name** provided. The third – **name** and **surname**, and the fourth – **name, surname**, and **age**.

In the program, we can create any number of constructors. Constructor overloading is useful when we want to create objects with different sets of properties. This makes our class more flexible and easier to adapt to various requirements.

3.4 Check yourself!

1. **Which of the following statements about classes and objects in Java is true?**
   a) A class is an object that can be created based on other objects.
   b) An object is an instance of a class that represents specific resources and behaviors.
   c) A method is an instance of an object that defines its properties and behaviors.
   d) A class is a collection of methods that can be called in other classes.
2. **Which of the following methods is a constructor in Java?**
   a) void calculate(int a, int b)
   b) int multiply(int a, int b)
   c) Calculator()
   d) String toString()
3. **In Java, what does the acronym OOP stand for?**
   a) Order of Operations in Programming
   b) Object - Oriented Programming
   c) Optimal Object Procedures
4. **In Java, what is "encapsulation"?**
   a) The process by which one class can inherit from another.

b) A mechanism that allows hiding the implementation details of a class.
c) A special method that initializes the state of an object.

3.5 Inheritance and Polymorphism

3.5.1 Inheritance

Inheritance occurs by creating a derived class that inherits the fields and methods of the base class. The derived class can also define new fields and methods that were not available in the base class.

Inheritance in Java is implemented using the **extends** keyword. It is also an example of the **IS - A** relationship, also known as the parent - child relationship.

Here is a simple example:

We have an **Animal** class and want to create a derived class **Cat** for it. The **Cat** class will have additional methods and fields specific only to cats. Below is the implementation of the mentioned classes:

```
public class Animal {
    private String name;
    private int age;

    public Animal(){}

    public Animal(String name, int age){
        this.name = name;
        this.age = age;
    }

    public void makeSound(){
        System.out.println("The animal
makes a sound!");
    }
}
```

Listing 3.38 Class ‘Animal’

```
public class Cat extends Animal {
    private String breed;

    public Cat(){}

    public Cat(String name, int age, String breed){
        super(name, age);
        this.breed = breed;
    }

    public void purr(){
        System.out.println("The cat purrs!");
    }
}
```

Listing 3.39 Class "Cat" Inheriting from Class "Animal"

In the above example, we have two classes: **Animal** and **Cat**. The **Animal** class is the base class, and the **Cat** class inherits from it, making it the derived class.

The **Animal** class has two private fields: **name** and **age**, and a public method **makeSound().** The constructor of this class takes two arguments: the **name** and **age** of the animal, and assigns them to the respective fields. The **makeSound()** method prints "**Animal makes a sound!"** to the console.

The **Cat** class inherits from the **Animal** class, meaning it has the same fields and methods as the **Animal** class. Additionally, the **Cat** class has an extra field: **breed.**

The constructor of the **Cat** class takes three arguments: the **name**, **age**, and **breed** of the cat. The invocation of the base class constructor is done using the **super** keyword.

The **Cat** class also has an additional method purr(), which prints **"Cat purrs!"** to the console.

Thanks to inheritance, the **Cat** class inherits from the **Animal** class, which means it has access to the fields and methods of the **Animal** class. As a result, the **Cat** class does not need to define the same fields and methods as the **Anima**l class, but can use those already defined in the base class.

Additionally, the **Cat** class can add its own fields and methods, allowing for the creation of more detailed and complex classes.

When it comes to inheritance, we distinguish three basic types of inheritance in Java:

- **Single inheritance** (class B inherits from class A),
- **Multiple inheritance** (class C inherits from class B, and class B inherits from class A),
- **Hierarchical inheritance** (both class C and class B inherit from class A).

Below are simple examples of each of these types of inheritance:

```
public class A {
   void methodA(){
      System.out.println("This is a method
of class A");
   }
}
public class B extends A {
   void methodB(){
      System.out.println("This is a method
of class B");
   }
}
public class Main {
   public static void main(String[] args){
      B classB = new B();
      classB.methodA();
      classB.methodB();
}
```

Listing 3.40 Example of Single Inheritance

```
public class A {
    void methodA(){
        System.out.println("This is a method
of class A");
    }
}
public class B extends A {
    void methodB(){
        System.out.println("This is a method
of class B");
    }
}
public class C extends B {
    void methodC(){
        System.out.println("This is a method
of class C");
    }
}
public class Main {
    public static void main(String[] args){
        C classC = new C();
        classC.methodA();
        classC.methodB();
        classC.methodC();
}
```

Listing 3.41 Example of Multiple Inheritance

```
public class A {
   void methodA(){
      System.out.println("This is a method
of class A");
   }
}
public class B extends A {
   void methodB(){
      System.out.println("This is a method
of class B");
   }
}
public class C extends A {
   void methodC(){
      System.out.println("This is a method
of class C");
   }
}
public class Main {
   public static void main(String[] args){
      B classB = new B();
      C classC = new C();
      classB.methodA();
      classB.methodB();
      classC.methodC();
      classB.methodC();
}
```

Listing 3.42 Example of Hierarchical Inheritance

In each example, the **Main** class contains methods available for the given object. This means that, for instance, in the last example, the **classC** object will not be able to use the **methodB** because it does not inherit from **classB**, and thus does not have access to it.

You might be wondering why multiple inheritance is not possible in Java, where, for example, **classC** could inherit from both **classA** and **classB**. Let's assume that **classC** inherits from these two classes, and both **classA** and **classB** have a method with the same name. If you wanted to call such a method, the program would have trouble choosing the method from **classA** or **classB** because both have the same name. This would make the call ambiguous, which is why in Java we can only inherit from one class.

Earlier in one of the examples, the keyword **@Override** appeared in yellow. Since you have already learned about inheritance, we can take a closer look at overridden methods, as this is what it pertains to.

Method overriding in Java, also known as method shadowing, is the process of replacing the implementation of a method inherited from the parent class with a new implementation in the derived class. To override a method, you need to create a method in the derived class with the same name, parameters, and return type as the inherited method. An example could be the **Animal** class with the **makeSound()** method:

```
public class Animal {
    public void makeSound(){
        System.out.println("The animal
makes a sound!");
    }
}
```

Listing 3.43 "Animal" with the "makeSound" Method

Now let's assume we have a **Cat** class that inherits from the **Animal** class, and we want to change the sound that the cat makes. To do this, we can override the **makeSound()** method in the **Cat** class:

```
public class Cat extends Animal {
    @Override
    public void makeSound(){
        System.out.println("Meow");
    }
}
```

Listing 3.44 Overriding the "makeSound" Method in the "Cat" Class Inheriting from the "Animal" Class

In this case, when we call the **makeSound()** method on an object of the **Cat** class, the overridden version of the method will be called, not the one from the parent class. This means that the result in the console will be **'Meow'.**

Thanks to this mechanism, we can change the behaviour of the inherited method and adapt it to the needs of the derived class.

A longer and more practical example would be the **GeometricFigure** class, where we find the **calculateArea()** method. Since each figure has its own formula for calculating the area, we cannot use a universal method.

Let's write the **GeometricFigure** class:

```
public class GeometricFigure{
   private int side;

   public GeometricFigure(){}

   public GeometricFigure(int side){
      this.side = side;
   }

   public int calculateArea(){
      return side;
   }
}
```

Listing 3.45 Class 'GeometricFigure'

This class has a private variable **side** of type int, two constructors, and a method **calculateArea().** As we can see, the **calculateArea** method only returns the value of the side. In derived classes, such as **Square** or **Triangle**, we need to override the **calculateArea()** method and adapt it to the specific figure.

For example, in the Square class, the **calculateArea()** method will have the following implementation:

```
public class Square extends GeometricFigure {
   private int side;

   public Square(int side){
      this.side = side;
   }

   @Override
   public int calculateArea(){
      return side * side;
   }
}
```

Listing 3.46 Class "Square" and Overriding the "calculateArea" Method of the Base Class

For the square, the **calculateArea()** method returns the appropriate calculation, which is: side times side. On the other hand, the **Triangle** class will look like this:

```
public class Triangle extends GeometricFigure {
   private int side;
   private int height;

   public Triangle(int side, int height){
      this.side = side;
      this.height = height;
   }

   @Override
   public int calculateArea(){
      return (side * height) / 2;
   }
}
```

Listing 3.47 Class "Triangle" and Overriding the "calculateArea()" Method of the Base Class

For the triangle, the area is calculated using the formula: ½*a*h Now, we will proceed to create objects of these figures in the Main class and call the methods of the respective classes. Below is an example code:

```
public class Main {
   public static void main(String[] args){
      GeometricFigure figure = new
GeometricFigure(2);
      Square square = new Square(5);
      Triangle triangle = new Triangle(3,4);
      System.out.println("The area of the figure
is: " + figure.calculateArea());
      System.out.println("The area of the square
is: " + square.calculateArea());
      System.out.println("The area of the triangle
is: " + triangle.calculateArea());
   }
}
```

Listing 3.48 Class "Main" with Objects of Previously Defined Classes and Their Methods

The result displayed in the console after running the program:

```
The area of the figure is: 2
The area of the square is: 25
The area of the triangle is: 6

Process finished with exit code 0
```

Figure 3.13 Displaying the Fields of Different Figures Using the "calculateArea" Method

In the case of the figure object, the method of the GeometricFigure class is called, of course. Similarly, this also happens for the square and triangle objects.

3.5.2 Polymorphism

The word polymorphism comes from two Greek words - **poly** and **morphs**, where **poly** means many, and **morphs** means form.

Thus, polymorphism means many forms. It is one of the important features of object - oriented programming that allows the creation of class hierarchies and the use of many types of objects as one kind. In Java, polymorphism refers to the ability to assign a reference of one type to an object of another type, provided that both types are related in the inheritance hierarchy.

Polymorphism allows writing code that can operate on many types of objects without the need to write separate code for each of these types. This makes the code more flexible and easier to modify. An example of polymorphism in the context of abstract classes and inheritance might look like this:

We have two abstract classes: **Animal** and **Bird**. The **Animal** class has an abstract method **makeSound(),** and the **Bird** class has an abstract method **fly().** Both types of animals have different implementations of these methods. It can be written like this:

```
abstract class Animal {
   public abstract void makeSound();
}
```

Listing 3.49 Abstract Class Animal with the "makeSound()" Method

```
abstract class Bird {
   public abstract void fly();
}
```

Listing 3.50 Abstract Class Bird with the "fly()" Method

Next, we create two classes inheriting from the **Animal** class: **Cat** and **Dog**. Both these animals have different ways of making sounds. Thus:

```
public class Cat extends Animal {
    @Override
    public void makeSound(){
        System.out.println("Meow!");
    }
}
```

Listing 3.51 Class "Cat" with the "makeSound()" Method, Inheriting from the "Animal" Class

```
public class Dog extends Animal {
    @Override
    public void makeSound(){
        System.out.println("Woof woof!");
    }
}
```

Listing 3.52 Class "Dog" with the "makeSound()" Method, Inheriting from the "Animal" Class

Additionally, we create a class inheriting from the **Bird** class - **Jay**:

```
public class Jay extends Bird {
    @Override
    public void fly(){
        System.out.println("Jay flies!");
    }
}
```

Listing 3.53 Class "Jay" with the "fly()" Method, Inheriting from the "Bird" Class

The **Jay** class has its own implementation of the **fly()** method. Now we can create an array of objects of type **Animal** and **Bird**, and then iterate over it, calling the **makeSound()** or **fly()** methods. Thanks to polymorphism, we can call these methods on different types of objects, and the methods will execute the appropriate implementations for each type. Here is the code for the example implementation:

```
public class Main {
   public static void main(String[] args){
      Animal[] animals = new Animal[2];
      animals[0] = new Cat();
      animals[1] = new Dog();

      Bird bird = new Jay();

      for(Animal animal : animals){
         animal.makeSound();
      }

      bird.fly();
   }
}
```

Listing 3.54 Class "Main" with Three Objects, Calling Specific Methods

As you can see, in the for loop, the **makeSound()** method is called on objects of type **Cat** and **Dog,** which inherit from the **Animal** class. Thanks to polymorphism, this method calls the appropriate implementations for each type of animal. Then, the **fly()** method is called on the **Jay** object, which inherits from the **Bird** class. This method also calls the appropriate implementation for the given type of object. The result of the program should be:

```
Meow!
Woof woof!
Jay flies!

Process finished with exit code 0
```

Figure 3.14 Result of the Above Program

3.6 Abstraction and interfaces

3.6.1 Abstraction

Since you are already familiar with the concepts of inheritance and method overriding, it's time to learn about abstract classes.

Abstract classes are classes that cannot be directly instantiated as objects but are used to define an interface for a group of derived classes.

Abstract classes define behaviour but leave the implementation details to the derived classes.

In Java, an abstract class is marked with the keyword **abstract.** Abstract classes are useful in situations where we have a group of classes that are related in some way and share certain behaviours but require different specific implementations. An example of such a class could be a **Vehicle** class, which has certain common features for all vehicles but requires different implementations depending on the type of vehicle.

An example of an abstract class in Java might look like this:

```
public abstract class Vehicle {
    private String name;

    public Vehicle(String name){
        this.name = name;
    }

    public String getName(){
        return name;
    }

    public abstract void drive();
}
```

Listing 3.55 Przykład klasy abstrakcyjnej

In the example above, the **Vehicle** class has a constructor that takes an appropriate **name** and a private field name that is accessible via a public **getter**.

The **Vehicle** class also contains an abstract method **drive(),** which has no implementation. Each derived class of the **Vehicle** class must implement this method according to the specific requirements of the class.

An example of a derived class of the abstract **Vehicle** class could be the **Car** class:

```
public class Car extends Vehicle {
   private String brand;

   public Car(String name, String brand){
      super(name);
      this.brand = brand;
   }

   @Override
   public void drive(){
      System.out.println("The car is driving!");
   }
}
```

Listing 3.56 Derived Class of the Abstract "Vehicle" Class

The **Car** class inherits from the abstract **Vehicle** class and implements the abstract method **drive().** Additionally, the **Car** class has a field brand, which is not available in the **Vehicle** class. Now, we will create another derived class that works similarly to the **Car** class. This will be the **Plane** class:

```
public class Airplane extends Vehicle {
   private String brand;

   public Airplane(String name, String brand){
      super(name);
      this.brand = brand;
   }

   @Override
   public void drive(){
      System.out.println("The airplane is flying!");
   }
}
```

Listing 3.57 Another Derived Class of the Abstract "Vehicle" Class

The **Plane** class, just like the **Car** class, has a private variable brand. It differs essentially only in the implementation of the **drive()** method.

By using abstract classes and inheritance, we can create class hierarchies that have certain common features and at the same time have specific implementations according to the requirements of particular applications.

Abstract classes allow us to define basic features and functionalities for a group of classes while enforcing them to conform to these requirements.

3.6.2 Interfaces

In addition to abstract classes in Java, we also have interfaces. Interfaces are another way to define a **contract** between classes.

An interface defines a set of methods that a class implementing the interface must implement.

Interfaces are defined by the keyword **interface** and consist of the interface name, a list of methods without their implementations, as well as constants and default methods. In Java, abstract classes and interfaces are tools for defining abstract concepts and frameworks that are implemented by derived classes. Here are some differences between them:

- **Implementation:** An abstract class can contain method implementations and fields, whereas an interface cannot contain any method implementations, only declarations. Additionally, a class can inherit from only one abstract class but can implement multiple interfaces.
- **Constructor:** An abstract class can have a constructor, whereas an interface cannot.
- **Inheritance:** An abstract class uses the keyword extends to be inherited by other classes, whereas an interface uses the keyword implements for the same purpose.
- **Nature:** An abstract class is a class, whereas an interface is a kind of contract between the class and the outside world.

An example of an abstract class could be the **Animal** class, which can have many methods and fields, such as **name, weight,** and **age**, but does not have a specific implementation because each animal has a different form and way of functioning.

The **Cat** class can inherit from the **Animal** class and adapt it to its needs. An example of a simple interface could be the **Quacking** interface for objects of type **Duck**.

This interface could contain one method **quack(),** which is implemented by different duck classes depending on their specific behaviours.

The **Quacking** interface might look like this:

```
public interface Quacking {
   void quack();
}
```

Listing 3.58 Example of interface

This interface has one method **quack().** Now, duck classes that want to implement this interface must implement the **quack()** method in their class body. For example:

```
public class WildDuck implements Quacking {
    public void quack(){
        System.out.println("Quack! Quack!");
    }
}
```

Listing 3.59 Example of a Class Implementing an Interface

The **WildDuck** class implements the Quacking interface by providing its own implementation of the **quack()** method. On the other hand, another class, **RubberDuck**, can implement the same interface in a different way, for example, by making a squeaking sound.

```
public class RubberDuck implements Quacking {
    public void quack(){
        System.out.println("Squeak!");
    }
}
```

Listing 3.60 Example of a Class Implementing an Interface

By using interfaces, we can ensure that different classes implementing the same interface have the same method but different implementations, allowing for various behaviors depending on the context of use. A class can, of course, implement multiple interfaces. In such a case, each additional interface is listed after a comma.

3.7 Composition and Aggregation

3.7.1 Aggregation

Aggregation is one of the mechanisms of relationships between objects in object - oriented programming. It describes a **"whole - part"** relationship between classes. In other words, one class (**the whole**) contains another class (**the part**), but objects of the latter class can exist independently.

This means that parts of the class can function on their own, regardless of the whole. Aggregation can create hierarchies of objects. In Java, aggregation can be divided into weak or strong. In the case of strong aggregation, the part object cannot belong to more than one whole.

Most often in Java, weak aggregation is used, which is implemented using object fields, where one class contains a field that is an object of another class. Below is an example of using aggregation. Let's start by creating the **School** class, the **Student** class, and the **Main** class:

```
public class School {}

public class Student {}

public class Main {
    public static void main(String[] args){

    }
}
```

Listing 3.61 Example of Using Aggregation

Let's start with the **Student** class. We will create two fields for it – name and **lockerNumber**, a constructor, and a method **getName().** So:

```
public class Student{
   private String name;
   private int lockerNumber;

   public Student(String name, int lockerNumber){
      this.name = name;
      this.lockerNumber = lockerNumber;
   }

   public String getName(){
      return name;
   }
}
```

Listing 3.62 Creating New Fields, Methods, and Constructor in the Student Class

The private variable **name** of type String represents the student's name, while the variable **lockerNumber** of type int stores the student's locker number. Next, the constructor, which is called when creating a new **Student** object, takes two parameters – our variables. The **getName** method will be used to return the student's name.

Now, let's move on to the **School** class:

```
public class School {
   private Student class1B;

   public School(Student class1B){
      this.class1B = class1B;
   }

   public void schoolInformation(){
      System.out.println("Class 1B has a student
named: " + class1B.getName());
   }
}
```

Listing 3.63 „School" Class

The **School** class represents a school and in this example has one student (subordinate class). The **Student** class represents a student in the school.

In the first line of the **School** class, we used aggregation.

We have a field **class1B** of type **Student**. This means that the school contains one student as its part. Then, a constructor was created in which we pass **Student** objects, creating a relationship between the school and the student. Additionally, we added the **schoolInfo()** method to display simple information about the school and the student.

Finally, we move on to the **Main** class, where we create an object of the **Student** class (student1) and an object of the **School** class (school), passing the student to the school:

```
public class Main {
   public static void main(String[] args){
      Student student = new
Student("Alan Milner",27);
      School school = new School(student);
      school.schoolInformation();
   }
}
```

Listing 3.64 The Main Class with an Object of the Student Class and an Object of the School Class

After running the program, we will get information about the school and one student:

```
Class 1B has a student named: Alan Milner

Process finished with exit code 0
```

Figure 3.15 Displaying Information About the Student Using the schoolInfo Method

In this way, through aggregation, we create a relationship between the school and student objects where the student is part of the school but can also exist independently of it. This allows for the creation of better - organized object structures.

3.7.2 Composition

In the case of composition, an object of one type becomes an integral part of an object of another type. There is a strong relationship between them, where the **part** object cannot function independently of the **whole** object.

In Java, it is somewhat like building a house from individual elements. The house consists of various parts, such as doors, walls, and a roof. In composition, one class is like one of these parts, and the parent class uses these parts to create something larger and more organized. In short, the parent class contains an object of the subordinate class.

Composition creates a strong dependency between classes. The subordinate class object cannot exist independently of the parent class object. Returning to the house example – doors are part of it, but they cannot exist and create anything on their own. Another example could be a car and an engine. For instance, if we have the **Engine** and **Car** classes, composition means that the **Car** class contains an object of the **Engine** class. The **car** not only has an **engine** but is dependent on it – without the engine, the car cannot function.

Let's illustrate this example in practice. First, let's create the **Engine** class, where we will create a field, constructor, and a **start** method. For example:

```
public class Engine {
   private String type;

   public Engine(String type){
      this.type = type;
   }

   public void start(){
      System.out.println("Engine started");
   }
}
```

Listing 3.65 The Engine Class with a Field, Constructor, and start Method

The **Engine** class has a field **type** that specifies the type of engine (petrol, diesel, etc.). The constructor of the **Engine** class initializes the engine type. The **start()** method displays a message about starting the engine.

Now, let's move on to the **Car** class:

```
public class Car{
   private Engine engine;

   public Car(Engine engine){
      this.engine = engine;
   }

   public void move(){
      engine.start();
      System.out.println("The car is moving");
   }
}
```

Listing 3.66 The Car Class with a Field Being an Object of the Engine Class, Constructor, and startCar Method Containing the start Method

The **Car** class contains a field engine, which is an object of the **Engine** class. This means that the car has an engine. The constructor in this class takes an **Engine** object as an argument and assigns it to the engine field. The **startCar()** method calls the **start()** method from the **Engine** class and displays the given message.

In the **Main** class, we will create objects and check the program's functionality. Let's write the following code:

```
public class Main {
    public static void main(String[] args){
        Engine gasolineEngine = new
Engine("Gasoline");
        Car myCar = new Car(gasolineEngine);
        myCar.move();
    }
}
```

Listing 3.67 The Main Class with Objects and Using the startCar Method

In the example, we create an object of the **Engine** class (petrolEngine) and an object of the **Car** class (myCar), thereby passing the engine to the car. After running the program, we will get a message that the engine is starting, followed by a message that the car is starting. As shown below:

```
Engine started
The car is moving

Process finished with exit code 0
```

Figure 3.16 Console Output of the startCar Method

Aggregation and composition make design more flexible. We can create complex structures that are both organized and understandable. Thanks to them, our programs are more prepared for changes. We can add new elements or adjust structures without much trouble.

Aggregation organizes the code, making it more readable and understandable. It separates responsibilities among different classes. Composition, on the other hand, allows for structuring the code, making it clear and comprehensible. It is also based on a strong relationship between classes.

3.8 Refactoring

We have reached the point where we can create a working program using various instructions, functions, and object - oriented programming concepts that form the structure of the program. When we want to create more advanced programs, we need to include more methods and fields. However, the more we expand the program, the harder it becomes to manage everything. Over time, the structure of the program can become complicated and difficult to understand.

This is where refactoring comes in – a process that helps improve the quality of our code without changing the program's functionality. Instead of rewriting everything from scratch, we simply simplify the existing code and modify it to be more readable, organized, and easier to maintain. We won't add new features, but we will improve them to be in the best possible form. Let's move on to some examples of code **refactoring** in Java.

The first example is method extraction. To start, we create a new class and a method within it, which we will then refactor:

```
public void calculateResult(int a, int b){
    int sum = a + b;
    int result = sum * 4;
    System.out.println("Result: " + result);
}
```

Listing 3.68 'calculateResult' Method

The **calculateResult()** method performs two operations. First, it adds two numbers, **a** and **b**, then multiplies the result by **4**, and finally prints it to the screen. Although the code works, it could be more readable. To achieve this, we will create a new method.

The code will look like this:

```
public void calculateResult(int a, int b){
    int sum = calculateSum(a,b)
    int result = sum * 4;
    System.out.println("Result: " + result);
}
private int calculateSum(int a, int b){
    return a + b;
}
```

Listing 3.69 Example of function refactoring

After refactoring, the **calculateResult()** function still does the same thing, but now it uses an additional method called **calculateSum(),** which has been extracted into a separate function. This process is known as method extraction.

It works as if we've separated a portion of the code into a **helper function** to improve readability and enable reuse.

Adding **calculateSum()** as a separate method helps with:

- **Code readability** – the method name 'calculateSum' clearly indicates what the function does, making the code easier to understand.

- **Reusability** – if we need to calculate the sum of two numbers elsewhere in the program, we can now use the 'calculateSum()' function instead of repeating the same code.

This is one of many approaches to refactoring, aimed at making the code more understandable, flexible, and easier to manage. The next approach will be splitting into classes.

Let's create a class called Calculator, and inside it we'll define:

```
public class Calculator {
    public int add(int a, int b){
        return a + b;
    }
    public int multiply(int a, int b){
        return a * b;
    }
}
```

Listing 3.70 A calss containing two methods

We have a **Calculator** class that contains two methods: **add()** and **multiply()**. This class performs two different functions – both addition and multiplication. While this is consistent with object - oriented programming principles, sometimes the code structure can be improved. We can split this class into two separate ones – for example, **Adder** and **Multiplier**.

So:

```
public class Adder {
    public int add(int a, int b){
        return a + b;
    }
}
```

Listing 3.71 The 'Multiplier' class with the 'multiply() method'.

Each of these classes now performs only one specific task – **Adder** adds numbers, and **Multiplier** multiplies them. This is beneficial for clarity and understanding. Each class has one clearly defined responsibility. When functions are split into two separate classes, managing them becomes easier. If a problem occurs with addition, we look into the **Adder** class; if it's with multiplication, we check the **Multiplier** class. If we want to add more mathematical operations in the future, we can easily create new classes without modifying the existing ones.

Another example of code refactoring involves improving variable names. In the new class, let's create a method called **calculateArea():**

```
public double calculateArea(int r){
    double p = 3.14;
    return p * r * r;
}
```

Listing 3.72 The calculateArea method returning 'p'

In the code above, we have a function that calculates the area of **p** circle based on its radius, but the variable p used as the name for the area is not very descriptive. Let's slightly modify this method:

```
public double calculateCircleArea(int radius){
    return Math.PI * radius * radius;
}
```

Listing 3.73 The 'calculateCircleArea' method returning 'circleArea'

Descriptive names for variables and functions help in understanding exactly what a piece of code does. A name like **p** could suggest a **point**, speed, or some other concept. The name **circleArea** leaves no doubt about what the variable represents.

It's important to maintain naming conventions, such as using **camelCase** (starting with a lowercase letter and capitalizing each subsequent word) and choosing descriptive variable names.

The final refactoring example we'll present involves using interfaces. As an example, let's create a class called **Square**, and then define a method **calculateArea()** that returns a double:

```
public class Square implements Figure {
    public double calculateArea(double side){
        return side * side;
    }
}
```

Listing 3.74 The' Square' class with the calculateArea() method

The **calculateArea()** method calculates the area of a square based on the length of its side.

Now, let's create an interface called **Shape** with a method **calculateArea()** of type double:

```
public interface Figure {
   double calculateArea(double side);
}
```

Listing 3.75 The Shape interface with the calculateArea() method

Let's add an implementation of the **Shape** interface to the **Square** class and override the **calculateArea()** method:

```
public class Square implements Figure {
   @Override
   public double calculateArea(double side){
      return side * side;
   }
}
```

Listing 3.76 The Square class implementing the Shape interface and overriding the calculateArea() method

After refactoring, we introduced the **Shape** interface, which defines the **calculateArea()** method. The **Square** class implements this interface, which means it must provide an implementation of the **calculateArea()** method. By using an interface, we separate the method definition from its implementation, making the code more concise. If we want to add more geometric shapes in the future, we can simply create new classes that implement the **Shape** interface. This gives us a more flexible code structure and makes it easier to add new geometric shapes.

To summarize, the goal of refactoring is primarily to improve code quality by eliminating unnecessary parts, enhancing variable and function names, and using clearer and more efficient constructs. These are key steps that help us improve our programs.

Refactoring is not just about technical fixes – it's also about gaining a deeper understanding of the code. Thanks to this, our projects become easier to develop and, most importantly, more friendly and transparent for other developers who will work with our code.

3.9 Check yourself!

1. **Which of the following statements about getters and setters in Java is true?**
   a) A getter is used to set the value of a class field, and a setter is used to retrieve the value.
   b) Getters and setters are methods that provide access to a class's private fields.
   c) Getters and setters are automatically generated by the compiler when the class is created.
   d) Getters and setters are only available for abstract classes.

2. **Which of the following keywords is used for class inheritance in Java?**
   a) new
   b) extends
   c) implements
   d) abstract

3. **What does the this keyword do in Java?**
   a) Refers to the object that invoked the method.
   b) Creates a new instance of a class.
   c) Closes a data stream.
   d) Provides access to static variables.

Task 4.9.1

Write a **Stack** class representing a stack data structure. The class should include the following methods:

- **push(element)**: Adds a new element to the top of the stack.
- **pop()**: Removes and returns the element at the top of the stack.
- **peek()**: Returns the element at the top of the stack without removing it.
- **isEmpty()**: Returns true if the stack is empty, otherwise false.

CHAPTER 5

CONCURRENT PROGRAMMING

4 Concurrent Programming

Multithreading is a key aspect of modern technology that plays an important role in our daily lives. Although many of us may not realize it, we experience its impact every day when using various devices such as computers, phones, or tablets.

Let's think about a situation where we're browsing the Internet on our computer. We can open multiple browser tabs at once, check our email, listen to music on a streaming platform, and write a work report simultaneously. Additionally, even without our knowledge, the time and weather information are being updated in real time. All these actions are possible thanks to multithreading, which allows multiple tasks to be executed simultaneously.

The same applies to our mobile phones. We can send text messages, browse social media, check the weather, and use GPS navigation all at once. Thanks to multithreading, our phones can handle multiple applications simultaneously, providing a smooth and responsive user experience.

Just as multi - core processors in our devices enable the execution of multiple operations at the same time, multithreading allows programs to perform many tasks concurrently, significantly increasing performance and efficiency. Similarly, multithreaded programming in Java gives us the tools to create applications that can process various tasks simultaneously.

With multithreaded programming in Java, we can build applications that fully utilize the potential of our computers, enabling simultaneous execution of computational tasks, input/output operations, and user interface handling. This means our applications can be more responsive, efficient, and scalable, resulting in better user experiences and more effective use of hardware resources.

In this chapter, we will explore the fundamentals of multithreaded programming in Java and learn about various techniques and tools that allow us to harness the power of multithreading. We will look at practical applications, as well as discuss well - known practices and design patterns that help us create efficient, scalable, and reliable applications in the Java environment.

4.1 Sequential Program vs. Concurrent Program

We've already learned what threads are and how powerful their benefits can be. Now we need to understand the fundamental difference between a sequential program and a concurrent program.

A sequential program is a traditional type of program that executes operations step by step. Each task must wait for the previous one to finish before it can begin. This is the most common type of program, and every topic discussed so far in this book has been written sequentially. However, this doesn't mean that threads are absent in such programs. In fact, every program runs within a single thread, known as the main thread.

A concurrent program, on the other hand, allows multiple tasks to be executed simultaneously using threads. Each thread can operate independently, which enables efficient use of system resources and increases application responsiveness.

The difference between these two types of programs can be illustrated with a real - life example. Imagine a queue at a store. The customers waiting at the checkout are tasks to be executed, and the cashier is a single thread. In a sequential program, there is only one open checkout. Everyone will eventually be served, but it may take a while. When more cashiers start working, the same number of customers can be served in a much shorter time.

4.2 Choosing Between Sequential and Concurrent Programming

In practice, the choice between a sequential and a concurrent program depends on the specific requirements of the project. The use of threads becomes important when dealing with simultaneous operations, such as handling multiple clients on a server or processing data in real time.

However, it's important to remember that concurrent programming also requires appropriate synchronization mechanisms to avoid conflicts and ensure the correctness of the application's behavior.

4.3 Parallelism vs. Concurrency, Process vs. Program, Interleaving

In computer science, there are many key concepts related to data processing and task execution. Parallelism, concurrency, process, program, and interleaving are fundamental terms for understanding how a computer executes instructions and manages tasks.

4.3.1 Parallelism vs. Concurrency

Parallelism and concurrency are two key concepts related to simultaneous processing. Parallelism refers to the actual simultaneous execution of multiple tasks on multiple processors or cores, which speeds up execution time. Concurrency, on the other hand, refers to the simultaneous handling of tasks, but not necessarily at the exact same moment.

In the context of Java, multithreading introduces elements of concurrency, allowing different threads to be processed simultaneously.

4.3.2 Process vs. Program

The distinction between a process and a program is very important. A process is an instance of a program running in an operating system, with its own memory space, resources, and state. It can contain multiple threads that execute different parts of the program simultaneously. A program, on the other hand, is an abstract concept that describes algorithms and data processing logic, independent of its actual execution.

4.3.3 Interleaving Mechanism

Interleaving is a technique in which different threads or processes are executed alternately, sharing CPU time. This mechanism allows for fair resource allocation and helps avoid blocking the entire program if one thread becomes unresponsive.

4.4 Creating Threads

Now that we've learned the theoretical meaning of multithreaded programming and its related definitions, we can move on to practical implementation. To begin with, it's important to know that threads have a lifecycle consisting of several stages:

- **New** – a newly created thread that is not yet performing any actions;
- **Runnable** – occurs after the thread has been started using a start method;
- **Terminated** – applies to any thread that has completed its execution;
- **Blocked** – a state in which the thread is paused or waiting for a resource;
- **Timed Waiting** – the thread is suspended for a specified amount of time;
- **Waiting** – the thread is suspended, for example, by using the join() method.

Creating new threads can be done in various ways depending on the needs of the application. We will try to implement them in three different ways.

4.4.1 Thread Class

Thread is a class provided by Java that is responsible for managing threads. We will use it to create our own thread. To do this, we need to override the run method, which will contain the instructions to be executed by our thread. Additionally, we'll use this class to start the thread.

Let's begin by creating our own class. We can name it Threads, and it's important that it extends the Thread class. Inside the class, we define the run method and provide its implementation. To start, we can display the name of our thread. The code should look like this:

```
public class MyThread extends Thread {

    public void run() {
      System.out.println(Thread.currentThread().getName());
    }
}
```

Listing 4.1 Returning the Name of the Current Thread

The methods used in the print statement are responsible for retrieving the current thread (currentThread) and extracting its name using getName.

Now let's move on to creating an object of our class and running the program. Let's name it thread1, and then call the run() method on it.

```
public static void main(String[] args) {
    MyThread thread1 = new MyThread();
    thread1.run();
}
```

Listing 4.2 Starting a thread using the run method

Let's run the program. In the console, we will get an output as shown below.

```
main

Process finished with exit code 0
```

Figure 4.1 Program output in the console

As you can see, the value "**main**" was displayed. As we remember, the **run** method we overrode is supposed to print the name of the current thread - and that's exactly what it did. We can improve this a bit. Let's assign a custom name to our thread using the setName() method. Add it to the code before calling watek1.run(); and set the new name to **MyThread**.

```
public static void main(String[] args) {

    MyThread thread1 = new MyThread();
    thread1.setName("MyNewThread");
    thread1.run();

}
```

Listing 4.3 Changing the thread name

We run the program again.

```
main

Process finished with exit code 0
```

Figure 4.2 Failed thread name change

Unfortunately, the program didn’t work. The name didn’t change, and the issue lies in calling the **run()** method on our thread. While it does indeed execute the thread’s logic, it does so within the main application thread – meaning it doesn’t run concurrently with the rest of the program. If we take a closer look at the **Thread** class (in the IDE, click on the class name with **Ctrl + Left Click**), we’ll see that it also has a start() method. This is the one we should use to run our object as a separate thread.So let’s make the necessary correction: we need to replace the call to **run()** with **start().**

```
public static void main(String[] args) {

    MyThread thread1 = new MyThread();
    thread1.setName("MyNewThread");
    thread1.start();

}
```

Listing 4.4 Changing the startup method from run to start

Let's run our program again.

```
MyNewThread

Process finished with exit code 0
```

Figure 4.3 Displaying the new name in the console

This time, the name we set was actually displayed. This means a new thread was successfully started. Let's do one more example. Remove the line where we set the thread's name, and then add two more objects of the Thread class. Name them **thread2** and **thread3**, and call the **start()** method on the first one and the **run()** method on the second.

```
public static void main(String[] args) {

    MyThread thread1 = new MyThread();
    MyThread thread2 = new MyThread();
    MyThread thread3 = new MyThread();
    thread1.start();
    thread2.start();
    thread3.run();
}
```

Listing 4.5 Creating multiple threads

Now let's run our program.

```
main
Thread-0
Thread-1

Process finished with exit code 0
```

Figure 4.4 Program output

As a result, we received **three thread names**. As you can see, one of them is the main thread – it comes from the **thread3** object. It might be surprising that it was displayed first. In general, multithreaded programming is highly dependent on the hardware on which the application is running. If we don't manage the execution order in any way, the results may vary even with identical input values.

We can use a method from the **Thread** class – namely **setPriority()** – which accepts the following values:

- **1** – for the lowest priority,
- **5** – for normal priority,
- **10** – for the highest priority.

However, there's no guarantee how much this will affect the actual thread priority. It's more of a suggestion to the system than a strict declaration. If we want to shorten the thread creation syntax and improve readability, we can also use a lambda expression. It might look like the example below.

```
public static void main(String[] args) {

    Thread thread = new Thread(() ->
            System.out.println("Thread name: " +
Thread.currentThread().getName()));

    thread.start();
}
```

Listing 4.6 Creating a new thread using a lambda expression

In situations where we're creating very short threads, this approach can be useful.

4.4.2 Runnable Interface

Let's start by creating a new class named, for example, **RunnableThread**. Then, indicate that the class implements Runnable. Inside the class, we need to provide an implementation for the run method. We'll want to observe how tasks from two (or more) threads are executed – in other words, we'll see whether multitasking actually occurs in the application. To do this, the best approach is to use a simple loop that prints the thread's name and the iteration number. The whole thing should look like the example below.

```
public class MyRunnableThread implements Runnable {
    public void run() {
        for (int i = 0; i < 99; i++) {

System.out.println(Thread.currentThread().getName() + ", 
i = " + i);
        }
    }
}
```

Listing 4.7 Overriding the run method from the Runnable interface

It's worth noting that to access the **currentThread()** method, we need to use the **Thread** class. We'll also need it to start the threads, since we'll be calling the run method we wrote through its object.

Let's move on to creating the objects. Start by creating two instances of the **RunnableThread** class, which we'll pass as parameters when creating two instances of the Thread class. Next, we can change the names of the threads we created using the **setName()** method – this will make it easier to analyze the output in the console. Finally, we call the **start()** method on the thread objects. The complete setup should look like the example below.

```
public static void main(String[] args) {

    MyRunnableThread myRunnableThread1 = new 
MyRunnableThread();
    MyRunnableThread myRunnableThread2 = new 
MyRunnableThread();

    Thread thread1 = new Thread(myRunnableThread1);
    Thread thread2 = new Thread(myRunnableThread2);

    thread1.setName("first");
    thread2.setName("second");

    thread1.start();
    thread2.start();

}
```

Listing 4.8 Running the program with two new threads

Now we can run our program. In the console, the loop iterations from both threads will be printed – but they will interleave with each other.

```
second, i = 0
second, i = 1
second, i = 2
first, i = 0
second, i = 3
first, i = 1
second, i = 4
first, i = 2
second, i = 5
first, i = 3
second, i = 6
first, i = 4
second, i = 7
first, i = 5
first, i = 6
first, i = 7
second, i = 8
first, i = 8
second, i = 9
second, i = 10
second, i = 11
first, i = 9
second, i = 12
first, i = 10
second, i = 13
```

Figure 4.5 Console output

As we can see, both threads are working simultaneously – but it's not always an even race. Depending on the CPU load at a given moment, there may be situations where one thread significantly outpaces the other. To observe this, it's worth running the program several times and watching the results. Even though the program code remains identical, the order of the output will almost always differ.

Here's an example where the second thread temporarily received more CPU time, allowing it to get ahead of the first thread.

```
first, i = 19
first, i = 20
second, i = 17
second, i = 18
second, i = 19
second, i = 20
second, i = 21
second, i = 22
second, i = 23
second, i = 24
second, i = 25
second, i = 26
second, i = 27
second, i = 28
second, i = 29
second, i = 30
second, i = 31
second, i = 32
second, i = 33
second, i = 34
first, i = 21
first, i = 22
```

Figure 4.6 Indicating the moment where one thread gains an advantage

4.4.3 ExecutorService Class

ExecutorService class is a tool that allows us to manage a thread pool for executing tasks in our applications. With it, we can control how many tasks are executed simultaneously and how they are processed. We can also decide whether we want our thread pool to be limited to a specific number of threads (for example, to avoid overloading the system) or to dynamically adjust to the application's workload.

To write a simple example, we'll use the **RunnableThread** class we created in the previous section. We'll only modify the class where the program is launched.

Start by creating two objects of our class and one object of the **ExecutorService** class. Next, define the number of available threads in the pool. To do this, assign the service object the value **Executors.newFixedThreadPool(2).** The **number 2** means that two threads will be available to execute tasks. Now, using the **submit()** method, add tasks to be executed. The complete setup should look like the example below.

```
public static void main(String[] args) {

    MyRunnableThread myRunnableThread1 = new
MyRunnableThread();
    MyRunnableThread myRunnableThread2 = new
MyRunnableThread();
    ExecutorService executorService;

    executorService= Executors.newFixedThreadPool(2);
    executorService.submit(myRunnableThread1);
    executorService.submit(myRunnableThread2);

}
```

Listing 4.9 Creating a thread pool

Now we can run our application.

```
pool-1-thread-1, i = 0
pool-1-thread-2, i = 0
pool-1-thread-1, i = 1
pool-1-thread-2, i = 1
pool-1-thread-1, i = 2
pool-1-thread-2, i = 2
pool-1-thread-1, i = 3
pool-1-thread-1, i = 4
pool-1-thread-1, i = 5
pool-1-thread-2, i = 3
pool-1-thread-1, i = 6
pool-1-thread-2, i = 4
pool-1-thread-2, i = 5
pool-1-thread-2, i = 6
pool-1-thread-2, i = 7
pool-1-thread-2, i = 8
pool-1-thread-2, i = 9
pool-1-thread-2, i = 10
pool-1-thread-1, i = 7
pool-1-thread-1, i = 8
```

Figure 4.7 Program output

As we can see, the application started working concurrently. However, let's take a closer look at the last line displayed in the console.

```
pool-1-thread-1, i = 90
pool-1-thread-1, i = 91
pool-1-thread-2, i = 98
pool-1-thread-1, i = 92
pool-1-thread-1, i = 93
pool-1-thread-1, i = 94
pool-1-thread-1, i = 95
pool-1-thread-1, i = 96
pool-1-thread-1, i = 97
pool-1-thread-1, i = 98
```

Figure 4.8 Missing line indicating program termination

The loop range we set in the **RunnableThread** class was **99**, so it seems that both threads completed their iterations. However, the program hasn't terminated. In a properly executed program, we should see the message: **Process finished with exit code 0.** But here, it's missing. Additionally, if we look at our IDE, the **Stop** button is still active above the editor, which indicates that the application is still running.

This is caused by the **ExecutorService**, which doesn't shut down automatically when the threads finish their work – it remains active. To fix this, we need to add the **shutdown()** instruction in the code.

```
public static void main(String[] args) {

    MyRunnableThread myRunnableThread1 = new
MyRunnableThread();
    MyRunnableThread myRunnableThread2 = new
MyRunnableThread();
    ExecutorService executorService;

    executorService= Executors.newFixedThreadPool(2);
    executorService.submit(myRunnableThread1);
    executorService.submit(myRunnableThread2);

    executorService.shutdown();
}
```

Listing 4.10 Adding a method to shut down the thread pool after task completion

If we now run the program again, it should terminate normally.

```
pool-1-thread-1, i = 94
pool-1-thread-1, i = 95
pool-1-thread-1, i = 96
pool-1-thread-1, i = 97
pool-1-thread-1, i = 98

Process finished with exit code 0
```

Figure 4. Program output showing proper termination

By using **ExecutorService**, we can build more efficient, scalable, and responsive applications – which makes it a better solution than using the **Thread** class alone.

4.5 Sleep() and Join() methods

In concurrent programming, using the **sleep()** and **join()** methods is important for effective thread management. Let's take a closer look at how they work to understand how they affect program execution.

The first thing to remember when using these methods is the need to handle the **InterruptedException**, which is thrown when another thread interrupts the current one.

4.5.1 Sleep() method

The **sleep()** method is used to pause the execution of a thread for a specified amount of time. While the thread is sleeping, other threads can continue their execution. This is useful when we want to introduce a delay in a thread's operation or control the processing pace.

For example, we can pause the main thread of the application for **4** seconds. To do this, we'll write a program that reads the start time and end time of the program, and then calculates the difference between them. We'll need to import the following classes: **Duration, LocalDateTime**, and **DateTimeFormatter**.
In the body of the method, we'll retrieve the current time into a variable and apply formatting for better readability.

```
LocalDateTime start = LocalDateTime.now();
DateTimeFormatter format =
DateTimeFormatter.ofPattern("HH:mm:ss");
```

Listing 4.11 Retrieving the current time and declaring a format for time display

Next, we place a **try – catch** block in which we specify how long the thread should sleep, and we add handling for the **InterruptedException**.

```
try {
    Thread.sleep(4000);
}
catch (InterruptedException e) {
    System.out.println(e);
}
```

Listing 4.12 Handling the InterruptedException with a try - catch block

Finally, we assign the current time to a new variable and calculate the difference between the start and end of the application's execution. It's a good idea to add a few print statements to make the console output easier to read. The complete code should look like the example below.

```
public static void main(String[] args){

    LocalDateTime start = LocalDateTime.now();
    DateTimeFormatter format =
DateTimeFormatter.ofPattern("HH:mm:ss");

    System.out.println("The program started working at: " +
start.format(format));

    System.out.println("Please wait...");

    try {
        Thread.sleep(4000);
    }
    catch (InterruptedException e) {
        e.printStackTrace();
    }

    LocalDateTime finish = LocalDateTime.now();
    System.out.println("Thread finished working at: " +
finish.format(format));

    Duration duration = Duration.between(start, finish);
    long difference = duration.getSeconds();
    System.out.println("Operating time: " + difference + "
s.");

}
```

Listing 4.13 The program is paused for four seconds

Now we can run the program.

```
The program started working at: 22:11:18
Please wait...
Thread finished working at: 22:11:22
Operating time: 4 s.

Process finished with exit code 0
```

Figure 4.9 Console output. Calculating program execution time

As we can see, right after launching the program, the first two lines were displayed in the console. Then, the program encountered the sleep instruction, which caused it to pause for **4 seconds**.

However, this is an example of pausing only the main thread of the application. Let's now try an example with two threads:

The first will print letters from **A** to **E** using a loop.The second will print numbers from **1** to **16**.We'll add the **sleep()** method with a value of **4000** ms for the thread displaying letters, and **1000** ms for the one displaying numbers. The program should look like the example below.

```
public static void main(String[] args) {

    Thread thread1 = new Thread(() -> {
        for (char c = 'A'; c <= 'E'; c++) {
            System.out.println("Thread 1: " + c);
            try {
                Thread.sleep(4000);
            } catch (InterruptedException e) {
                e.printStackTrace();
            }
        }
    });
    thread1.start();

    Thread thread2 = new Thread(() -> {
        for (int i = 1; i <= 17; i++) {
            System.out.println("thread 2: " + i);
            try {
                Thread.sleep(1000);
            } catch (InterruptedException e) {
                e.printStackTrace();
            }
        }
    });
    thread2.start();
}
```

Listing 4.14 Preview of a program executing two tasks concurrently with different sleep durations

Our goal is for both threads to run simultaneously, but with different delays. When counting the number of elements to display, the numbers thread has **4 times** more items, but the letters thread has a sleep duration 4 times longer. This means both threads should finish their work at roughly the same time.

Let's run the program.

```
thread 2: 1
Thread 1: A
thread 2: 2
thread 2: 3
thread 2: 4
Thread 1: B
thread 2: 5
thread 2: 6
thread 2: 7
thread 2: 8
Thread 1: C
thread 2: 9
thread 2: 10
thread 2: 11
thread 2: 12
Thread 1: D
thread 2: 13
thread 2: 14
thread 2: 15
thread 2: 16
Thread 1: E
thread 2: 17

Process finished with exit code 0
```

Figure 4.10 Wynik końcowy z konsoli Final console output

By observing the messages appearing in the console, we can see that the numbers are displayed every second, while the letters appear every 4 seconds.

4.5.2 Join() method

The **join()** method is used to wait for the completion of another thread. The main thread (or any other executing thread) calls **join()** on another thread and is suspended until that thread finishes its execution. This is especially useful when an operation in the main thread depends on the completion of another thread.

We'll write a program where the main thread runs a loop that prints its name and the current iteration. When the iteration reaches a certain number, the **join()** method will be called, and the progress will be paused until the second thread finishes its execution.

Let's start by creating a thread that loops **10 times** using a for loop, printing its name and the current iteration number. For better readability, we'll assign it a custom name.

Next, we'll write a second loop as part of the main thread. It will also run **10 times** and print its name and iteration number. However, we'll add a conditional statement that checks if i == 5. When this condition is true, the program will enter a **try - catch** block, start the previously created thread, and pause execution until that thread finishes.

The complete program should look like the example below.

```
public static void main(String[] args) {

    Thread thread1 = new Thread(()-> {
        for(int i = 1; i < 11; i++){
System.out.println(Thread.currentThread().getName() + " i =
" + i );
        }
    });

    thread1.setName("New thread");

    for (int i = 1; i < 11; i++) {
        System.out.println(Thread.currentThread().getName()
+ " i = " + i);
        if (i == 5) {
            try {
                thread1.start();
                thread1.join();
            } catch (InterruptedException e) {
                System.out.println("The main thread has
been interrupted!");
            }
        }
    }
}
```

Listing 4.15 A program demonstrating the operation of the join() method

The line **thread1.start();** is placed inside the **try - catch** block so that it's easier to see in the console when the main thread is interrupted. Let's run the program.

```
main i = 1
main i = 2
main i = 3
main i = 4
main i = 5
New thread i = 1
New thread i = 2
New thread i = 3
New thread i = 4
New thread i = 5
New thread i = 6
New thread i = 7
New thread i = 8
New thread i = 9
New thread i = 10
main i = 6
main i = 7
main i = 8
main i = 9
main i = 10

Process finished with exit code 0
```

Figure 4.11 Program output

As we can see, the program started running, and when the iteration reached **5**, the thread was paused. It resumed only after the **new thread** finished its execution.

4.6 Synchronization

One of the challenges in concurrent programming is ensuring consistency and correctness of application behavior when multiple threads try to access shared resources simultaneously. Without proper thread synchronization mechanisms, situations may arise where one thread modifies data while others attempt to read or modify the same data, which can lead to errors.

One way to deal with the lack of synchronization is by using the synchronized keyword, which can be applied to various parts of the code, such as entire methods or specific code blocks. It is recommended not to overuse synchronization when it's not necessary. While it solves many problems during application development, it can also introduce other issues, which we will discuss a bit later.

Let's now write a program that will demonstrate a problem with simultaneous data access by two threads. Then, we'll fix it using the method described earlier.

We'll start by creating a new class representing a bank account. In it, we'll declare an int field representing the account balance. Then, we'll add three methods responsible for depositing, withdrawing, and checking the account balance. The class should look like the one below.

```
public class BankAccount {

    private int bankBalance;

    public void deposit(int amount) {
        bankBalance += amount;
    }

    public void withdraw(int amount) {
        bankBalance -= amount;
    }

    public int getBankBalance() {
        return bankBalance;
    }
}
```

Listing 4.16 Class BankAccount

Now we'll write the logic in which we create two threads – one will perform deposits and the other will perform withdrawals from the account. Since errors don't occur every time, we need to operate on many repetitions in a loop. Let's assume we perform **1000** deposits and 1000 withdrawals. At the end, we display the final account balance. The program code may look as follows.

```
public static void main(String[] args) {

    BankAccount account = new BankAccount();

    Thread thread1 = new Thread(() -> {
        for (int i = 0; i < 1000; i++) {
            account.deposit(10);
        }
    });

    Thread thread2 = new Thread(() -> {
        for (int i = 0; i < 1000; i++) {
            account.withdraw(5);
        }
    });

    thread1.start();
    thread2.start();

    try {
        thread1.join();
        thread2.join();
    } catch (InterruptedException e) {
        e.printStackTrace();
    }

    System.out.println("The balance of the account after
operations: " + account.getBankBalance());
}
```

Listing 4.17 The main method with transaction - handling logic

In the code above, **thread1** will deposit money into the account **1000 times**, each time depositing **10**, which gives us a total of **10,000**. Meanwhile, **thread2** will withdraw money from the account 1000 times, each time withdrawing **5**, resulting in a total of **5,000**. From this, we can calculate that after all transactions, the account balance should be **5,000**. So, let's run our program.

```
The balance of the account after operations: 3740

Process finished with exit code 0
```

Figure 4.12 Incorrect value caused by lack of synchronization in resource access

As we can see, the value returned by the program is different from what we expected. This means that an error occurred during execution, leading to incorrect calculations. We're dealing here with a problem known as a race condition, which is a real conflict over access to shared resources. Now let's try to protect our application against such situations.

We need to ensure that while one thread is making changes, no other thread can modify the data. To do this, we must go back to the BankAccount class and use the synchronized keyword to secure the places where the field is being modified. It should look like the example below.

```
public class BankAccount {
    private int bankBalance;
    public void deposit(int amount) {
        synchronized (this) {
            bankBalance += amount;
        }
    }
    public void withdraw(int amount) {
        synchronized (this) {
            bankBalance -= amount;
        }
    }
    public int getBankBalance() {
        return bankBalance;
    }
}
```

Listing 4.18 Adding the synchronized instruction to vulnerable methods

We'll try running the application again.

```
The balance of the account after operations: 5000

Process finished with exit code 0
```

Figure 4.13 Correct program output

Now the value returned in the console matches our expectations.

4.7 The Lock class and ReentrantLock implementation

Managing synchronization of access to shared resources in applications is also possible using the Lock class and the ReentrantLock implementation, which allow for more fine - grained control over locking and help ensure data consistency. Proper use of these mechanisms can significantly improve the reliability and performance of multithreaded applications, minimizing the risk of deadlocks and race conditions.

The structure is similar to the synchronized keyword described earlier, so we'll use the same example with only minor modifications. We'll start with the **BankAccount** class. In it, we need to add the field **private**

Lock lock = new ReentrantLock(); and replace all synchronized blocks with **try - finally** blocks.

```
lock.lock();
try {
    bankBalance += amount;
} finally {
    lock.unlock();
}
```

Listing 4.19 Konstrukcja try - finally dla blokady dostępu

This will cause access to the bankBalance (account balance) variable to be locked until it is explicitly released. We do the same for the **withdraw** method. The complete implementation should look like the example below.

```
import java.util.concurrent.locks.Lock;
import java.util.concurrent.locks.ReentrantLock;

class BankAccount {
    private int bankBalance;
    private Lock lock = new ReentrantLock();

    public void deposit(int amount) {
        lock.lock();
        try {
            bankBalance += amount;
        } finally {
            lock.unlock();
        }
    }
    public void withdraw(int amount) {
        lock.lock();
        try {
            bankBalance -= amount;
        } finally {
            lock.unlock();
        }
    }
}
```

Listing 4.20 The BankAccount class adapted for lock usage

Now let's move on to the class where we implement the logic. We don't need to change it, because we'll be using the same class as before and applying the same values. So it should look like the example below.

```
public static void main(String[] args) {

    BankAccount account = new BankAccount();

    Thread thread1 = new Thread(() -> {
        for (int i = 0; i < 1000; i++) {
            account.deposit(10);
        }
    });

    Thread thread2 = new Thread(() -> {
        for (int i = 0; i < 1000; i++) {
            account.withdraw(5);
        }
    });

    thread1.start();
    thread2.start();

    try {
        thread1.join();
        thread2.join();
    } catch (InterruptedException e) {
        e.printStackTrace();
    }

    System.out.println("The balance of the account after 
operations: " + account.getBankBalance());
}
```

Listing 4.21 The main method with transaction handling

Now we'll run the program.

```
The balance of the account after operations: 5000

Process finished with exit code 0
```

Figure 4.14 Correct console output

As we can see, the program finished its execution with the correct result, which means that no resource access conflicts occurred.

4.8 Synchronization Issues: Deadlock and Livelock

4.8.1 Deadlock

Deadlock is a situation in which multiple threads are unable to continue their execution because each one is waiting for resources that are locked by other threads at the same time. As a result, none of them can complete their work or release the resources they are holding, leading to a standstill in the application.

An example of a situation where a **Deadlock** occurs is shown in the class below.

```
public class Deadlock {

    private static final Object value1 = new Object();
    private static final Object value2 = new Object();

    public static void main(String[] args) {

        Thread thread1 = new Thread(() -> {
            synchronized (value1) {
                System.out.println("Thread 1: Holds the
value 1...");
                try { Thread.sleep(100); } catch
(InterruptedException e) {}
                System.out.println("Thread 1: Waits for the
value 2...");
                synchronized (value2) {
                    System.out.println("Thread 1: Holds the
value 1 and 2...");
                }
            }
        });

        Thread thread2 = new Thread(() -> {
            synchronized (value2) {
                System.out.println("Thread 2: Holds the
value 2...");
                try { Thread.sleep(100); } catch
(InterruptedException e) {}
                System.out.println("Thread 2: Waits for the
value 1...");
                synchronized (value1) {
                    System.out.println("Thread 2: Holds the
value 2 and 1...");
                }
            }
        });

        thread1.start();
        thread2.start();
    }
}
```

Listing 4.22 Example of a Deadlock Occurrence in a Program

As you can see, each thread holds one resource and needs to acquire the other. Unfortunately, it cannot do so because the other resource is already locked. At this point, the program will no longer complete its execution.

4.8.2 Livelock:

Livelock is a situation similar to the previously mentioned **Deadlock**, in which threads are unable to continue their work. However, unlike deadlock, the threads are not completely blocked – instead, they are actively responding to each other and continuously changing their state, but still unable to make progress. **Livelock** can be difficult to detect and diagnose because the threads remain active and may perform certain operations, yet they cannot complete their tasks.

An example of a **Livelock** situation can be observed in the example below.

```
public class Livelock {

    static class Person {
        public synchronized void action(Person
secondPerson) {
            try {
                Thread.sleep(100);
            } catch (InterruptedException e) {
                e.printStackTrace();
            }

System.out.println(Thread.currentThread().getName() + " is
trying to perform an action");
            secondPerson.action(this);
        }
    }

    public static void main(String[] args) {
        final Person person1 = new Person();
        final Person person2 = new Person();

        new Thread(() -> person1.action(person2), "Thread
1").start();
        new Thread(() -> person2.action(person1), "Thread
2").start();
    }
}
```

Listing 4.23 Example of a Livelock Occurrence in a Program

The issue in this example arises from the fact that each thread wants to perform a task within the **action** method. This method is marked as synchronized, which means that other threads cannot access it until the current one finishes its execution. Unfortunately, one of the instructions involves calling this method on the other thread, which is not possible and will never happen. As a result, both threads are stuck in an infinite loop.

4.9 The Dining Philosophers Problem

The Dining Philosophers Problem is a classic example of a synchronization and concurrency issue in computer science. It involves a scenario where five philosophers sit around a circular table, with a fork placed between each pair of philosophers. Philosophers can either eat or think. To eat, a philosopher must pick up the two forks located to their left and right.

The challenge is to design an algorithm that ensures no philosopher starves (i.e., is unable to eat), while also avoiding deadlock (a situation where all philosophers hold one fork and wait indefinitely for the other).

Solutions to the Dining Philosophers Problem often rely on resource hierarchy algorithms or asymmetric fork strategies. In the resource hierarchy approach, philosophers always pick up the lower - numbered fork first, then the higher - numbered one. In the asymmetric fork strategy, one philosopher picks up the left fork first, while the others pick up the right fork first.

An example solution is shown below.

```
public class Philosopher {
    public static void main(String[] args) {
        Object[] forks = new Object[5];

        for (int i = 0; i < 5; i++) {
            forks[i] = new Object();
        }

        for (int i = 0; i < 5; i++) {
            final int number = i;
            Thread philosopher = new Thread(() -> {
                while (true) {
                    try {
                        System.out.println("Philosopher " +
number + " thinks");
                        Thread.sleep((long) (Math.random()
* 1000));
                        synchronized (forks[number]) {
                            synchronized (forks[(number +
1) % 5]) {

System.out.println("Philosopher " + number + " eats");
                                Thread.sleep((long)
(Math.random() * 1000));
                            }
                        }
                    } catch (InterruptedException e) {
                        e.printStackTrace();
                    }
                }
            });
            philosopher.start();
        }
    }
}
```

Listing 4.24 Dining Philosophers Problem – Example Solution

In this particular case, the solution is based on a resource hierarchy – each philosopher tries to pick up the left fork first, and then the right one. This is a simpler solution than the asymmetric fork strategy, as it doesn't require additional coordination between threads or the use of extra synchronization mechanisms. Each philosopher operates independently, attempting to pick up their forks in a fixed order. Thanks to this approach, deadlocks are avoided, and each philosopher is guaranteed to eat when both forks become available.

To summarize, the Dining Philosophers Problem is an important topic in computer science because it illustrates the challenges of synchronization and concurrency in multiprocessor systems.

4.10 Best Practices in Concurrent Programming

Concurrent programming can be challenging, but following certain practices can help minimize the risk of errors. Here are some useful tips for writing concurrent code:

1. **Minimize concurrency:** If possible, avoid using multithreading in areas where it's not necessary. Limit it to parts of the code that truly require parallel execution.
2. **Avoid shared variables:** Concurrency can lead to synchronization issues, so the use of shared variables should be minimized.
3. **Synchronize access to shared resources:** If shared variables must be used, ensure that operations on them are properly synchronized using mechanisms such as **synchronized** or the **Lock class**.
4. **Avoid blocking:** Try to avoid long - lasting locks that can cause delays and potentially lead to **application deadlocks**.
5. **Testing and debugging:** Concurrent programming can be difficult to test due to unpredictable behavior, so it's important to test returned results and continuously improve the code.
6. **Monitor and optimize performance:** Regularly monitor the application for performance issues and identify areas where concurrency problems occur. Optimize code and resources in those areas to ensure the best possible performance.

7. **Documentation:** Document how synchronization and concurrency are handled in the code so others can easily understand its behavior. Clearly communicate any assumptions about concurrency in the code.

Applying these practices can help reduce problems related to concurrent programming and ensure the stability and performance of applications running in multithreaded environments.

4.11 Check yourself!

1) What is a thread in Java?

- An independent sequence of instructions executed concurrently with other instruction sequences in a program.
- A special class that represents a unit of work in a program.
- A collection of objects that manages the execution of different parts of a program at specific times.

2) What is thread synchronization and why is it important?

- Thread synchronization means running multiple threads simultaneously.
- Thread synchronization involves controlling access to shared resources by multiple threads, ensuring safe operations on them.
- Thread synchronization means limiting the number of available threads in a program.

3) What is the main purpose of the sleep() method in Java?

- The sleep() method is used to pause a thread for a specified amount of time.
- The sleep() method is used to put all threads in a program to sleep.
- The sleep() method is used to remove threads from memory.

Task 5.1

Write a program that creates two threads.The first thread adds even numbers from 1 to 100, and the second adds odd numbers from **1** to **100**. Each thread should run concurrently, and their results (the sum of even numbers and the sum of odd numbers) should be displayed after both threads have finished executing.

CHAPTER 6

MOBILE APPLICATIONS

5 Mobile Applications

5.1 Introduction to Mobile Applications

5.1.1 Mobile Applications

A mobile application is software that runs on portable devices such as smartphones and tablets.

Initially, mobile applications served primarily utility functions. These included apps for browsing websites (web browsers), email clients, calendars, and apps for playing videos or music files.

The rapid development of portable devices – smartphones and tablets – has also driven the growth of mobile applications.

Among the most popular apps are those for mobile banking, apps from major retail chains that replace traditional loyalty cards, apps offering discount coupons in restaurants, games, and messaging apps.

Most social media platforms have mobile app versions that complement their web applications.

The first mobile phone considered to have a built - in application was the **Psion Organizer,** created by the British company **Psion** in 1984. This pocket computer was based on an 8 - bit Hitachi 6301 processor and had 2 KB of RAM. It was the first device in history to be based on a database and came equipped with a calculator and clock application.

The first mobile operating system was **Symbian**, which debuted in 2001 and was developed by Nokia.

Today, mobile applications are easily accessible and can be downloaded from **Google Play** (for Android devices) and the **App Store** (for Apple devices). Most are free, although some require account registration.

5.1.2 Android Operating System

Android is an operating system dedicated to mobile applications. It was created by the American startup **Android Inc**. The company's three founders worked intensively on developing an operating system that would compete with Symbian. In July 2005, the company was acquired by the tech giant Google for $50 million. Android is based on the Unix kernel and is mostly available under the GNU GPL license. It is an open system, meaning it is not dedicated to specific devices (unlike the iPhone). All Android system versions are named after sweets, with names starting with successive letters of the alphabet. The first phone to feature the Android system was the HTC Dream. Today, Android is used to develop applications not only for smartphones and tablets but also for TVs and smartwatches.

5.2 Android Studio

Android Studio is the official development environment for creating mobile applications for the Android operating system. It was introduced in 2013 and replaced Eclipse, which had been the most popular environment at the time. Android Studio is built on the commercial software IntelliJ IDEA, developed by JetBrains. It is available under the Apache License, which means it is free software that can be downloaded from the Internet and installed on a personal computer without any legal consequences. The environment allows for software development in Java, C++, and Kotlin, and can be installed on Windows, macOS, and Linux operating systems. At the time of writing this book (April 2024), the current version of Android Studio is Iguana, version 2023.1.2, released in March 2024.

5.2.1 Android Studio Installation

We can download Android Studio from this webside:

https://developer.android.com/studio

We simply click the **Download Android Studio Iguana** button, as shown in the illustration below.

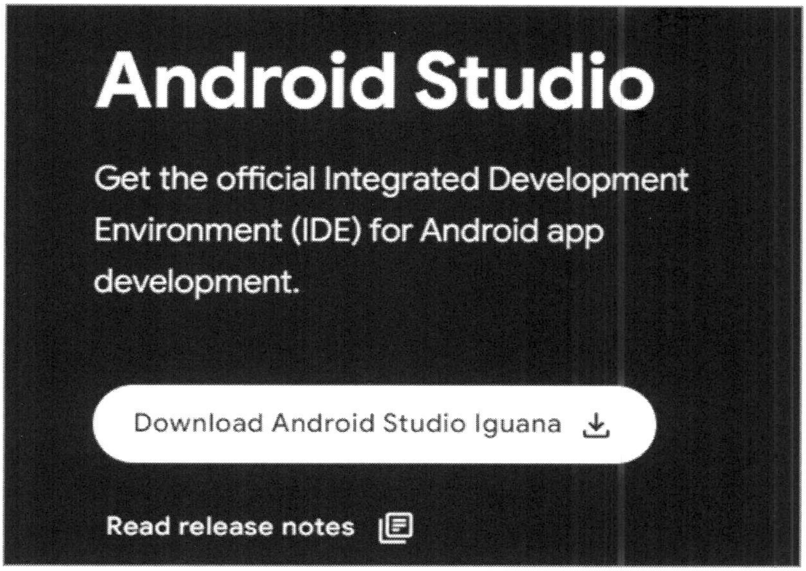

Figure 5.1 Official Android Developers Website

A license agreement window appears, which must be accepted. Then, we check the box and click the button responsible for downloading the software. Once downloaded, the package must be installed. However, before installing Android Studio, the Java package should be installed first. It can be safely downloaded from the following website: **https://www.oracle.com/pl/java/technologies/downloads/#jdk19 - windows.** After launching Android Studio, we will see the start screen, as shown in the illustration below.

Figure 5.2 Android Studio Start Screen

Once the application has loaded, we are presented with a view like the one shown in the illustration below.

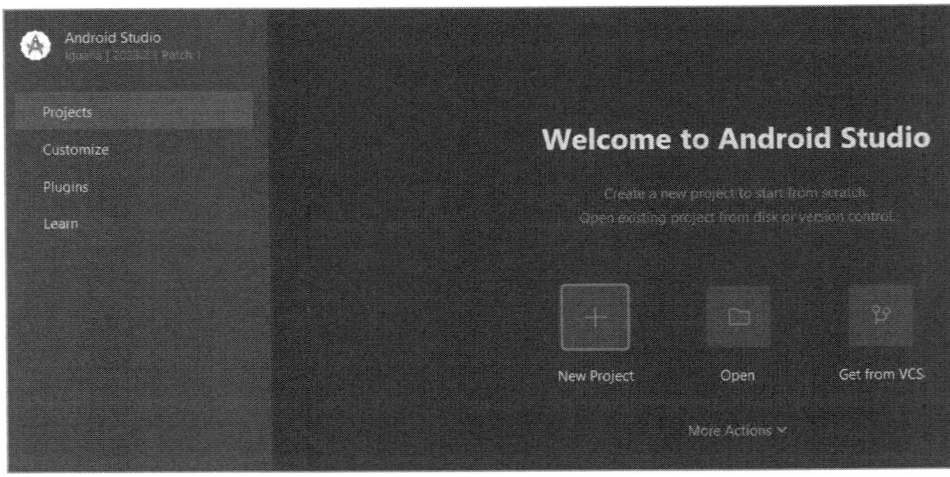

Figure 5.3 Application Selection Window in Android Studio

We have the option to load one of the recently edited applications. Alternatively, we can create a new project using the **New Project** button, or open an application saved on the disk using the **Open** option.

5.2.2 Creating Your First Application

To begin, we'll create a simple project. To do this, click **New Project**. You'll see the activity selection window. On the left side, in the **Templates** panel, you can choose the type of device for which you want to create the application. **Android Studio** allows you to develop apps for devices such as:Phone and Tablet, Wear OS (smartwatches), Android TV (televisions), Automotive (car dashboards)

On the right side of the window, you select the type of activity. For starters, choose **Empty Views Activity** and mark that option. Then click the **Next** button.

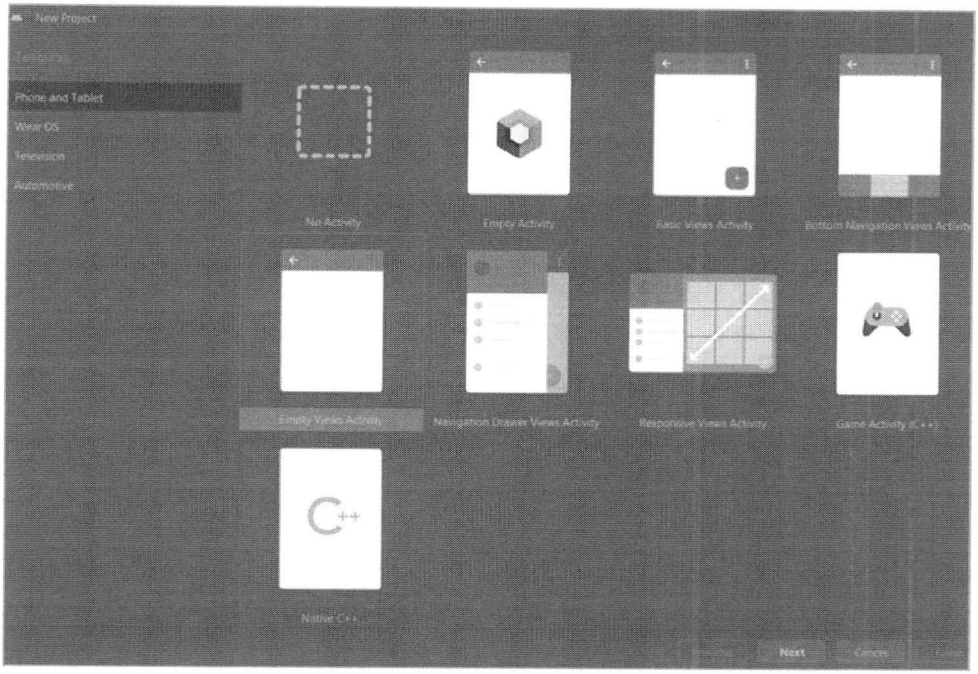

Figure 5.4 Activity Selection Window in Android Studio

A window for creating an application appears on the screen. In this window, we fill in the following fields:

- **Name** – enter the name of the application, e.g., Application1;
- **Package name** – enter the name of the package where the application will be placed, e.g., example.app1;
- **Save location** – choose the location on the disk where the application will be saved. Android Studio creates a folder;named AndroidStudioProjects, and all applications can be stored there;
- **Language** – select the programming language you want to use to create the application. You can choose between Java and Kotlin. Initially, we select Java as the programming language;

Minimum SDK – choose the Android version (API level) for which the application will be developed. According to the latest Android guidelines, applications should be created using the highest available API level, as they will still work properly on devices with older Android versions.

After filling in the application creation window, click Finish. The application components will then be loaded.

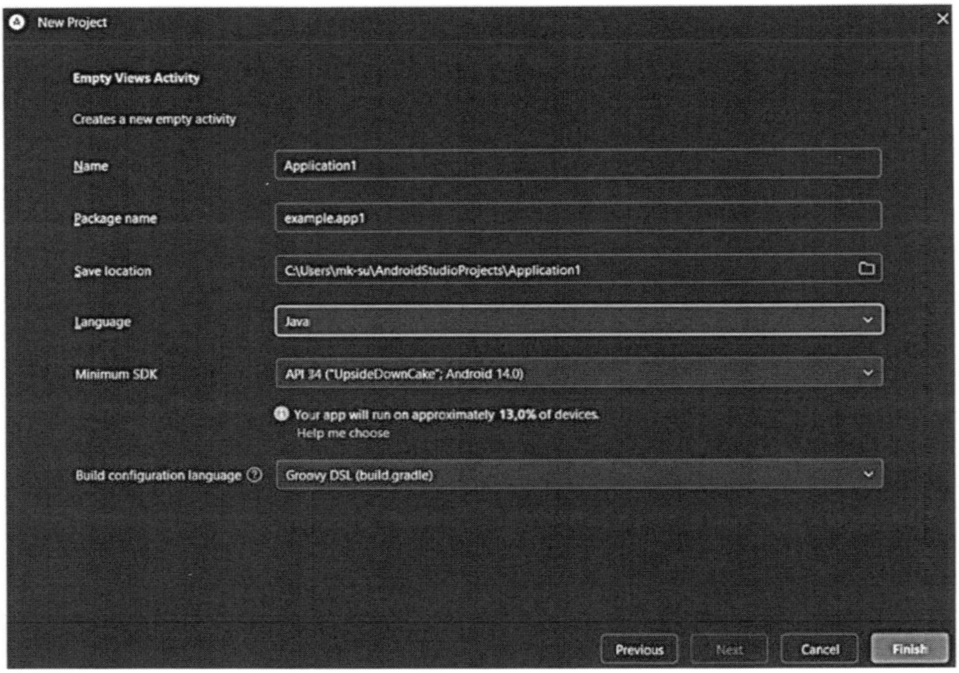

Figure 5.5 New Application Creation Window

After a moment, a window similar to the one shown in the illustration below appears on the screen.

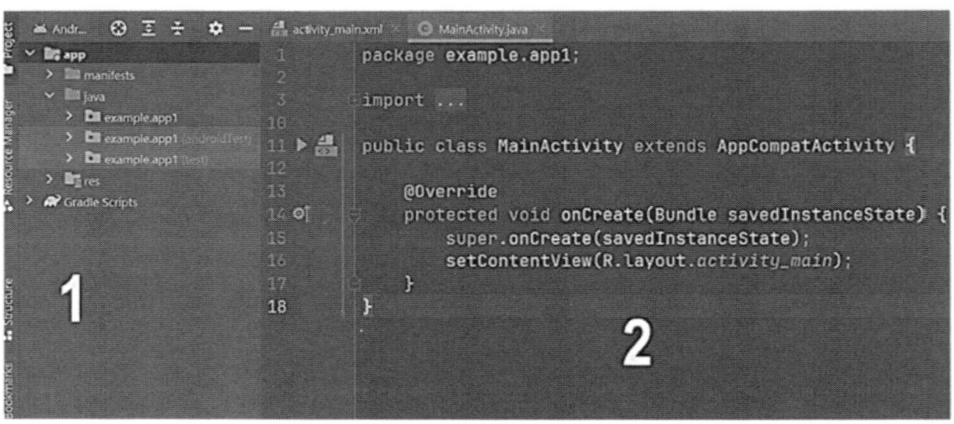

Figure 5.6 Main Window of Android Studio

In the area marked as **number 1**, you can find the application directory tree. An Android application consists of several files, each with its own unique purpose. Their usage will be discussed later in the book.

In the area marked as **number 2**, there is the code editor window. This is where we will write the code for our application. The visible project consists of two windows, which are presented as tabs located at the top of the window.

5.2.3 Changing the GUI Appearance

In Android Studio, it's possible to change the user interface. First, you can choose between the older version of the GUI and a newer, more modern one. If the newer interface version doesn't appear after installation, you can switch to it manually. To do this, click the gear icon located in the top right corner of the application.

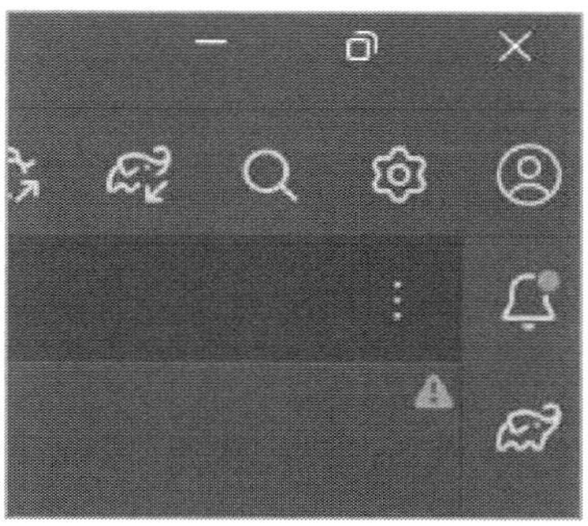

Figure 5.7 SDK Manager Icon

From the dropdown menu, select the option: **SDK Manager**.

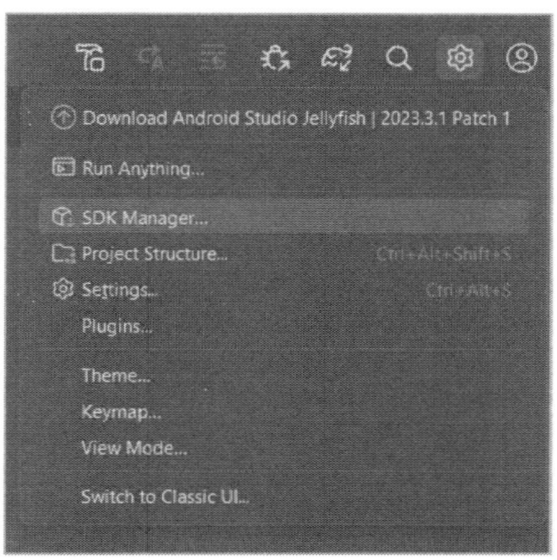

Figure 5.8 Context Menu – Basic Operations in Android Studio

Go to the **Appearance & Behavior** tab and select **New UI**. In the next step, check the box labeled **Enable New UI** and click the **OK** button.

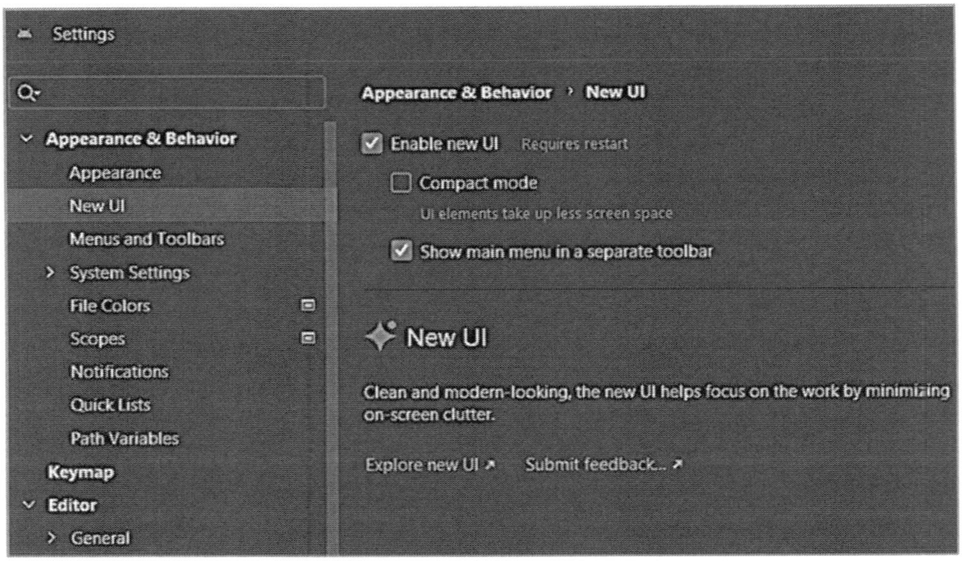

Figure 5.9 Settings window

The program will ask if you want to restart Android Studio. Click Restart.

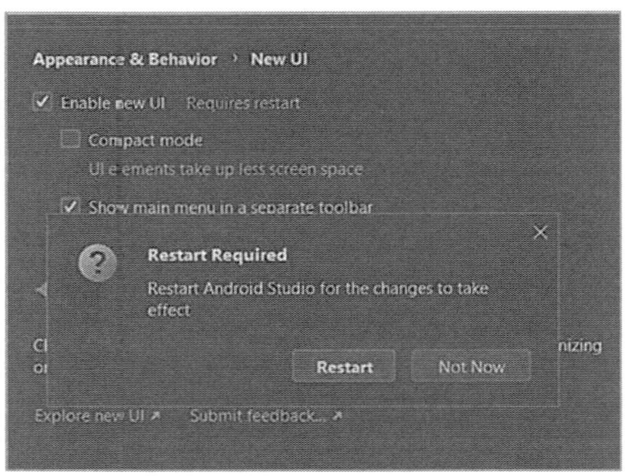

Figure 5.10 Restart Required: Confirming Android Studio Restart

The program will close and reopen with the new UI. Its appearance is shown in the illustration below.

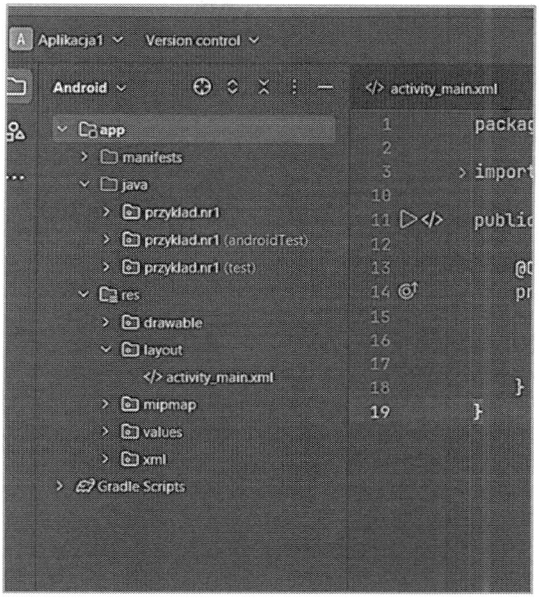

Figure 5.11 Main Window of Android Studio After Applying the New UI

Switching back to the older version of the GUI is a reverse operation. Go to the **Appearance & Behavior** tab and select **New UI**. Uncheck the box labeled **Enable New UI** and click the **OK** button. The program will once again ask if you want to restart it.

5.2.4 Changing the Application Theme

Android Studio allows you to set either a dark or light theme.

Now we'll switch to the light theme. From the **New UI** menu, go to **Appearance**. In this tab, you can choose the theme and also configure other elements such as the font size and type.

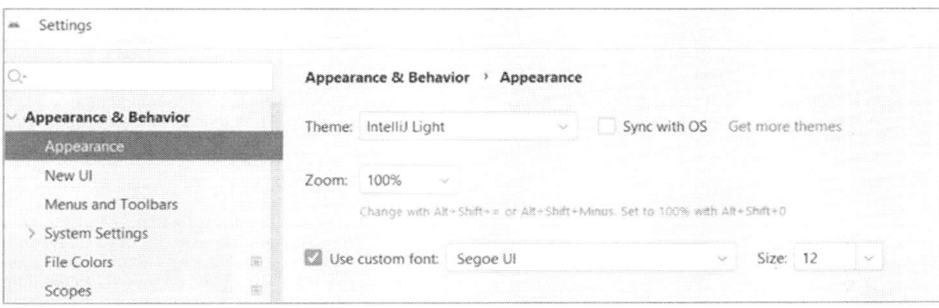

Figure 5.12 Setting the Light SDK Theme

In this book, we will use the **IntelliJ Light** theme. From the dropdown menu, select this option and click **OK**. Android Studio will now appear as shown in the illustration below.

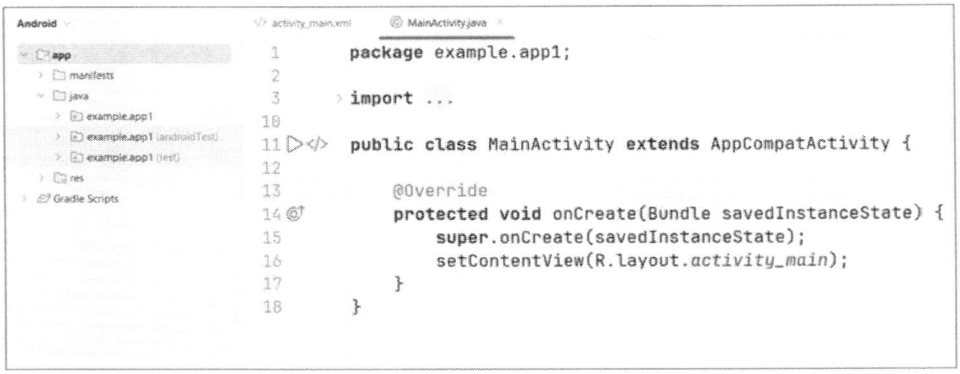

Figure 5.13 Android Studio Window with the Light Theme Applied

5.2.5 Emulator

After creating an application, every developer wants to see the result of their work. Most programming languages have their own development environments - applications that allow you to create, edit code, compile, and run programs.
In Android Studio, to run an application, you'll need a tool called an **Emulator**.

An emulator is a virtual operating system that lets you view your application as if it were running on a real device, without needing to connect a physical phone. You can also connect your own phone and see the app running on it. I'll explain how to do that in the next step. For now, let's focus on the emulator.

To use the emulator, you first need to launch it and connect it to your project. On the right side of the **SDK**, there is a tab called **Device Manager**. Clicking it will open the **Device Manager**, where all running emulators are visible. From this window, you can also add a new emulator.

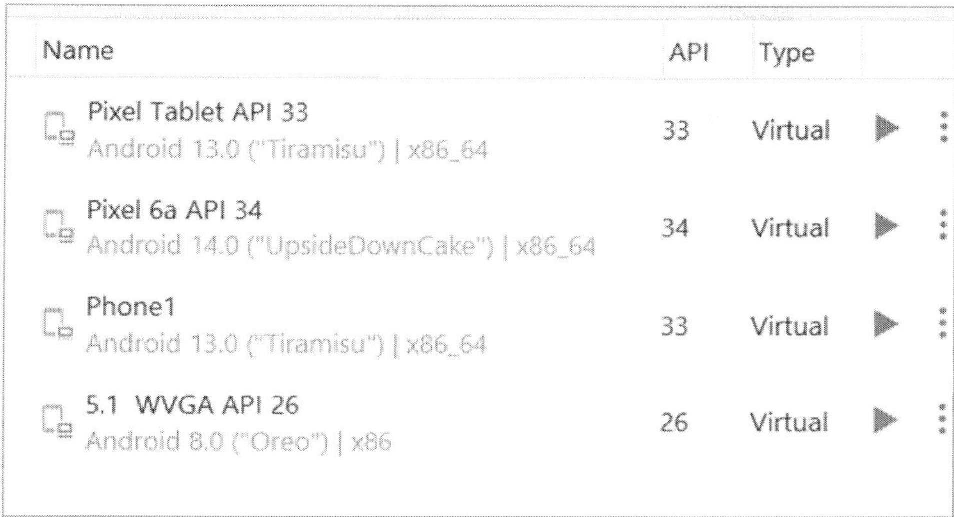

Figure 5.14 Device Manager Window – List of Installed Emulators

In the illustration, you can see a list of all installed emulators. The first column shows their names. In the API column, you can see the **API** level of each emulator. The triangle icon allows you to start the selected system. To create a new environment, start by clicking the **Create Virtual Device** button, which is shaped like a plus sign.

Figure 5.15 Button for Adding a New Emulator

After clicking this button, a device selection window will appear. Android Studio allows you to prepare applications for various types of devices, such as phones, tablets, or TVs. For now, we'll focus on preparing an application for a phone.

Select the **Phone** category. From the list of devices, choose for example **Pixel 6a**. Highlight the name and click the **Next** button.

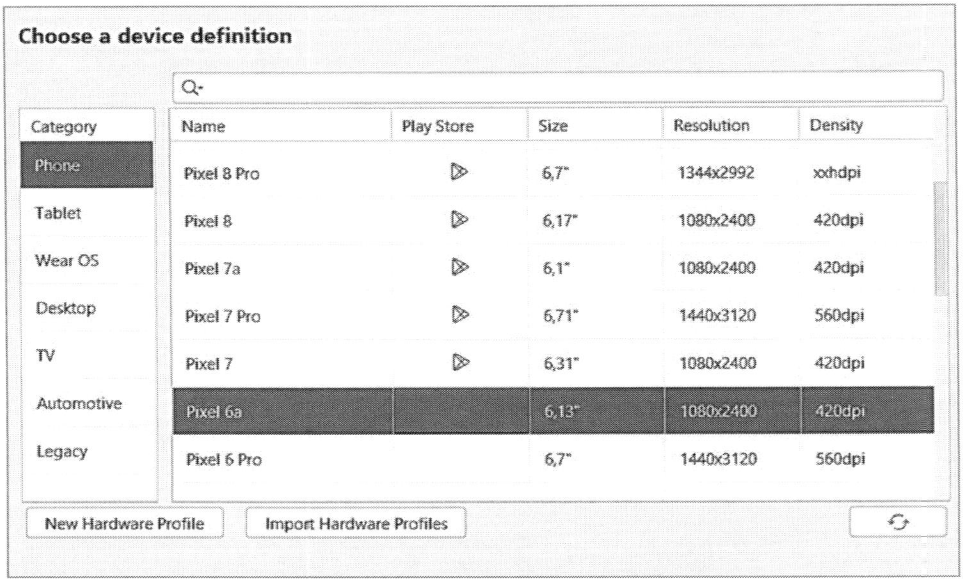

Figure 5.16 Device Selection Window

In the next window, **System Image**, you choose the API level, which corresponds to the system version. If you haven't previously created an emulator for a specific version, you'll first need to download the appropriate packages. Click the small arrow button and wait until the required files are downloaded in the next window.

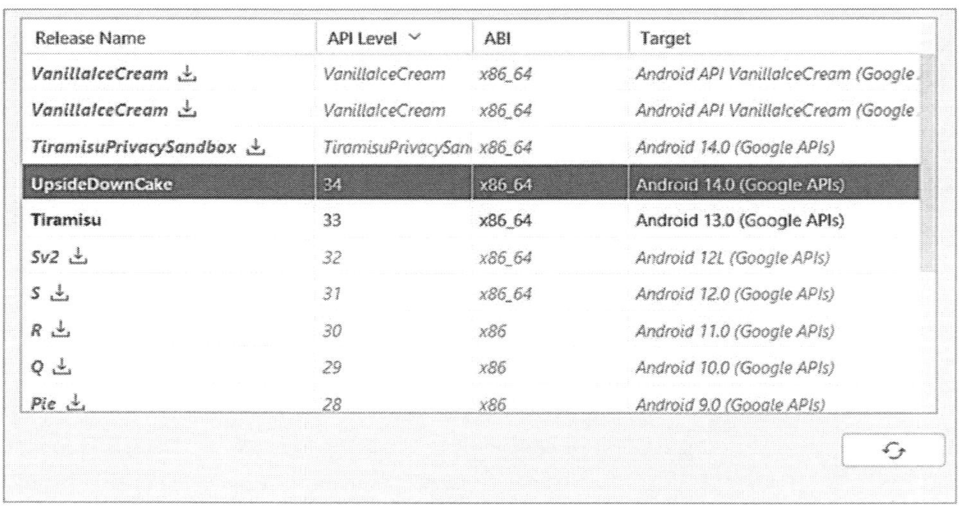

Figure 5.17 API Level Selection Window

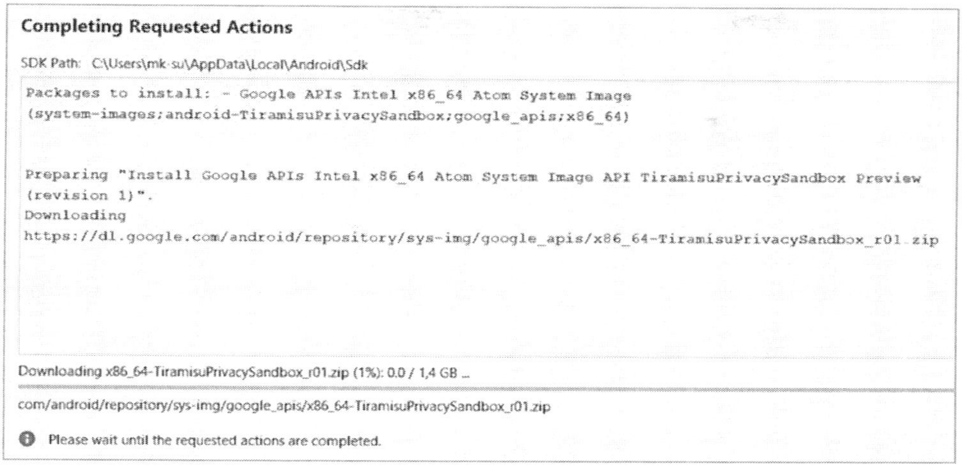

Figure 5.18 Downloading API 34 Installation Files

After the packages are loaded, click the **Finish** button. You'll return to the **System Image** window. There, click the Next button. The next window that will open is **Verify Configuration**.

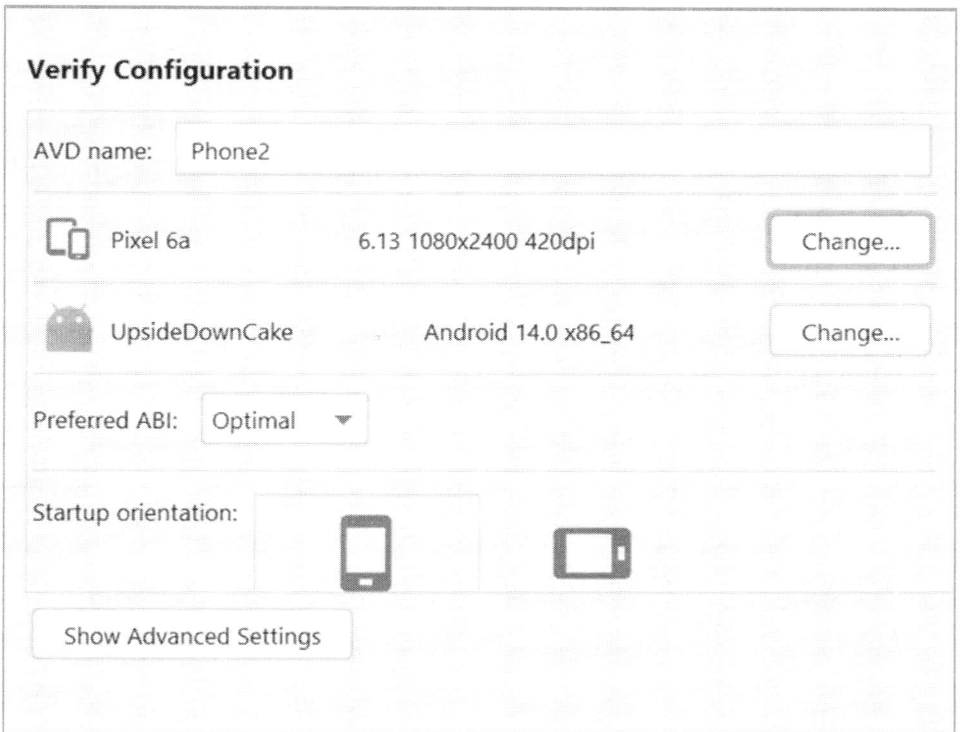

Figure 5.19 Editing Settings for the New Virtual Device – Emulator

Here, you can change the device name by entering it in the **AVD Name** field. Clicking the **Finish** button will create the emulator. After completing all these steps, you can run the application by clicking the green triangle icon.

Figure 5.20 Run Icon

Figure 5.21 Device Manager Window with the Newly Installed Emulator

To view the emulator simulation, select the **Running Devices** tab, which can be found on the right side of the main panel.

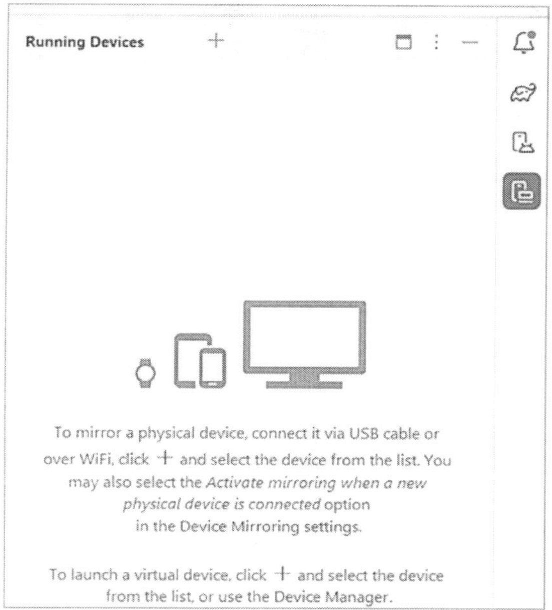

Figure 5.22 Running Devices Window.

You'll find the application code in the folder named **Application1**. Remember to place all application files in the Android Studio directory located within the folder created by the application.

Figure 5.23 Emulator After Launching the Default Application

5.2.6 the Application on a Physical Device

Applications created in **Android Studio** can also be run on a physical phone. The IDE installs the app directly onto the connected device, and the application runs on the phone itself.

If you have an Android phone nearby, you can connect it to Android Studio. The first step is to prepare the phone. The device you want to connect must be set to Developer Mode or Developer Options. You can find instructions for this on your smartphone manufacturer's website.

If you have a Samsung phone, you can follow these steps:

1. Open Settings.
2. Go to the **About Phone** section and tap to open it.
3. Tap on Software Information.
4. Find the **Build Number** section and tap it seven times.
5. A message will appear confirming that Developer Mode has been enabled.
6. Connect the phone to your computer using a USB cable.
7. Search for **Developer Options** in your phone's settings.
8. Go to the **Debugging** section and toggle the **USB Debugging** switch.
9. The phone will ask for permission.
10. Allow USB Debugging access.

The next steps are done in Android Studio. Go to the **Device Manager** tab located on the right side of the window. Your phone should appear in the list of devices. It stands out from the emulators because the Type field is set to **Physical**.

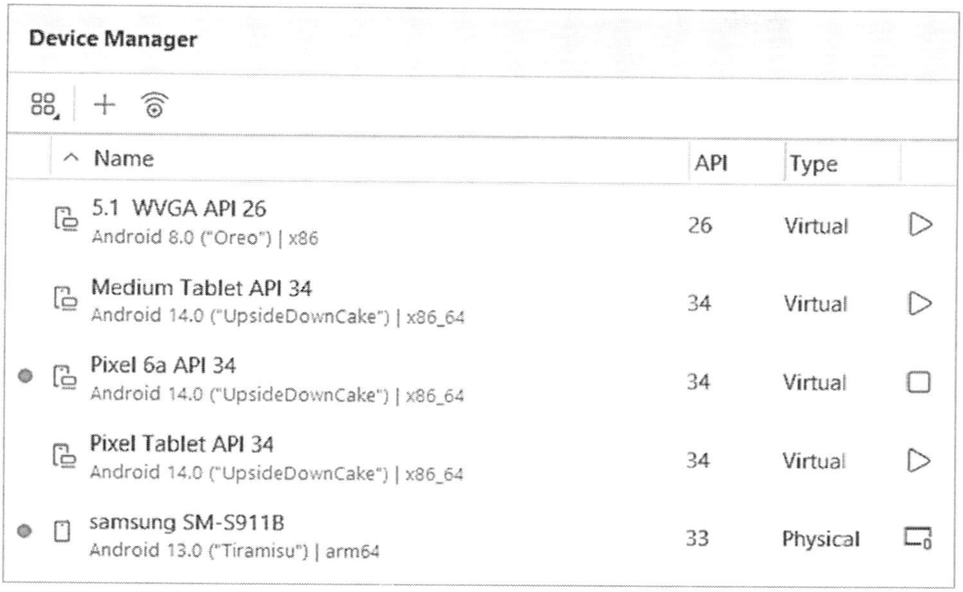

Figure 5.24 Device Manager Window with a Physical Device Installed

How do you run the application on your phone? Simply go to the application you want to launch. In the device selection window, choose your phone. Click the **green arrow** icon next to it. Android Studio will install the application on your phone.

If you want to open the app again later, just **tap its icon on your physical device**. This can be done even when the phone is not connected to the computer – the app remains installed on the device until it is manually removed by the user.

If you want to disable Developer Mode on your phone, simply toggle the **Switch** in the **Developer Options** window.

5.3 Creating an Application

Now we will move on to creating our own application. To start, we will create a simple application containing some **text** and a single button, known as a **Button**.

5.3.1 Creating an Application from an Open Window

To start creating a new application, begin by opening a **new project**. In the top - left corner of the window, select the **File** tab, then choose **New** and **New Project.**

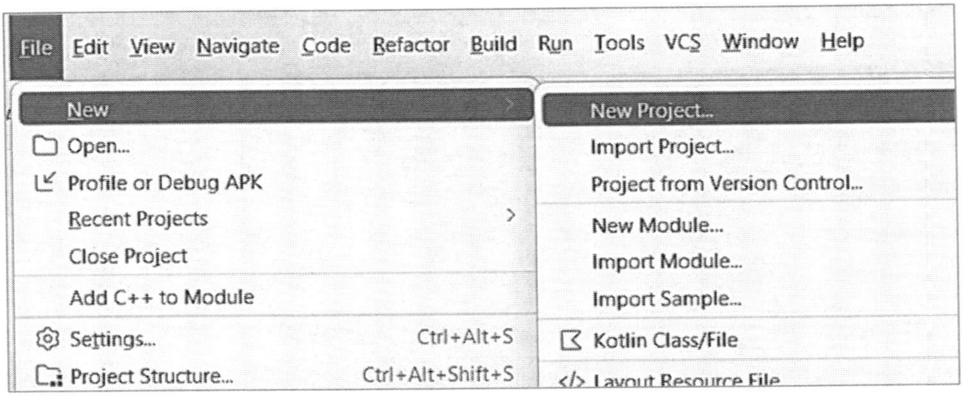

Figure 5.25 a New Project from Within the Application

As the application template, select **Empty Views Activity**. If the task does not specify a different template, this will always be the one to choose. Fill in the application creation window and click **Finish**.

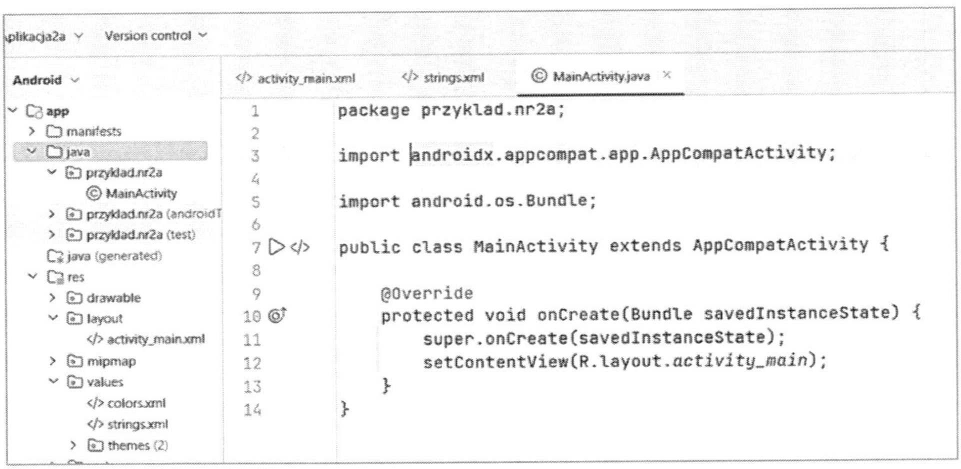

Figure 5.26 View of a New (Empty) Application After Creating a New Project

In the center of the window, you can see the editor for the activity file **MainActivity.java**. In the second tab, there is a graphical editor for the layout file.

The **layout of an application** refers to the arrangement of elements placed within the app. The layout is what the user sees when launching the application. In mobile applications, layouts are created using **XML**, a language somewhat similar to CSS. You can edit the layout in two ways:

- **Graphically** – by dragging, positioning, or resizing elements using the mouse
- **Textually** – by entering appropriate XML commands in the text editor

You can switch between views by clicking the corresponding tab:

- **Code tab** – allows for textual editing of the file
- **Design tab** – opens the graphical editor
- **Split tab** – combines both editors

Figure 5.27 Tabs for Changing the Layout View

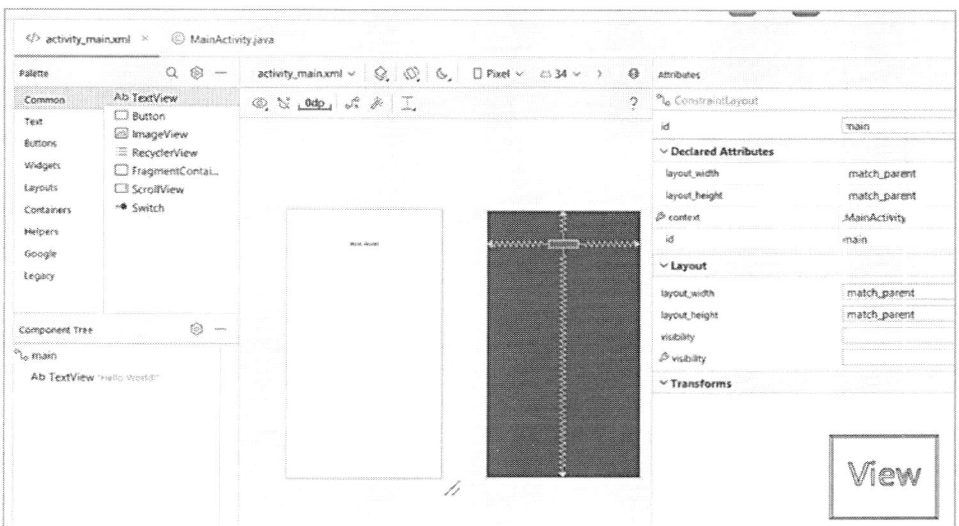

Figure 5.28 Graphical Layout Editor

```
<?xml version="1.0" encoding="utf-8"?>
<androidx.constraintlayout.widget.ConstraintLayout xmlns:android="http:
    xmlns:app="http://schemas.android.com/apk/res-auto"
    xmlns:tools="http://schemas.android.com/tools"
    android:layout_width="match_parent"
    android:layout_height="match_parent"
    tools:context=".MainActivity">

    <TextView
        android:layout_width="wrap_content"
        android:layout_height="wrap_content"
        android:text="Hello World!"
        app:layout_constraintBottom_toBottomOf="parent"
        app:layout_constraintEnd_toEndOf="parent"
        app:layout_constraintStart_toStartOf="parent"
        app:layout_constraintTop_toTopOf="parent" />

</androidx.constraintlayout.widget.ConstraintLayout>
```

Figure 5.29 Text Layout Editor

In this part of the manual, we will create the layout using the text editor. The graphical editor is the default view, which means that every newly opened application will initially open in that view.

5.3.2 Bacic Concepts

To begin programming mobile applications, we need to become familiar with the basic concepts that will appear throughout this book.

Layout – A layout defines how elements are arranged within an application. Android Studio allows you to create several types of layouts, each with its own specific properties and use cases. The files containing layout code are located in the **res/layout** directory and always have the .xml extension.

Activity – An activity represents an action performed by the application. This could be a response to a user pressing a button or selecting an option from a dropdown list. Activities are found in the Java directory. These are files with the **.java extension** and are programmed in the Java language.

View – (also called a widget or component) is an element placed within a layout. Examples of views include a text field (**TextView**) and a button (**Button**).

These concepts will appear frequently throughout this guide, which is why their definitions are introduced at the very beginning of your journey with Android.

5.3.3 Linear Layout

You can find the code for the application being created in the **Application2** folder. The first layout we will discuss is the Linear Layout. Its characteristic feature is that each element (component) added to the project is arranged one after another in the order in which it appears in the layout file.

We will start by creating the "**frame**" of our layout, which means defining the linear layout. In the **activity_main.xml** file, insert the code from the listing below.

```
<?xml version="1.0" encoding="utf-8"?>
<LinearLayout
xmlns:android="http://schemas.android.com/apk/res/android"
    xmlns:tools="http://schemas.android.com/tools"
    android:layout_width="match_parent"
    android:layout_height="wrap_content"
    android:orientation="vertical"
    tools:context=".MainActivity">

</LinearLayout>
```

Listing 5.1 Linear Layout

The most important elements:

```
xmlns:android="http://schemas.android.com/apk/res/android"
xmlns:tools=http://schemas.android.com/tools
```

Listing 5.2 Adding a Namespace to the Application

With these lines of code, we add a **so - called namespace** to the application, which enables us to use the **XML** language.

```
android:layout_width="match_parent"
android:layout_height="wrap_content"
```

Listing 5.3 Setting the Width and Height of the View

We set the width and height of the layout.

```
android:orientation="vertical"
```

Listing 5.4 Linear Layout

We set the orientation of the elements in the layout. This attribute can take two values:

- **Verical** – the elements are placed one below the other
- **Horizontal** – the elements are arranged side by side

```
tools:context=".MainActivity">
```

Listing 5.5 Linking to the Activity File

We connect the layout file to the activity file (by default, this should be **MainActivity.java**). All of the attributes mentioned above (except for android:orientation) are present in every application, regardless of the layout type used.

The attributes android:**layout_width and android**:**layout_height** can take different values:

- **match_parent** – adjusts the size of the layout to match its parent element, which in the case of a layout is the application window
- **wrap_content** – adjusts the size of the element to fit its content, such as a text label

These attributes can also be assigned a numeric value, e.g., **25dp**. At this point, the application does not yet contain any visible elements. We have only created the basic frame. Now let's add a simple text element.

To display text in the application, we use the **TextView** widget. Our text should be placed inside the **LinearLayout** view, so in the code, it must be inserted between the layout tags.

```
<LinearLayout

</LinearLayout>
```

Listing 5.6 Linera Layout

Placing the Cursor and Adding a TextView Widget Place **the cursor just below the line** containing **tools:context=".MainActivity">.** Click to position the **cursor** and start typing <**T**. The program will automatically suggest what you should enter. From the dropdown list, select **TextView** and click it. The program will automatically generate the widget with the required attributes.

Figure 5.30 Autocomplete Window

We complete the values of the attributes **android:layout_width** and **android:layout_height** by setting them to match_parent. We also add the attribute android:text, where we place the text that will be displayed on the application screen.

Now we will add two buttons to the application. Buttons are inserted using the Button widget. Below the TextView element, we place the following code in the layout file. The layout will now look as follows:

```
<?xml version="1.0" encoding="utf-8"?>
<LinearLayout
xmlns:android="http://schemas.android.com/apk/res/android"
    xmlns:tools="http://schemas.android.com/tools"
    android:layout_width="match_parent"
    android:layout_height="wrap_content"
    android:orientation="vertical"
    tools:context=".MainActivity">
    <TextView
        android:layout_width="match_parent"
        android:layout_height="match_parent"
        android:text="Hello world"
        />
    <Button
        android:layout_width="match_parent"
        android:layout_height="match_parent"
        android:text="This is Button1" />
    <Button
        android:layout_width="wrap_content"
        android:layout_height="wrap_content"
        android:text="This is Button2"
        />
</LinearLayout>
```

Listing 5.7 Linear Layout

After launching, the application will look like the illustration below.

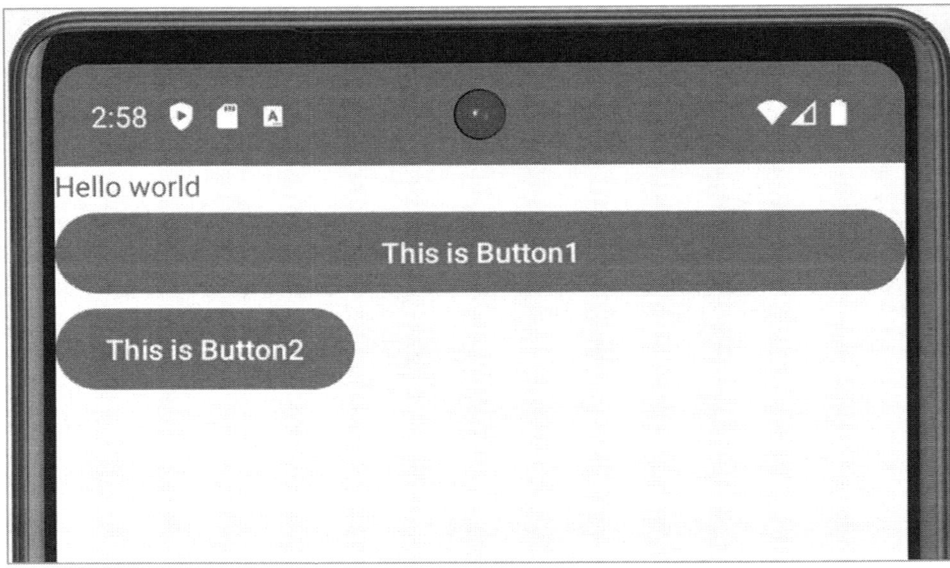

Figure 5.31 An application demonstrating the behavior of the match_parent and wrap_content properties.

In the application, you can observe different ways the buttons are displayed. **Button 1** is stretched to the full width of the layout because the android:layout_width attribute is set to **match_parent**. The button's width is adjusted to match the width of the layout. **Button 2** is significantly narrower because its width is set to wrap_content. The button's width is adjusted to fit the length of the text. If we replace the text "**This is Button2**" with "**Button2**", its width will adjust accordingly to the new content length.

5.3.4 Restarting the application after making changes to the code.

If we make changes to the application and want to preview the edits, we need to refresh the app in the emulator. To do this, click the **green rounded arrow** icon at the top of the editor.

Figure 5.32 Application restart button

5.3.5 File storing string resources – strings.xml

You can find the modified application code in the folder named **Application2a**. In the previous exercise, we placed several elements in the layout. Each of them included the **android:text** attribute. The text displayed in the application was entered directly as the value of this attribute. Let's open the editor and check the **warning messages** that appeared there.

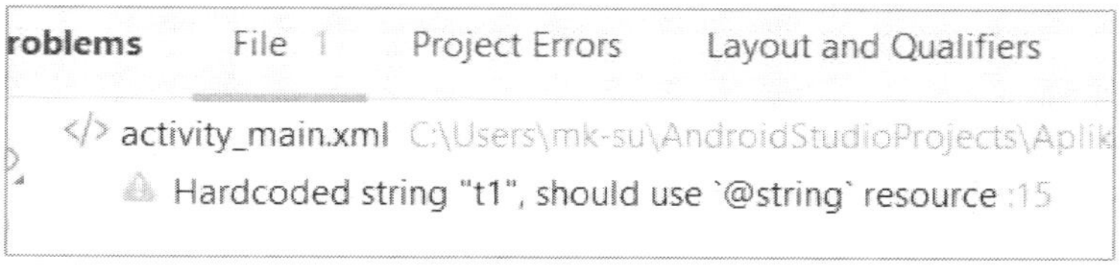

Figure 5.33 Warning message content: Hardcoded text

As shown in the illustration, the **TextView** element we inserted raises a warning. The message reads: **Hardcoded text**. **Hardcoding** is a type of programming practice where data is placed directly into the target element within the code. As we can see, Android Studio doesn't necessarily treat this as an error, but rather as a warning. If we take a closer look, Android will suggest what we should do to fix this issue.

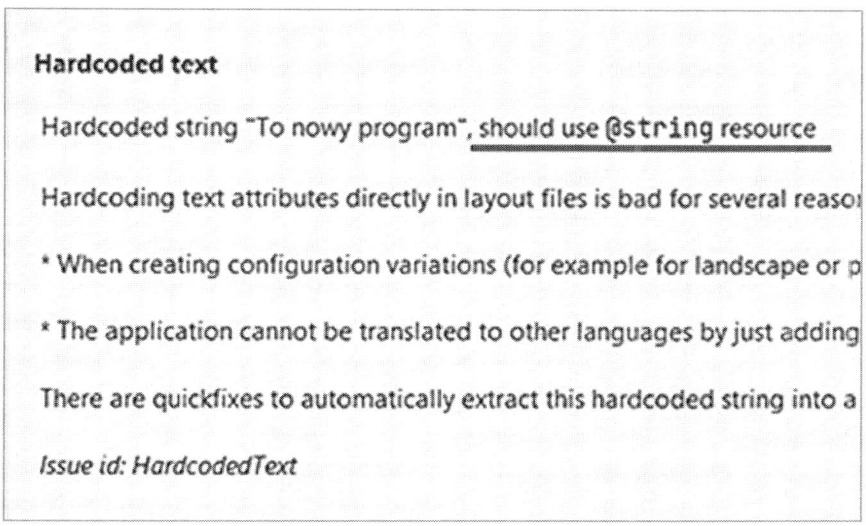

Figure 5.34 System suggestion for a possible solution

Android suggests that we should use text from the **@string** resource file. The **strings.xml** file can be found in the application tree – the list of files and folders that make up our project. If we click the **Project** tab on the **right side of**

the editor, a file list will open. The three most important folders are: **manifest, java,** and **res.** The **strings.xml** resource file is located in the **res** folder, specifically in its subfolder named values. Clicking on the file will add a tab to the editor and allow us to edit it.

Figure 5.35 Application Tree with the strings.xml File

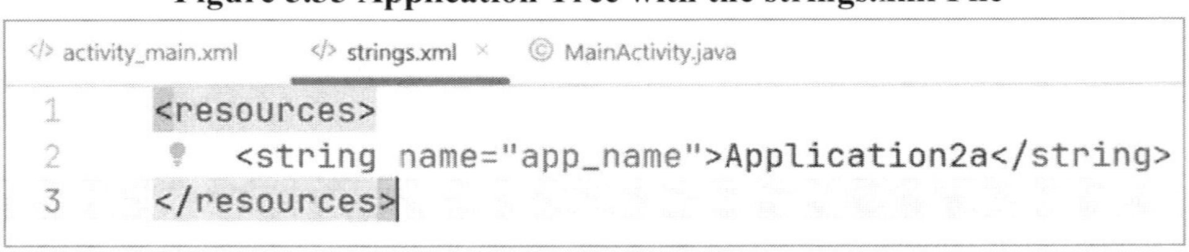

Figure 5.36 Initial Content of the strings.xml File

All entries related to strings should be placed between the **<resources>** and **</resources>** tags. An empty **strings.xml** file contains the following code:

```
<resources>
    <string name="app_name">Application2a</string>
</resources>
```

Listing 5.8 trings.xml file

The previously mentioned **<resources>** tags appear here, along with the **app_name** string, which is assigned the name of our application. We will now complete the file's code with the strings that label our views.

```
<resources>
    <string name="app_name">Application2a</string>
    <string name="text1">Hello world</string>
    <string name="btn1">This is Button 1</string>
    <string name="btn2">This is Button 2</string>
</resources>
```

Listing 5.9 The strings.xml file with completed values

Now we need to place references to the strings in the layout file. We move on to the **activity_main.xml** file and fill in the **android:text** attributes with the following entries.

```
<?xml version="1.0" encoding="utf-8"?>
<LinearLayout

xmlns:android="http://schemas.android.com/apk/res/android"
    xmlns:tools="http://schemas.android.com/tools"
    android:layout_width="match_parent"
    android:layout_height="wrap_content"
    android:orientation="vertical"
    tools:context=".MainActivity">
    <TextView
        android:layout_width="match_parent"
        android:layout_height="match_parent"
        android:text="@string/text1"
        />
    <Button
        android:layout_width="match_parent"
        android:layout_height="match_parent"
        android:text="@string/btn1"
        />
    <Button
        android:layout_width="wrap_content"
        android:layout_height="wrap_content"
        android:text="@string/btn2"
        />
</LinearLayout>
```

Listing 5.10 File with Configured Views: TextView and Button

We replace the text with a reference to the strings.xml file. The @ symbol indicates that we are referencing another file. The name following the @ symbol specifies the file where the resource is located. In this exercise, it refers to the string resources file. After the / symbol, we enter the name of the string that defines the text. The appearance of the application will not change in this case. Only the warnings in the editor will disappear.

5.3.6 Warning and Error

In the previous exercise, we encountered a so - called "**warning**." This is a notification about certain irregularities in the code that we should correct.

However, even very advanced programmers make more serious mistakes. Android Studio will catch all code issues and report them as errors. So, what is the difference between a **Warning** and an **Error**?

As mentioned several times, a **Warning** is just a caution – like a yellow card for the programmer. In fact, this type of message is displayed in yellow. Warnings should be corrected, but they do not significantly affect the functioning of the application. The emulator successfully launched the first application despite the warnings.

With an **Error**, it's a completely different story. First of all, an **Error** is marked in **red**. Its occurrence has a significant impact on the application's functionality, and unfortunately, the **emulator** will not run an application that contains an **error.**

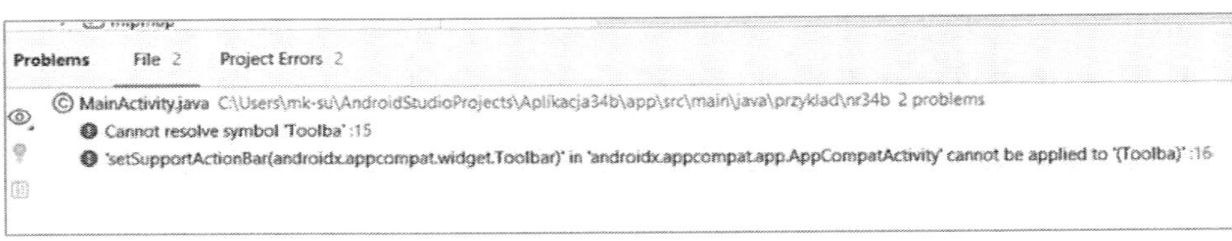

Figure 5.37 Errors Reported by Android Studio

The illustration shows a fragment of code after the removal of the **LinearLayout** tag. In the top - left corner, we see a red warning. Much of the code has also turned slightly "red." If we try to run the application with the above error, the **emulator** will refuse to cooperate. The application will not launch, and the following messages will appear on the screen.

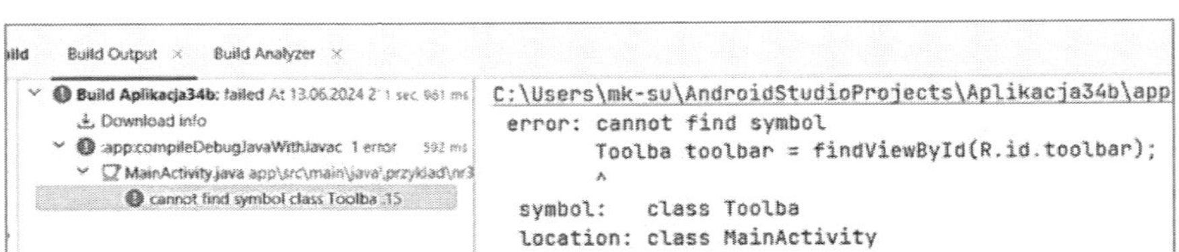

Figure 5.38 Program After Launching the Application with Errors

5.4 Activity

You can find the application code in the folder named **Application3**.

All Android applications consist of at least two components. The first is the **layout**, and the second is the **activity**. The **activity** is responsible for the app's behavior – reacting to button presses, displaying messages, etc.

Layouts are defined in files with the **.xml extension** – the main one is usually **activity_main.xml.** Activities are defined in files with the **.java** or **.kt extension**, depending on whether the code is written in **Java** or **kt.** The main activity file is typically named **MainActivity.java** (or **MainActivity.kt** for **Kotlin**). Activities and layouts form pairs.

Let's create a new application. Its complete code can be found in the folder named **Application3**. We'll start by inserting a button that responds to user interaction. We place it inside a **LinearLayout.** The layout code in **activity_main.xml** will look as follows:

```
<?xml version="1.0" encoding="utf-8"?>
<LinearLayout
xmlns:android="http://schemas.android.com/apk/res/android"
    xmlns:tools="http://schemas.android.com/tools"
    android:layout_width="match_parent"
    android:layout_height="match_parent"
    android:orientation="vertical"
    tools:context=".MainActivity">

    <Button
        android:layout_width="wrap_content"
        android:layout_height="wrap_content"
        android:layout_margin="25dp"
        android:text="@string/Btn1"
        android:onClick="write"/>

</LinearLayout>
```

Listing 5.11 Application3 Layout Code

A new attribute here is **android:layout_margin**, which is set to a value of **25dp**. The **dp** unit is specific to the Android system. **1dp** represents a distance or length of **1 pixel**, regardless of screen density. This makes it independent of the resolution of the device on which the application is running.

The attribute itself creates a margin between the view and the edge of the screen or another element. Before launching the application, make sure to complete the **strings.xml** file. After launching, the application looks like the image shown below.

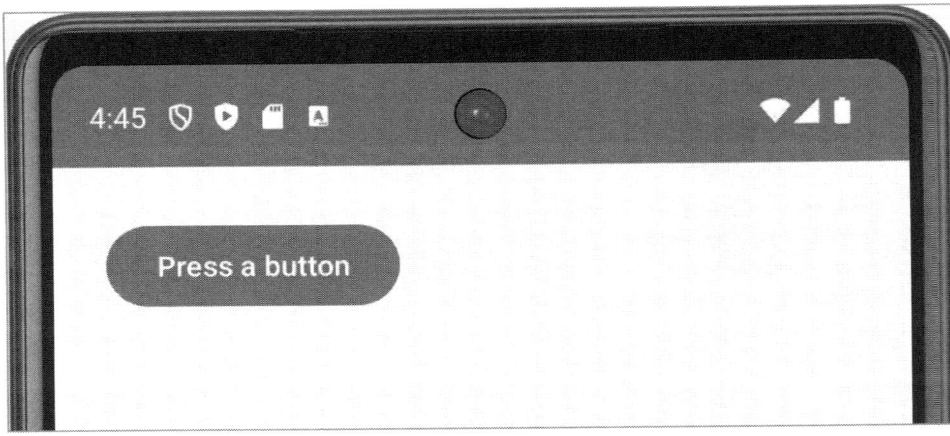

Figure 5.39 Application Window After Completing the Layout Code

Before we start programming the activity, let's take a look at the elements of the activity file. The activity file should open as a tab in the editor. If it doesn't appear, you'll need to open it manually. It is located in the **Java** directory and is named **MainActivity**.

```
package example.app3;

import androidx.appcompat.app.AppCompatActivity;
import android.os.Bundle;

public class MainActivity extends AppCompatActivity {

    @Override
    protected void onCreate(Bundle savedInstanceState) {
        super.onCreate(savedInstanceState);
        setContentView(R.layout.activity_main);
    }
}
```

Listing 5.12 Application3 Code

Each line means the following:

- **Package** – this is the so - called package. The name displayed is the name of the project. If you don't remember the package name, you can always check it in the project tree on the left side of the editor.

- **Import** – allows you to include classes in the application that are added to the project. The more complex the application (specifically the activity), the more classes are imported. The editor highlights in gray the classes that are included but not used in the current project. In this application, two classes are imported at the beginning:
- **androidx.appcompat.app.AppCompatActivity** – imports the base class. It is a subclass of Activity that enables the use of Android features available in older API versions.
- **android.os.Bundle** – responsible for communication between components in the application and for storing data during the app's runtime.

The next line of code defines the main class of the application, where we will write everything that happens in the activity. The MainActivity class inherits from the AppCompatActivity class.

- **@Override** – this is an instruction to the compiler that the class is overriding a method (you can find more detailed information about overriding in the Java section).
- **protected void onCreate(Bundle savedInstanceState)** – the onCreate method is called when the activity is created for the first time.
- **setContentView(R.layout.activity_main)** – in this line, we tell the activity which layout file to use (in simple terms, this connects the activity to a specific layout).

Let's now take a closer look at the final line of code, which includes the **letter R**, as it plays a very important role in activity creation.

The **letter R** is essentially a link to the **R.java** file. This file is located in the application directory at: **app/build/generated/source/r/debug**

If needed, you can open this file and check its contents. The **R.java** file is automatically updated during app development. It contains definitions of all elements included in your application.

Now that we've reviewed the basic structure of the activity file, we can move on to editing the application. We'll start by modifying the layout code to add a function that allows the **Button** to respond to clicks.

```
android:onClick="write"
```

Listing 5.13 Assigning a Method to the Button

Adding the following line to the **activity_main.xml** file, in the section related to the button, will cause a method named **write** to be triggered when the button is clicked. The definition of this method will be placed in the **MainActivity.java** file.

We want the application to display text when the button is pressed. To show text on the screen, we first need to prepare a space for it. In the layout file, we need to add a **TextView** element. The completed code will look as follows:

```
<?xml version="1.0" encoding="utf-8"?>
<LinearLayout
xmlns:android="http://schemas.android.com/apk/res/android"
    xmlns:tools="http://schemas.android.com/tools"
    android:layout_width="match_parent"
    android:layout_height="match_parent"
    android:orientation="vertical"
    tools:context=".MainActivity">

    <Button
        android:layout_width="wrap_content"
        android:layout_height="wrap_content"
        android:layout_margin="25dp"
        android:text="@string/Btn1"
        android:onClick="write"/>

    <TextView
        android:id="@+id/txt1"
        android:layout_width="wrap_content"
        android:layout_height="wrap_content"
        android:textSize="30sp"
        android:text="" />
```

Listing 5.14 Layout Code with a TextView Element

The TextView element is initially empty. If we want text to appear there before the button is pressed, we need to prepare a string for it in the strings.xml file. In the **TextView** view, new attributes have also appeared:

```
android:id="@+id/txt1"
```

Listing 5.15 Assigning an ID

This attribute assigns an ID to the view – a unique name. Using this name, we can reference the view in the activity file.

```
android:textSize="30sp"
```

Listing 5.16 Setting Font Size

This attribute sets the font size. Here, it is set to **30sp.** The sp unit is used in Android and is very similar to **dp**, with the difference that it respects the user's system font size settings. This makes it more suitable for text, ensuring accessibility and readability across different devices.

Since we've already made changes to the layout file, we now move on to editing the activity. To do this, we open the **MainActivity.java** file.

We'll start by writing a method that will respond to the button click. As specified in the layout file, the method will be named **write**. We'll place it inside the MainActivity class, below the **onCreate** method.

The method will be of type **View**. In Android, the View class represents UI elements (or widgets) that can be added to the app. One such widget is the Button. Other widgets will be introduced later in the book. The MainActivity.java file with the empty write method will look like this:

```
package example.app3;

import androidx.appcompat.app.AppCompatActivity;
import android.os.Bundle;
import android.view.View;
import android.widget.TextView;
public class MainActivity extends AppCompatActivity {

    @Override
    protected void onCreate(Bundle savedInstanceState) {
        super.onCreate(savedInstanceState);
        setContentView(R.layout.activity_main);
    }
    public void write (View view) {

    }
}
```

Listing 5.17 Main Activity Code

We complete the code so that when the button is pressed, a message appears.

```
TextView txt = findViewById(R.id.txt1);
```

Listing 5.18 Creating a Reference to an Element from the Layout File

In the **write** class, we declare an object of type **TextView** and name it txt. We assign this object a reference to the TextView element. Using the **findViewById** function, we locate the appropriate element in the layout file. Note that we are searching for an element with a specific ID. In this code snippet, the ID is named **txt1**, which is the name we assigned to the **TextView** element in the layout file.

```
txt.setText("The button is pressed");
```

Listing 5.19 Setting a String

The purpose of this method is to assign a text string to the variable using **setText**, which will be displayed after pressing the button. Below is the complete code of both files. Check if the code matches what you have written, and then run the application. Code of the **write** method:

```
public void write (View view) {
    TextView txt = findViewById(R.id.txt1);
    txt.setText("The button is pressed");
}
```

Listing 5.20 Definition of the write method

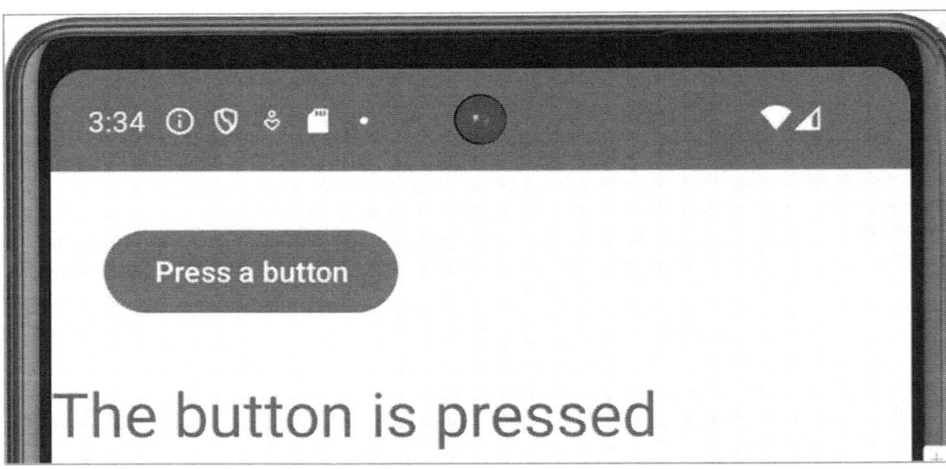

Figure 5.40 Application window after launching the activity

5.5 Toast Message

You can find the application code in the folder named **Application4**. A **Toast message** is a short piece of information that appears at the bottom of the application. We use it for quick communication with the user. We are creating an application that contains a single **Button**. The layout code will look like this:

```
<?xml version="1.0" encoding="utf-8"?>
<LinearLayout
xmlns:android="http://schemas.android.com/apk/res/android"
    xmlns:tools="http://schemas.android.com/tools"
    android:layout_width="match_parent"
    android:layout_height="match_parent"
    android:orientation="vertical"
    tools:context=".MainActivity">

    <Button
        android:layout_width="wrap_content"
        android:layout_height="wrap_content"
        android:layout_margin="25dp"
        android:text="@string/Btn1"
        android:onClick="toast"/>

</LinearLayout>
```

Listing 5.21 Application4 layout file.

In the activity file, we define a method called toast, which will respond to the button press. The method definition will contain the following code:

```
String text = "You have launched a toast";
```

Listing 5.22 Defining a string

A variable of type **String** will store the content of the message.

```
int duration = Toast.LENGTH_SHORT;
```

Listing 5.23 The duration variable with an assigned value. The duration of the Toast message.

An int type variable is assigned the message duration, which is determined using the **LENGTH_SHORT** value.

```
Toast toast = Toast.makeText(this, text, duration);
```

Listing 5.24 Creating a Toast object.

We assign the result of the **makeText** method to the variable toast, which is an object of type **Toast**. This method takes three parameters:

The first is the so - called **Context**, which refers to the environment in which the method will be executed. Since we are calling this method inside a class that already has access to the context, we set it to this.

The second parameter is the name of the variable that stores the message to be displayed in the **Toast** popup.

The third parameter is the **duration** variable, which stores the length of time the message will be shown.

The duration parameter can take two values:

- **LENGTH_SHORT** – short display time
- **LENGTH_LONG** – longer display time

The final task is to display the Toast message, which is done using the show method.

```
toast.show();
```

Listing 5.25 Launching the Toast message

The complete activity code will look as follows:

```
package example.app4;

import androidx.appcompat.app.AppCompatActivity;
import android.os.Bundle;
import android.view.View;
import android.widget.Toast;

public class MainActivity extends AppCompatActivity {

    @Override
    protected void onCreate(Bundle savedInstanceState) {
        super.onCreate(savedInstanceState);
        setContentView(R.layout.activity_main);
    }
    public void toast(View view) {
        String text = "You have launched a toast";
        int duration = Toast.LENGTH_LONG;
        Toast toast = Toast.makeText(this, text, duration);
        toast.show();
    }
}
```

Listing 5.26 Application4 activity code

After launching the application and pressing the button, a **Toast** message will appear at the bottom of the screen.

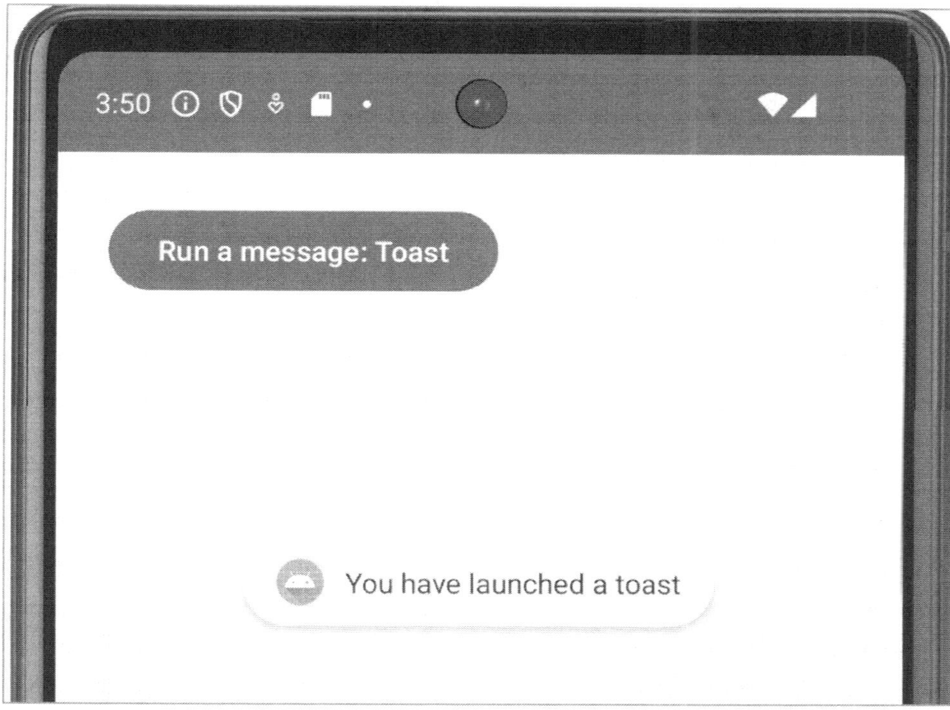

Figure 5.41 Toast message

5.6 Views

We mentioned views in the previous chapter. These included, among others: buttons (**Button**) and text fields **(TextView).** Now we will explore other types of views that will be useful when working on applications.

An important piece of information is that all widgets are elements of the GUI - Graphical User Interface. These are components that are derived from the already familiar **View** class.

5.6.1 EditText - text field

You can find the application code in the folder named **Application5**. The first GUI element will be a text field. It is a box where we can enter text. In Android Studio, the text field is represented by the widget **EditText**. The code that places the **EditText** element in the layout will look as follows:

```
<?xml version="1.0" encoding="utf-8"?>
<LinearLayout

xmlns:android="http://schemas.android.com/apk/res/android"
    xmlns:tools="http://schemas.android.com/tools"
    android:layout_width="match_parent"
    android:layout_height="match_parent"
    android:orientation="vertical"
    tools:context=".MainActivity">
    <EditText
        android:id="@+id/editText1"
        android:layout_width="wrap_content"
        android:layout_height="wrap_content"
        android:hint="@string/edt1"
        android:inputType="textCapSentences"
        android:textColorHint="#8D6E63"
        />
</LinearLayout>
```

Listing 5.27 view defined in the layout file

New attributes:

```
android:hint="@string/edt1"
```

Listing 5.28 Attribute for setting a hint

This is known as a hint. The text in quotation marks will be displayed when the application starts, before the user enters anything. Its content is defined in the **strings.xml** file.

```
android:inputType="textCapSentences"
```

Listing 5.29 Declaring the inputType attribute

The inputType attribute defines the type of data that can be entered into the field. Possible options for this attribute are listed in the table below:

Value	Type of Input
Number	Allows entering numbers
Phone	Allows entering a phone number
textPassword	Allows entering a password; each character is masked

textCapSentences	Allows entering text; each new sentence starts with a capital letter
textAutoCorrect	Allows entering text; automatically corrects mistakes

Table 4.1: Possible values of the android:inputType attribute

```
android:textColorHint="#8D6E63"
```

Listing 5.30 Attribute for setting hint text color

This attribute defines the color of the hint text displayed in the EditText field. The color is set using hexadecimal notation. Now run the application and check how it looks.

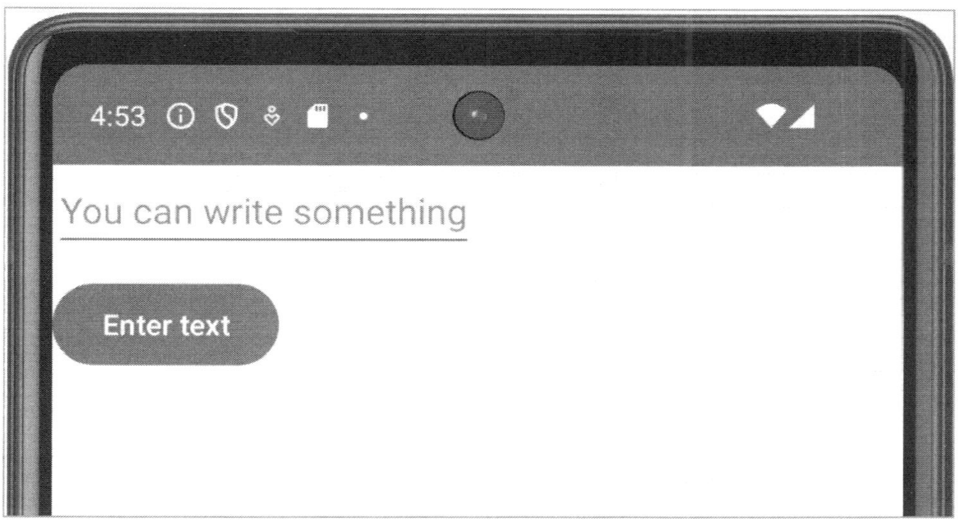

Figure 5.42 EditText input field

We will now use the **EditText** view in the activity file. The application will retrieve text from the text field and display it on the screen. To create this application, we will need the following components: **EditText**, **TextView**, and a **Button**. You can find the layout file of the application below:

```
<?xml version="1.0" encoding="utf-8"?>
<LinearLayout

xmlns:android="http://schemas.android.com/apk/res/android"
    xmlns:tools="http://schemas.android.com/tools"
    android:layout_width="match_parent"
    android:layout_height="match_parent"
    android:orientation="vertical"
    tools:context=".MainActivity">
    <EditText
        android:id="@+id/editText1"
        android:layout_width="wrap_content"
        android:layout_height="wrap_content"
        android:hint="@string/edt1"
        android:inputType="textCapSentences"
        android:textColorHint="#8D6E63"
        />
     <Button
        android:layout_width="wrap_content"
        android:layout_height="wrap_content"
        android:id="@+id/przycisk1"
        android:text="@string/btn1"
        android:layout_marginTop="10dp"
        android:onClick="enterText"
        />
     <TextView
        android:layout_width="wrap_content"
        android:layout_height="wrap_content"
        android:id="@+id/t1"
        android:text=""
        android:layout_marginTop="10dp"/>
 </LinearLayout>
```

Listing 5.31 Full layout code

Now we will work with the activity file **MainActivity.java.** To retrieve text from the text field, we will need objects of type **EditText** and **TextView** from the layout file. We will also use a variable named pobrany, which will be of type String. This variable will retrieve and store the text entered by the user.

```
EditText text = findViewById(R.id.editText1);
String downloadedText = text.getText().toString();
TextView text1 = findViewById(R.id.t1);
text1.setText(downloadedText);
```

Listing 5.32Creating references to layout elements: EditText and TextView

The first line creates an **EditText** object named tekst and links it to the layout element with the ID edit **Text**. In the second line, we assign the text retrieved from the text field to a variable named pobrany. This is done using the **getText()** method. The **toString()** function converts the user - entered text into a string. Next, we need to insert the retrieved text into the **TextView**. To do this, we create a reference to the appropriate view using the **findViewById** method.

In the final step, we set the text using the **setText()** method. Since the application should respond when the button is pressed, the code for retrieving and displaying the text must be placed inside the method assigned to the **Button**.

Full activity code:

```
package example.app5;

import androidx.appcompat.app.AppCompatActivity;
import android.os.Bundle;
import android.view.View;
import android.widget.EditText;
import android.widget.TextView;

public class MainActivity extends AppCompatActivity {

    @Override
    protected void onCreate(Bundle savedInstanceState) {
        super.onCreate(savedInstanceState);
        setContentView(R.layout.activity_main);
    }
    public void enterText (View view) {
        EditText text = findViewById(R.id.editText1);
        String downloadedText = text.getText().toString();
        TextView text1 = findViewById(R.id.t1);
        text1.setText(downloadedText);
    }
}
```

Listing 5.33 Program activity code Activity5.

After launching the application and entering text in the **EditText** field, then pressing the button, the application window will look like in the image below.

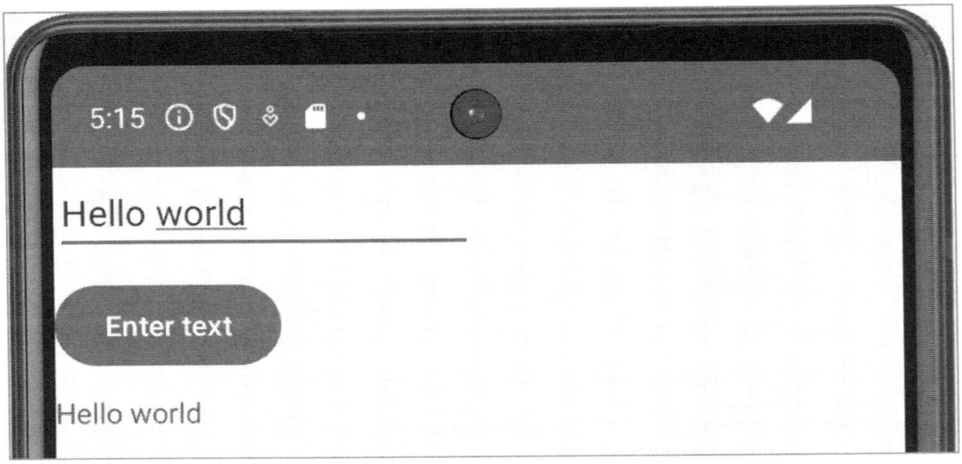

Figure 5.43 Application5 after launch

5.6.2 Inserting Graphics - ImageView

You can find the application code in the **Application6** folder. To make the application look more attractive, we can insert an image into it. For the next application, prepare a small - sized image. If you don't have a photo, for example, you can download a graphic from the Internet. Just remember to respect copyright laws. To begin, we create a linear layout in which we will place an **ImageView**.

```
<?xml version="1.0" encoding="utf-8"?>
<LinearLayout

xmlns:android="http://schemas.android.com/apk/res/android"
    xmlns:tools="http://schemas.android.com/tools"
    android:layout_width="match_parent"
    android:layout_height="match_parent"
    tools:context=".MainActivity" >

    <ImageView
        android:layout_width="match_parent"
        android:layout_height="wrap_content"
        android:src="@drawable/pic1"
        android:contentDescription="@string/pic1"/>

</LinearLayout>
```

Listing 5.34 ImageView in the Layout File

The following code:

```
android:src="@drawable/pic1"
```

Listing 5.35 Reference to the Image File

This tells us that we will insert an image named pic1 and retrieve it from the **drawable** directory.For the image to be visible in the application, it must be placed in the drawable folder. This folder is created automatically with the project and is located within the application's files. You can find it by following the appropriate access path or by clicking on the folder name in the project tree and selecting “**Open in Explorer**.”

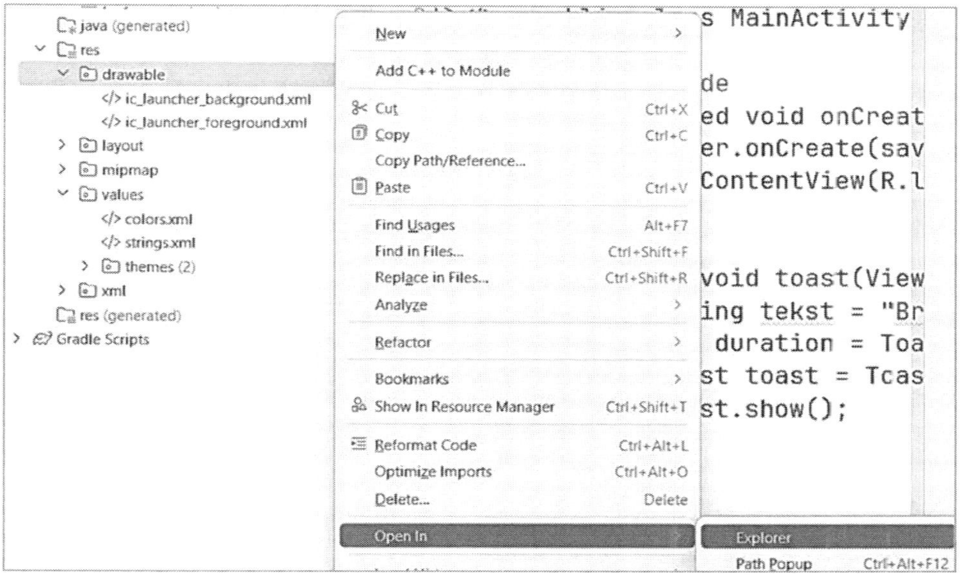

Figure 5.44 Opening the drawable Folder from the Application Window

On your computer, the res directory will open. You just need to go into the **drawable** folder and paste the image there. It’s important that the image name matches the name used in the application code and starts with a letter. Files with the extensions **.jpg** and **.png** are accepted. When the image is placed inside the folder, you can run the application.

Figure 5.45 Application with an ImageView

5.6.3 ToggleButton

The next widget will be a **ToggleButton**.Below is the code you can use to insert it into your application.

```
<ToggleButton
    android:id="@+id/toggle_button"
    android:layout_width="200dp"
    android:layout_height="wrap_content"
    android:textOff="@string/on"
    android:textOn="@string/off" />
```

Listing 5.36 ToggleButton Element in the Layout File

The new attributes used in this code are:

```
android:textOff="@string/on"
android:textOn="@string/off"
```

Listing 5.37 Attributes textOff and textOn

These attributes define the text displayed on the button when it is turned off and on, respectively. The above labels are defined in the strings.xml file, which contains the following code:

```
<resources>
    <string name="app_name">Application7</string>
    <string name="on">Give your consent</string>
    <string name="off">Withdraw your consent</string>
    <string name="t1">Do you give your marketing consent?
</string>
</resources>
```

Listing 5.38 strings.xml file

The **ToggleButton** will appear in the application as shown in the image below. The first one is in the **ON** state, and the second one is **OFF**.

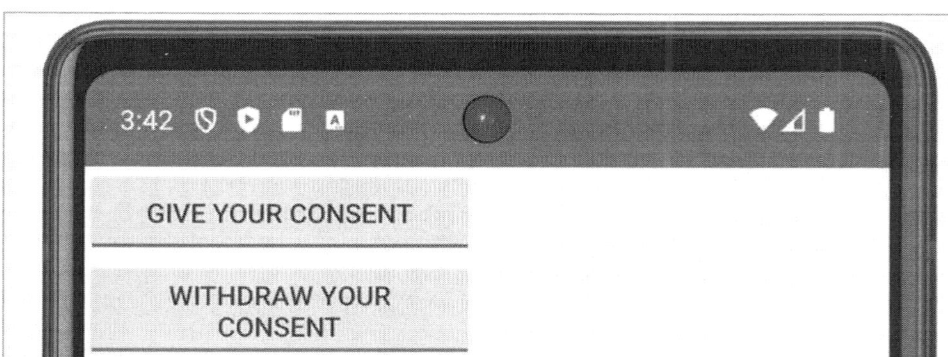

Figure 5.46 ToggleButton Switch

To demonstrate how the **ToggleButton** switch works, we will prepare an application. You can find the application code in the folder named **Application7.** The application will display information about the user's consent to receive advertisements. In the layout file, we will place two views: a **ToggleButton** and a **TextView**, which will change depending on whether the user gives marketing consent.

The layout file will look as follows:

```
<?xml version="1.0" encoding="utf-8"?>
<LinearLayout

xmlns:android="http://schemas.android.com/apk/res/android"
    xmlns:tools="http://schemas.android.com/tools"
    android:layout_width="match_parent"
    android:layout_height="match_parent"
    android:orientation="vertical"
    tools:context=".MainActivity">

    <ToggleButton
        android:id="@+id/toggle_button"
        android:layout_width="200dp"
        android:layout_height="wrap_content"
        android:textOff="@string/on"
        android:textOn="@string/off"
        android:onClick="activated"/>

    <TextView
        android:layout_width="wrap_content"
        android:layout_height="wrap_content"
        android:id="@+id/t1"
        android:text="@string/t1"
        android:textSize="30sp"
        android:layout_marginTop="10dp"/>

</LinearLayout>
```

Listing 5.39 Application Layout File

Just like a regular Button, the **ToggleButton** also has the **onClick** attribute, and we will use it in this application. We assign it the value activated, which will also be the name of the method that is triggered when the button is clicked. The method **activated** will have the following code:

```
public void activated(View view) {
    TextView t1 = findViewById(R.id.t1);
    boolean isCh = ((ToggleButton) view).isChecked();
if (isCh) {
   t1.setText("You have given your marketing consent");
    }
else {
   t1.setText("You haven't given your marketing consent.");
    }
```

Listing 5.40 Definition of the activated Method

First, we create a **TextView** object and name it **t1**, then retrieve a reference to the view from the layout file. We will also need a **boolean** variable. Such a variable can hold one of two values: **true** or **false**. It will take the appropriate value depending on the state of the **ToggleButton** – whether it is **On** or **Off**. To do this, we use the **isChecked** method. If the button is checked (i.e., turned on), the variable will be set to **true**; otherwise, it will be false. We will use this variable in an **if** conditional statement. Both options will display the appropriate text depending on the user's decision.

The activity code will look as follows:

```
package example.app7;

import androidx.appcompat.app.AppCompatActivity;
import android.os.Bundle;
import android.view.View;
import android.widget.TextView;
import android.widget.ToggleButton;

public class MainActivity extends AppCompatActivity {

    @Override
    protected void onCreate(Bundle savedInstanceState) {
        super.onCreate(savedInstanceState);
        setContentView(R.layout.activity_main);
    }

    public void activated(View view) {
        TextView t1 = findViewById(R.id.t1);
        boolean isCh = ((ToggleButton) view).isChecked();
        if (isCh) {
            t1.setText("You have given your marketing
consent");
        } else {
            t1.setText("You haven't given your marketing
consent.");
        }
    }
}
```

Listing 5.41 Activity Code for the Application Application7

The result of the application's operation can be seen in the image below.

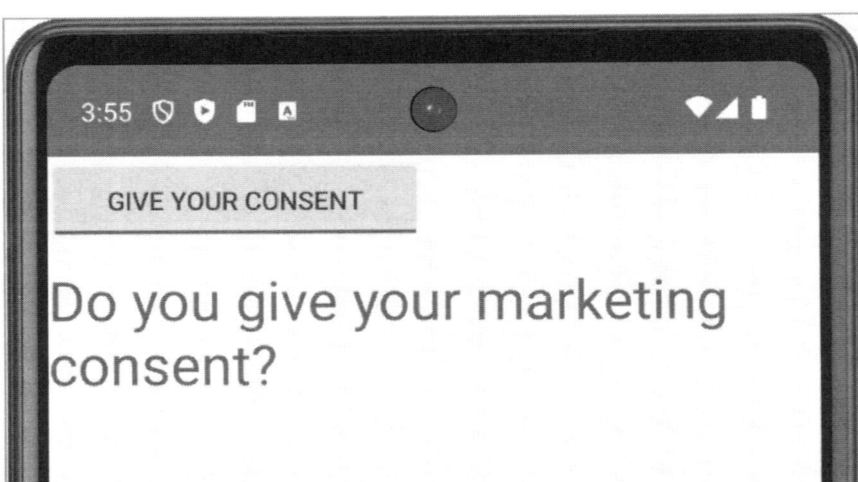

Figue 5.47 Application After Pressing the ToggleButton

5.6.4 Switch Toggle

You can find the application code in the folder named **Application8**. This button also operates in two states. The only difference from the **ToggleButton** is its appearance – it is a sliding switch. This element is called a **Switch**. The code used to insert it into the layout file looks as follows:

```
<Switch
android:id="@+id/switch1"
android:layout_width="wrap_content"
android:layout_height="wrap_content"
/>
```

Listing 5.42 Switch Toggle

The activity code in which we will use the Switch will be similar to the one from the previous exercise. The layout file will include two elements: a **Switch** and a **TextView**.

```
<?xml version="1.0" encoding="utf-8"?>
<LinearLayout

xmlns:android="http://schemas.android.com/apk/res/android"
    xmlns:tools="http://schemas.android.com/tools"
    android:layout_width="match_parent"
    android:layout_height="match_parent"
    android:orientation="vertical"
    tools:context=".MainActivity">

    <Switch
        android:id="@+id/switch1"
        android:layout_width="wrap_content"
        android:layout_height="wrap_content"
        android:onClick="switchOn"
        />

    <TextView
        android:layout_width="wrap_content"
        android:layout_height="wrap_content"
        android:id="@+id/tekst1"
        android:text="@string/t1"
        android:textSize="30sp"
        android:layout_marginTop="10dp"/>

</LinearLayout>
```

Listing 5.43 Application8 Layout Code

```
package example.app8;
import androidx.appcompat.app.AppCompatActivity;
import android.os.Bundle;
import android.view.View;
import android.widget.Switch;
import android.widget.TextView;

public class MainActivity extends AppCompatActivity {

    @Override
    protected void onCreate(Bundle savedInstanceState) {
        super.onCreate(savedInstanceState);
        setContentView(R.layout.activity_main);
    }
    public void switchOn(View view) {
        TextView t1 = findViewById(R.id.t1);
        boolean isCh = ((Switch) view).isChecked();
        if (isCh) {
            t1.setText("You have given your marketing
consent");
        } else {
            t1.setText("You haven't given your marketing
consent.");
        }
    }
}
```

Listing 5.44 Main Activity Code

5.6.5 Checkbox

Application Code Can Be Found in the Folder Named **Application9.** Now we'll take a closer look at selection fields. The first type is a **CheckBox** – a small square that can have two states. We often encounter checkboxes when confirming acceptance of Terms and Conditions or giving marketing consent while filling out an online form. The code that allows us to place a **checkbox** in the application looks as follows:

```
<CheckBox
    android:id="@+id/delivery"
    android:layout_width="wrap_content"
    android:layout_height="wrap_content"
    android:text="@string/delivery"
    android:textSize="12pt"
    android:onClick="count"
    />
```

Listing 5.45 CheckBox Widget in the Layout File

We will use it in an application that calculates additional order costs. The layout will include three **checkboxes**: **delivery, cash on delivery, and gift wrapping,** as well as two **TextView** elements. The full layout code will look as follows:

```
<?xml version="1.0" encoding="utf-8"?>
<LinearLayout
xmlns:android="http://schemas.android.com/apk/res/android"
    xmlns:tools="http://schemas.android.com/tools"
    android:layout_width="wrap_content"
    android:layout_height="wrap_content"
    android:orientation="vertical"
    tools:context=".MainActivity">
    <TextView
        android:id="@+id/t2"
        android:layout_width="wrap_content"
        android:layout_height="wrap_content"
        android:textSize="12pt"
        android:text="@string/additional_services"/>
    <CheckBox
        android:id="@+id/delivery"
        android:layout_width="wrap_content"
        android:layout_height="wrap_content"
        android:text="@string/delivery"
        android:textSize="12pt"
        android:onClick="count"/>
    <CheckBox
        android:id="@+id/payment"
        android:layout_width="wrap_content"
        android:layout_height="wrap_content"
        android:text="@string/payment"
        android:textSize="12pt"
        android:onClick="count"/>
    <CheckBox
        android:id="@+id/packaging"
        android:layout_width="wrap_content"
        android:layout_height="wrap_content"
        android:text="@string/packaging"
        android:textSize="12pt"
        android:onClick="count"/>
    <TextView
        android:id="@+id/t1"
        android:layout_width="wrap_content"
        android:layout_height="wrap_content"
        android:textSize="12pt"
        android:text=""/>
</LinearLayout>
```

Listing 5.46 Full Layout Code

For the **CheckBox** field, you can assign the **onClick** attribute. In this application, it will be the method named calculate, which we will define in the main activity. Its code will look as follows:

```
public void count(View view) {
    boolean checked = ((CheckBox) view).isChecked();
    switch((view.getId()) ) {
        case R.id.delivery:
            if (checked)
                amount = amount + 10;
            else
                amount = amount - 10;
            break;

        case R.id.payment:
            if (checked)
                amount = amount + 5;
            else
                amount = amount -5;
            break;

        case R.id.packaging:
            if (checked)
                amount = amount + 20;
            else
                amount = amount - 20;
            break;
    }
    TextView textView = findViewById(R.id.t1);
    textView.setText("To be paid additionally " + amount +
" $");
}
```

Listing 5.47 Definition of the count Method

We start by creating a variable of type boolean.

```
boolean checked = ((CheckBox) view).isChecked();
```

Listing 5.48 Declaration of the checked Variable

It will check whether the checkbox is selected. Next, we use a switch statement The switch statement defined in the code above will check the option's ID using the method **view.getId()** and respond accordingly to the checkbox selection. Inside each case, there is a conditional statement. If the checkbox is selected, the corresponding amount will be added to the order. If the user deselects the option, the amount will be subtracted.

```
TextView textView = findViewById(R.id.t1);
textView.setText("To be paid additionally " + amount + "
$");
```

Listing 5.49 Setting a Reference to the TextView Element and Displaying Text

The **reference** to the **TextView** field will retrieve the text, and the **setText** method will set the message to be displayed. In the string, you will find the name of the variable **amount** – this is the value that will be calculated based on the selected options. The variable amount must be declared in the main class.

```
int amount = 0;
```

Listing 5.50 Declaration of the amount Variable

We will also need the strings.xml file in this application.

```
<resources>
    <string name="app_name">Application9</string>
    <string name="delivery">Delivery to address</string>
    <string name="payment">Cash on delivery</string>
    <string name="packaging">Decorative packaging</string>
    <string name="additional_services">Select additional
services to order \n</string>
</resources>
```

Listing 5.51 strings.xml file

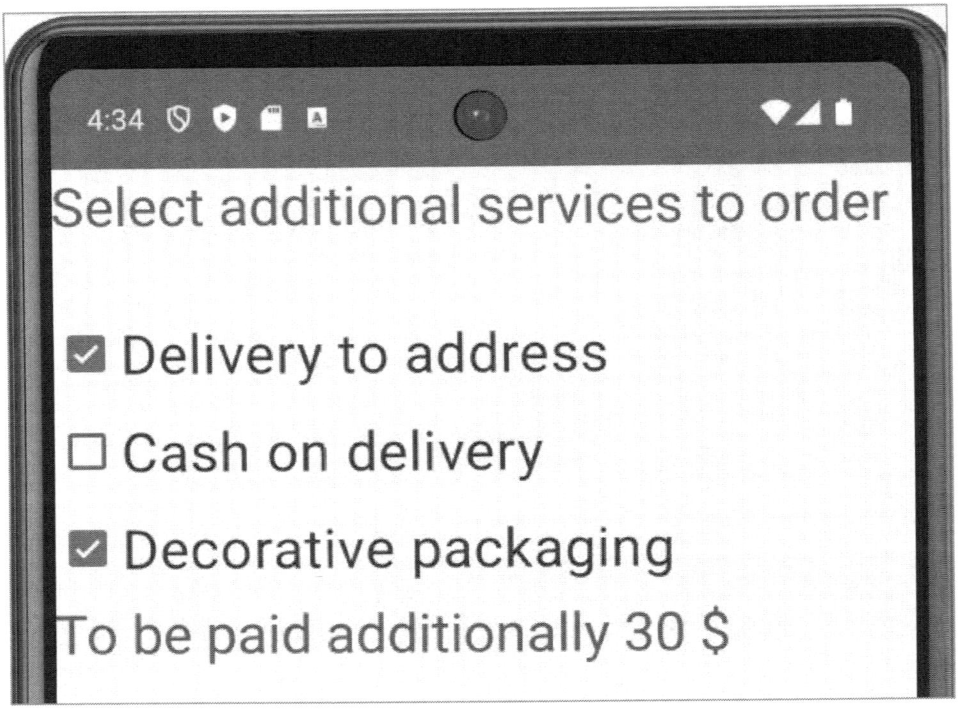

Figure 5.48 Application Demonstrating the Functionality of the CheckBox View

5.6.6 Radio Option Buttons

Radio option buttons, like **checkboxes**, allow you to select a specific option. The difference is that within a group of radio buttons, only one option can be selected at a time. With **checkboxes**, you can select multiple options simultaneously. You can find the application code in the folder named **Application10**. To insert a radio option field, you first need to create a group of buttons – a **RadioGroup**.

```
<RadioGroup android:id="@+id/radio_group"
    android:layout_width="match_parent"
    android:layout_height="wrap_content"
    android:orientation="vertical">
</RadioGroup>
```

Listing 5.52 RadioGroup Widget in the Layout File

The code above creates only the button group. To display the radio option buttons, you need to place **RadioButton** elements inside the **RadioGroup**.

```
<RadioGroup android:id="@+id/radio_group"
    android:layout_width="match_parent"
    android:layout_height="wrap_content"
    android:orientation="vertical">

    <RadioButton android:id="@+id/red"
        android:layout_width="wrap_content"
        android:layout_height="wrap_content"
        android:text="@string/red"
        android:onClick="marked" />
    <RadioButton
        android:id="@+id/green"
        android:layout_width="wrap_content"
        android:layout_height="wrap_content"
        android:text="@string/green"
        android:onClick="marked" />
    <RadioButton
        android:id="@+id/blue"
        android:layout_width="wrap_content"
        android:layout_height="wrap_content"
        android:text="@string/blue"
        android:onClick="marked" />
</RadioGroup>
```

Listing 5.53 RadioButton Fields in the Layout File

The next application will change the color of a text label depending on which **radio** option is selected. First, we will prepare a layout file that includes a **RadioGroup** containing three RadioButton fields. We will also add a TextView element, which will change its color based on the user's selection. The layout file will look as follows:

```
<?xml version="1.0" encoding="utf-8"?>
<LinearLayout

xmlns:android="http://schemas.android.com/apk/res/android"
    xmlns:tools="http://schemas.android.com/tools"
    android:layout_width="match_parent"
    android:layout_height="match_parent"
    tools:context=".MainActivity"
    android:orientation="vertical">

    <RadioGroup android:id="@+id/radio_group"
        android:layout_width="match_parent"
        android:layout_height="wrap_content"
        android:orientation="vertical">

        <RadioButton android:id="@+id/red"
            android:layout_width="wrap_content"
            android:layout_height="wrap_content"
            android:text="@string/red"
            android:onClick="marked" />
        <RadioButton
            android:id="@+id/green"
            android:layout_width="wrap_content"
            android:layout_height="wrap_content"
            android:text="@string/green"
            android:onClick="marked" />
        <RadioButton
            android:id="@+id/blue"
            android:layout_width="wrap_content"
            android:layout_height="wrap_content"
            android:text="@string/blue"
            android:onClick="marked" />
    </RadioGroup>
    <TextView
        android:id="@+id/t1"
        android:layout_width="wrap_content"
        android:layout_height="wrap_content"
        android:text="@string/t1"
        android:textSize="25dp"
        />
</LinearLayout>
```

Listing 5.54 Linear layout using radio buttons

In the activity file, we will define a method called **'marked'** that will respond to button selection and change the text color.

```
RadioGroup radioGroup = findViewById(R.id.radio_group);
int id = radioGroup.getCheckedRadioButtonId();
TextView text1 = findViewById(R.id.t1);
```

Listing 5.55 Creating references to the RadioGroup view and the TextView field

First, we create **references** in the layout file for the **RadioGroup** and **TextView** elements. We also create an integer variable that will retrieve the **ID** of the selected button. This ID value will be used in a switch statement.

```
switch(id) {
    case R.id.red:
        text1.setTextColor(Color.parseColor("#FF0000"));
        break;
```

Listing 5.56 Switch statement in the activity code

Inside each **case** option, we use the **setTextColor** method to change the current text coluor to the selected one. The **parseColor** method converts a hexadecimal color code into an **integer** value. Below is the full activity code.

```
package example.app10;

import androidx.appcompat.app.AppCompatActivity;
import android.annotation.SuppressLint;
import android.graphics.Color;
import android.os.Bundle;
import android.view.View;
import android.widget.RadioGroup;
import android.widget.TextView;

public class MainActivity extends AppCompatActivity {

    @Override
    protected void onCreate(Bundle savedInstanceState) {
        super.onCreate(savedInstanceState);
        setContentView(R.layout.activity_main);
    }
    @SuppressLint("NonConstantResourceId")
    public void marked(View view) {

   RadioGroup radioGroup = findViewById(R.id.radio_group);
   int id = radioGroup.getCheckedRadioButtonId();
   TextView text1 = findViewById(R.id.t1);

     switch(id) {
       case R.id.red:
        text1.setTextColor(Color.parseColor("#FF0000"));
                break;
       case R.id.green:
        text1.setTextColor(Color.parseColor("#00FF00"));
                break;
       case R.id.blue:
        text1.setTextColor(Color.parseColor("#0000FF"));
                break;
        }
    }
}
```

Listing 5.57 Application10 activity code

When the application is launched, it will look like in the illustration below:

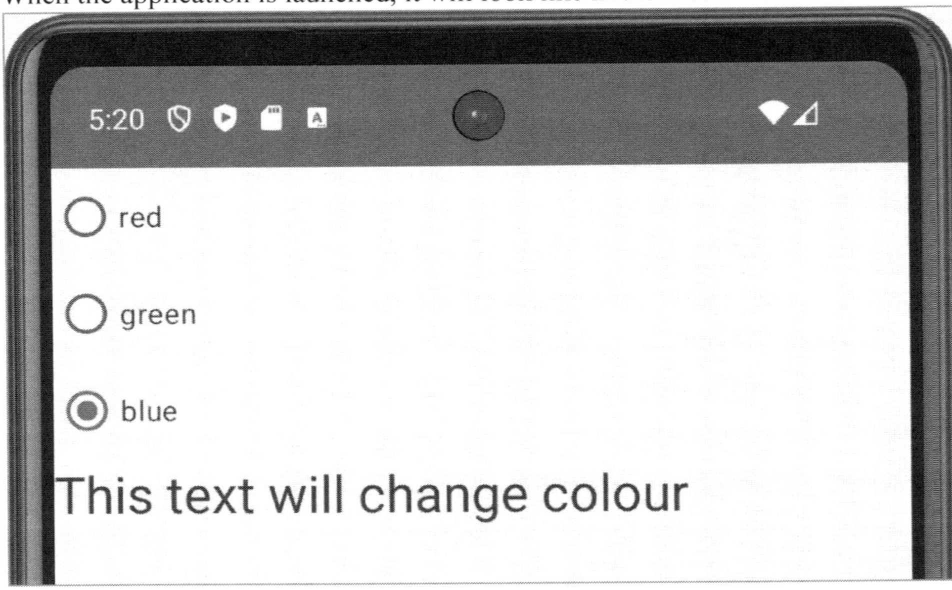

Figure 5.49 An application demonstrating the functionality of the RadioButton field

5.6.7 Dropdown List – Spinner

Android Studio allows you to create a **dropdown selection list**. You can insert the list into your application using the **Spinner** element.You'll find the application code in the **Application11** folder. We're creating an application that uses the **Spinner control**. First, we place the **Spinner** component in the layout file. This can be done using the following code.

```
<Spinner
    android:id="@+id/spinner"
    android:layout_width="wrap_content"
    android:layout_height="wrap_content"
    android:entries="@array/listOptions"
    android:layout_marginTop="25dp"/>
```

Listing 5.58 Spinner view in the layout file

The above code creates a component in the layout. We still need to add options to the dropdown list. This can be done in the **strings.xml file.** The attribute responsible for linking the list to the **strings.xml** file is:

```
android:entries="@array/listOptions"
```

Listing 5.59 Reference to the array element

The **entries** attribute allows you to define the options that will appear in the list. An **array** represents a set of options that lets us add items to the list. The **strings.xml** file will look as follows:

```
<resources>
    <string name="app_name">Application11</string>
    <string name="question">What color is the
grass?</string>
    <string name="btn1">Check the answer</string>
    <string-array name="listOptions">
        <item>red</item>
        <item>green</item>
        <item>blue</item>
        <item>yellow</item>
    </string-array>

</resources>
```

Listing 5.60 Strings.xml file with the declaration of items included in the Spinner dropdown list

Each entry between the **<item>** and **</item>** tags creates a single selectable option. It's important that the name value matches the name used after **@array/.** Once the application is launched, the dropdown list will look like this:

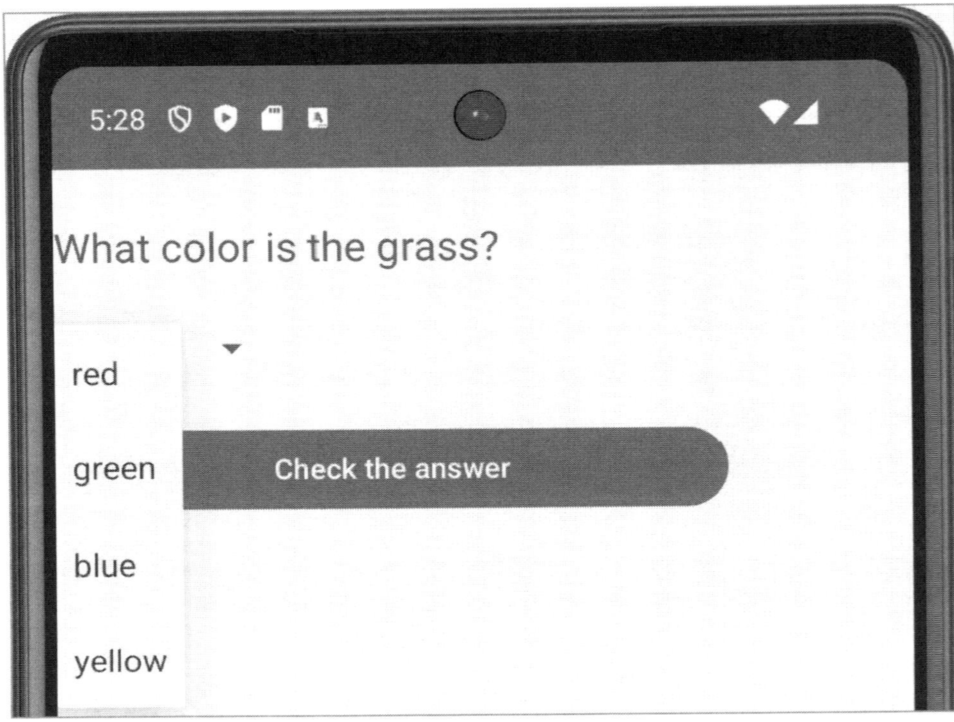

Figure 5.50 Spinner dropdown list with selectable options

Now we'll use the **Spinner** component in the activity file. We'll add a **TextView** and a **Button** to the layout. The completed layout code will look as follows:

```
<?xml version="1.0" encoding="utf-8"?>
<LinearLayout
xmlns:android="http://schemas.android.com/apk/res/android"
    xmlns:tools="http://schemas.android.com/tools"
    android:layout_width="match_parent"
    android:layout_height="match_parent"
    android:orientation="vertical"
    tools:context=".MainActivity">
    <TextView
        android:id="@+id/t1"
        android:layout_width="wrap_content"
        android:layout_height="wrap_content"
        android:text="@string/question"
        android:textSize="20sp"
        android:layout_marginTop="25dp" />
    <Spinner
        android:id="@+id/spinner"
        android:layout_width="wrap_content"
        android:layout_height="wrap_content"
        android:entries="@array/listOptions"
        android:layout_marginTop="25dp"/>
    <Button
        android:id="@+id/btn1"
        android:layout_width="323dp"
        android:layout_height="wrap_content"
        android:layout_marginTop="25dp"
        android:onClick="checkTheAnswer"
        android:text="@string/btn1" />
</LinearLayout>
```

Listing 5.61 Application11 layout code

In the **TextView** field, the question will appear: **"What color is the grass?"** The application will check whether the selected answer is correct. We need to define a method called **checkTheAnswer**, which will be triggered when the user selects an answer and presses the button.

We'll start by defining two Toast messages:

- The first will be displayed when the user selects the correct answer.
- The second will be shown when the user's answer is incorrect.

```
String text1 = "Correct answer";
String text2 = "Wrong answer";
int duration = Toast.LENGTH_LONG;
Toast toast = Toast.makeText(this, text1, duration);
Toast toast2 = Toast.makeText(this, text2, duration);
```

Listing 5.62 Definition of Toast message elements

Next, we'll retrieve the selected value from the **Spinner** component.

```
Spinner color = findViewById(R.id.spinner);
String  choice= String.valueOf(color.getSelectedItem());
```

Listing 5.63 Reference to the Spinner element

The variable **color** will retrieve a reference to the **Spinner control** located in the layout file. A second variable of type **String** will store the user's selection – that is, it will set its value to the option selected from the list.Now, we need to use the retrieved value to trigger the appropriate **Toast** message.A simple conditional statement will be useful here.

```
if(choice.equals("green"))
     toast.show();
else
     toast2.show();
```

Listing 5.64 Conditional statement checking the user's selection

The statement will check whether the option selected by the user is equal to **green**.If so, **Toast message #1** will be displayed.Otherwise – if the user selects a different option – **Toast message #2** will be shown. Here is the full activity code:

```
package example.app11;
import androidx.appcompat.app.AppCompatActivity;
import android.os.Bundle;
import android.view.View;
import android.widget.Spinner;
import android.widget.Toast;

public class MainActivity extends AppCompatActivity {

    @Override
    protected void onCreate(Bundle savedInstanceState) {
        super.onCreate(savedInstanceState);
        setContentView(R.layout.activity_main);
    }
public void checkTheAnswer(View view) {
  Spinner color = findViewById(R.id.spinner);
  String  choice= String.valueOf(color.getSelectedItem());
        String text1 = "Correct answer";
        String text2 = "Wrong answer";
        int duration = Toast.LENGTH_LONG;
      Toast toast = Toast.makeText(this, text1, duration);
      Toast toast2 = Toast.makeText(this, text2, duration);
        if(choice.equals("green"))
            toast.show();
        else
            toast2.show();
    }
 }
```

Listing 5.65 Full activity code for the Application11 app

When the application is launched, it will look like this:

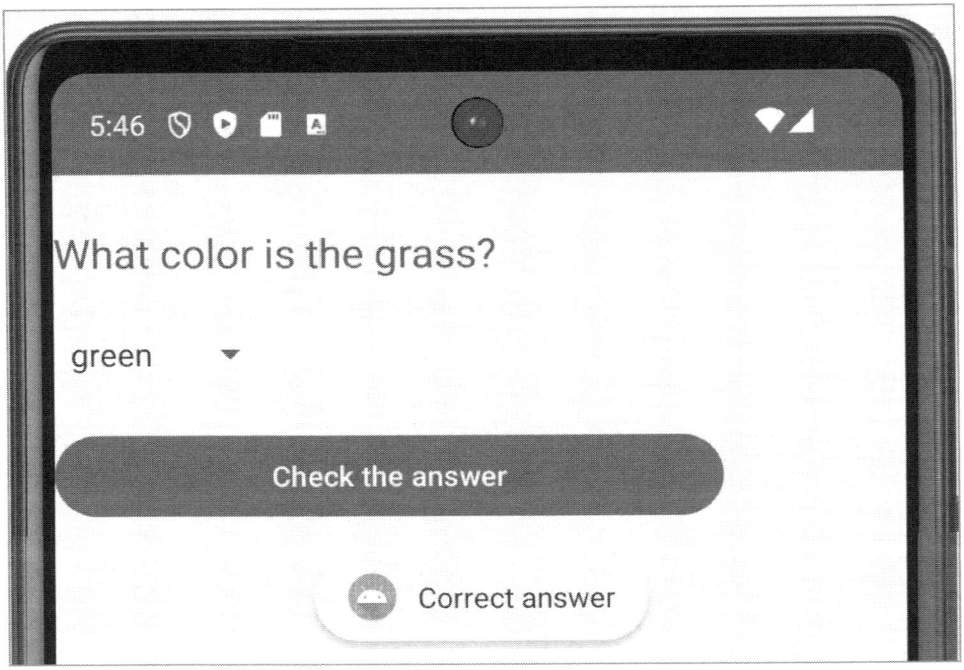

Figure 5.51 Toast message displayed after selecting the correct answer to the question

5.6.8 ListView

You'll find the application code in the folder **Application12**. The **ListView** container displays information in the form of a list. Its code is similar to the **Spinner container**. The layout code will look like the following:

```
<?xml version="1.0" encoding="utf-8"?>
<LinearLayout
xmlns:android="http://schemas.android.com/apk/res/android"
    xmlns:tools="http://schemas.android.com/tools"
    android:layout_width="match_parent"
    android:layout_height="match_parent"
    android:orientation="vertical"
    tools:context=".MainActivity" >

    <ListView
        android:id="@+id/list"
        android:layout_width="wrap_content"
        android:layout_height="wrap_content"
        android:entries="@array/options" />
</LinearLayout>
```

Listing 5.66 Layout code containing the ListView element

Next, we'll define the options that will appear in the list. We'll do this in the strings.xml file – similar to how it's done with the **Spinner**. The code placed in the **strings.xml** file will look like this:

```
<resources>
    <string name="app_name">Application12</string>
    <string-array name="options">
        <item>red</item>
        <item>green</item>
        <item>blue</item>
        <item>yellow</item>
    </string-array>
</resources>
```

Listing 5.67 Contents of the strings.xml file

After launching, the application window should resemble the illustration below.

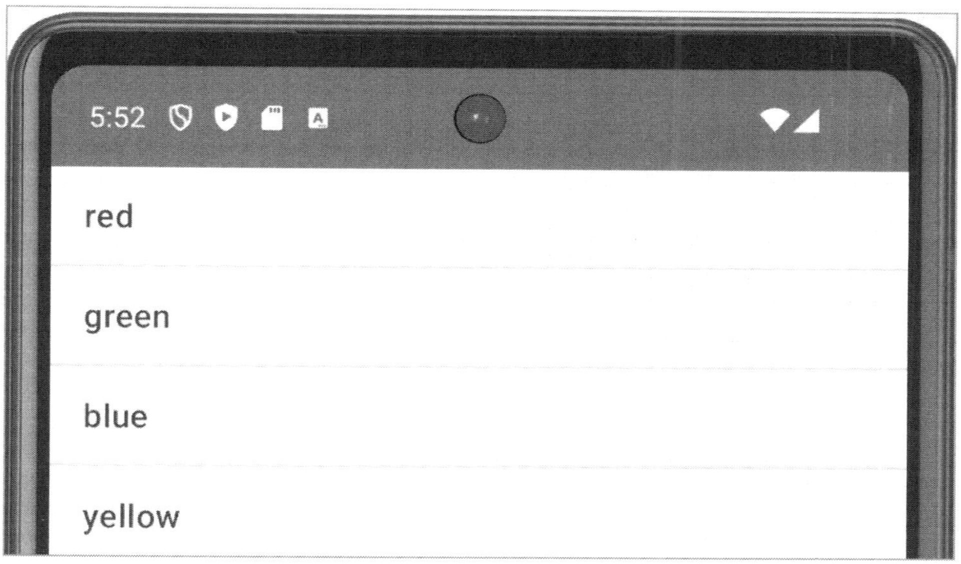

Figure 5.52 An application demonstrating the functionality of ListView

This is a control designed to display suggestions to the user. The suggestions are sourced from an array prepared by the application developer. You can find the application code in the **Application13** folder.

As a first step, we will create the layout file **activity_main.xml,** in which we will place two views:**TextView** and**AutoCompleteTextView.**

5.6.9 AutoCompleteTextView

```
<?xml version="1.0" encoding="utf-8"?>
<LinearLayout
xmlns:android="http://schemas.android.com/apk/res/android"
    android:layout_width="match_parent"
    android:layout_height="match_parent"
    android:orientation="vertical">
    <TextView
        android:layout_width="wrap_content"
        android:layout_height="wrap_content"
        android:text="Select month "
        android:id="@+id/text1"
        android:textSize="25sp" />
    <AutoCompleteTextView
        android:id="@+id/text2"
        android:layout_width="match_parent"
        android:layout_height="wrap_content"
        android:completionThreshold="1"/>
</LinearLayout>
```

Listing 5.68 Layout code with an AutoCompleteTextView view

The **android:completionThreshold** attribute specifies after how many entered characters the suggestion will be displayed. Now we will create the activity code. First, we need to prepare a list from which the user will be able to select a month.

```
private static final String[] Month = {
        "January",
        "February",
        "March",
        "April",
        "May",
        "June",
        "July",
        "August",
        "September",
        "October",
        "November",
        "December",
};
```

Listing 5.69 Array defining the list items

This is a private static array of strings. Each item in the list is enclosed in quotation marks and separated by commas. Next, we define the adapter and create an object to handle the **AutoCompleteTextView** component. At this point, we should mention the **adapter**. What is an adapter and why do we use it?

An **adapter** is essentially a connector. It links the data source with the view placed in the layout. In our application, we connect a **String** array from the activity file with the **AutoCompleteTextView** component located in the layout file. We won't need an adapter if the data comes from another XML file, such as **strings.xml** – as is the case with a Spinner. In the activity file, we create an adapter for **String** data, which looks as follows:

```
ArrayAdapter<String> adapter = new ArrayAdapter<>(this,
android.R.layout.simple_dropdown_item_1line, Month);
```

Listing 5.70 Adapter for String data

We use the generic **ArrayAdapter** class for the **String** type. The resource **android.R.layout.simple_dropdown_item_1line** is used to create the list entries. This is a predefined layout file that we use as a ready - made component, although we could define a similar resource ourselves.

The last argument is **Month**, which is the name of the array containing the suggestions for the list. All that remains is to obtain a reference to the control using the **findViewById** method, where we provide the ID assigned in the layout file.

The final line of code sets the **adapter**. The complete activity file will look as follows:

```
package example.app13;

import androidx.appcompat.app.AppCompatActivity;
import android.os.Bundle;
import android.widget.ArrayAdapter;
import android.widget.AutoCompleteTextView;
public class MainActivity extends AppCompatActivity {
    private static final String[] Month = {
            "January",
            "February",
            "March",
            "April",
            "May",
            "June",
            "July",
            "August",
            "September",
            "October",
            "November",
            "December",
    };
@Override
protected void onCreate(Bundle savedInstanceState) {
super.onCreate(savedInstanceState);
setContentView(R.layout.activity_main);
ArrayAdapter<String> adapter = new ArrayAdapter<>(this,
android.R.layout.simple_dropdown_item_1line, Month);
AutoCompleteTextView textView = findViewById(R.id.text2);
  textView.setAdapter(adapter);
    }
}
```

Listing 5.71 Activity code for the application named Application13

The result of the application's operation is shown in the illustration below.

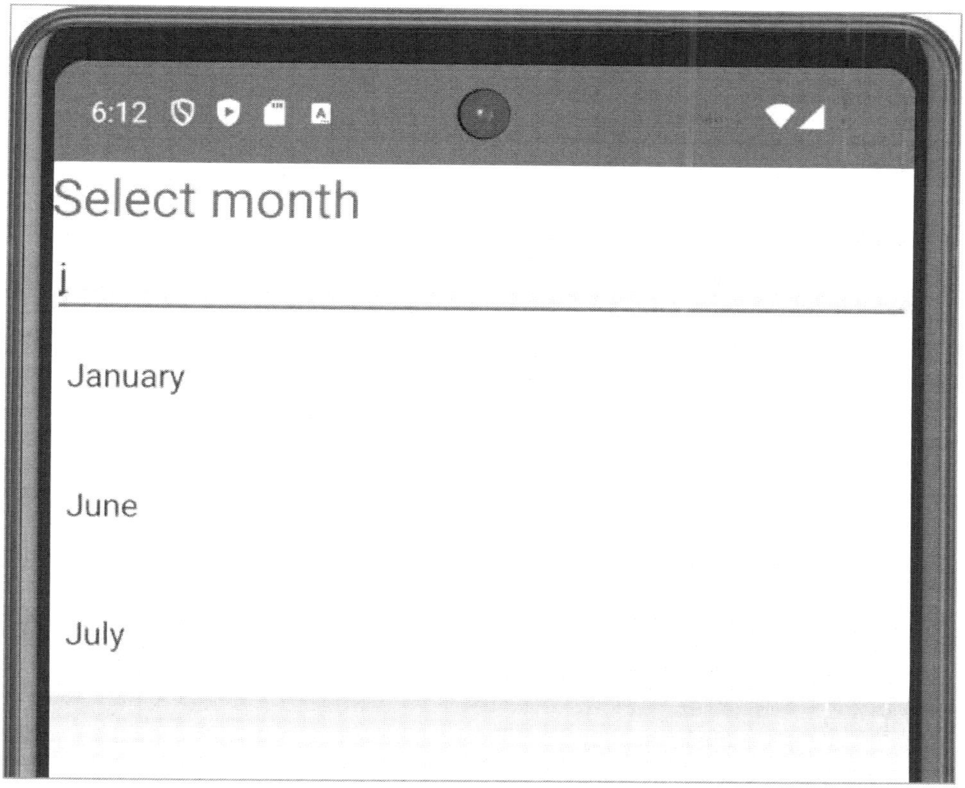

Figure 5.53 Functionality of the AutoCompleteTextView control

5.6.10 ProgressBar

You can find the application code in the **Application14** folder.

When an application occasionally needs more time to respond, we may need icons that appear on the screen during the waiting period. The first widget of this type is the **ProgressBar**. It will appear as a rotating, colorful segment of a circle. We place it as a view in the layout. A sample code will be presented in the listing below:

```
<ProgressBar
    android:id="@+id/progressBar"
    style="?android:attr/progressBarStyle"
    android:layout_width="110dp"
    android:layout_height="wrap_content"
    android:layout_weight="1"
/>
```

Listing 5.72 ProgressBar in the layout file

One noteworthy **attribute** here is style. Other style options include, for example:

- Widget.ProgressBar.Horizontal;
- Widget.ProgressBar.Small;
- Widget.ProgressBar.Large;
- Widget.ProgressBar.Inverse;
- Widget.ProgressBar.Small.Inverse;
- Widget.ProgressBar.Large.Inverse;

It's worth testing all available styles. Application after launch:

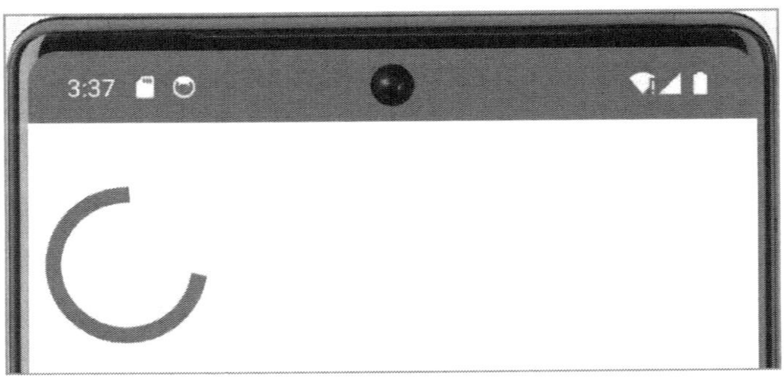

Figure 5.54 ProgressBar progress indicator

5.6.11 SeekBar

SeekBar is a type of **slider**.It features a horizontal line and a round thumb that can be dragged. You can find the application code in the **Application15** folder. In the layout code, **SeekBar** looks like this:

```
<?xml version="1.0" encoding="utf-8"?>
<LinearLayout
    xmlns:android="http://schemas.android.com/apk/res/android"
    xmlns:tools="http://schemas.android.com/tools"
    android:layout_width="match_parent"
    android:layout_height="match_parent"
    tools:context=".MainActivity">

    <SeekBar
        android:id="@+id/seekBar"
        android:layout_width="wrap_content"
        android:layout_height="wrap_content"
        android:layout_weight="1" />
</LinearLayout>
```

Listing 5.73 SeekBar element in the layout file

the application, it will look as follows:

Figure 5.55 SeekBar progress indicator

Using the **activity**, we can add a Toast message to the **SeekBar** element, which will inform the user about the percentage of the total that is currently selected through the view.

The layout code will resemble the example below:

```
<?xml version="1.0" encoding="utf-8"?>
<LinearLayout
    xmlns:android="http://schemas.android.com/apk/res/android"
    xmlns:tools="http://schemas.android.com/tools"
    android:layout_width="match_parent"
    android:layout_height="match_parent"
    tools:context=".MainActivity">

    <SeekBar
        android:id="@+id/seekBar"
        android:layout_width="wrap_content"
        android:layout_height="wrap_content"
        android:layout_weight="5"
        android:max="1000"
        android:progress="150"/>

</LinearLayout>
```

Listing 5.74 Application15 layout code

Notable attributes of the **SeekBar** view include:

- **android:max** – defines the maximum value the user can select.
- **android:progress** – sets the initial value when the application starts.

A sample application code will look like this:

```
package example.app15;

import androidx.appcompat.app.AppCompatActivity;
import android.os.Bundle;
import android.widget.SeekBar;
import android.widget.Toast;
public class MainActivity extends AppCompatActivity {
    @Override
    protected void onCreate(Bundle savedInstanceState) {
        super.onCreate(savedInstanceState);
        setContentView(R.layout.activity_main);
        SeekBar seekbar;
        seekbar = findViewById(R.id.seekBar);
        seekbar.setOnSeekBarChangeListener(new
SeekBar.OnSeekBarChangeListener() {
            int prg = 1;
public void onProgressChanged(SeekBar seekBar, int
progress, boolean fromUser) {
                prg = progress;
            }
public void onStartTrackingTouch(SeekBar seekBar) {

 }
public void onStopTrackingTouch(SeekBar seekBar) {
 Toast.makeText(MainActivity.this, "The maximum price is: "
+ prg + " $",
 Toast.LENGTH_SHORT).show();
            }
        });
    }}
```

Listing 5.75 Sample activity code using the SeekBar element

First, we create an object of the **SeekBar** class:

```
SeekBar seekbar;
```

Listing 5.76 Declaration of a SeekBar object

We assign a **reference to** the **SeekBar** object from the layout file to the variable seekbar.

```
seekbar=findViewById(R.id.seekBar);
```

Listing 5.77 Reference to the SeekBar element

Next, we set a so - called listener object (**setOnSeekBarChangeListener**), which will respond to changes on the bar. An **integer variable** named **prg** will store the numeric value.

```
seekbar = findViewById(R.id.seekBar);
seekbar.setOnSeekBarChangeListener(new
SeekBar.OnSeekBarChangeListener() {
    int prg = 1;
```

Listing 5.78 Listener object: setOnSeekBarChangeListener

Next, we use three methods. The first one is:

```
public void onProgressChanged(SeekBar seekBar, int
progress, boolean fromUser) {
    prg = progress;
}
```

Listing 5.79 Definition of the onProgressChanged method

This method takes the following parameters:

- **an object of the SeekBar class** – the one the application is working with;
- **an integer variable** – which stores the value selected by the component;
- **a boolean variable** – which depends on user interaction and changes as the slider is moved.

In this method, we assign the value retrieved from the **SeekBar** to the variable progress.

The second method is **public void onStartTrackingTouch(SeekBar seekBar)**. It has one parameter, which is a **SeekBar** object. This function defines the moment when the user starts interacting with **the SeekBar**.

The final method is **void onStopTrackingTouch(SeekBar seekBar)**. Like the previous one, it also takes a single parameter – the name of the **SeekBar** object the application is working with. This function is triggered when the user finishes adjusting the slider. In this method, we create and display a Toast message.

```
Toast.makeText(MainActivity.this, "The maximum price is: "
+ prg + " $",
        Toast.LENGTH_SHORT).show();
```

Listing 5.80 Definition of the Toast element

After launching the application and moving the slider, a Toast message will appear at the bottom of the screen.

The complete activity code is as follows:

```
package example.app15;

import androidx.appcompat.app.AppCompatActivity;
import android.os.Bundle;
import android.widget.SeekBar;
import android.widget.Toast;
public class MainActivity extends AppCompatActivity {
    @Override
    protected void onCreate(Bundle savedInstanceState) {
        super.onCreate(savedInstanceState);
        setContentView(R.layout.activity_main);
        SeekBar seekbar;
        seekbar = findViewById(R.id.seekBar);
        seekbar.setOnSeekBarChangeListener(new
SeekBar.OnSeekBarChangeListener() {
            int prg = 1;
public void onProgressChanged(SeekBar seekBar, int
progress, boolean fromUser) {
                prg = progress;
            }
 public void onStartTrackingTouch(SeekBar seekBar) {

  }
 public void onStopTrackingTouch(SeekBar seekBar) {
  Toast.makeText(MainActivity.this, "The maximum price is: "
 + prg + " $",
  Toast.LENGTH_SHORT).show();
            }
        });
    }}
```

Listing 5.81 Full activity code

5.6.12 RatingBar

RatingBar allows users to give a rating. It appears as five stars. You can find the application code in the **Application16** folder.

In the layout file, we place the RatingBar as follows:

```
<LinearLayout
    xmlns:android="http://schemas.android.com/apk/res/android"
    xmlns:tools="http://schemas.android.com/tools"
    android:layout_width="match_parent"
    android:layout_height="match_parent"
    tools:context=".MainActivity">

<RatingBar
  android:id="@+id/RatingBar"
  style="@style/Widget.AppCompat.RatingBar"
  android:layout_width="wrap_content"
  android:layout_height="wrap_content"
  android:numStars="5"
  android:stepSize="0.5"/>
</LinearLayout>
```

Listing 5.82 Layout containing the RatingBar element

Let's take a look at the key attributes:

- **android:numStars** – defines the maximum number of stars to be displayed.
- **android:stepSize** – determines the increment by which the rating can be increased. In this example, the value is half a star.

The application will look like in the illustration below:

Figure 5.56 RatingBar rating system

5.7 Intents

In this exercise, we will focus on communication between activities. Every mobile application typically consists of multiple activities. To enable communication between two activities, we use intents.

5.7.1 Intent without passing values

We'll start with a simple example. We'll write an application in which we first place a **Button.** You can find the code for this example in the folder named **Application17**.

The layout code will look as follows:

```
<?xml version="1.0" encoding="utf-8"?>
<LinearLayout

xmlns:android="http://schemas.android.com/apk/res/android"
    xmlns:tools="http://schemas.android.com/tools"
    android:layout_width="match_parent"
    android:layout_height="match_parent"
    tools:context=".MainActivity">

    <Button
        android:layout_width="wrap_content"
        android:layout_height="wrap_content"
        android:text="@string/btn1"
        android:onClick="intent"/>
</LinearLayout>
```

Listing 5.83 Layout code with a Button

As mentioned earlier, an **intent** is used to transfer data between activities. This means that the application will require a second **activity** and a second **layout file**. So, we move to the left side of the editor. From the resource tree, expand the **java branch**. Right - click on it and select the following options: **New → Activity → Empty Views Activity**

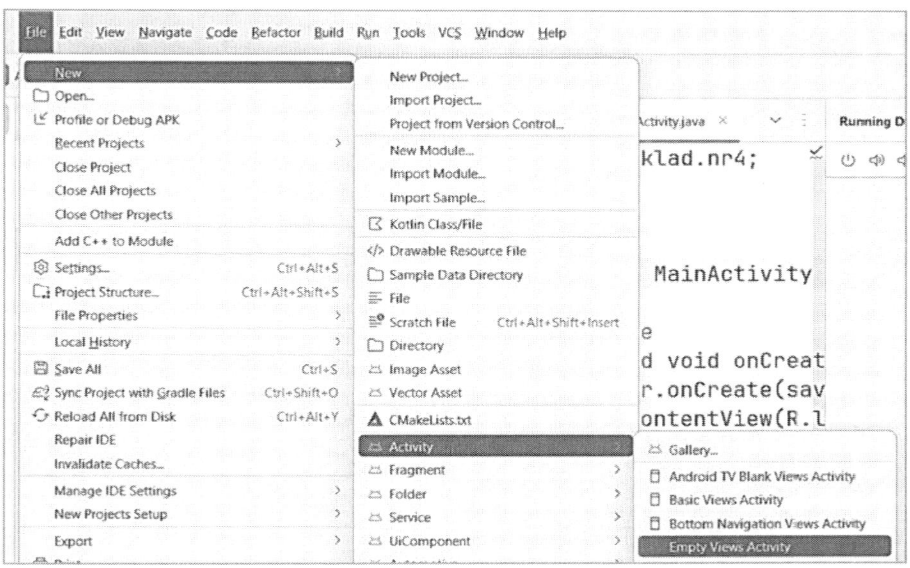

Figure 5.57 Creating a new activity

In the window that opens, enter the name of the new activity: **SecondActivity**. Note that along with the activity, a layout file named **activity_second_activity.xml** is also created. This layout will be associated with our activity. Simply click **Finish.** Now the project contains **two activities** and **two layout** files.

When we open the layout file **activity_second_activity.xml** and the activity file **SecondActivity.java,** we can see that they are connected to each other.

```
<?xml version="1.0" encoding="utf-8"?>
<LinearLayout
    xmlns:android="http://schemas.android.com/apk/res/android"
    xmlns:tools="http://schemas.android.com/tools"
    android:layout_width="match_parent"
    android:layout_height="match_parent"
    tools:context=".SecondActivity">

    <TextView
        android:layout_width="wrap_content"
        android:layout_height="wrap_content"
        android:text="A second Intent was launched"
        android:textSize="20sp"
        />
</LinearLayout>
```

Figure 5.58 Layout code of activity_second_activity.xml with a highlighted reference to the activity file

```
package example.app17;


import ...

public class SecondActivity extends AppCompatActivity {

    @Override
    protected void onCreate(Bundle savedInstanceState) {
        super.onCreate(savedInstanceState);
        setContentView(R.layout.activity_second);
    }
}
```

Figure 5.59 Activity Code SecondActivity.java with a highlighted reference to the layout file

Now we will create the layout for the second activity. Since we will be cisplaying text, we will need a **TextView** view. Code for the second layout:

```
<?xml version="1.0" encoding="utf-8"?>
<LinearLayout

xmlns:android="http://schemas.android.com/apk/res/android"
    xmlns:tools="http://schemas.android.com/tools"
    android:layout_width="match_parent"
    android:layout_height="match_parent"
    tools:context=".SecondActivity">

    <TextView
        android:layout_width="wrap_content"
        android:layout_height="wrap_content"
        android:text="@string/int1"
        android:textSize="20sp"/>
</LinearLayout>
```

Listing 5.84 Layout file activity_second_activity.xml

Now we will work on the main activity file. In it, we define a method called **intent**, which will be triggered when the **Button** is pressed.

```
public void intent(View view) {
    startActivity(new Intent(this, SecondActivity.class));
}
```

Listing 5.85 Declaration of the intencja method

We launch the intent using **startActivity**. We create an object of the **Intent** class. The **constructor** of this class takes two arguments: the first is the **activity** from which we are launching the **intent**, and the second is the name of the **target activity** – the one to which we are sending the **intent**.

```
package example.app17;
import androidx.appcompat.app.AppCompatActivity;
import android.content.Intent;
import android.os.Bundle;
import android.view.View;
public class MainActivity extends AppCompatActivity {

    @Override
    protected void onCreate(Bundle savedInstanceState) {
        super.onCreate(savedInstanceState);
        setContentView(R.layout.activity_main);
    }
    public void intent(View view) {
     startActivity(new Intent(this, SecondActivity.class));
    }
}
```

Listing 5.86 Activity Code

We launch the program. The application will look as follows:

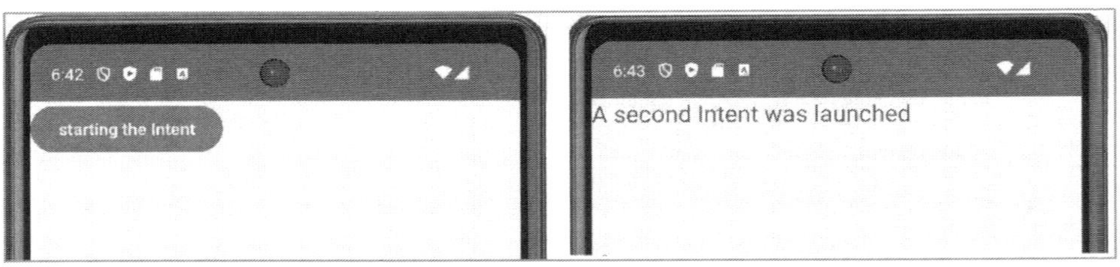

Figure 5.60 The application before (image on the left) and after (image on the right) triggering the intent.

5.7.2 Intent for Passing Data

Another application will also use **intents**. However, this time, information will be passed between activities. You can find the application code in the folder **Application17a**. The program will collect input from the user via a text field and send it to the second activity.

In the layout file **activity_main.xml**, we will place two **EditText** fields and a Button. In the layout **activity_second_activity.xml**, the received data will be displayed in two **TextView** fields. Layout code for **activity_main.xml**:

```
<?xml version="1.0" encoding="utf-8"?>
<LinearLayout

xmlns:android="http://schemas.android.com/apk/res/android"
    xmlns:tools="http://schemas.android.com/tools"
    android:layout_width="match_parent"
    android:layout_height="match_parent"
    android:orientation="vertical"
    tools:context=".MainActivity">

    <EditText
        android:id="@+id/street"
        android:layout_width="match_parent"
        android:layout_height="wrap_content"
        android:hint="@string/hint1"
        android:inputType="textCapSentences" />
    <EditText
        android:id="@+id/house_number"
        android:layout_width="match_parent"
        android:layout_height="wrap_content"
        android:hint="@string/hint2"
        android:inputType="number"/>
    <Button
        android:layout_width="wrap_content"
        android:layout_height="wrap_content"
        android:text="@string/btn1"
        android:onClick="intent"/>
</LinearLayout>
```

Listing 5.87 Full main layout code

Layout code for activity_second_activity.xml:

```
<?xml version="1.0" encoding="utf-8"?>
<LinearLayout

xmlns:android="http://schemas.android.com/apk/res/android"
    xmlns:tools="http://schemas.android.com/tools"
    android:layout_width="match_parent"
    android:layout_height="match_parent"
    android:orientation="vertical"
    tools:context=".SecondActivity">
    <TextView
        android:layout_width="wrap_content"
        android:layout_height="wrap_content"
        android:text="@string/t1"
        android:textSize="20sp"/>
    <TextView
        android:layout_width="wrap_content"
        android:layout_height="wrap_content"
        android:id="@+id/t2"
        android:text=" "
        android:textSize="20sp"/>
</LinearLayout>
```

Listing 5.88 Full layout code of the second activity

Now we will move on to the main activity file **MainActivity.java**. We will define a method called **intent,** which will be triggered when the **Button** is pressed.

```
public void intent(View view) {
    EditText str = findViewById(R.id.street);
    EditText hn = findViewById(R.id.house_number);
    String str2 = str.getText().toString();
int nrd2 = Integer.parseInt(String.valueOf(hn.getText()));
Intent newIntent = new Intent(this, SecondActivity.class);
    newIntent.putExtra("street", str2);
    newIntent.putExtra("house_number", nrd2);
    startActivity(newIntent);
}
```

Listing 5.89 of the intencja method for passing data

We create references to the **EditText** fields that collect data from the user. Then, the retrieved values need to be converted to the appropriate types.

```
EditText str = findViewById(R.id.street);
EditText hn = findViewById(R.id.house_number);
```

Listing 5.90 Creating references to EditText fields

For the street, the data type will be **String**. For the **house number**, it will be a numeric value of type **int**.

```
String str2 = str.getText().toString();
int nrd2 = Integer.parseInt(String.valueOf(hn.getText()));
```

Listing 5.91 Conversion of Retrieved Data

We create an intent named **newIntent.**

```
Intent newIntent = new Intent(this, SecondActivity.class);
```

Listing 5.92 Creating the Intent

The next step is to prepare the **intent** for passing data. You will need the **putExtra** method, which sends values to the **second activity**.

```
newIntent.putExtra("street", str2);
newIntent.putExtra("house_number", nrd2);
```

Listing 5.93 Intent for Passing Information

The first argument is the so - called **key** – a name used to identify the data. The **second argument** is the value that is passed to the second activity. In this application, these are the names of two variables that store the data.

```
startActivity(newIntent);
```

Listing 5.94 Launching the Intent

The **activity** that receives the **intent** – the **SecondActivity.java** class – will look as follows:

```
package example.app17a;

import androidx.appcompat.app.AppCompatActivity;
import android.os.Bundle;
import android.widget.TextView;

public class SecondActivity extends AppCompatActivity {

    @Override
    protected void onCreate(Bundle savedInstanceState) {
        super.onCreate(savedInstanceState);
        setContentView(R.layout.activity_second);
        Bundle bundle = getIntent().getExtras();
        TextView announcement = findViewById(R.id.t2);
        if (bundle != null) {
            String text = bundle.getString("street");
            int number = bundle.getInt("house_number");
 announcement.setText("Your place of residence is \n " +
     text +  " Street: " + " "+ number);
        }
    }
}
```

Listing 5.95 Code of the SecondActivity.java file

All key operations take place in the **onCreate** method. First, we create a **Bundle** object, which retrieves the **intent** and the additional information.

```
Bundle bundle = getIntent().getExtras();
```

Listing 5.96 Creating a Bundle object to retrieve data from the intent

Next, we create a reference to the text field where the information received from the main activity will be displayed.

```
TextView announcement = findViewById(R.id.t2);
```

Listing 5.97 Creating a reference to a layout element

A **conditional statement** will check whether the user has entered data. If so, the values from the first activity will be assigned to two variables: **String text** and **int number**. This operation will be handled by two methods: getString and **getInt**.

```
if (bundle != null) {
    String text = bundle.getString("street");
    int number = bundle.getInt("house_number");
```

Listing 5.98 Conditional Statement Checking if the User Filled Out the Form

The methods **getString** and **getInt** are, in a way, the counterparts of the methods used in the first activity: **putString** and **putInt**. Methods with the **put** prefix send data, while those with the **get** prefix retrieve it. The final task is to display the retrieved data in a TextView. You can see how the application works in the illustration below:

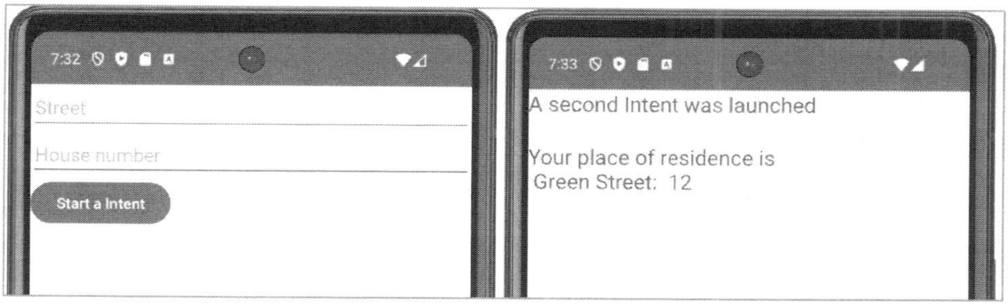

Figure 5.61 Result of the application using intents with data transfer.

5.7.3 Implicit Intent

In the example we just discussed, we dealt with what is known as an **explicit intent.** An explicit intent is a type of intent that targets a specific, predefined destination. In our case, that destination was the **second activity**. The intent was sent **from the first activity to the second one**. The place where the **intent** was received was **explicit** and predetermined – we provided the **intent** with information about which **class** to launch.

```
Intent newIntent = new Intent(this, SecondActivity.class);
```

Listing 5.99 Creating an Intent

When developing mobile applications, there are situations where we create an **intent** without knowing exactly where it will be delivered. This happens when we send an intent to another application.

Imagine that the app we're building is supposed to send a message. We only know that it should be a text message – but we don't know whether it will be an **SMS** or an **email**. When the user clicks the send button, a list of available apps will appear on the screen, allowing them to choose how to send the message – for example, using an email app.

In the case of an **implicit intent**, it is Android that decides which activity should handle it. This decision is guided by an intent filter, which is defined in the **manifest file.** Its code will look similar to the example below.

```
<intent-filter>
<action android:name="android.intent.action.MAIN" />
<category
android:name="android.intent.category.LAUNCHER"/>
</intent-filter>
```

Listing 5.100 Declaration of an Implicit Intent Filter

An implicit intent is created using the following code, which is placed in the appropriate activity.

```
Intent newIntent = new Intent(action);
```

Listing 5.101 Creating an Implicit Intent

When defining the action, we specify the type of operation that should occur after the intent is triggered – for example, **Intent.ACTION_VIEW** or **Intent.ACTION_SEND.** The first constant is useful for displaying a view, while the second allows sending a message, such as an email or SMS.

5.8 Layouts

So far, we have used only one type of **layout** – the **LinearLayout**. However, applications can also be built using other available layout types.We will begin by reviewing and thoroughly discussing the LinearLayout.

5.8.1 Linear Layout

The basic principle of a linear layout is that elements are arranged **one below the other** or **side by side**, in the order they appear in the **XML file**. When it comes to how the elements are displayed, the most important parameter is android:orientation.

5.8.2 FrameLayout

FrameLayout is another type of layout. Its characteristic feature is that elements are stacked on top of each other **in reverse order** compared to how they are listed in the **XML layout** file. We can think of elements in a FrameLayout as layers in a graphic file – each new element is placed above the previous one.

To illustrate how FrameLayout works, let's use an example. We have an application in which we place **three images**, each a square of a specific color: blue, red, and green. In the layout file, they are arranged as shown in the code below. You can find the application code in the folder **Application18**.

```
<?xml version="1.0" encoding="utf-8"?>
<FrameLayout
    xmlns:android="http://schemas.android.com/apk/res/android"
    xmlns:tools="http://schemas.android.com/tools"
    android:layout_width="match_parent"
    android:layout_height="match_parent"
    tools:context=".MainActivity">
    <ImageView
        android:layout_width="wrap_content"
        android:layout_height="wrap_content"
        android:src="@drawable/blue"
        />
    <ImageView
        android:layout_width="wrap_content"
        android:layout_height="wrap_content"
        android:src="@drawable/red"
        />
    <ImageView
        android:layout_width="wrap_content"
        android:layout_height="wrap_content"
        android:src="@drawable/green"
        />
</FrameLayout>
```

Listing 5.102 FrameLayout Layout

When the application is launched, it looks like the illustration below:

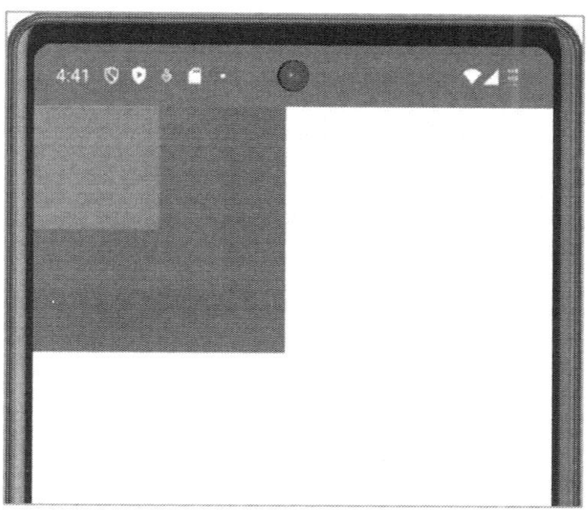

Figure 5.62 Application Using a Linear Layout – FrameLayout

At the bottom, there is a blue square, which is placed first in the layout file. If we looked at the image from the side – as if we were holding the phone horizontally – the **FrameLayout** would appear as shown in the illustration below.

Figure 5.63 Arrangement of Elements in a Linear Layout in a 3D Model

5.8.3 RelativeLayout

RelativeLayout defines the position of layout elements based on the position of components relative to other elements. This is known as a relative way of arranging elements. In a **RelativeLayout**, we can position views in relation to their parent elements. This becomes especially important when designing applications for devices with different screen resolutions and sizes, such as smartphones and tablets. On both types of devices, the application should look the same – or at least similar.

5.8.3.1 Positioning Elements Relative to the Layout

The application code is located in a folder named **Application19**. The parent element (also called the "container") for a view is usually the layout itself. Therefore, the position of a button, for example, will be defined relative to the RelativeLayout.

In the example below, we will place three buttons – **Button1, Button2**, and **Button3** – in three different positions using **RelativeLayout**. But first, let's take a look at the result of how the **layout** works.

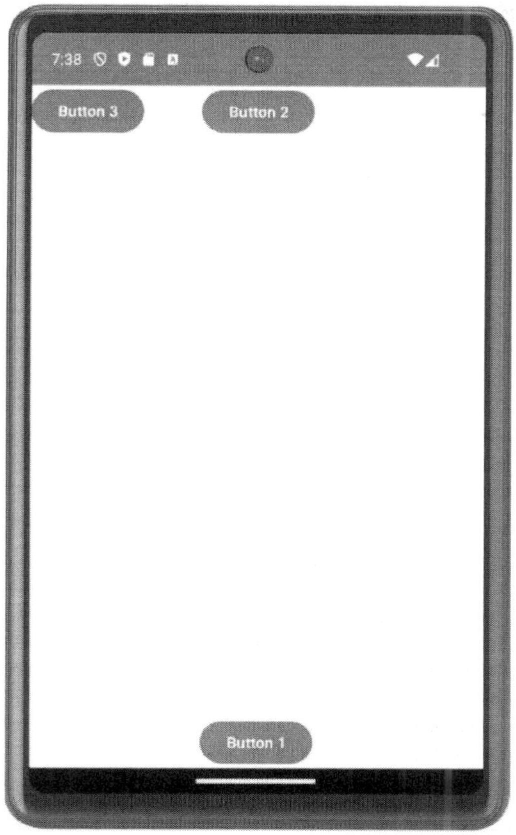

Figure 5.64: Button arrangement after applying the RelativeLayout layout

The layout code might look like this:

```
<?xml version="1.0" encoding="utf-8"?>
<RelativeLayout

xmlns:android="http://schemas.android.com/apk/res/android"
    xmlns:tools="http://schemas.android.com/tools"
    android:layout_width="match_parent"
    android:layout_height="match_parent"
    tools:context=".MainActivity">
    <Button
        android:layout_width="wrap_content"
        android:layout_height="wrap_content"
        android:id="@+id/btn1"
        android:text="@string/btn1"
        android:layout_alignParentBottom="true"
        android:layout_centerHorizontal="true"/>
    <Button
        android:layout_width="wrap_content"
        android:layout_height="wrap_content"
        android:id="@+id/btn2"
        android:text="@string/btn2"
        android:layout centerHorizontal="true"/>
    <Button
        android:id="@+id/btn3"
        android:layout_width="wrap_content"
        android:layout_height="wrap_content"
        android:layout_alignParentLeft="true"
        android:text="@string/btn3" />
</RelativeLayout>
```

Listing 5.103 RelativeLayout layout

The position of elements in the layout is determined by the lines that contain the following entries:

```
android:layout_alignParentLeft="true"
android:layout_centerHorizontal="true"
android:layout_alignParentBottom="true"
android:layout_centerHorizontal="true".
```

Listing 5.104 Relative layout attributes.

All of the above parameters are set to true. The default value for these attributes is false, so if we want to activate them, we need to change their value to the opposite. Note that in the case of **RelativeLayout,** the order of elements in the layout file does not matter.

Button1 has the **alignParentBottom** attribute set, which places the element at the bottom of the screen. Additionally, the **centerHorizontal** option is also included, which centers the element horizontally. As you can see, these options can be combined. The following table presents the list of available options for the android:layout... attribute:

Atribute	Action
android:layout_alignParentBottom	Places the element at the bottcm of the layout
android:layout_alignParentTop	Places the element at the top cf the layout
android:layout_alignParentLeft	Places the element on the left side
android:layout_alignParentRight	Places the element on the right side
android:layout_centerInParent	Places the element exactly in the center of the layout
android:layout_centerHorizontal	Centers the element horizontally within the layout
android:layout_centerVertical	Centers the element vertically within the layout

Table 5.1 Attribute values used in the RelativeLayout layout

These are the most commonly used options in the **RelativeLayout** layout. Now compare the application code with the table. Are the attributes assigned to the views consistent with the table?

5.8.3.2 Positioning elements relative to each other

You can find the application code in the **Application19a** folder. If we need to place two elements in a group, for example side by side, we can also use **RelativeLayout**. We just need to specify which element the second one depends on. Let's design two buttons that are dependent on each other – arranged one below the other.

The code for such an application should be similar to the one shown in the listing below:

```
<?xml version="1.0" encoding="utf-8"?>
<RelativeLayout

xmlns:android="http://schemas.android.com/apk/res/android"
    xmlns:tools="http://schemas.android.com/tools"
    android:layout_width="match_parent"
    android:layout_height="match_parent"
    tools:context=".MainActivity">
    <Button
        android:layout_width="wrap_content"
        android:layout_height="wrap_content"
        android:id="@+id/btn1"
        android:text="@string/btn1"
        android:layout_centerInParent="true"/>
    <Button
        android:layout_width="wrap_content"
        android:layout_height="wrap_content"
        android:id="@+id/btn2"
        android:text="@string/btn2"
        android:layout_alignLeft="@id/btn1"
        android:layout_below="@id/btn1"
        android:layout_centerHorizontal="true"/>

</RelativeLayout>
```

Listing 5.105 RelativeLayout with elements dependent on each other

We will treat **Button1** as the parent element. It is positioned in the center of the screen using the attribute **android:layout_centerInParent**. The second button is linked to it using two attributes:

- **android:layout_alignLeft="@+id/button1"** – this aligns the second button to the left edge of Button1, and
- **android:layout_below="@+id/button1"** – this places the second button below Button1.

Other attributes used to position elements relative to each other are listed in the table below:

Atribute	Action
layout_above	Places the view above the referenced element
Layout_below	Places the view below the referenced element
Layout_alignTop	Aligns views to the top edge
Layout_alignBottom	Aligns views to the bottom edge
Layout_alignLeft, Layout_alignStart	Aligns views to the left side
Layout_alignRight, Layout_alignEnd	Aligns views to the right side

Layout_toLeftOf, Layout_toStartOf	Places the element to the left of the referenced element
Layout_toRightOf, Layout_toEndOf	Places the element to the right of the referenced element

Table 5.2 RelativeLayout attribute values.

Figure 5.65 Arrangement of buttons in a RelativeLayout layout positioned relative to each other.

5.8.4 TableLayout

Table layout presents the structure in the form of a **table**. We can create the layout by adding **rows** to it. Each element added to a row creates a cell. The width of the cell is equal to the width of the widest element.

The application code is located in the folder named **Application20**. Let's create a simple table layout consisting of:

- the first row containing a label and a text input field,
- the second row with two buttons: Send and Clear,
- the third row with a label,
- the fourth row with three checkbox selection fields.

The layout will look like in the image below:

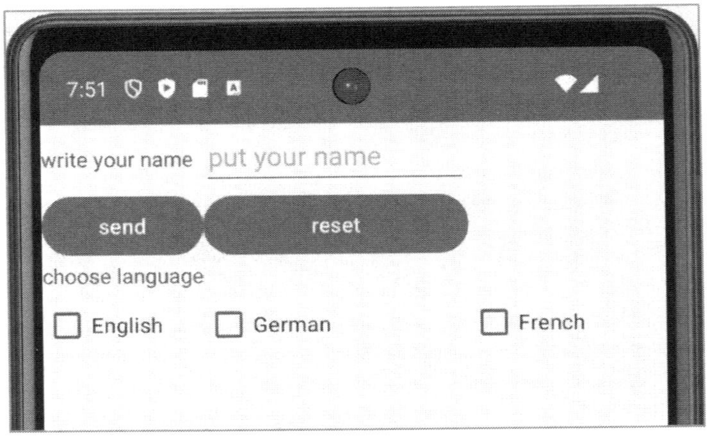

Figure 5.66 Views arranged using the TableLayout layout

As shown in the illustration, four rows of elements have been created. Each **row** is divided into **columns**. Every newly added element in a row creates a column. Pay attention to the middle column – it has been widened to **175dp**, and therefore all elements in this column have the same width, because the text field in the first row is the widest element in the column.

The layout code will look like the one shown below:

```
<?xml version="1.0" encoding="utf-8"?>
<TableLayout
xmlns:android="http://schemas.android.com/apk/res/android"
    xmlns:tools="http://schemas.android.com/tools"
    android:layout_width="match_parent"
    android:layout_height="wrap_content"
    tools:context=".MainActivity">
    <TableRow
        android:layout_width="match_parent"
        android:layout_height="match_parent">
        <TextView
            android:id="@+id/name"
            android:layout_column="0"
            android:text="@string/t1" />
        <EditText
            android:id="@+id/answer"
            android:layout_width="175dp"
            android:layout_height="wrap_content"
            android:layout_column="1"
            android:hint="@string/hint1"
            android:inputType="textAutoCorrect" />
    </TableRow>
    <TableRow
        android:layout_width="match_parent"
        android:layout_height="match_parent">
        <Button
            android:id="@+id/button1"
            android:layout_width="wrap_content"
            android:layout_height="wrap_content"
            android:layout_column="0"
            android:text="@string/t2" />
        <Button
            android:id="@+id/button2"
            android:layout_width="wrap_content"
            android:layout_height="wrap_content"
            android:layout_column="1"
            android:text="@string/t3" />
    </TableRow>
    <TableRow
        android:layout_width="match_parent"
        android:layout_height="match_parent">
        <TextView
            android:id="@+id/text"
            android:layout_width="match_parent"
            android:layout_height="match_parent"
            android:layout_column="0"
            android:text="@string/t4"/>
    </TableRow>
    <TableRow
        android:layout_width="match_parent"
        android:layout_height="match_parent">
 <CheckBox
            android:id="@+id/eng"
            android:layout_width="match_parent"
            android:layout_height="match_parent"
            android:layout_column="0"
            android:text="@string/t5" />
        <CheckBox
            android:id="@+id/ger"
            android:layout_width="match_parent"
            android:layout_height="match_parent"
            android:layout_column="1"
            android:text="@string/t6" />
        <CheckBox
            android:id="@+id/fr"
            android:layout_width="match_parent"
            android:layout_height="match_parent"
            android:layout_column="2"
            android:text="@string/t7" />
    </TableRow>
</TableLayout>
```

Listing 5.106 TableLayout layout

A new attribute is: **android:layout_column**. It is assigned successive values starting from 0. These values indicate the order in which the element is placed within the row.

5.8.5 GridLayout

The code for the following application can be found in the folder named **Applicaion21a**. **GridLayout** is a grid - based layout. It creates a grid of rows and columns in which elements can be placed.

Similar to TableLayout, **GridLayout** arranges elements into cells. The difference is that in GridLayout, each element is assigned both a **column number and** a **row number**. There is no need to separate rows manually as in the previous layout.

The illustration shows the appearance of the application, containing the same elements as in the previous exercise, with the difference that here we use **GridLayout**.

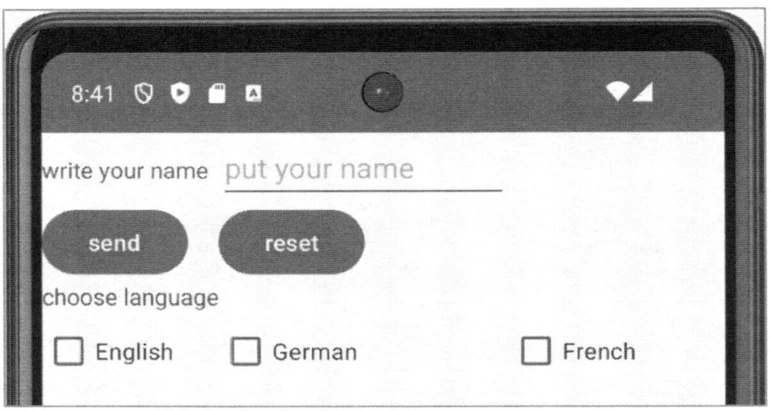

Figure5.67 Views arranged using the GridLayout layout

As you can see, the layout looks exactly the same as in the previous exercise. Now take a look at the application code based on **GridLayout:**

```
<?xml version="1.0" encoding="utf-8"?>
<GridLayout

xmlns:android="http://schemas.android.com/apk/res/android"
    xmlns:tools="http://schemas.android.com/tools"
    android:layout_width="wrap_content"
    android:layout_height="wrap_content"
    tools:context=".MainActivity"
    android:columnCount="3"
    android:rowCount="4">

    <TextView
        android:text="@string/t1"
        android:id="@+id/t1"
        android:layout_column="0"
        android:layout_row="0"/>
    <EditText
        android:hint="@string/hint1"
        android:layout_width="175dp"
        android:layout_height="wrap_content"
        android:id="@+id/answer"
        android:layout_column="1"
        android:layout_row="0"
        android:inputType="textAutoCorrect" />
    <Button
        android:layout_width="wrap_content"
        android:layout_height="wrap_content"
        android:text="@string/t2"
        android:id="@+id/btn1"
        android:layout_column="0"
        android:layout_row="1"/>
    <Button
        android:layout_width="wrap_content"
        android:layout_height="wrap_content"
        android:id="@+id/btn2"
        android:text="@string/t3"
        android:layout_column="1"
        android:layout_row="1"/>
    <TextView
        android:text="@string/t4"
        android:layout_width="match_parent"
        android:layout_height="match_parent"
        android:id="@+id/t4"
        android:layout_column="0"
        android:layout_row="2"/>
    <CheckBox
        android:text="@string/t5"
        android:layout_width="match_parent"
        android:layout_height="match_parent"
        android:id="@+id/eng"
        android:layout_column="0"
        android:layout_row="3"/>
    <CheckBox
        android:text="@string/t6"
        android:layout_width="match_parent"
        android:layout_height="match_parent"
        android:id="@+id/ger"
        android:layout_column="1"
        android:layout_row="3"/>
    <CheckBox
        android:text="@string/t7"
        android:layout_width="match_parent"
        android:layout_height="match_parent"
        android:id="@+id/fr"
        android:layout_column="2"
        android:layout_row="3"/>

</GridLayout>
```

Listing 5.107 GridLayout layout

In a grid layout, all elements are placed within a single section without dividing them into separate rows. In each view, we add an extra line of code: **android:layout_row**, and just like with **android:layout_column**, we assign values starting from 0. Each new row gets a value that is one greater than the previous.

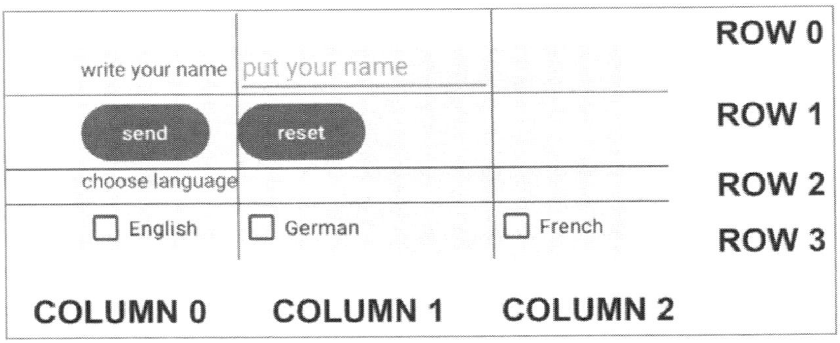

Figure 5.68 View layout scheme

Looking at our **layout**, it's easy to notice that it has some drawbacks. Since the second column has a larger width, the other cells (especially in the second and third rows) are too wide. However, **GridLayout** gives us the ability to merge two cells, just like in a spreadsheet or word processor.

Imagine our layout as a table. If we consider that the EditText looks better when it's wider, the table would look approximately like the diagram below:

<table>
<tr><td>TextView</td><td colspan="2">EditText</td></tr>
<tr><td>Button1</td><td>Button2</td><td></td></tr>
<tr><td colspan="3">TextView</td></tr>
<tr><td>CheckBox1</td><td>CheckBox2</td><td>CheckBox3</td></tr>
</table>

Table 5.3 GridLayout layout

You can find the application code in the folder named Applicatio21b. Let's now try to adjust our layout to make it look better.

We will use the attribute: **android:layout_columnSpan="2"** This attribute indicates that the cell will occupy the space of two columns. The final activity code after applying these changes will look like this:

```
<EditText
    android:hint="@string/hint1"
    android:layout_width="250dp"
    android:layout_height="wrap_content"
    android:id="@+id/answer"
    android:layout_column="1"
    android:layout_row="0"
    android:layout_columnSpan="2"
    android:inputType="textAutoCorrect" />
```

Listing 5.108 GridLayout with the use of the attribute android:layout_columnSpan

And after launching, the application now looks like this:

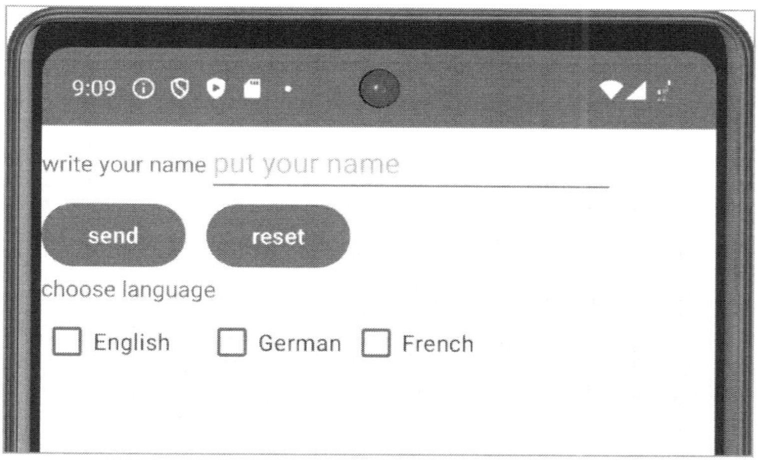

Figure 5.69 Arrangement of views using the columnSpan attribute

5.8.6 Nested layouts

You can find the code for the created application in the folder named **Application22**. Let's try to create the layout shown in the illustration below:

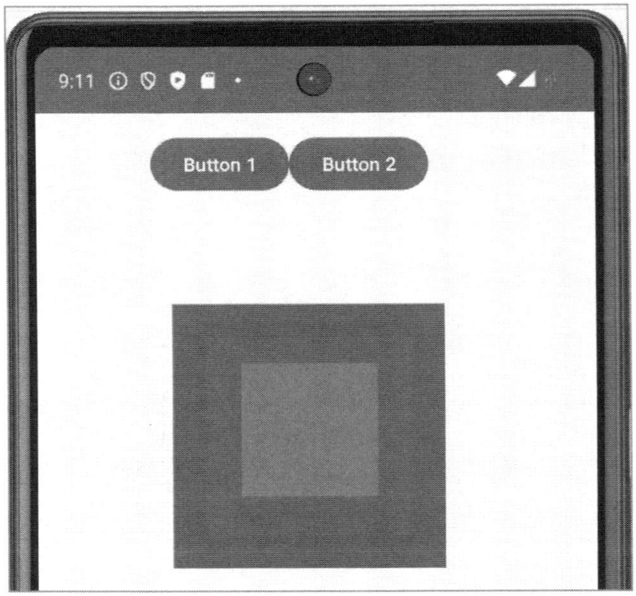

Figure 5.70 Nested layout

We have two buttons: **BUTTON1** and **BUTTON2**, as well as three colorful images containing three colored squares. The images are stacked on top of each other. Therefore, the simplest solution is to use a **FrameLayout** for the images. To arrange the buttons, we will use a **LinearLayout**.

When combining layouts like this, it's best to use nested layouts. Nesting layouts means placing one layout inside another. Before we start writing the code for the layout above, let's try to use the following diagram.

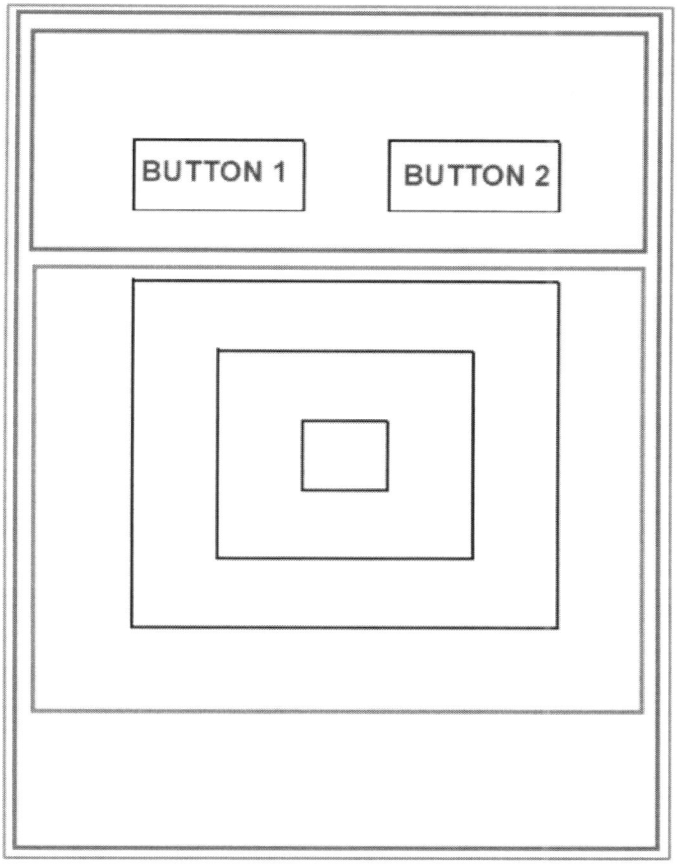

Figure 5.71 Layout structure showing nested views

In the activity file, we will have **three layouts**. The first one (marked in red) will be the **main layout** – a **LinearLayout with vertical orientation.** We want the **two inner layouts** to be arranged one below the other. This layout will consist of two elements: A **LinearLayout** (marked in blue) with **horizontal** orientation, because we want the buttons to be placed side by side. A **FrameLayout** (marked in green) in which we will place three images. We also need to adjust the positioning of the elements using **margin** parameters.

The layout code may look like the listing below:

```xml
<?xml version="1.0" encoding="utf-8"?>
<LinearLayout
xmlns:android="http://schemas.android.com/apk/res/android"
    xmlns:tools="http://schemas.android.com/tools"
    android:layout_width="match_parent"
    android:layout_height="match_parent"
    android:orientation="vertical"
    tools:context=".MainActivity">

    <LinearLayout
        android:layout_width="match_parent"
        android:layout_height="145dp"
        android:orientation="horizontal">

        <Button
            android:id="@+id/btn1"
            android:layout_width="wrap_content"
            android:layout_height="wrap_content"
            android:layout_marginLeft="85dp"
            android:layout_marginTop="15dp"
            android:text="@string/btn1" />

        <Button
            android:id="@+id/btn2"
            android:layout_width="wrap_content"
            android:layout_height="wrap_content"
            android:layout_marginLeft="0dp"
            android:layout_marginTop="15dp"
            android:text="@string/btn2" />
    </LinearLayout>

    <FrameLayout
        android:layout_width="match_parent"
        android:layout_height="257dp"
        android:layout_marginLeft="0dp"
        android:layout_marginTop="0dp">

        <ImageView
            android:layout_width="wrap_content"
            android:layout_height="wrap_content"
            android:layout_marginLeft="100dp"
            android:layout_marginTop="0dp"
            android:src="@drawable/blue" />
        <ImageView
            android:layout_width="wrap_content"
            android:layout_height="wrap_content"
            android:layout_marginLeft="125dp"
            android:layout_marginTop="25dp"
            android:src="@drawable/red" />

        <ImageView
            android:layout_width="wrap_content"
            android:layout_height="wrap_content"
            android:layout_marginLeft="150dp"
            android:layout_marginTop="45dp"
            android:src="@drawable/green" />
    </FrameLayout>
</LinearLayout>
```

Listing 5.109 Application code with a nested layout

5.8.7 ConstraintLayout

The application code can be found in the folder named **Applicatio23**. **ConstraintLayout**, or the layout with constraints, is a layout in which elements are arranged using a **graphical editor**, rather than by manually writing **XML** code as we've done so far. Let's now create a new project. By default, the layout will be set to **ConstraintLayout.** Its code looks like the one shown below:

```
<?xml version="1.0" encoding="utf-8"?>
<androidx.constraintlayout.widget.ConstraintLayout
    xmlns:android="http://schemas.android.com/apk/res/android"
    xmlns:tools="http://schemas.android.com/tools"
    xmlns:app="http://schemas.android.com/apk/res-auto"
    android:layout_width="match_parent"
    android:layout_height="match_parent"
    tools:context=".MainActivity">
  </androidx.constraintlayout.widget.ConstraintLayout>
```

Listing 5.110 ConstraintLayout

Let's add a simple text view to the layout. We'll use a **TextView** to display the text "**Good morning**".

```
<?xml version="1.0" encoding="utf-8"?>
<androidx.constraintlayout.widget.ConstraintLayout

xmlns:android="http://schemas.android.com/apk/res/android"
    xmlns:app="http://schemas.android.com/apk/res-auto"
    xmlns:tools="http://schemas.android.com/tools"
    android:layout_width="match_parent"
    android:layout_height="match_parent"
    tools:context=".MainActivity">

    <TextView
        android:id="@+id/textView2"
        android:layout_width="wrap_content"
        android:layout_height="0dp"
        android:layout_marginTop="260dp"
        android:text="@string/t1"
        app:layout_constraintStart_toStartOf="parent"
        app:layout_constraintTop_toTopOf="parent" />
</androidx.constraintlayout.widget.ConstraintLayout>
```

Listing 5.111 ConstraintLayout with a TextView view

When we look at the application, we notice an **error**. The error message is: **<TextView>: Missing Constraints in ConstraintLayout**. This means that the **TextView** element has no **constraints** defined – in other words, it's missing the necessary positioning rules.

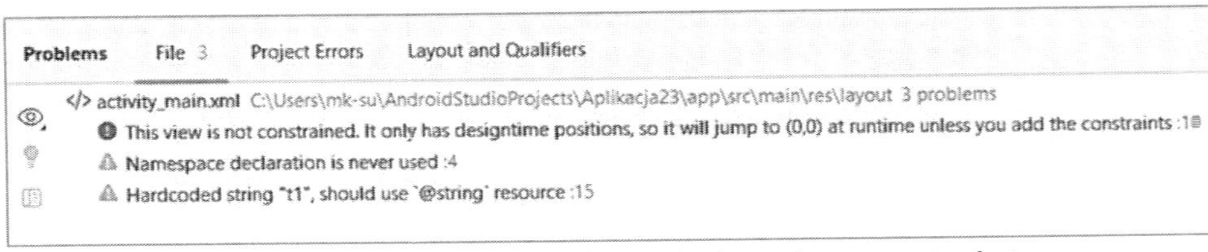

Figure 5.72 Error indicating missing view constraints

Let's now remove the **error** by adding constraints to the **element**. To do this, we need to switch the **XML file view.** Go to the **Design** tab located in the upper right corner of the editor.

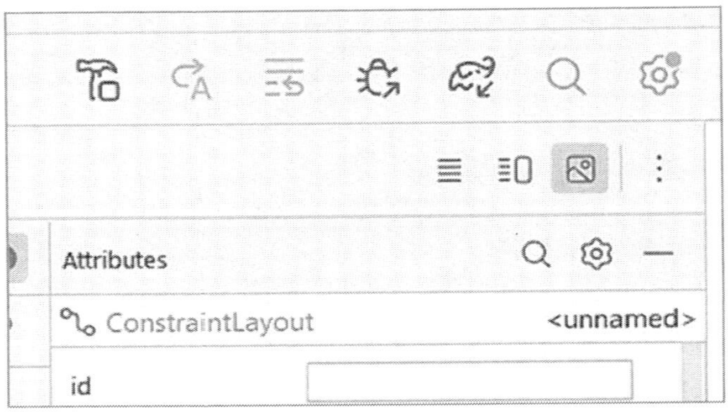

Figure 5.73 Icons that allow navigation between layout editors (text, split, graphical)

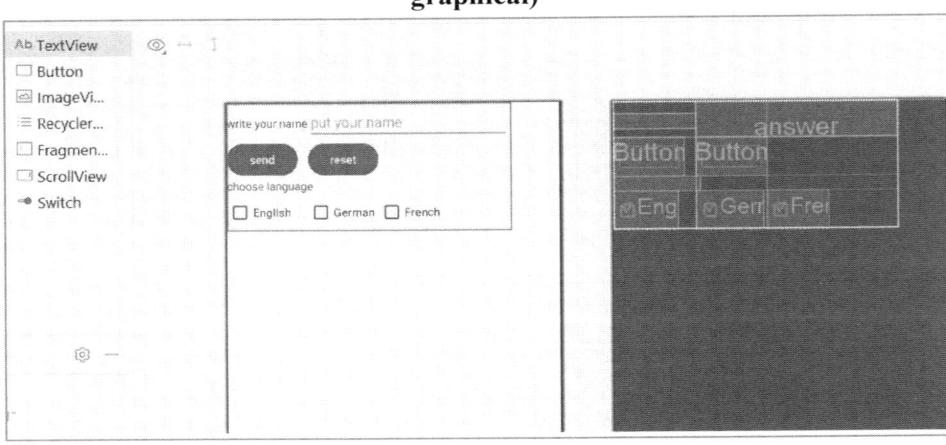

Figure 5.74 Graphical layout editor

In the window, we can see our TextView element. It is located in the top - left corner. We need to assign constraints to it. Click on the view to select it. On the right side of the window, a section named Layout will appear.

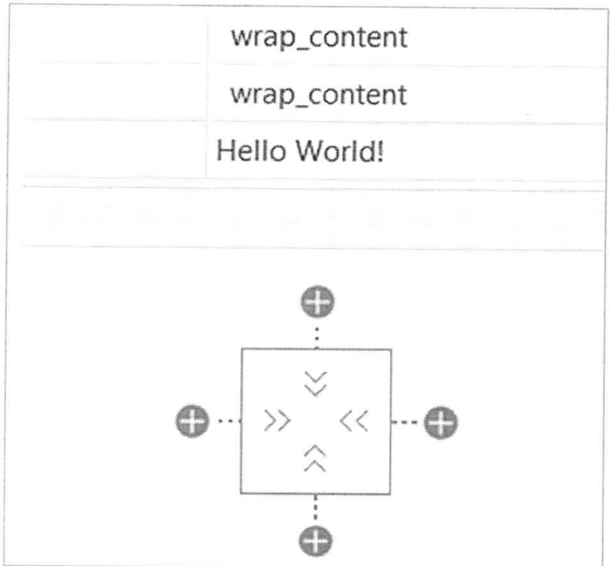

Figure 5.75 Window for setting view constraints

We assign constraints by clicking the **blue plus icon**. We must set at least two constraints: one vertical and one horizontal. We can also assign constraints for all four sides: **top, bottom, left,** and **right**.

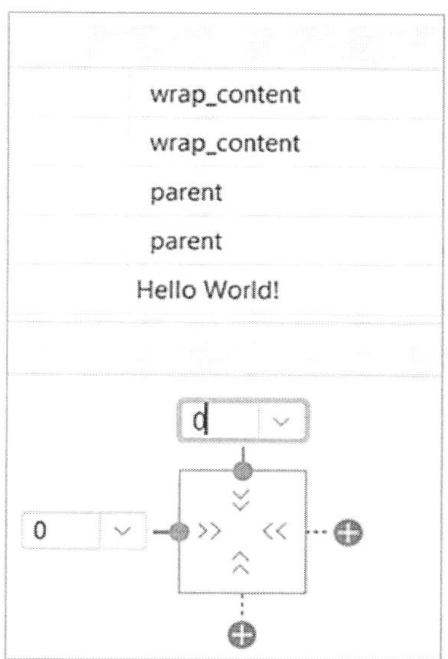

Figure 5.76 Setting constraints for a view

Once constraints are added, the **error** about missing constraints **disappears.** In the **Layout** window, we can see the position of the view. Currently, it is set to default values of **0** and **0**, which represent the margins – the distance from the left and top edges. You can move the element by selecting a margin value from the dropdown list, or by manually dragging the element in the editor.

Click on the element and position the cursor **in its center**. While **holding down the mouse button, drag** the element to any location. The margin values will update according to the new position. You can also preview these changes in the text editor. The layout code will look like the one shown below:

```
<?xml version="1.0" encoding="utf-8"?>
<androidx.constraintlayout.widget.ConstraintLayout
    xmlns:android="http://schemas.android.com/apk/res/android"
    xmlns:app="http://schemas.android.com/apk/res-auto"
    xmlns:tools="http://schemas.android.com/tools"
    android:layout_width="match_parent"
    android:layout_height="match_parent"
    tools:context=".MainActivity">

    <TextView
        android:layout_width="wrap_content"
        android:layout_height="0dp"
        android:layout_marginStart="176dp"
        android:layout_marginTop="260dp"
        android:text="@string/t1"
  app:layout_constraintStart_toStartOf="parent"
  app:layout_constraintTop_toTopOf="parent" />
</androidx.constraintlayout.widget.ConstraintLayout>
```

Listing 5.112 ConstraintLayout layout in the text editor

Note that the attributes app: **layout_constraintStart_toStartOf** and app:**layout_constraintTop_toTopOf were** present by default when we created the project.

Now let's add another element using the constraint - based layout and the graphical editor. Switch to the **Design** tab. On the left side of the editor, you'll see a list of available views. Browse through it to explore the available options. We'll insert a **button**. Select **Button** from the list and, while holding down the mouse button, drag the button onto the layout area.

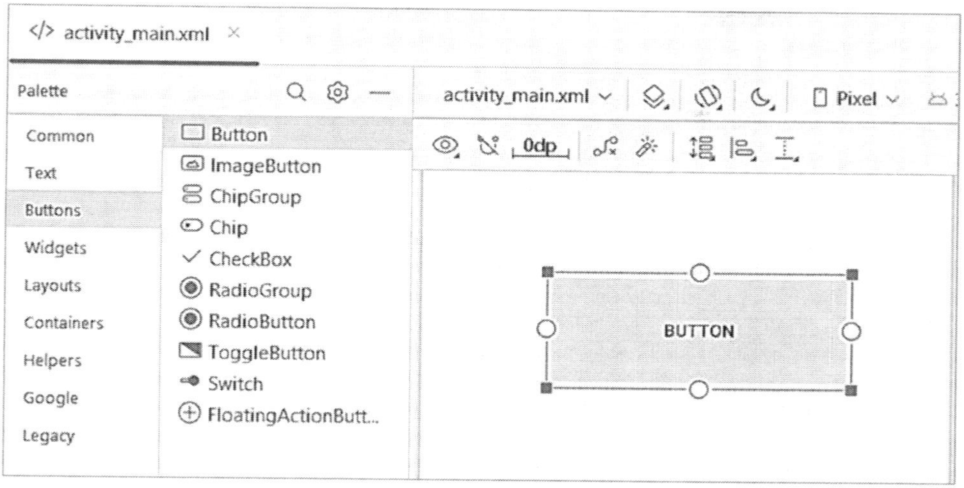

Figure 5.77 Inserting a Button into the layout

Now we can set the position of the button, but first we need to assign constraints to it. We proceed in exactly the same way as we did with the TextView.

5.9 Styles

We want to create an application consisting of **nine buttons** arranged in three rows and three columns. The buttons should have alternating colors – so that they resemble a chessboard. In the layout code, we will place nine **Button** elements and assign appropriate settings to each of them. This approach has two drawbacks. First, it **multiplies the code**, as each button must be described separately. Second, if a **small change is needed** in one element, we would have to apply that change to each element individually. We can use **styles** here. Styles (similar to cascading style sheets in CSS) allow us to group settings in one place and assign a specific style to a view.

5.9.1 Creating Styles

The application code is located in a folder named **Application24**. We are creating a new application. To arrange the elements, we will use **GridLayout**. In the layout, we will place nine buttons. Initially, the code of the **activity_main.xml** file will look as follows:

```
<?xml version="1.0" encoding="utf-8"?>
<GridLayout
    xmlns:android="http://schemas.android.com/apk/res/android"
    xmlns:tools="http://schemas.android.com/tools"
    android:layout_width="match_parent"
    android:layout_height="match_parent"
    tools:context=".MainActivity">

    <Button
        android:text="1"
        android:layout_column="0"
        android:layout_row="0"
        />
    <Button
        android:layout_column="1"
        android:layout_row="0"
        android:text="2" />
    <Button
        android:text="3"
        android:layout_column="2"
        android:layout_row="0"
        />
    <Button
        android:layout_column="0"
        android:layout_row="1"
        android:text="4" />
    <Button
        android:text="5"
        android:layout_column="1"
        android:layout_row="1"
        />
    <Button
        android:layout_column="2"
        android:layout_row="1"
        android:text="6" />
    <Button
        android:text="7"
        android:layout_column="0"
        android:layout_row="2"
        />
    <Button
        android:text="8"
        android:layout_column="1"
        android:layout_row="2"
        />
    <Button
        android:text="9"
        android:layout_column="2"
        android:layout_row="2"
        />
</GridLayout>
```

Listing 5.113 Initial Layout Code of the Application

The only differences will be in the values of the parameters android:**layout_column** and **android:layout_row**. Once launched, the application will look like this:

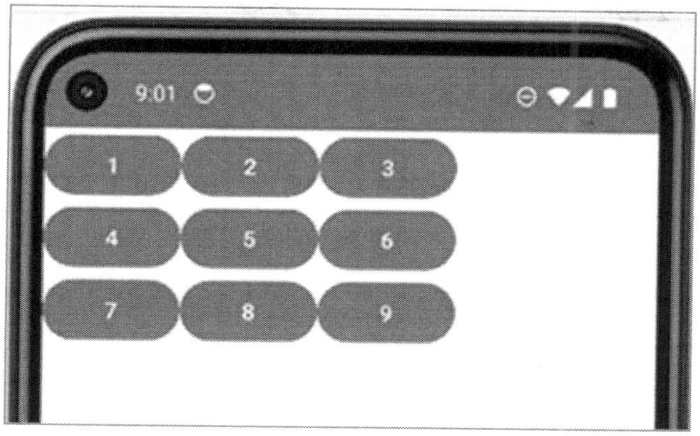

Figure 5.78 Application with Default Style

Styles can be created in the **styles.xml** file. This is an application resource file and can be found in the tree on the left side. If the file is not there, it must be created manually. Right - click on the **values branch** and from the menu that appears, select **New → Values Resource File**.

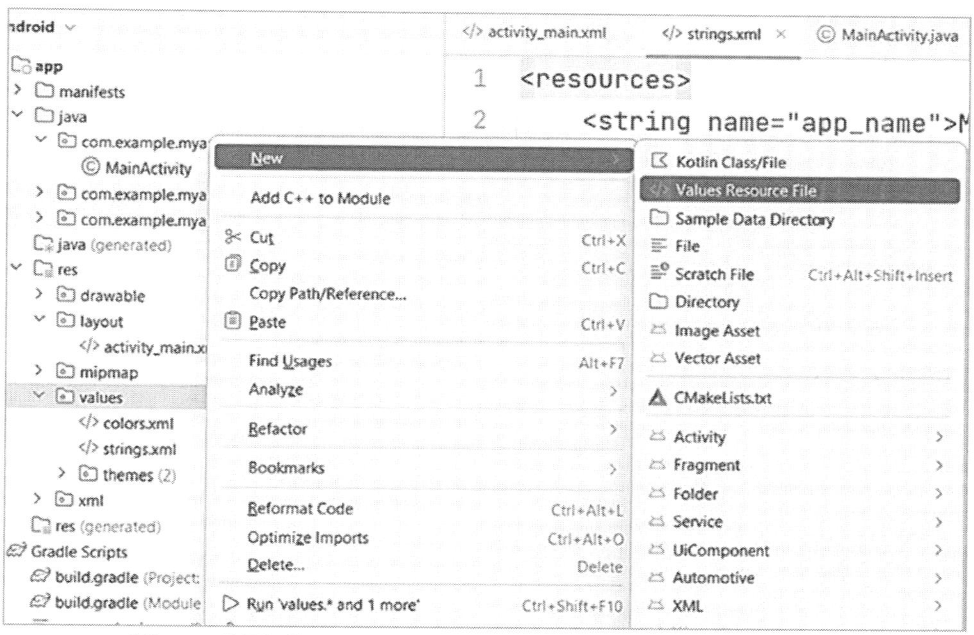

Figure 5.79 Creating a New Resource File – styles.xml

We name the file **styles**. The **.xml** extension will be added automatically. We will create a style named **Chessboard**.

```
<style name="Chessboard">
    <item name="android:layout_width">130dp</item>
    <item name="android:layout_height">130dp</item>
    <item name="android:background">#FFFFFF</item>
    <item name="android:textColor">#EDE906</item>
    <item name="android:typeface">serif</item>
    <item name="android:textSize">55sp</item>
</style>
```

Listing 5.114 Definition of the "Chessboard" Style

First, we assign a name to the style: **name="Chessboard".** The following attributes define the **width** and **height** of the view. The background color is determined by the **android:background** attribute. It is set to white because we want all buttons to be white. You can change the color by clicking the **small square** located **on the left side** of the window.

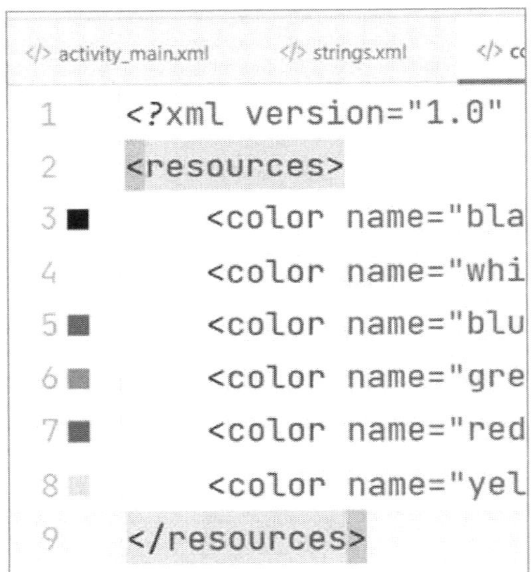

Figure 5.80 Contents of the colors.xml File

Clicking will display a color **palette**.

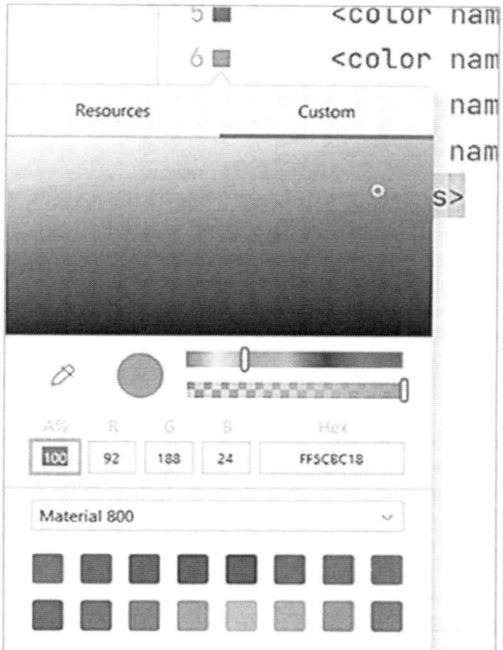

Figure 5.81 color Selection Window

You choose a color by clicking on the **desired area**. You can also do this by adjusting the **available sliders**. The first slider controls the **hue**, and the second controls **transparency**. You can also use a predefined list or **manually** enter **RGB** values. For white, the value is **255, 255, 255**. In the **styles.xml** file, the color is saved in **hexadecimal format.**

The next attributes define the text color settings:

```
<item name="android:textColor">#FF0000</item>
```

Listing 5.115 Font color Settings

This defines the font family:

```
<item name="android:typeface">serif</item>
```

Listing 5.116 Font Family Setting

This defines the font size:

```
<item name="android:textSize">55sp</item>
```

Listing 5.117 Font Size Setting

In the layout file, we can now assign styles to the appropriate squares. We will do this using the following code:

```
style="@style/StyleName"
```

Listing 5.118 Assigning a Style to a View

In place of **StyleName**, we enter the name **Chessboard**. We will change the style setting for the first button. The button code will look as follows:

```
<Button
    style="@style/Chessboard"
    android:text="1"
    android:layout_column="0"
    android:layout_row="0"/>
```

Listing 5.119 Button code with a declared style

After launching, the application should resemble the illustration below:

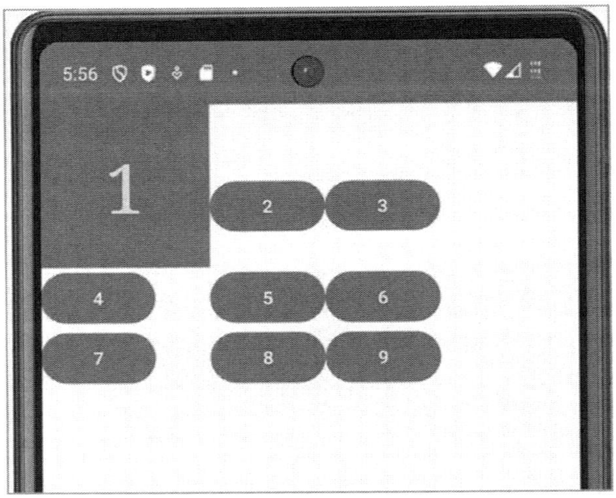

Figure 5.82 Button 1 after applying the style

In the illustration, you can see that the button has changed its **size** and **shape**. The font **size** and **color** have also changed. However, the **button's background color** has not changed. The application is running with the default style, which is defined in the **Manifest.xml** file. Therefore, we need to change this setting. First, we need to define our own application theme. In the **styles.xml** file, we place the following code:

```
<style name="MyTheme" parent="Theme.AppCompat.Light.NoActionBar">
</style>
```

Listing 5.120 Creating a new application style

We create a new **style** named **NewTheme**. In the **parent** attribute, we enter the name of the **parent** style – the one that slightly changes the appearance of the application.Theme settings will be discussed in more detail in the next chapter. For now, the two lines above are sufficient. Next, we go to the **manifest** file and change the theme name there.

```
<application
    android:allowBackup="true"

android:dataExtractionRules="@xml/data_extraction_rules"
    android:fullBackupContent="@xml/backup_rules"
    android:icon="@mipmap/ic_launcher"
    android:label="@string/app_name"
    android:roundIcon="@mipmap/ic_launcher_round"
    android:supportsRtl="true"
    android:theme="@style/MyTheme"
    tools:targetApi="31">
```

Listing 5.121 Manifest file fragment

In the **android:theme** attribute, we change the default name to the name of our style, which is: **NewTheme**. After launching the application, our button will change to the correct color.

Figure 5.83 Application after applying a custom theme

You can also notice changes to the other buttons, as well as a change in the color of the status bar. This is because we changed the entire color theme of the application.

5.9.2 Style inheritance

The code for the application below can be found in the folder **Application24a**. When creating larger and more complex applications, using a single group of styles may be insufficient. Often, multiple style groups are needed, which may differ only in certain elements. In such cases, we can reuse some attributes from one style. As an example, we will modify the previous application. First, let s assign the style **Chessboard** to all views in the layout. The application will look like the illustration below.

Figure 5.84 Application using a custom style

All fields are **white**. Now we need to find the simplest and fastest way to make changes in the code. We will use style inheritance for this purpose. As mentioned earlier, **inheritance** allows us to **change** only **selected parameters**, leaving the rest unchanged. We create a style named **Chessboard.Black.** The name indicates that the main style is Chessboard, and the dot signifies that the **Black** style inherits from it. In the **Chessboard.Black** style, we define the background color that the view should have. The styles.xml file will look like the example below:

```
<?xml version="1.0" encoding="utf-8"?>
<resources>
    <style name="NewTheme"
parent="Theme.AppCompat.Light.NoActionBar">
    </style>
    <style name="Chessboard">
        <item name="android:layout_width">130dp</item>
        <item name="android:layout_height">130dp</item>
        <item name="android:background">#FFFFFF</item>
        <item name="android:textColor">#FF0000</item>
        <item name="android:typeface">serif</item>
        <item name="android:textSize">55sp</item>
    </style>
    <style name="Chessboard.Black">
        <item name="android:background">#000000</item>
    </style>
</resources>
```

Listing 5.122 Definition of the inherited style named Chessboard.Black

In the layout file, we need to add information about the **new style for views** that should have a **black** background. After the changes, the layout file will look as follows:

```
<Button
    style="@style/Chessboard"
    android:text="1"
    android:layout_column="0"
    android:layout_row="0"/>
<Button
    style="@style/Chessboard.Black"
    android:layout_column="1"
    android:layout_row="0"
    android:text="2" />
```

Listing 5.123 Fragment of the layout with assigned styles

The application will look like in the illustration below:

Figure 5.85 An application using style inheritance

5.10 Themes and motifs

Themes or motifs were already discussed in the previous chapter. This topic is somewhat broader, and we will explore it further in this chapter. A **theme** or **motif** is a **style** applied in an **application**. Like a style, a theme can be defined and used throughout the entire program. Styles are typically used for parts of the application, such as a **view**. A theme, on the other hand, is applied to the entire application. These are graphical appearance settings for activities: **colorus, font types**, and also the **colors of bars within the window**.

5.10.1 Using built - in themes

We create a new application with a layout file containing a **text field** and a **button**.

```
<?xml version="1.0" encoding="utf-8"?>
<androidx.constraintlayout.widget.ConstraintLayout

xmlns:android="http://schemas.android.com/apk/res/android"
    xmlns:app="http://schemas.android.com/apk/res-auto"
    xmlns:tools="http://schemas.android.com/tools"
    android:layout_width="match_parent"
    android:layout_height="match_parent"
    tools:context=".MainActivity">

    <TextView
        android:id="@+id/textView"
        android:layout_width="wrap_content"
        android:layout_height="wrap_content"
        android:layout_marginBottom="32dp"
        android:text="Hello World!"
        app:layout_constraintBottom_toBottomOf="parent"
        app:layout_constraintEnd_toEndOf="parent"
        app:layout_constraintStart_toStartOf="parent"
        app:layout_constraintTop_toTopOf="parent"
        app:layout_constraintVertical_bias="0.125"
        android:textSize="25pt"/>

    <Button
        style="@style/Button"
        android:layout_width="260dp"
        android:layout_height="97dp"
        android:layout_marginTop="150dp"
        android:text="Button"
        app:layout_constraintBottom_toBottomOf="parent"
        app:layout_constraintEnd_toEndOf="parent"
        app:layout_constraintHorizontal_bias="0.498"
        app:layout_constraintStart_toStartOf="parent"
        app:layout_constraintTop_toTopOf="parent"
        app:layout_constraintVertical_bias="0.071" />

</androidx.constraintlayout.widget.ConstraintLayout>
```

Listing 5.124 Application layout file

Next, we add the **styles.xml** file. A **manifest** file will also be needed. In **styles.xml**, we create a new **theme**. Let's name it **NewTheme2**, and we will use this name in the manifest file. The **styles.xml** file should now look like this:

```
<?xml version="1.0" encoding="utf-8"?>
<resources>
    <style name="NewTheme" parent="Theme.AppCompat">
    </style>
</resources>
```

Listing 5.125 Creating a new style

In the **parent** attribute, we can choose from many available application themes. The best choice would be **themes** from the **Material3** collection. These are very modern and based on **Material Design version 3** technology. Below are examples of applications using various built - in themes.

Theme.AppCompat:

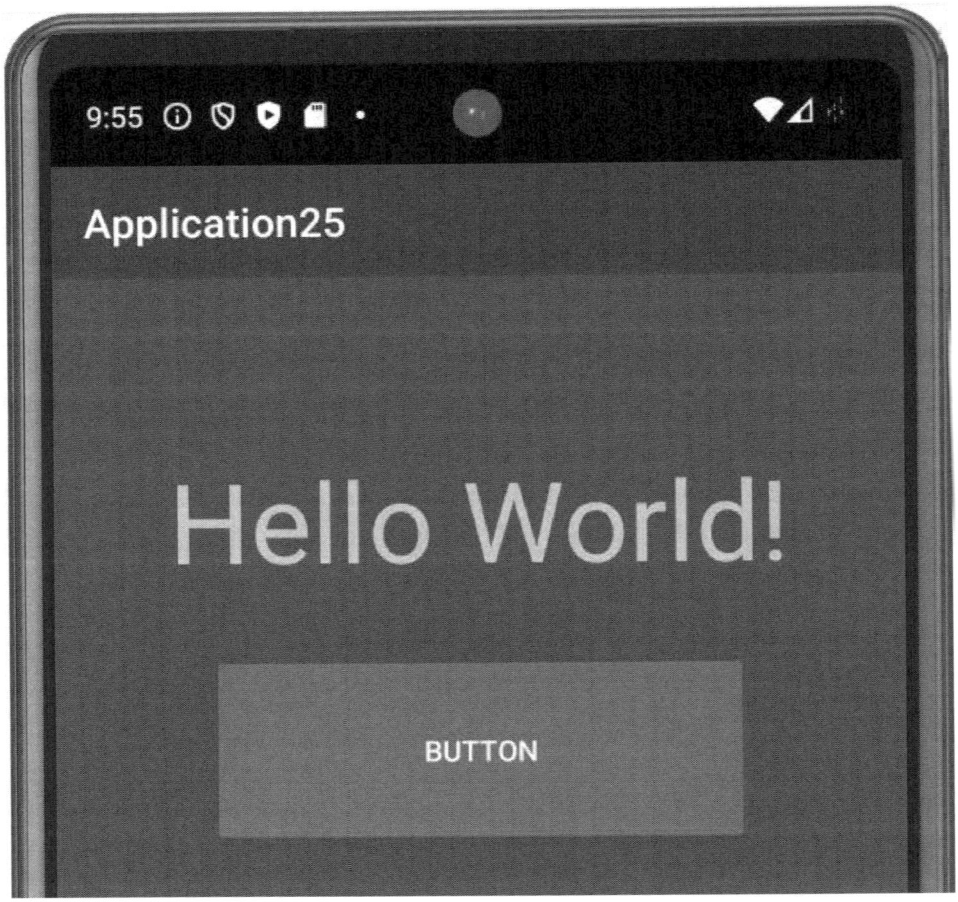

Figure 5.86 The application after applying the 'Theme.AppCompat' theme

Theme.Material3.DynamicColors.Light:

Figure 5.87 The application after applying the 'Theme.Material3.DynamicColors.Light' theme

Theme.Material3.Dark:

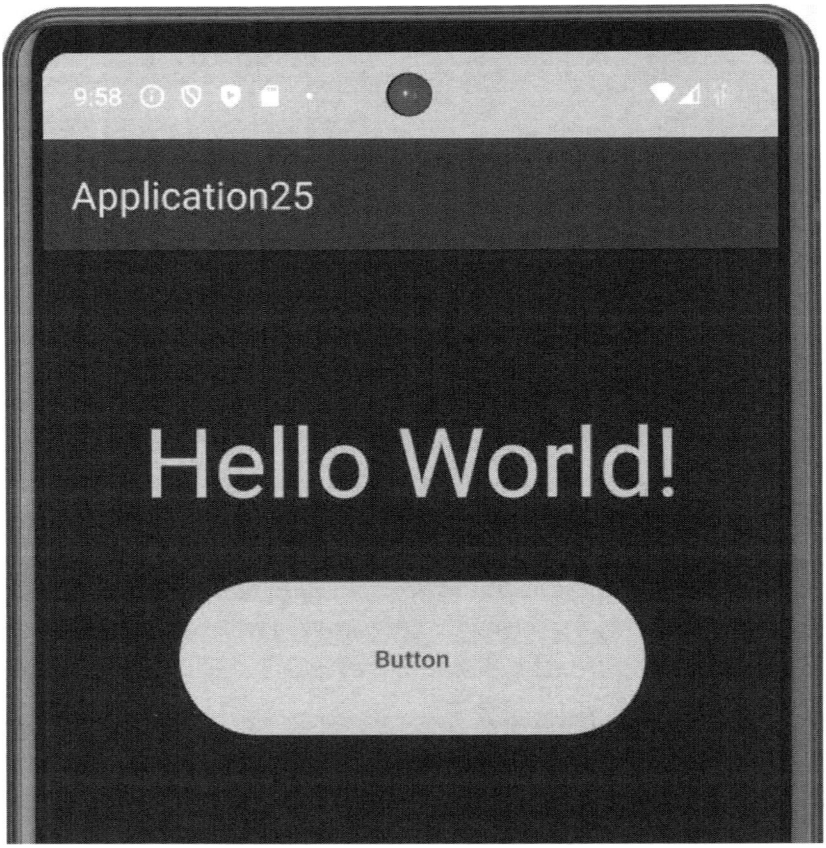

Figure 5.88 The application after applying the "Theme.Material3.Dark"

5.10.2 Creating a custom theme

The application code is located in a folder named **Application25**. Creating a custom **theme** should begin by setting one of the default themes. This is done in the **styles.xml** file. Remember to also add the **main style name** in the **manifest** file.

All the colors that will be used in the application should first be declared and set in the **colors.xml** file. This file is located in the application's tree under the **Values** branch. You can add new values to the ones already present in the file. We will now edit this file. We will create bold, expressive colors that strongly emphasize the application's elements. Add the following colors:

```
<?xml version="1.0" encoding="utf-8"?>
<resources>
    <color name="black">#FF000000</color>
    <color name="white">#FFFFFFFF</color>
    <color name="green">#7CB342</color>
    <color name="red">#D50000</color>
    <color name="yellow">#FFD600</color>
    <color name="lightblue">#55B7F1</color>
    <color name="darkblue">#283593</color>
    <color name="purple">#D1119C</color>
</resources>
```

Listing 5.126 colors.xml file

Next, in the **styles.xml** file, we change the color settings of the elements used in the application. The code in the **styles.xml** file looks like the example below:

```
<?xml version="1.0" encoding="utf-8"?>
<resources>
  <style name="NewTheme" parent="Theme.AppCompat">
<item name="android:windowBackground">@color/green</item>
<item name="colorPrimary">@color/yellow</item>
<item name="colorPrimaryDark">@color/red</item>
<item name="android:textColor">@color/lightblue</item>
<item name="colorAccent">@color/darkblue</item>
<item name="android:textColorPrimary">@color/purple</item>
    </style>
    <style name="Button">
<item name="android:background">@color/darkblue</item>
<item name="android:textColor">@color/lightblue</item>
    </style>
</resources>
```

Listing 5.127 styles.xml file with a custom style defined

We have also created an additional **style** for the **button**. In the illustration, we can see where in the application the declared colors have been applied.

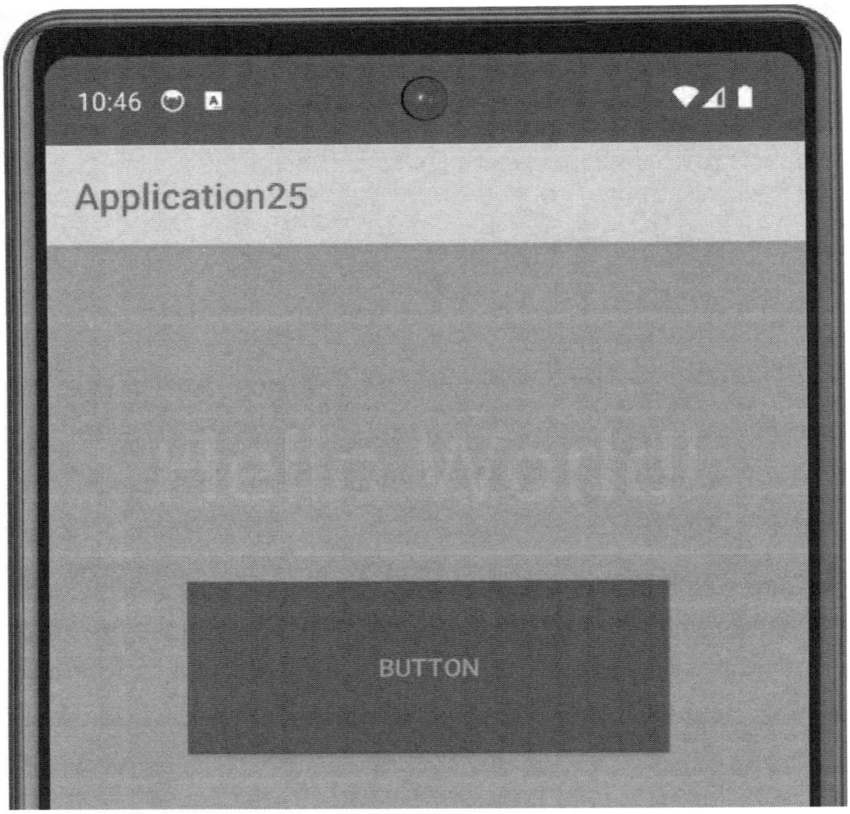

Figure 5.89 Application with a custom theme

As we can see, **colorPrimary** is the color located at the top of the application, known as the **ToolBar**. **ColorPrimaryDark** is the color of the bar at the very top of the application. **Android:windowBackground** is the background color of the entire application, and **android:textColor** is the color of the text. These settings will work similarly for individual views. In this application, **the Button** is used as an example.

5.11 Activity Lifecycle

Every activity that is launched by the operating system begins its lifecycle. An application can exist in several different states:

- **Active state** – the activity is visible in the foreground;
- **Paused state** – the application is partially visible, but can still be resumed (it hasn't been closed);

- **Stopped state** – the application is no longer visible, but not all resources have been released yet;
- **Destroyed state** – the activity ends its operation.

When the application starts, the **onCreate** method is triggered. It is defined in the activity file. The **onCreate** method "brings the activity to life" and enables its operation. When the activity ends, the **onDestroy** method is called. This is the final method in the activity lifecycle. Its purpose is to clean up the data used by the application. When the application is closed, all resources it used are released, and the activity enters the destroyed state.

However, while using the application, there are situations when its operation is not stopped but must be **temporarily interrupted**. Such a situation may occur, for example, when a phone call is received during app usage. The application enters a **sleep state**. Good examples include games, listening to music, or watching a video on a mobile device. In such cases, additional lifecycle methods help ensure the application continues to function properly without disruption. Before discussing these methods, let's analyze the activity lifecycle diagram shown below.

Launching an activity triggers the **onCreate()** method. When the activity (and primarily the application) begins to operate, but is not necessarily visible in the foreground, the **onStart()** method is called. Once the application is visible in the foreground, the **onResume()** method begins to work.

When the user closes the application, several methods ensure the process completes correctly. The first is **onPause(),** which is triggered when the app disappears from the foreground – for example, when the user answers a phone call or opens another app. If the app is resumed, the **onResume()** method is called again. However, if the user decides to close the app, the next method triggered is **onStop().**
At the end of the application's lifecycle, the **onDestroy()** method is called, which clears all resources reserved by the app.

If, for any reason, the user decides to resume the application and bring it back to the foreground, the **onRestart()** method is triggered. This method runs just before the app resumes, followed by another call to **onStart().**

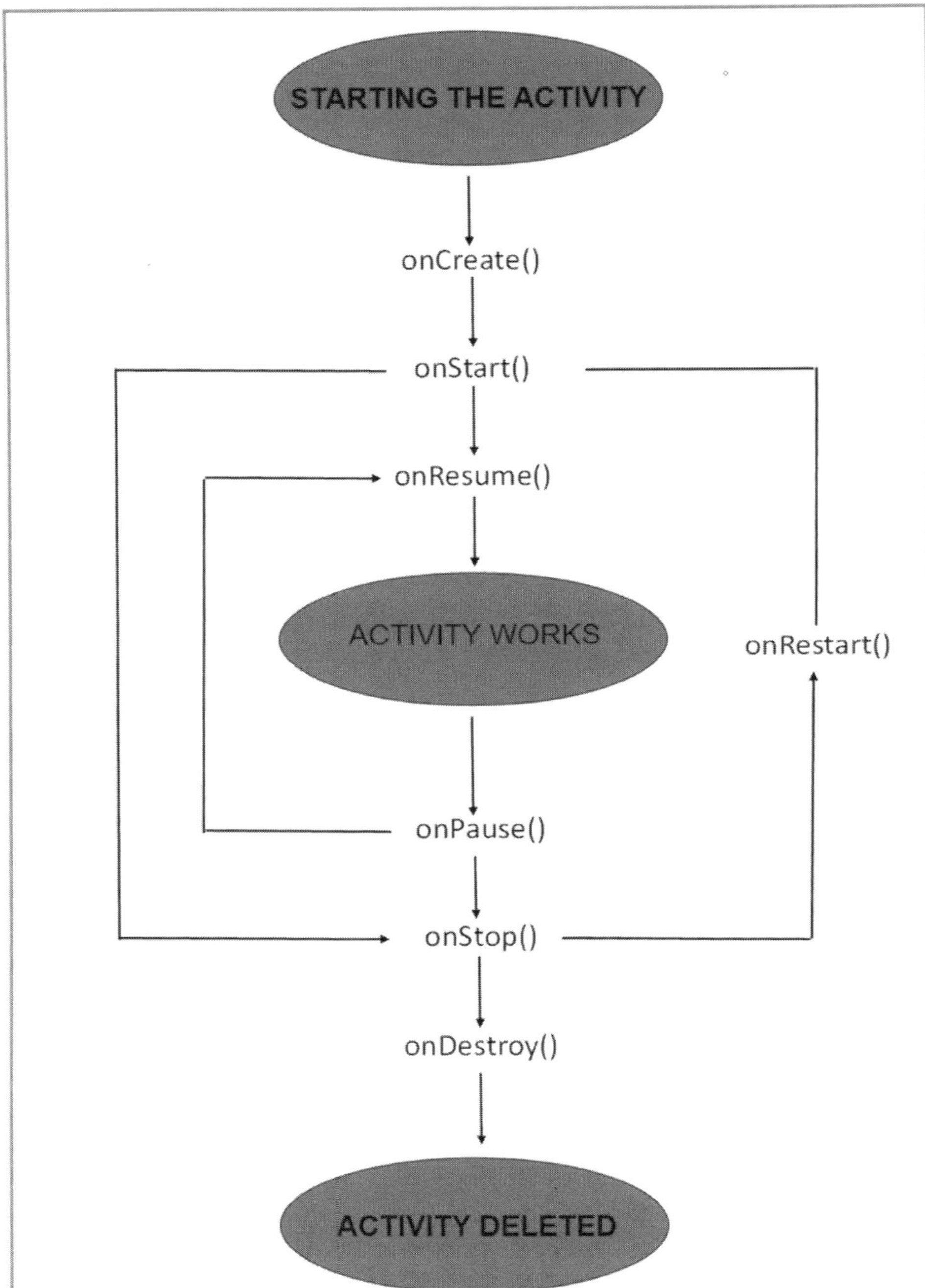

Figure 5.90 Activity Lifecycle Diagram

5.12 Fragments

For better organization and functionality of the application, the layout can be divided into smaller parts. A part of the **layout** is simply called a **fragment**. Fragments, like layouts, are defined in layout files with the ***.xml** extension.

To demonstrate how fragments work, let's prepare another application. The layout of the application will be divided into **three parts**, so we will create **three layout files and three new activities** with the following names: **fragment_1.xml, fragment_2.xml, fragment_3.xml, Fragment1.java, Fragm ent2.java, Fragment3.java.**

We'll start by adding **fragments** to the project. Open the project tree located on the left side of the **Android Studio window**. Expand it and right - click on the **layout** folder located inside the **res directory**.

Create a **new fragment: New → Fragment → Fragment (Blank)** In the fragment creation window, enter the name **Fragment1** and confirm by clicking **Finish**. In the Java files (in the project tree), a **new class Fragment1.java** will appear, and in the layout resources folder, a new layout file named **fragment_1.xml** will be created.

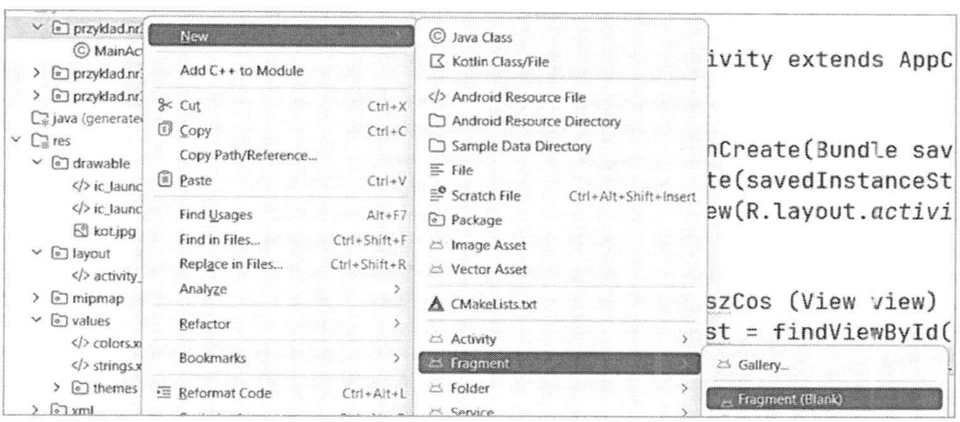

Figure 5.91 Creating a New Fragment

Repeat the operation **three times** to create **fragments named Fragment1, Fragment2, and Fragment3.** The added files will be visible in the project tree. The application code is located in the folder named **Application6.**

We will start by defining **Fragment1**, beginning with its **layout** file. A fragment is physically a part of an **activity**, so it can be defined similarly to an activity – for example, by assigning it the same types of **layouts** and attributes used in activities. The first fragment will be defined using a **LinearLayout** containing a text view with the message: **"I am the first fragment",** and a button labeled **"Fragment1".** To distinguish this fragment from the others, we will also give it a **green background**.

The second fragment will use a **FrameLayout** and will contain an image with white text saying: **"I am the second fragment".** The background color of this fragment will be **blue**.

The third fragment will be defined using a **RelativeLayout**. It will contain a **TextView** with the message: **"It's me, Fragment no. 3"** and a **yellow background.** The text will be centered both **vertically and horizontally** within the layout.

The code for all fragments will look as follows: File: fragment_1.xml

```
<?xml version="1.0" encoding="utf-8"?>
<LinearLayout

xmlns:android="http://schemas.android.com/apk/res/android"
    xmlns:tools="http://schemas.android.com/tools"
    android:layout_width="match_parent"
    android:layout_height="match_parent"
    android:background="@color/green"
    android:orientation="vertical"
    tools:context=".Fragment1">
    <TextView
        android:layout_width="wrap_content"
        android:layout_height="wrap_content"
        android:text="I'm the first fragment"/>
    <Button
        android:layout_width="wrap_content"
        android:layout_height="wrap_content"
        android:text="Fragment1"/>
</LinearLayout>
```

Listing 5.128 Layout file of the first fragment

File: fragment_2.xml

```
<?xml version="1.0" encoding="utf-8"?>
<FrameLayout
xmlns:android="http://schemas.android.com/apk/res/android"
    xmlns:tools="http://schemas.android.com/tools"
    android:layout_width="match_parent"
    android:layout_height="match_parent"
    android:background="@color/blue"
    tools:context=".Fragment2">
    <ImageView
        android:layout_width="150dp"
        android:layout_height="350dp"
        android:layout_marginLeft="25dp"
        android:src="@drawable/pic12" />
    <TextView
        android:layout_width="wrap_content"
        android:layout_height="wrap_content"
        android:text="I'm the second fragment"/>
</FrameLayout>
```

Listing 5.129 Layout file of the second fragment

File: fragment_3.xml

```
<?xml version="1.0" encoding="utf-8"?>
<RelativeLayout

xmlns:android="http://schemas.android.com/apk/res/android"
    xmlns:tools="http://schemas.android.com/tools"
    android:layout_width="match_parent"
    android:layout_height="match_parent"
    android:background="@color/yellow"
    tools:context=".Fragment3">
    <TextView
        android:layout_width="wrap_content"
        android:layout_height="wrap_content"
        android:layout_centerInParent="true"
        android:text="This is fragment number 3"/>
</RelativeLayout>
```

Listing 5.130 Layout file of the third fragment

The next task is to edit the activity files so that our classes become fragment handling classes.The code for the **Fragment1.java** file will look as follows:

```
package example.app26;
import android.os.Bundle;
import androidx.fragment.app.Fragment;
import android.view.LayoutInflater;
import android.view.View;
import android.view.ViewGroup;

public class Fragment1 extends Fragment {
    @Override
 public View onCreateView(LayoutInflater inflater,
ViewGroup container, Bundle savedInstanceState) {
return inflater.inflate(R.layout.fragment_1, container,
false);
    }
}
```

Listing 5.131 Activity file for the first fragment

First, we need to import the necessary **classes for this fragment**. Next, we create the **Fragment1 class**, which will inherit from the **built - in Fragment** class.

The **onCreateView** method is triggered when the fragment appears on the screen It contains three parameters:

- **Inflater** – places the appropriate layout within the fragment;
- **Container** – the parent component that connects all controls used in the fragment;
- **savedInstanceState** – responsible for restoring the previous state of the fragment.

In the first parameter of the **inflate method**, we specify the layout file that should be used for our fragment. That's why the **fragment_1 file** is included in this code. The other fragment files **(Fragment2.java and Fragment3.java)** will have similar initial code and will look as follows:

```
package example.app26;
import android.os.Bundle;
import androidx.fragment.app.Fragment;
import android.view.LayoutInflater;
import android.view.View;
import android.view.ViewGroup;

public class Fragment2 extends Fragment {
    @Override
    public View onCreateView(LayoutInflater inflater,
ViewGroup container, Bundle savedInstanceState) {
 return inflater.inflate(R.layout.fragment_2, container,
false);
    }
}
```

Listing 5.132 Activity file for the second fragment

Fragment3.java

```
package example.app26;

import android.os.Bundle;
import androidx.fragment.app.Fragment;
import android.view.LayoutInflater;
import android.view.View;
import android.view.ViewGroup;

public class Fragment3 extends Fragment {
    @Override
    public View onCreateView(LayoutInflater inflater,
ViewGroup container, Bundle savedInstanceState) {
        return inflater.inflate(R.layout.fragment_3,
container, false);
    }
}
```

Listing 5.133 Activity file for the third fragment

Now we need to combine our **fragments** into a complete layout. To do this, we will edit the main layout file: **activity_main.xml.** We want our **fragments** to be arranged as shown in the illustration below. The best approach is to use a nested **LinearLayout**. The activity code will look like this:

```
<?xml version="1.0" encoding="utf-8"?>
<LinearLayout

xmlns:android="http://schemas.android.com/apk/res/android"
    android:layout_width="match_parent"
    android:layout_height="match_parent"
    android:orientation="vertical">
    <LinearLayout
        android:layout_width="wrap_content"
        android:layout_height="wrap_content"
        android:orientation="horizontal">
        <fragment
            android:id="@+id/fragment1"
            android:name="example.app26.Fragment1"
            android:layout_width="match_parent"
            android:layout_height="match_parent"/>
        <fragment
            android:id="@+id/fragment2"
            android:name="example.app26.Fragment2"
            android:layout_width="280dp"
            android:layout_height="wrap_content"/>
    </LinearLayout>
    <fragment
        android:id="@+id/fragment3"
        android:name="example.app26.Fragment3"
        android:layout_width="match_parent"
        android:layout_height="match_parent"/>
</LinearLayout>
```

Listing 5.134 Activity_main.xml file with embedded fragments

After launching, the application will resemble the one shown in the illustration below.

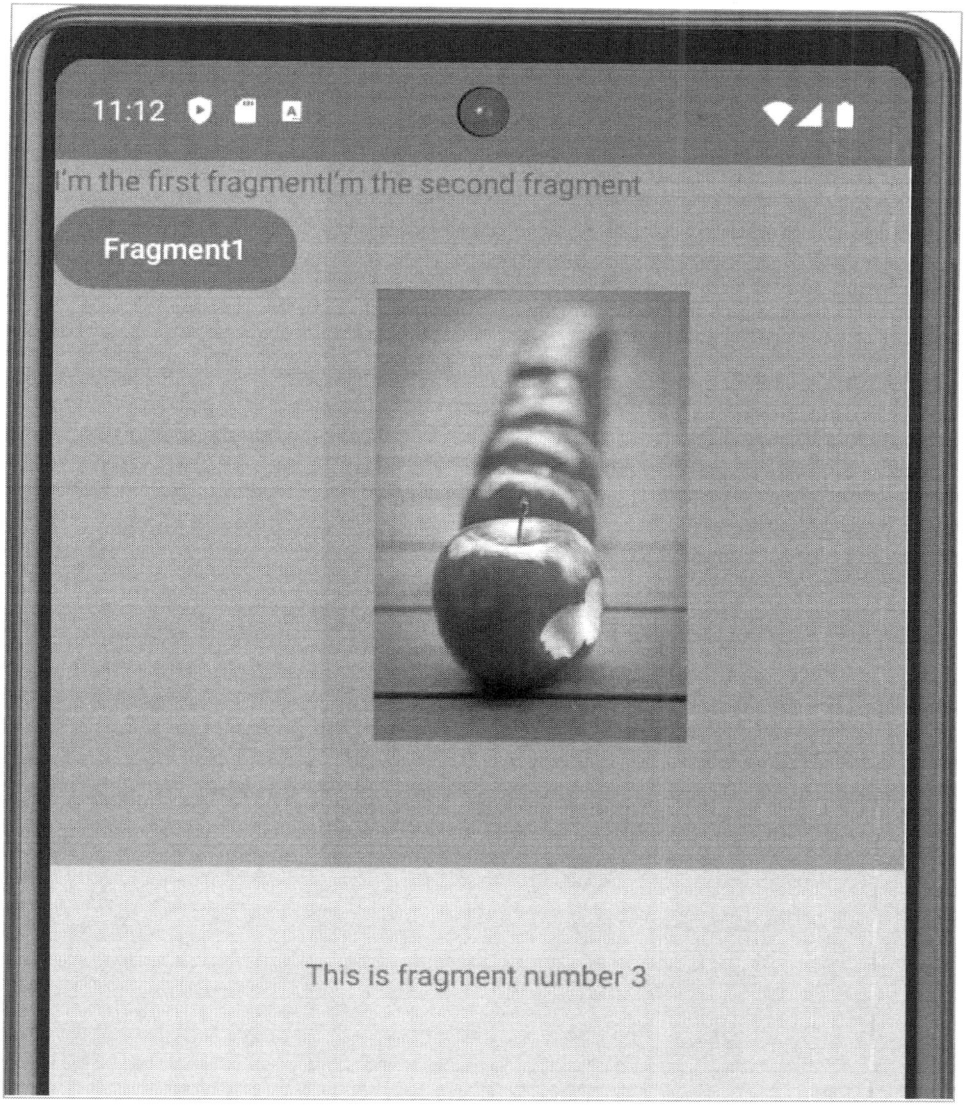

Figure 5.92 Application using three fragments

5.13 Notifications

Notifications in a mobile app are short messages delivered by the system to the user. A notification can be, for example, an alert about a **received email or a calendar reminder.** A small window with the message appears on the screen, and an icon pops up in the status bar.

The application code is located in a folder named **Application27**. To create a simple notification, we'll start by preparing the layout file. We'll place a **Button** that will trigger the notification, and **two TextView elements.** The first will display the message: **"Are notifications enabled?"** The second will display the answer: **yes** or **no**.

This behaviour is due to changes introduced in **API level 34**, which aim to give users more control over blocking unwanted notifications. Before the app can display a notification, the user must grant permission. If permission is granted, the notification will appear automatically.

The layout code will look as follows:

```
<?xml version="1.0" encoding="utf-8"?>
<androidx.appcompat.widget.LinearLayoutCompat

xmlns:android="http://schemas.android.com/apk/res/android"
    xmlns:tools="http://schemas.android.com/tools"
    android:layout_width="match_parent"
    android:layout_height="match_parent"
    android:orientation="vertical"
    android:padding="16dp"
    tools:context=".MainActivity">

    <Button
        android:id="@+id/przycisk1"
        android:layout_width="wrap_content"
        android:layout_height="wrap_content"
        android:layout_gravity="center"
        android:text="Show  the notification"
        android:onClick="start"/>
    <LinearLayout
        android:layout_width="match_parent"
        android:layout_height="match_parent"
        android:orientation="horizontal"
        android:padding="8dp">
    <TextView
        android:layout_width="wrap_content"
        android:layout_height="wrap_content"
        android:layout_weight="1"
        android:gravity="center"
        android:text="Is the notification on?" />
    <TextView
        android:id="@+id/text1"
        android:layout_width="wrap_content"
        android:layout_height="wrap_content"
        android:layout_weight="1"
        android:gravity="center"
        tools:text="YES" />

    </LinearLayout>
</androidx.appcompat.widget.LinearLayoutCompat>
```

Listing 5.135 Activity_main.xml layout file

Now we'll move on to the **activity** file. We'll begin creating the **notification** by **declaring the necessary variables**.

```
private static final String CHANNEL_ID = "channel_01";
private static ActivityResultLauncher<String>
requestPermissionsLauncher;
private NotificationManager notificationManager;
```

Listing 5.136 Variable declaration

The **first** variable, **CHANNEL_ID**, creates the ID for the notification channel. The **second** variable will store information about whether the user has granted permission to display notifications. The **third** variable creates the notification manager. The next step is to complete the **onCreate** method.

```
notificationManager =
getSystemService(NotificationManager.class);

requestPermissionsLauncher = registerForActivityResult(new
ActivityResultContracts.RequestPermission(), isGranted -> {
    refreshUI();
    if (isGranted) sendNotification();
});
```

Listing 5.137 Code to complete the onCreate method and initialize the notification manager

We create a **new object** that checks whether notifications are enabled. A **conditional statement** will verify if permission has been granted. If so, the **sendNotification** method will be triggered – its task is to launch the notification. We'll discuss the definition of this method shortly.

```
createNotificationChannel();
refreshUI();
```

Listing 5.138 Calling the method that creates the notification channel

We create a notification channel and use the **refreshUI** method to display a message indicating whether the user has granted permission for notifications.

```
public void uruchom(View view){
    if (ActivityCompat.checkSelfPermission(this,
android.Manifest.permission.POST_NOTIFICATIONS) !=
PackageManager.PERMISSION_GRANTED) {

requestPermissionsLauncher.launch(android.Manifest.permi
ssion.POST_NOTIFICATIONS);
        return;
    }
    sendNotification();
}
```

Listing 5.139 Definition of the run Method

The **run** method is triggered when the **Button** is pressed. It checks whether the user has granted the necessary permission. If such permission is granted, a notification will be triggered. Another method will then create the **notification channel.**

```
private void createNotificationChannel() {
 CharSequence name = "notification_channel";
 String description =
"notification_channel_description";
 int importance =
NotificationManager.IMPORTANCE_DEFAULT;
NotificationChannel channel = new
NotificationChannel(CHANNEL_ID, name, importance);
    channel.setDescription(description);

notificationManager.createNotificationChannel(channel);
}
```

Listing 5.140 Definition of the Method Creating a Notification Channel

CharSequence name assigns a **name to the channel**, which is necessary for its creation. The **importance** variable sets the **priority** level of the channel, determining its significance when multiple channels exist within the same application.

An object of the **NotificationChannel** class, for example named **channel**, creates the notification channel. It uses parameters defined earlier in the code: the **channel ID, name,** and **description**. Finally, the channel is activated using the notification manager **notificationManager**.

```
private void refreshUI() {
TextView textView = findViewById(R.id.tekst1);

textView.setText(notificationManager.areNotificationsEna
bled() ? "TAK" : "NIE");
}
```

Listing 5.141 Declaration of the refreshUI Method

The **refreshUI** method is responsible for displaying either **YES** or **NO** depending on whether the user has granted permission for notifications. The response will be shown in a **TextView**, for which a reference will be obtained. If the application does not have the required permissions, it will prompt the user to grant them.

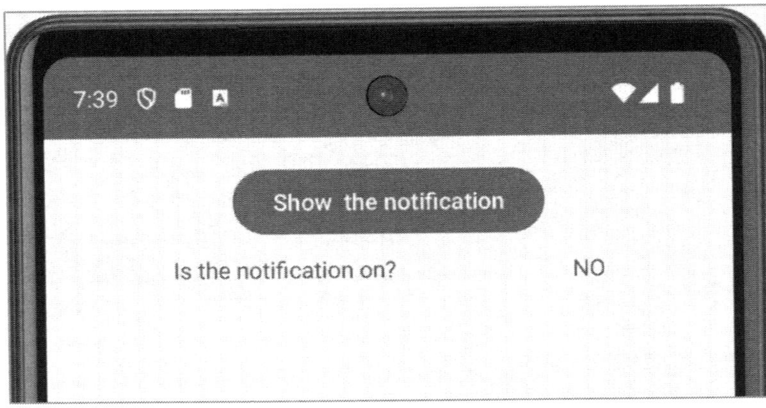

Figure 5.93 The application after launching

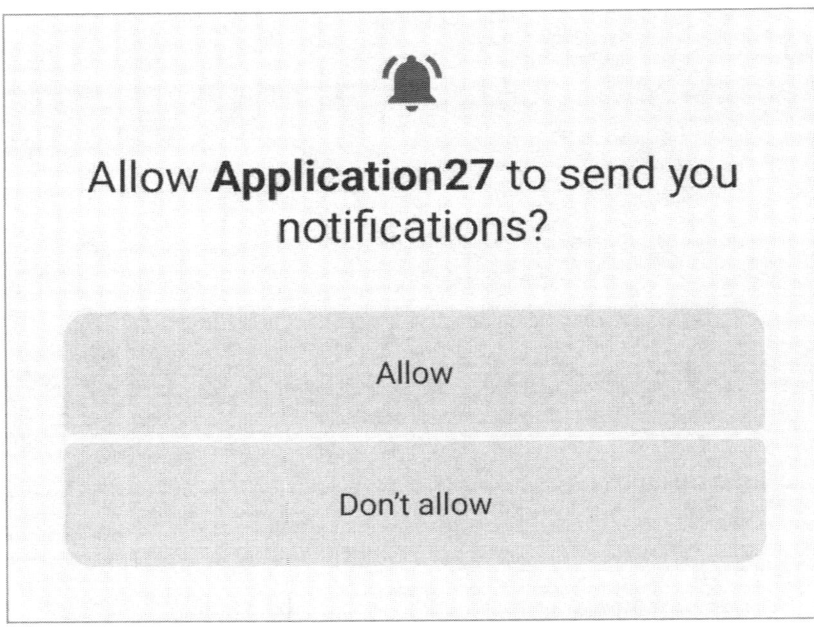

Figure 5.94 Android asks the user whether they consent to enabling notifications.

```
private void sendNotification() {
NotificationCompat.Builder builder = new
NotificationCompat.Builder(this, CHANNEL_ID)
.setSmallIcon(R.drawable.ic_launcher_foreground)
.setContentTitle("Powiadomienie")
.setContentText("Udało Ci się utworzyć
powiadomienie.")
.setPriority(NotificationCompat.PRIORITY_DEFAULT)
;
notificationManager.notify(1, builder.build());
}
```

Listing 5.142 Creating a Simple Notification

The final class, **sendNotification**, will create a notification. To build the notification, we'll use the **NotificationCompat.Builder** class. We'll need two parameters: the **first** is the so - called context, with the value **this**. The second parameter is **CHANNEL_ID**, which is the unique ID of the channel created earlier.

Just like any view, notifications should include some basic settings. These are:

- A small icon displayed at the top of the app – **setSmallIcon**;
- The notification title – **setContentTitle**;
- The notification content – **setContentText**.

All these elements are included in the sample code shown in the listing above.

Another setting presented is the so - called **notification priority**. It indicates how important the notification is compared to others. There are seven levels of priority, each assigned a numerical value representing its importance:

- IMPORTANCE_MAX - 5;
- IMPORTANCE_HIGH - 4 ;
- IMPORTANCE_DEFAULT - 3 ;
- IMPORTANCE_LOW - 2 ;
- IMPORTANCE_MIN - 1 ;
- IMPORTANCE_NONE – 0;
- IMPORTANCE_UNSPECIFIED - 1000.

There are many more notification settings available. However, this example covers only the mandatory ones. The last line of the sample code:

```
notificationManager.notify(NOTIFICATION_ID,builder.build
());
```

Listing 5.143 Launching the Notification in an Activity

This step triggers the previously created notification. The parameter **NOTIFICATION_ID** is a unique **ID** assigned to the notification. The **second** parameter is an object of the **NotificationCompat** class, created earlier. As you can see, the last line of the code is highlighted in red and reports an error.

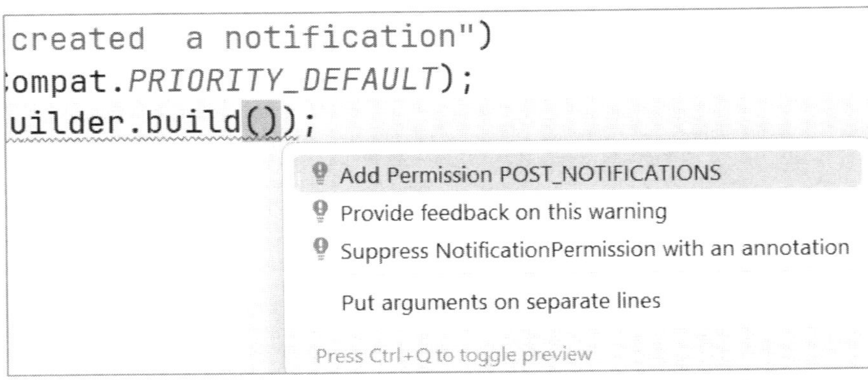

Figure 5.95 Application Error and Suggested Solution

This happens because the app must include permission to send notifications in the **manifest** file. If you click on the underlined part of the code and select the option **"Add Permission POST_NOTIFICATION",** the program will automatically add the appropriate entry to the manifest file. After launching, the application looks as follows:

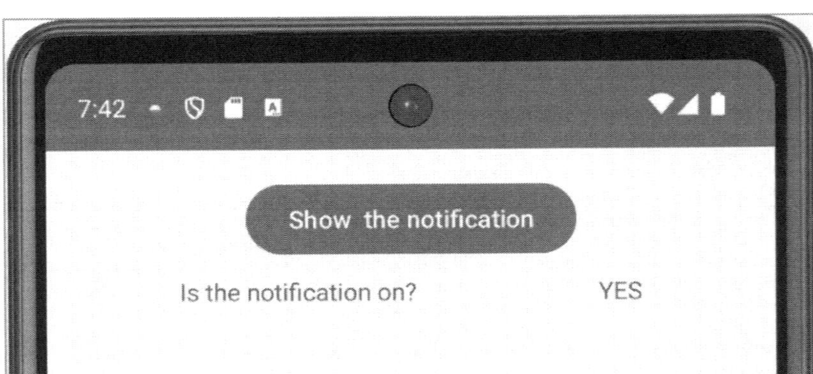

Figure 5.96 The application after the user grants permission to launch notifications

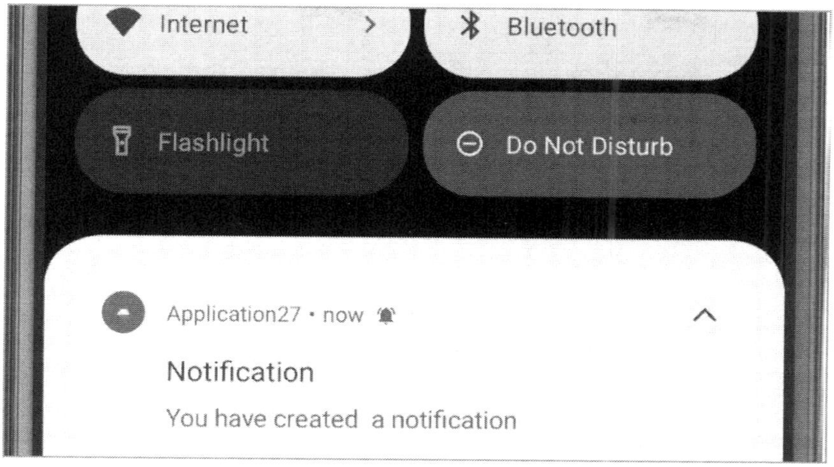

Figure 5.97 The notification window launched

5.14 Dialog Windows

Dialog windows are used for communication between the application and the user. These are simple pop - up windows that appear during the operation of the app.

5.14.1 Information Window

The application code is located in the folder **Application28**. In the next example, we create a simple **button**. In the activity file, we place the following code:

```
package example.app28;

import androidx.appcompat.app.AppCompatActivity;
import android.app.AlertDialog;
import android.os.Bundle;
import android.view.View;
public class MainActivity extends AppCompatActivity {

    @Override
    protected void onCreate(Bundle savedInstanceState) {
        super.onCreate(savedInstanceState);
        setContentView(R.layout.activity_main);
    }
    public void dialog1(View view) {
        AlertDialog.Builder dialogBuilder = new
AlertDialog.Builder(this);
  dialogBuilder.setTitle("Information window");
  dialogBuilder.setMessage("The application is launched");
        AlertDialog announcement = dialogBuilder.create();
        announcement.show();
    }
}
```

Listing 5.144 Activity File with Code Creating a Dialog Window

In the **onClick** method, we create an object of the **AlertDialog** class.

```
AlertDialog.Builder dialogBuilder = new
AlertDialog.Builder(this);
```

Listing 5.145 Creating a New Dialog Object

Using the **setTitle** method, we assign, a title to the dialog window, and with **setMessage,** we define the message to be displayed.

```
dialogBuilder.setTitle("Information window");
dialogBuilder.setMessage("The application is launched");
```

Listing 5.146 Setting Up the Dialog Window

We create an **object** named **message**, and then display it using the **show method**.

```
AlertDialog announcement = dialogBuilder.create();
announcement.show();
```

Listing 5.147 Launching the Dialog Window

The application window will look as shown below:

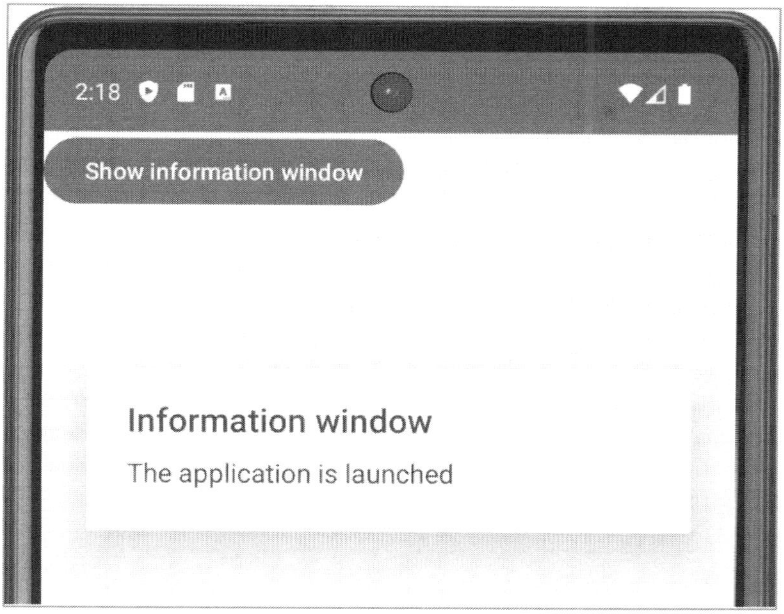

Figure 5.98 Application with an Active Information Dialog Window

5.14.2 Information Dialog Reacting to User Interaction

The application code is located in the folder named **Application28a.**

In the previous example, we launched a simple information dialog, but it didn't allow the user to respond. The next example will show how to handle user **interaction**. The application will consist of a **simple layout with one button and a TextView field**. **When the button is pressed**, a dialog window will appear. This dialog will contain a **message** and **two buttons** for the user: **Yes** and **No**. After selecting either button, a corresponding message will be displayed in the application window, and the dialog will close.

The activity code will look like the listing below:

```
package example.app28a;

import androidx.appcompat.app.AppCompatActivity;
import android.app.AlertDialog;
import android.os.Bundle;
import android.view.View;
import android.widget.TextView;

public class MainActivity extends AppCompatActivity {

    @Override
    protected void onCreate(Bundle savedInstanceState) {
        super.onCreate(savedInstanceState);
        setContentView(R.layout.activity_main);
    }
public void dialog1(View view) {
AlertDialog.Builder dialogBuilder = new
AlertDialog.Builder(this);
 dialogBuilder.setTitle("I will ask you a question");
 dialogBuilder.setMessage("Are you in a good mood today?");
dialogBuilder.setCancelable(false);
dialogBuilder.setPositiveButton("Yes", (dialog, which) -> {
      TextView text = findViewById(R.id.info);
      String text2 = "You have chosen yes";
      text.setText(text2);
        });
 dialogBuilder.setNegativeButton("No", (dialog, which) -> {
            TextView text = findViewById(R.id.info);
            String text2 = "You have chosen no";
            text.setText(text2);
        });
        AlertDialog dialog = dialogBuilder.create();
        dialog.show();
    }
}
```

Listing 5.148 Activity Code with a Dialog Window Awaiting User Response

What happens in the code? We've extended the code from the previous application by adding methods that respond to the user pressing specific buttons. These methods are:

- **dialogBuilder.setPositiveButton** – responds when the answer is positive;
- **dialogBuilder.setNegativeButton** – responds when the answer is negative.

```
dialogBuilder.setPositiveButton("Yes", (dialog, which) -> {
    TextView text = findViewById(R.id.info);
    String text2 = "You have chosen yes";
    text.setText(text2);
});
```

Listing 5.149 Definition of the onClick Class Triggered by User Interaction

Both methods have **two parameters**. The **first** is a string **that defines the text** displayed on the button – in this case, **Yes** and **No**. The **second** parameter is an **OnClickListener** object.

Inside each method, there is another method called **onClick**, which is executed exactly when the user presses a response button. In these functions, a **reference to the TextView** from the layout file is retrieved, and then it is updated with the appropriate message depending on which button was clicked.

The application will look similar to the one shown in the illustration below:

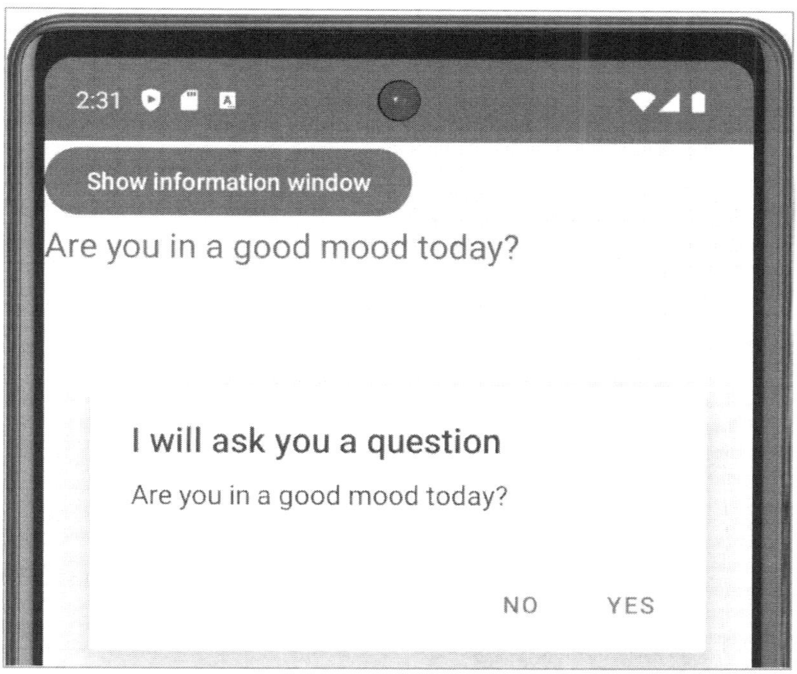

Figure 5.99 Information Dialog Requiring User Interaction

5.15 Animations

5.15.1 Frame - by - Frame Animation

The application code is located in a folder named **Application29**. **Android Studio** allows you to create a simple animation consisting of several images. The program switches images one after another at a specified time interval, creating an animation effect.

We'll start building the application by preparing the images. There will be seven **.png files**. Each one will contain the word **ANDROID**. The background of the images will be black, and the original color of the letters will be white. In each image, a single letter will be displayed in a different color.

The illustration shows the graphics needed to create the animation.

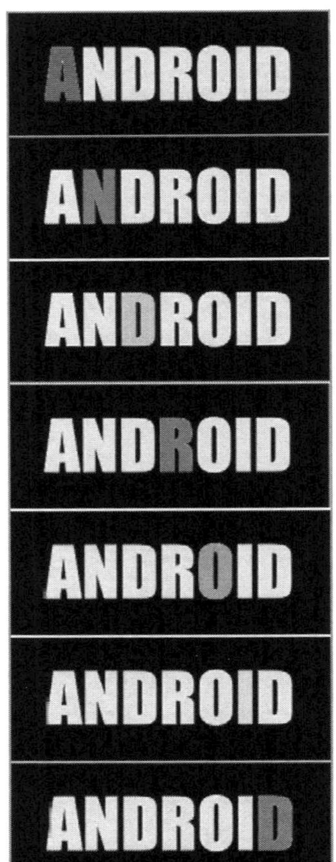

Figure 5.100 Animation Frames

The prepared images are placed in the **drawable** directory.The next step is to prepare the **layout file**. The only element we'll include there is an **ImageView widget**. You don't need to reference a specific image file in the layout code – all of that will be handled in the **MainActivity.java** file.

For this application, we'll also need a file to manage the animation. We'll create it in the **drawable directory**. To do this, **right - click on** the drawable folder in the **project tree,** select New from the dropdown menu, and then choose **Drawable Resource File**.Name the new file animation. A new **XML** file will appear in the project tree.

We'll then fill this file with the following code:

```
<animation-list
    xmlns:android="http://schemas.android.com/apk/res/android"
    android:oneshot="false">
<item android:drawable="@drawable/p1"android:duration="250" />
<item android:drawable="@drawable/p2"android:duration="250" />
<item android:drawable="@drawable/p3"android:duration="250" />
<item android:drawable="@drawable/p4"android:duration="250" />
<item android:drawable="@drawable/p5"android:duration="250" />
<item android:drawable="@drawable/p6"android:duration="250" />
<item android:drawable="@drawable/p7"android:duration="250" />
</animation-list>
```

Listing 5.150 Animation.xml file

The attribute **android:oneshot** is set to **false**, which means the animation will loop endlessly. Changing the value to true will cause the animation to play **only once**.

Each **item** tag contains two pieces of information: A reference to an image in the **drawable** directory; The **android:duration** attribute, which defines the duration of each frame in milliseconds. In our application, this means each image will be displayed for **250 ms, or ¼ of a second.** The last step is to complete the code in the **MainActivity.java** file.

```
package example.app29;

import androidx.appcompat.app.AppCompatActivity;
import android.graphics.drawable.AnimationDrawable;
import android.os.Bundle;
import android.widget.ImageView;

public class MainActivity extends AppCompatActivity {
    @Override
    protected void onCreate(Bundle savedInstanceState) {
        super.onCreate(savedInstanceState);
        setContentView(R.layout.activity_main);
        ImageView imageView = findViewById(R.id.pic);

imageView.setBackgroundResource(R.drawable.animation);
AnimationDrawable anim = (AnimationDrawable)
imageView.getBackground();
        anim.start();
    }
}
```

Listing 5.151 Activity Code Launching Frame - by - Frame Animation

In the **onCreate** method, we create several objects. The first is an **ImageView** object, for which we create a **reference**. Next, we set it as the background of the **ImageView** component from the layout file. As the target resource, we specify the name of the animation file.

5.15.2 Animating Views

The application code is located in the folder named **Application30**. Android allows several graphical operations that can be performed on views. Animations can be applied in four areas using four tags:

- **alpha** – controls the fading of an element;
- **scale** – used to change the size of an element;
- **translate** – responsible for moving an element;
- **rotate** – used to trigger rotation.

Animation 1: The layout file will contain a **Button** and an **ImageView**. An image is placed in the drawable folder.

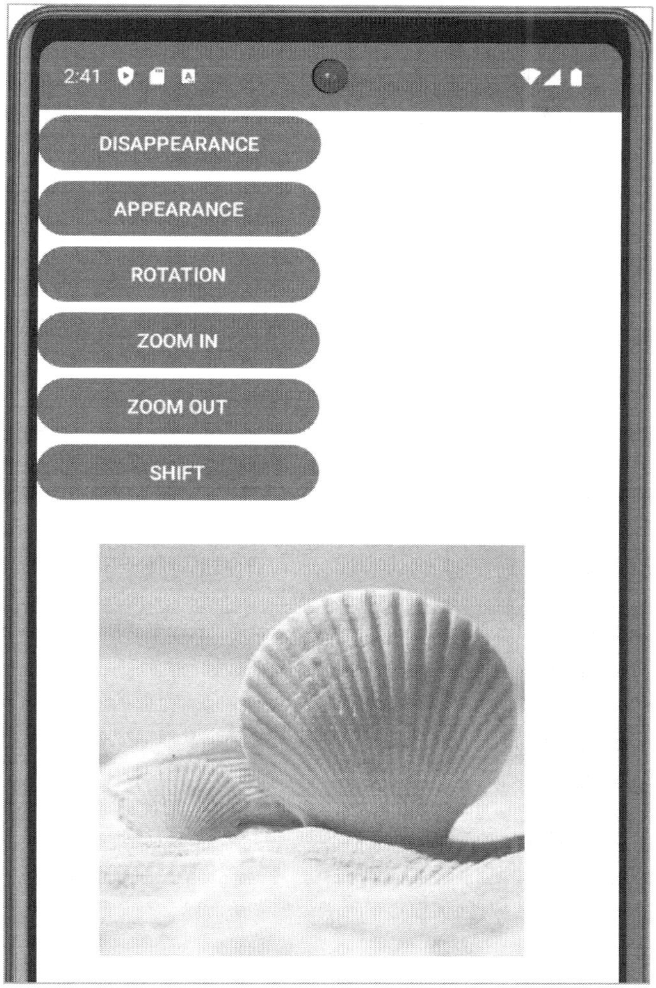

Figure 5.101 Application After Launch

Since the application will consist of several animations, we'll create a special directory named **anim.** This directory will be placed within the project tree.

To begin, position the cursor where the **res** folder is located. **Right - click** and select **New → Android Resource Directory**.

In the window that appears after clicking the button, enter the name of the directory. In the first field of the form, type **anim**, and in the next field, select the type of resource – also choose **anim**. Click **OK**, and the newly created directory will appear in the project tree.

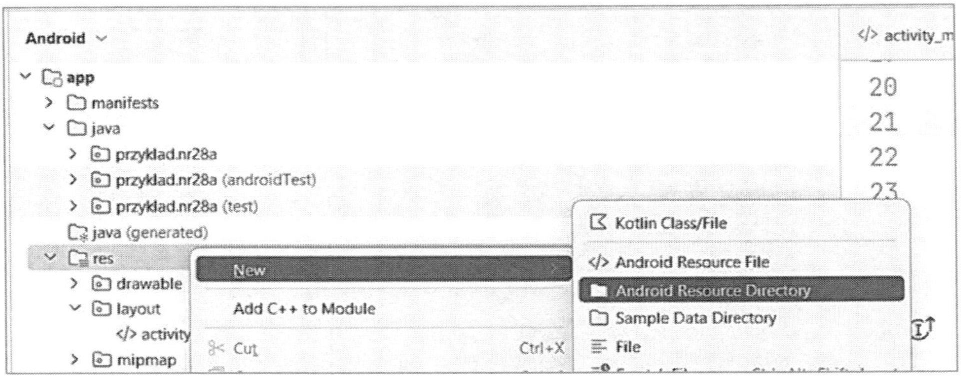

Figure 5.102 Creating a New Application Resource Folder

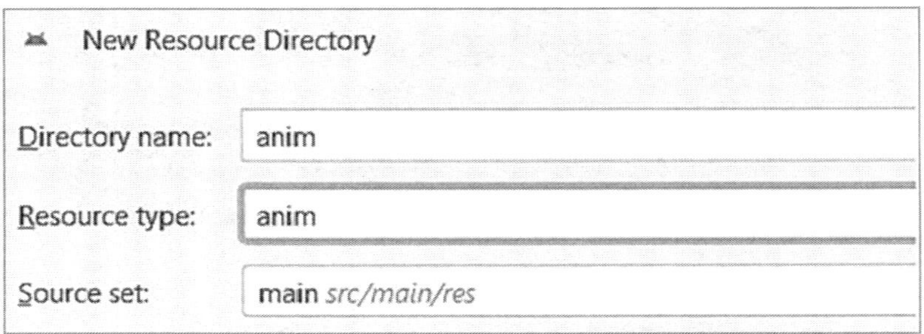

Figure 5.103 Creating the anim Folder

In the newly created **anim** directory, we create the first file named **animation1.xml**. Right - click on the folder, select **New**, and then choose **Animation Resource File**. In the dialog window, enter the file name: **animation1**. For the **Root element**, leave the default value as **set**.

After clicking **OK**, the newly created **XML** file will appear in the project tree.

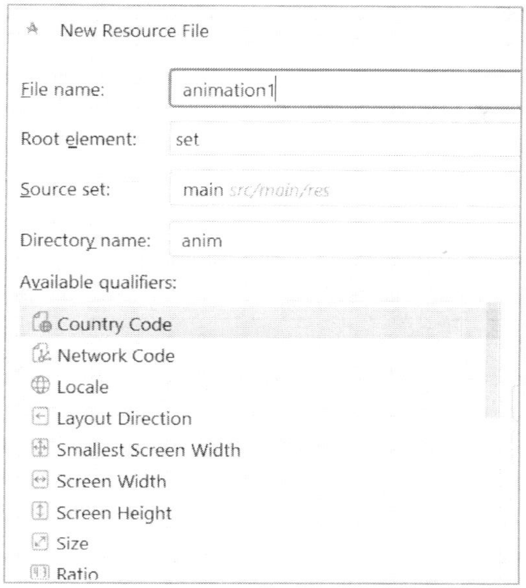

Figure 5.104 Creating the animation1.xml Resource File

Now we need to fill the file with the following code:

```
<set
xmlns:android="http://schemas.android.com/apk/res/android" >
    <alpha
        android:duration="5000"
        android:fromAlpha="1.0"
        android:toAlpha="0.0" />
</set>
```

Listing 5.152 animation1.xml File with Defined Animation Action

The **set** tag allows you to configure the following properties in the application. The **first animation** will cause the displayed image to **fade out**. This operation involves changing the **alpha channel** value over time, which is why the alpha tag appears in this part of the code.

The first attribute, **android:duration**, defines the total duration of the animation, expressed in milliseconds. In this example, the image will fade out over **5 seconds**.

The next **attribute**, android:**fromAlpha**, sets the initial alpha value, and **android:toAlpha** defines the value at which the animation ends. This animation will create the impression that the image is disappearing.

The next step is to edit the code in the **MainActivity.java** file. We'll define an **onClick** method that will be triggered when the button is pressed. Since we'll be programming additional actions beyond fading, we'll use the same name for the **onClick** attribute as the file name in the anim folder – in this case, **anim1**. The **anim1** class code will look like the listing below:

```
public void anim1(View view){
    Animation anim1= AnimationUtils.loadAnimation(this,
R.anim.animation1);
    ImageView pic = findViewById(R.id.picture);
    pic.startAnimation(anim1);
}
```

Listing 5.153 Launching the Animation in the Activity File

In the application, we'll use the **Animation** class. We create an **object** of this class named **anim1** and assign it the data loaded from the **fade** file located in the **anim** directory. Next, we create a **reference** to the image located in the **layout file**. We start the animation using the **startAnimation** method. When the application is launched and the **FADE** button is pressed, the image will gradually **disappear** from the screen.

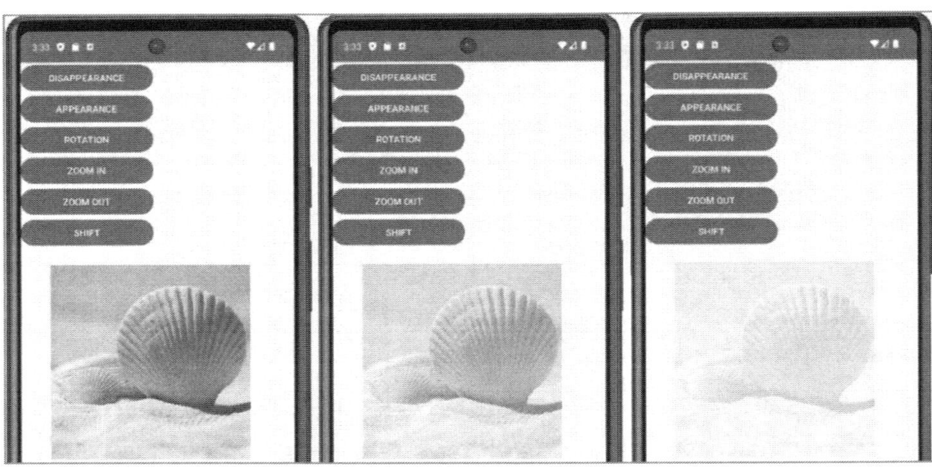

Figure 5.105 Fade - In Animation

Animation 2:

Let's add another animation to the application. This time, it will be an animation where the image appears gradually. The procedure is exactly the same as in the first example. We add a file named **animation2.xml** to the anim directory and fill it with code that performs the opposite effect of the previous example.

Next, we add another button to the **activity_main.xml layout** with the label **FADE IN**. We also need to define a class responsible for launching the animation. Clicking the button should cause the image to appear in the application. The class defined for the **FADE IN** button will look like the listing below:

```
public void anim2(View view){
    Animation  anim1= AnimationUtils.loadAnimation(this,
R.anim.animation2);
    ImageView pic = findViewById(R.id.picture);
    pic.startAnimation(anim1);
}
```

Listing 5.154 Code of the anim2 Method

The **animation2.xml** file will contain the following code:

```
<set
xmlns:android="http://schemas.android.com/apk/res/android" >
    <alpha
        android:duration="5000"
        android:fromAlpha="0.0"
        android:toAlpha="1.0" />
</set>
```

Listing 5.155 animation2.xml File with Defined Animation Action

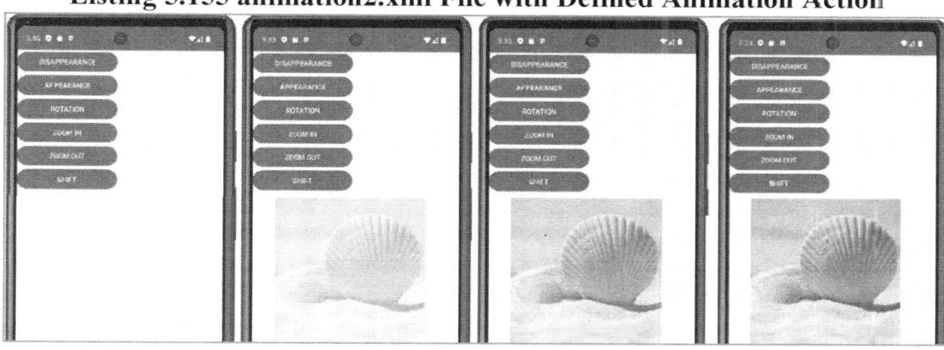

Figure 5.106 Fade - In Animation

Animation 3:

Now we'll define additional files in the **anim** directory. The **animation3**.xml file is shown in the listing below:

```
<set
xmlns:android="http://schemas.android.com/apk/res/android">
<rotate
    android:fromDegrees="0"
    android:toDegrees="360"
    android:duration="1000" >
</rotate>
</set>
```

Listing 5.156 animation3.xml File with Defined Animation Action

The code will rotate the image by **360 degrees**. It starts from **point 0**, which is set using the **android:fromDegrees attribute**. The number of degrees can be greater than **360** – any **multiple** will **result in more than one full rotation.** For example, if the android:**toDegrees** attribute is set to **720** (i.e., 2 × 360), the image will rotate twice.

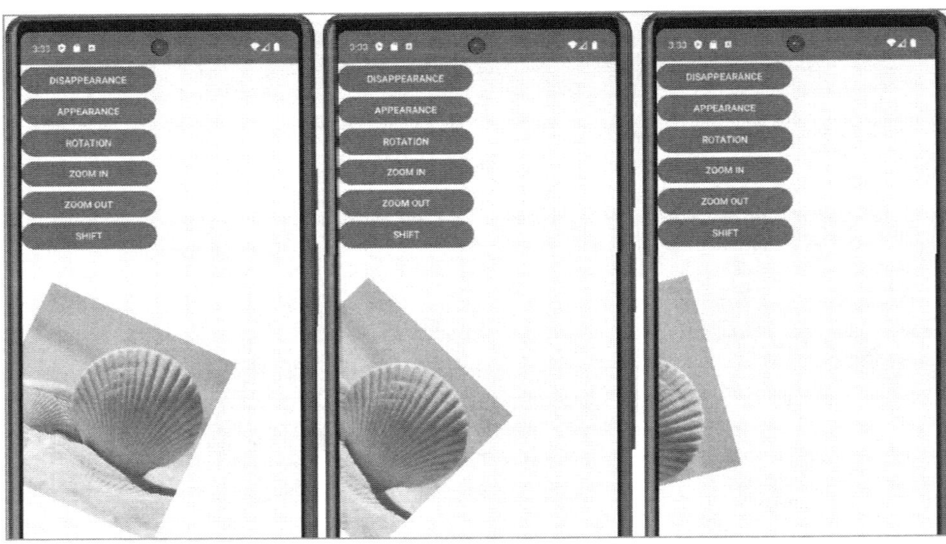

Figure 5.107 Rotation animation. Rotation axis set to the top - left corner

To change the rotation axis, we can use the attributes **ndroid:pivotX** and **android:pivotY**. The first attribute shifts the rotation axis horizontally, and the second one vertically. The unit to be used here is a percentage value. Using the notation **android:pivotX="50%"** will move the rotation axis to the center of the top edge.

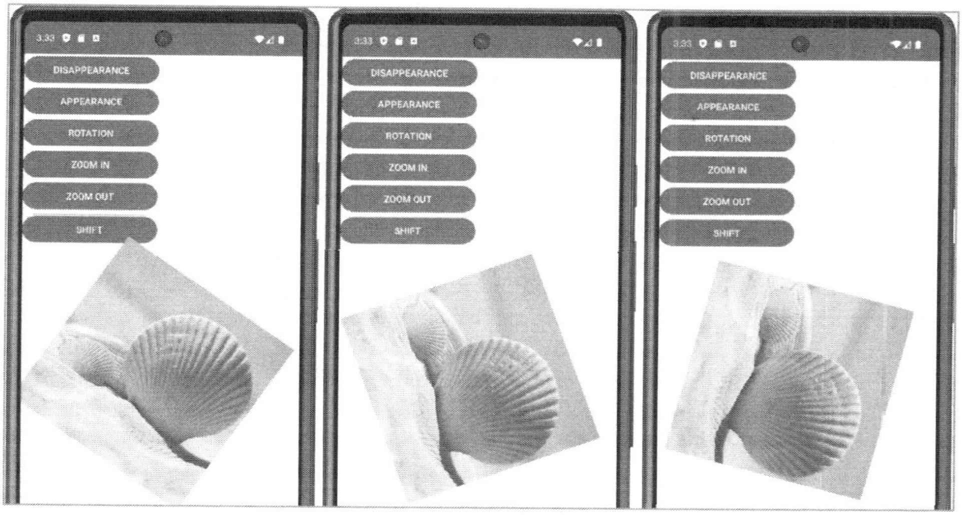

Figure 5.108 Rotation animation. Rotation axis set to the center of the image

Animation 4 i Animation 5:

The code for the file **animation4.xml** will look like this:

```
<set
xmlns:android="http://schemas.android.com/apk/res/android" >
    <scale
        android:duration="1000"
        android:fromXScale="0.5"
        android:fromYScale="0.5"
        android:toXScale="1"
        android:toYScale="1" >
    </scale>
</set>
```

Listing 5.157 The file animation4.xml with a defined animation action

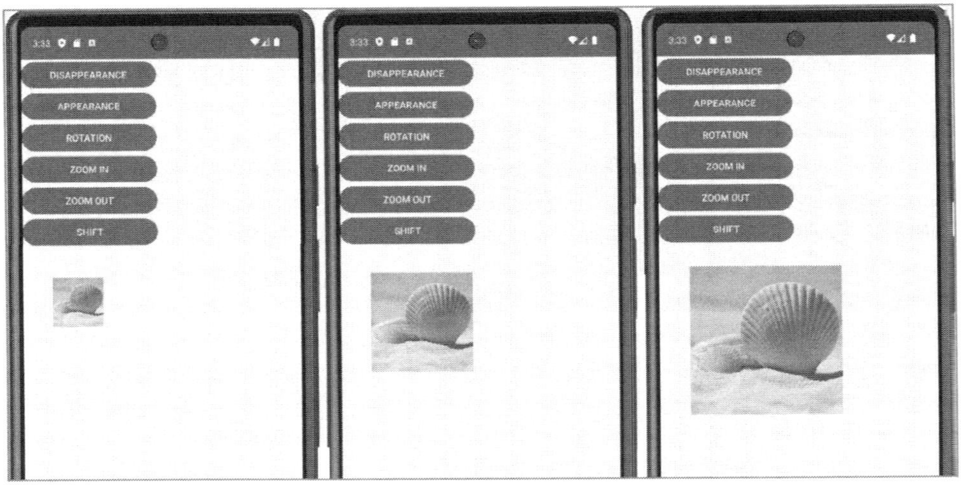

Figure 5.109 Zoom animation

The code for the file animation5.xml:

```
<set
xmlns:android="http://schemas.android.com/apk/res/android" >
    <scale
        android:duration="1000"
        android:fromXScale="1"
        android:fromYScale="1"
        android:toXScale="0.5"
        android:toYScale="0.5" >
    </scale>
</set>
```

Listing 5.158 The file animacja5.xml with a defined animation action

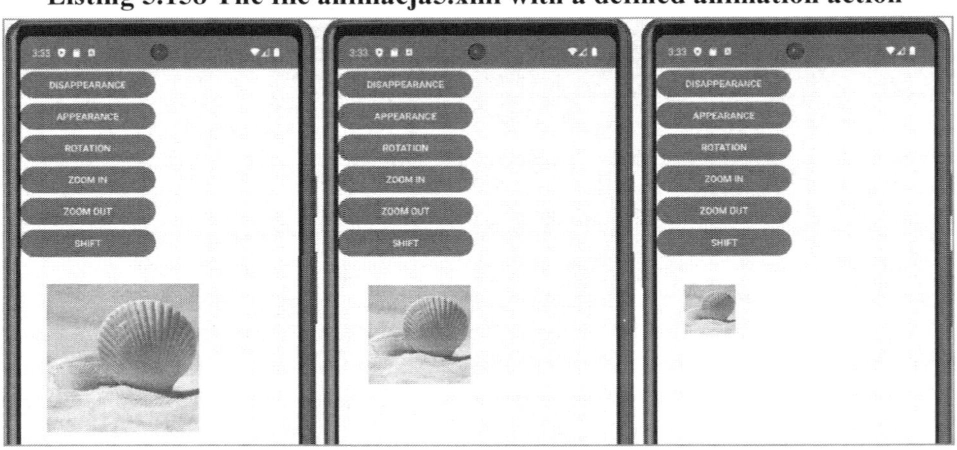

Figure 5.110 Shrink animation

New attributes appear here. The first one, **android:fromXScale**, defines the horizontal size of the image at the start of the animation. A value of **1.0** corresponds to **100%** of the original size, while **0.5** means **50%**. The attribute android:fromYScale works the same way, except it defines the vertical size of the image. The attributes **android:toXScale** and **android:toYScale** specify how large the image should be at the end of the animation.

Zoom in and zoom out operations start from the top - left corner of the image. If we want to move this point, we use the **pivot** attributes.

Animation 6 The code for the file animation6.xml will look like this:

```
<set
xmlns:android="http://schemas.android.com/apk/res/android" >
    <translate
        android:fromXDelta="0%"
        android:toXDelta="70%"
        android:fromYDelta="0%"
        android:toYDelta="70%"
        android:duration="1000" />
</set>
```

Listing 5.159 The file animation6.xml with a defined animation action

The attributes **fromXDelta** and **fromYDelta** specify what percentage of the image should be hidden at the moment the application starts. The first attribute refers to the **X** axis – the horizontal axis, while the second refers to the **Y** axis the vertical axis. These values are expressed as percentages. The next two attributes, **toYDelta** and **toXDelta**, define the point at which the animation will stop. In our application, the image will be shifted from **0%** both vertically and horizontally to **70%** of the image. The point where the movement begins is again the top - left corner.

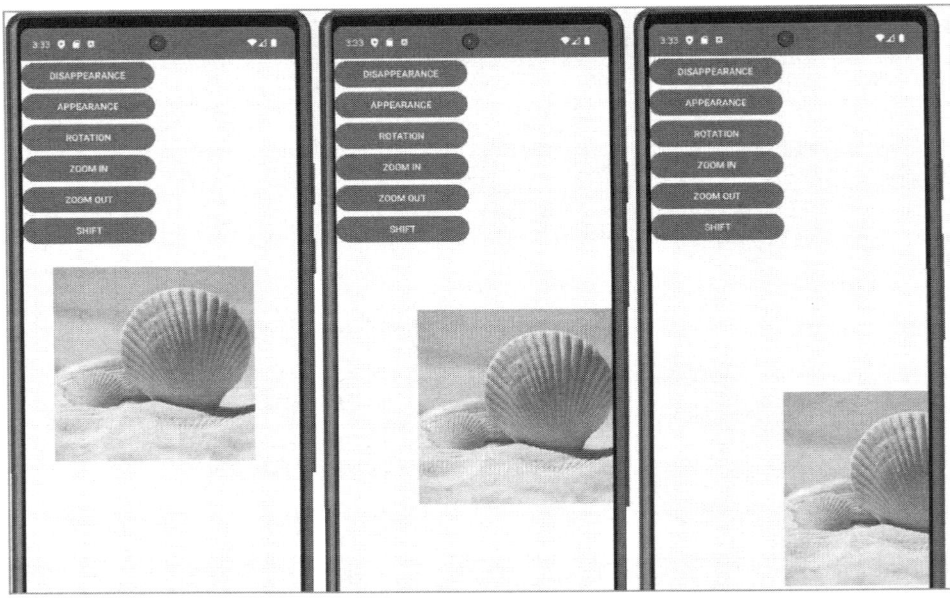

Figure 5.111 Translation Animation

Other important attributes that can be used when animating elements:

- **fillAfter** – This attribute can take two values: true and false. A value of true means that after the animation stops, the element will remain in its final position, and restarting the animation will begin from where it stopped. A value of false will return the element to its original position after the animation ends.
- **repeatCount** – Specifies the number of times the animation should repeat. If the parameter is set to - 1, the animation will repeat indefinitely.
- **repeatMode** – If the repeatCount attribute is set to a value other than zero (meaning the animation should repeat), the repeatMode parameter determines how the animation will be restarted.

This parameter can take the following values: Two values are available:

- **restart** – the animation will start a new cycle from the beginning (this is the default value).
- **reverse** – the animation will play in reverse.

- **startOffset** – delay. This parameter specifies how much time should pass after the animation is triggered before it starts. The unit is time expressed in milliseconds.

Code of the activity activity_main.xml file:

```
<?xml version="1.0" encoding="utf-8"?>
<LinearLayout
xmlns:android="http://schemas.android.com/apk/res/android"
    android:layout_width="match_parent"
    android:layout_height="match_parent"
    android:orientation="vertical">
    <Button
        android:layout_width="200dp"
        android:layout_height="wrap_content"
        android:text="@string/anim1"
        android:id="@+id/anim1"
        android:onClick="anim1" />
    <Button
        android:layout_width="200dp"
        android:layout_height="wrap_content"
        android:text="@string/anim2"
        android:id="@+id/anim2"
        android:onClick="anim2"/>
    <Button
        android:layout_width="200dp"
        android:layout_height="wrap_content"
        android:text="@string/anim3"
        android:id="@+id/anim3"
        android:onClick="anim3"/>
    <Button
        android:layout_width="200dp"
        android:layout_height="wrap_content"
        android:text="@string/anim4"
        android:id="@+id/anim4"
        android:onClick="anim4"/>
    <Button
        android:layout_width="200dp"
        android:layout_height="wrap_content"
        android:text="@string/anim5"
        android:id="@+id/anim5"
        android:onClick="anim5"/>
    <Button
        android:layout_width="200dp"
        android:layout_height="wrap_content"
        android:text="@string/anim6"
        android:id="@+id/anim6"
        android:onClick="anim6" />
    <ImageView
        android:id="@+id/picture"
        android:layout_width="300dp"
        android:layout_height="300dp"
        android:scaleType="centerCrop"
        android:src="@drawable/pic1"
        android:layout_marginLeft="45dp"
        android:layout_marginTop="45dp"/>
</LinearLayout>
```

Listing 5.160 Application layout code

Main activity code: **MainActivity.java.**

```
package example.app30;
import androidx.appcompat.app.AppCompatActivity;

import android.os.Bundle;
import android.view.View;
import android.view.animation.Animation;
import android.view.animation.AnimationUtils;
import android.widget.ImageView;

public class MainActivity extends AppCompatActivity {
    @Override
    protected void onCreate(Bundle savedInstanceState) {
        super.onCreate(savedInstanceState);
        setContentView(R.layout.activity_main);
    }
    public void anim1(View view){
        Animation anim1= AnimationUtils.loadAnimation(this,
R.anim.animation1);
        ImageView pic = findViewById(R.id.picture);
        pic.startAnimation(anim1);
    }
    public void anim2(View view){
        Animation  anim1=
AnimationUtils.loadAnimation(this, R.anim.animation2);
        ImageView pic = findViewById(R.id.picture);
        pic.startAnimation(anim1);
    }
    public void anim3(View view){
        Animation  anim1=
AnimationUtils.loadAnimation(this, R.anim.animation3);
        ImageView pic = findViewById(R.id.picture);
        pic.startAnimation(anim1);
    }
    public void anim4(View view){
        Animation anim1= AnimationUtils.loadAnimation(this,
R.anim.animation4);
        ImageView pic = findViewById(R.id.picture);
        pic.startAnimation(anim1);
    }
    public void anim5(View view){
        Animation  anim1=
AnimationUtils.loadAnimation(this, R.anim.animation5);
        ImageView pic = findViewById(R.id.picture);
        pic.startAnimation(anim1);
    }
    public void anim6(View view){
Animation  anim1= AnimationUtils.loadAnimation(this,
R.anim.animation6);
        ImageView pic = findViewById(R.id.picture);
        pic.startAnimation(anim1);
    }
}
```

Listing 5.161 Activity code

The **strings.xml** file will also be needed.

```
<resources>
    <string name="app_name">Application30</string>
    <string name="anim1">DISAPPEARANCE</string>
    <string name="anim2">APPEARANCE</string>
    <string name="anim3">ROTATION</string>
    <string name="anim4">ZOOM IN</string>
    <string name="anim5">ZOOM OUT</string>
    <string name="anim6">SHIFT</string>
</resources>
```

Listing 5.162 strings.xml file

5.16 RecyclerView and CardView Containers

RecyclerView is a more advanced form of list view. It allows the creation of layouts using **CardView**. It takes the form of **scrollable cards** on which other views can be placed as a repeating group. Creating this type of view is more complex than a regular list, as it requires the developer to create a **custom adapter**. However, it offers a more visually appealing design and is easier and more convenient to edit.

You can find the application code in the **Application31** folder. In this project, we will need four images placed in the **drawable** directory. In this example, they will be photos of colorful salads.

We will start building the application by editing the **activity_main.xml** layout file. Inside it, we will place a **RelativeLayout**, within which we will use the **RecyclerView widget**. The layout code will look as follows:

```
<?xml version="1.0" encoding="utf-8"?>
<RelativeLayout

xmlns:android="http://schemas.android.com/apk/res/android"
    xmlns:tools="http://schemas.android.com/tools"
    android:layout_width="match_parent"
    android:layout_height="match_parent"
    tools:context=".MainActivity">

    <androidx.recyclerview.widget.RecyclerView
        android:id="@+id/view1"
        android:scrollbars="vertical"
        android:layout_width="wrap_content"
        android:layout_height="wrap_content"/>
</RelativeLayout>
```

Listing 5.163 Layout code using the RecyclerView container

The next step is to define the appearance of a single card. The card layout will be defined in a separate layout file. Therefore, we create a new layout file named **salad.xml**. This file will be located in the same directory as the main activity layout file **activity_main.xml**, which is the **layout** folder. As the layout, we will use a **CardView** container. We will declare it using the following code:

```
<?xml version="1.0" encoding="utf-8"?>
<androidx.cardview.widget.CardView
xmlns:android="http://schemas.android.com/apk/res/android"
xmlns:card_view="http://schemas.android.com/apk/res-auto"
    android:id="@+id/card_view"
    android:layout_width="match_parent"
    android:layout_height="250dp"
    android:layout_margin="4dp"
    card_view:cardElevation="2dp"
    card_view:cardCornerRadius="20dp">
    <LinearLayout
        android:layout_width="match_parent"
        android:layout_height="match_parent"
        android:orientation="vertical">
        <ImageView
            android:id="@+id/pic1"
            android:layout_height="200dp"
            android:layout_width="match_parent"/>
        <TextView
            android:id="@+id/name"
            android:layout_marginLeft="4dp"
            android:layout_marginBottom="4dp"
            android:textSize="10pt"
            android:textColor="@color/black"
            android:layout_height="wrap_content"
            android:layout_width="match_parent"/>
    </LinearLayout>
</androidx.cardview.widget.CardView>
```

Listing 5.164 CardView Container – salad.xml file

In the above code snippet, new **attributes** appear that directly define the appearance of the card. The first attribute, **card_view:cardElevation**, will display a shadow beneath the card. The second one, **card_view:cardCornerRadius**, will round the corners of the card. Both attributes serve aesthetic purposes.

Inside the CardView widget, we will place a LinearLayout, which will contain an image (ImageView) and a simple label in the form of a **TextView**. This means that each card will include an image and a label, arranged in a linear layout. Both views need to be connected, and the individual card elements (image and text) must be defined.

All these tasks will be performed in the **MainActivity.java** file. To begin, we create three objects:a **RecyclerView** object of the **RecyclerView** class, a layout manager responsible for the proper appearance of the layout, and a list that will store information about the images and salad names.

```
RecyclerView RecyclerView;
private RecyclerView.LayoutManager menager1;
ArrayList<Salad> salad;
```

Listing 5.165 Creating a data list

Inside the built - in **onCreate** method:

We assign the **RecyclerView** object a **reference** to the view placed in the layout file (**activity_main.xml**) with the ID **view1**, which is a **RecyclerView** widget.

```
RecyclerView = findViewById(R.id.view1);
```

Listing 5.166 Reference to the RecyclerView element

We create an object called **salad,** which will store data retrieved using the method **makeSalad();** – this method will be defined later in the code.

```
salad = makeSalad();
```

Listing 5.167 Creating the salad object

We assign the **menager1** object a new instance of the **GridLayoutManager** method, which is a grid layout manager. Here, we use the **class constructor** that takes two parameters. The **first** one, called **Context**, indicates from which class the data should be retrieved. Since we are using it within the current class, we use the keyword **this**. The **second** parameter is an integer that defines how many columns the layout should be divided into.

```
menager1 = new GridLayoutManager(this,1);
```

Listing 5.168 Creating a GridLayoutManager object

Next, using the **setLayoutManager** method of the **RecyclerView** object, we set the **layout** manager to our **menager1** object.

```
RecyclerView.setLayoutManager(menager1);
```

Listing 5.169 Using the setLayoutManager method

We create an adapter named **adapter** of the class **Adapter1**, and then we create a new instance called **salad**. Next, we assign it to the **RecyclerView** object using the **setAdapter** method.

```
Adapter1 adapter = new Adapter1(salad);
RecyclerView.setAdapter(adapter);
```

Listing 5.170 Creating the adapter

The next component is a **class** named **Salad**. It will define the elements that we will use on each card in the view.

```
private static class Salad {
    int pic1;
    String name;
    public Salad (int picture1, String name1){
        this.pic1 = picture1;
        this.name = name1;
    }
```

Listing 5.171 Definition of the Salatka class

We will need an **integer** variable to store the image **ID,** and a **string variable** to hold the **text** displayed in the description (name) of the salad. We also need to create a constructor for the class. The next task is to create an array that stores the data for each **card**.

```
private ArrayList<Salad> makeSalad(){
    ArrayList<Salad>salatka = new ArrayList<>();
salatka.add(new Salad(R.drawable.egg, "Salad with egg"));
salatka.add(new Salad(R.drawable.caprese, "Caprese salad"));
salatka.add(new Salad(R.drawable.shrimp, "Salad with shrimp"));
salatka.add(new Salad(R.drawable.fruit, "Fruit salad"));
    return salatka;
}
```

Listing 5.172 Array storing card data

Using the **add** method, we add a single object to the array, consisting of a **reference** to an image and a **text** label that describes the salad. In this application, we have a four - element array. Next, we create the **adapter** class.

```
public static class Adapter1 extends
RecyclerView.Adapter<ViewHolder> {
```

Listing 5.173 Creating the Adapter class

In this class, we create an **array**:

```
ArrayList<Salad> s1;
```

Listing 5.174 Declaration of the s1 array

This adapter still needs a few **more methods** to function properly. The first one is the **constructor**.

```
public Adapter1(ArrayList<Salad> salad3) {
    s1 = salad3;
}
```

Listing 5.175 Definition of the Adapter1 method

This **constructor** will contain only one object of type **Array**, which will be our **array** storing the list of salads. The next method is **onCreateViewHolder**.

```
public ViewHolder onCreateViewHolder(ViewGroup parent, int
viewType) {
View v =
LayoutInflater.from(parent.getContext()).inflate(R.layout.salad,
parent, false);
    return new ViewHolder(v);
}
```

Listing 5.176 Definition of the ViewHolder method

Here, we create the so - called **ViewHolder** pattern. It defines how a single item – a single card – should look. That's why there is a reference to the layout file **salad.xml.** The **onBindViewHolder** method connects the data with the view.

```
public void onBindViewHolder(ViewHolder holder, int
position) {
    Salad salad2 = s1.get(position);
    holder.saladPicture.setImageResource(salad2.pic1);
    holder.saladName.setText(salad2.name);
}
```

Listing 5.177 Definition of the onBindViewHolder method

In this method, the position of the item in the list is retrieved. The final method will be **getItemCount**.

```
public int getItemCount() {
    return s1.size();
}
```

Listing 5.178 Definition of the getItemCount method

This method retrieves the number of items that the **list** will contain.

```
private static class ViewHolder extends
RecyclerView.ViewHolder {
    public ImageView saladPicture;
    public TextView saladName;
public ViewHolder(View v) {
        super(v);
        saladPicture = v.findViewById(R.id.pic1);
        saladName =  v.findViewById(R.id.name);
    }
}
```

Listing 5.179 Definition of the ViewHolder class

The final class will be the **ViewHolder** class, which inherits from the **RecyclerView** class. In this class, references from the layout file are retrieved into the holder objects. For the image, this will be the **ImageView** with the **ID** from the **salad.xml** file. For the text, it will be the name the **TextView ID** from the same layout file. At first, the code may seem quite complex. The full content of the **MainActivity.java** activity is shown below.

```
package example.app31;

import android.os.Bundle;
import android.view.LayoutInflater;
import android.view.View;
import android.view.ViewGroup;
import android.widget.ImageView;
import android.widget.TextView;
import androidx.appcompat.app.AppCompatActivity;
import androidx.recyclerview.widget.GridLayoutManager;
import androidx.recyclerview.widget.RecyclerView;
import java.util.ArrayList;

public class MainActivity extends  AppCompatActivity  {
    RecyclerView RecyclerView;
    private RecyclerView.LayoutManager menager1;
    ArrayList<Salad> salad;
    @Override
    protected void onCreate(Bundle savedInstanceState) {
        super.onCreate(savedInstanceState);
        setContentView(R.layout.activity_main);
        RecyclerView = findViewById(R.id.view1);
        salad = makeSalad();
        menager1 = new GridLayoutManager(this,1);
        RecyclerView.setLayoutManager(menager1);
        Adapter1 adapter = new Adapter1(salad);
        RecyclerView.setAdapter(adapter);
    }
    private static class Salad {
        int pic1;
        String name;
        public Salad (int picture1, String name1){
            this.pic1 = picture1;
            this.name = name1;
        }
    }
    private ArrayList<Salad> makeSalad(){
private ArrayList<Salad> makeSalad(){
    ArrayList<Salad>salad2 = new ArrayList<>();
salad2.add(new Salad(R.drawable.egg, "Salad with egg"));
salad2.add(new Salad(R.drawable.caprese, "Caprese salad"));
salad2.add(new Salad(R.drawable.shrimp, "Shrimp salad"));
salad2.add(new Salad(R.drawable.fruit, "Fruit salad"));
    return salad2;
}
    public static class Adapter1 extends
RecyclerView.Adapter<ViewHolder> {
 ArrayList<Salad> s1;
        public Adapter1(ArrayList<Salad> salad3) {
            s1 = salad3;
        }
        @Override
        public ViewHolder onCreateViewHolder(ViewGroup
parent, int viewType) {
View v = LayoutInflater.from(parent.getContext())
.inflate(R.layout.salad, parent, false);
            return new ViewHolder(v);
        }
        @Override
  public void onBindViewHolder(ViewHolder holder, int
position) {
            Salad salad2 = s1.get(position);
    holder.saladPicture.setImageResource(salad2.pic1);
    holder.saladName.setText(salad2.name);
        }
        @Override
        public int getItemCount() {
            return s1.size();
        }
    }
     private static class ViewHolder extends
 RecyclerView.ViewHolder {
         public ImageView saladPicture;
         public TextView saladName;
         public ViewHolder(View v) {
             super(v);
             saladPicture = v.findViewById(R.id.pic1);
             saladName =  v.findViewById(R.id.name);
         }
     }
 }
```

Listing 5.180 MainActivity.java activity code

When the application is launched, it will look like in the illustration below:

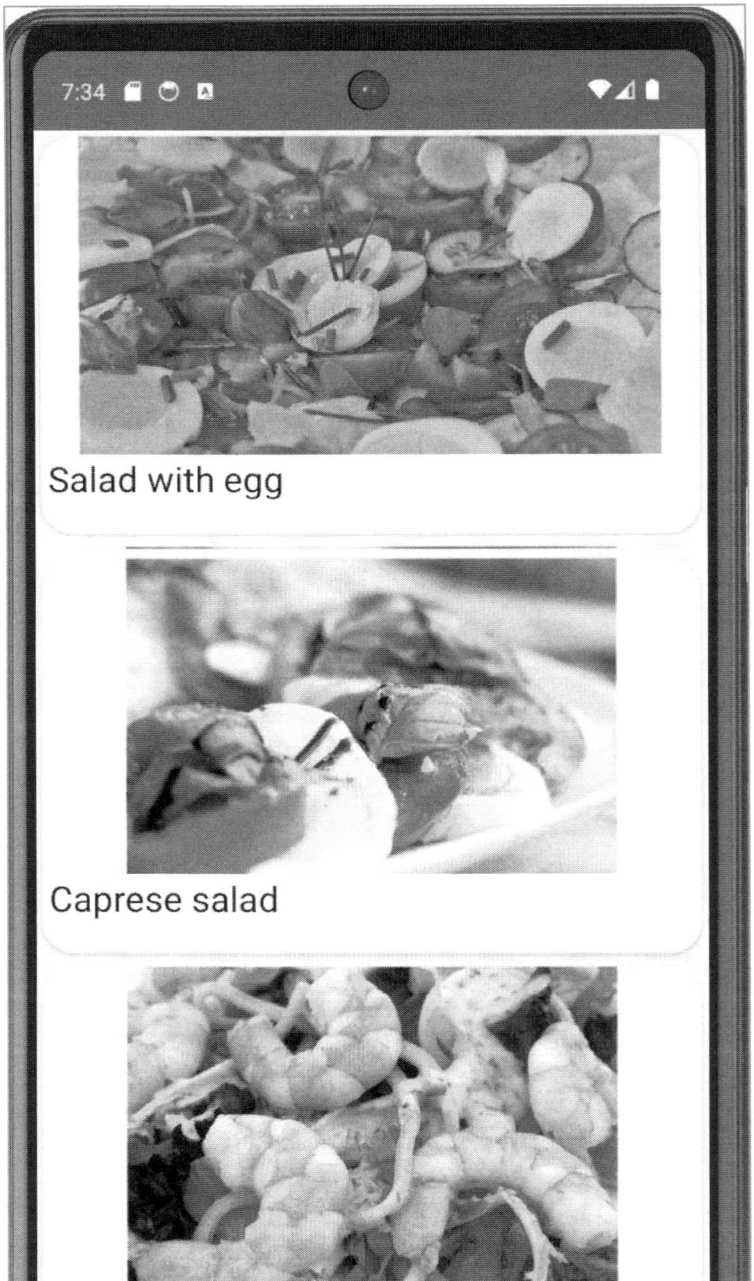

Figure 5.112 Application using CardView containers

Only three images with descriptions are visible on the screen at the same time. The card view includes a scrolling feature. Simply scroll the application screen, and the last item on the list will appear.

5.17 Multimedia

A modern application, in addition to intuitive operation and a visually appealing design, should also include multimedia elements. In previous chapters, we have already inserted images and applied animations to them. We also created frame - by - frame animations. In an application, we can also use sound and video.

5.17.1 Playing music

The application code and the resources needed for it are located in the folder **Application32**.

In the following example, we will create a simple application for playing audio files. We will need:

- A short music file in **.wav** or **.mp3** format;
- Three small images that will serve as buttons: **Start, Stop**, and **Pause**.

We will begin building the application by preparing the three images. In this example, the images will have the following dimensions: **height** 100px, **width** 100px each. It is best if the background of the images is transparent.

Figure 5.113 Icons used in the music playback application

We create a **LinearLayout** with **horizontal** orientation. Inside the layout, we insert three **ImageButton** widgets. These views work the same way as standard **Button** widgets and have the same attributes – including the **onClick** attribute, which will be essential in this application.

The difference is that in an **ImageButton**, instead of text, we can insert an image. Therefore, the **android:text** attribute is replaced with **android:src**, where we insert a reference to the image located in the drawable folder. The layout file will look like the following:

```
<LinearLayout
xmlns:android="http://schemas.android.com/apk/res/android"
    xmlns:tools="http://schemas.android.com/tools"
    android:layout_width="match_parent"
    android:layout_height="match_parent"
    android:orientation="horizontal"
    tools:context=".MainActivity" >
    <ImageButton
        android:id="@+id/button1"
        android:layout_width="100dp"
        android:layout_height="100dp"
        android:layout_marginLeft="5dp"
        android:src="@drawable/play2"
        android:onClick="Play" />
    <ImageButton
        android:id="@+id/button2"
        android:layout_width="100dp"
        android:layout_height="100dp"
        android:layout_marginLeft="10dp"
        android:src="@drawable/stop2"
        android:onClick="Stop" />
    <ImageButton
        android:id="@+id/button3"
        android:layout_width="100dp"
        android:layout_height="100dp"
        android:layout_marginLeft="10dp"
        android:src="@drawable/pause2"
        android:onClick="Pause"/>
</LinearLayout>
```

Listing 5.181 Application layout code

The sound file must be placed in a new directory, which needs to be created within the application's resources. To create the directory, right - click on the res branch in the project tree. Select **New**, then **Android Resource Directory**.

Figure 5.114 Creating a New Resource Directory

In the **Resource type** field, select **raw**. The **Directory type** name will update automatically. Just click **OK**, and a new folder will appear in the directory tree.

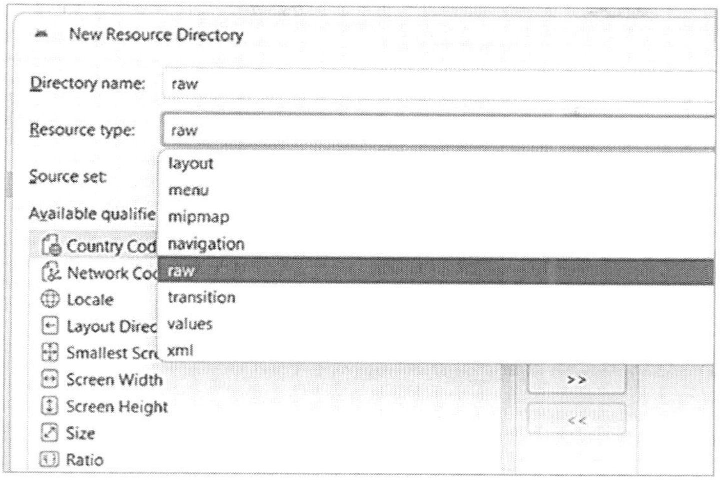

Figure 5.115 Creating a Raw Resource Directory

Locate the **raw** directory on your computer's disk and place the audio file you want to use in the application inside it. You can also use the **Open in Explorer** option. Now it's time to edit the **MainActivity.java** activity file. To handle audio files, you'll need the **MediaPlayer** library. Start by creating a **MediaPlayer** object, which should be defined in the main activity class.

```
MediaPlayer music;
```

Listing 5.182 Creating a MediaPlayer Object

Next, link the created object to the appropriate audio file placed in the raw directory. This is done in the onCreate method.

```
music = MediaPlayer.create(this, R.raw.music2);
```

Listing 5.183 Defining the Music Object

The **create** method of the **MediaPlayer** object takes two arguments. The first one is the **context**, which is why we use the keyword this here (this notation has been discussed many times before). The second argument is the **audio file**. It is located in the **raw** directory and, in this example, is named **music2**. To handle the buttons, you need to create three methods: **Play, Stop**, and **Pause**.

The **Play** method will start the audio. The **Stop** method will stop playback and prevent restarting. The **Pause** method will pause the audio but allow it to resume from the same position when the **Play** button is clicked again. These methods are very simple to implement, and their code will look as follows:

```
public void Play(View view)
{
    music.start();
}
public void Stop(View view)
{
    music.stop();
}
public void Pause(View view)
{
    music.pause();
}
```

Listing 5.184 Defining Methods for Audio Playback

The complete activity code looks like this:

```
package example.app32;

import android.media.MediaPlayer;
import android.os.Bundle;
import android.view.View;

import androidx.appcompat.app.AppCompatActivity;

public class MainActivity extends AppCompatActivity {

    MediaPlayer music;
    @Override
    protected void onCreate(Bundle savedInstanceState) {
        super.onCreate(savedInstanceState);
        setContentView(R.layout.activity_main);
        music = MediaPlayer.create(this, R.raw.music2);
    }
    public void Play(View view)
    {
        music.start();
    }
    public void Stop(View view)
    {
        music.stop();
    }
    public void Pause(View view)
    {
        music.pause();
    }
}
```

Listing 5.185 Application Activity Code

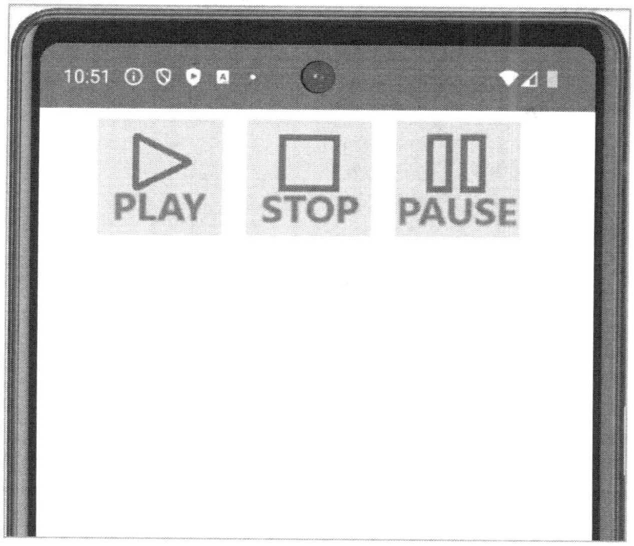

Figure 5.116 Application on Launch

5.17.2 Video Playback

The application code is located in the **Application33** folder. **Android Studio** allows for video file playback. In this case, the **VideoView** class will be useful. We will now write a simple application that plays a video. In the **Video** application, we will use a short video placed in the app's rescurces.

Just like in the previous task, we need to create a directory for storing multimedia files. Again, this will be the **raw** directory located in the **res** rescurce folder. Place the video file in the newly created directory. In the layout file, add a view that enables video playback – this will be a **VideoView**. The layout file will look like in the code below.

```
<LinearLayout
xmlns:android="http://schemas.android.com/apk/res/android"
    xmlns:tools="http://schemas.android.com/tools"
    android:layout_width="match_parent"
    android:layout_height="match_parent"
    android:orientation="vertical"
    tools:context=".MainActivity">

    <VideoView
        android:id="@+id/film"
        android:layout_width="match_parent"
        android:layout_height="250dp" />
</LinearLayout>
```

Listing 5.186 Application Layout Code with VideoView Element

In the activity file, we add a **VideoView** object and assign it to the corresponding element from the layout file. Next, we link the object to the video file located in the **raw** directory. Now, we simply start the video using the **start** method. The entire code is placed inside the **onCreate** method. The code for the **MainActivity.java** file is shown below:

```
package example.app33;

import androidx.appcompat.app.AppCompatActivity;
import android.net.Uri;
import android.os.Bundle;
import android.widget.MediaController;
import android.widget.VideoView;
public class MainActivity extends AppCompatActivity {
    @Override
    protected void onCreate(Bundle savedInstanceState) {
        super.onCreate(savedInstanceState);
        setContentView(R.layout.activity_main);
        VideoView video = findViewById(R.id.film);
        video.setVideoURI(Uri.parse("android.resource://" +
getPackageName() + "/" + R.raw.film1));
        video.start();
        MediaController mediaController = new
MediaController(this);
        video.setMediaController(mediaController);
    }
}
```

Listing 5.187 Application Activity Code

You can add a playback control panel to the application. To do this, simply include the following lines in the activity file:

```
MediaController mediaController = new
MediaController(this);
video.setMediaController(mediaController);
```

Listing 5.188 Adding a Video Navigation Bar to the Application

The application with a controller will look like in the illustration below:

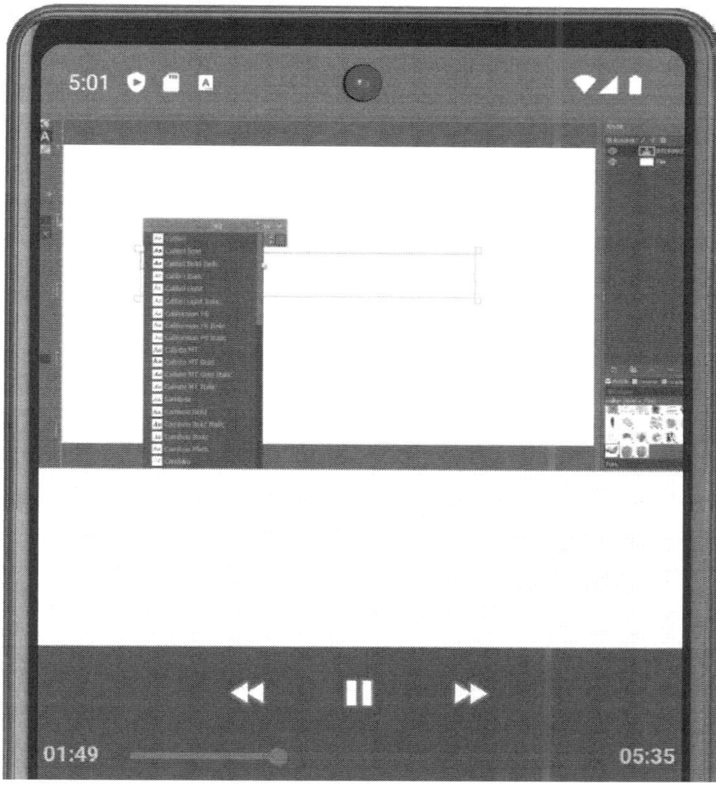

Figure 5.117 Application with Video Playback

5.18 Navigation and Menu Creation

A mobile application consists of several activities. To navigate it efficiently, a **menu** and **intuitive navigation** are needed. A good solution in this case is to use the **Toolbar** component.

5.18.1 Toolbar

Let's start from the beginning. The first navigation tool used was the **AppBar**, also known as the application bar. It's simply a colored area at the top of the window, with its main element being the **title**. A simple menu button could also be added to it.

The successor to AppBar is the **ActionBar**, which was introduced in **API level 11**. **ActionBar** could be customized to suit the needs of the application by adding elements such as the app icon, action buttons, and an extended menu or a navigation drawer. **Toolbar**, or the tool bar, is the successor to **ActionBar**. It's a more modern and functional version, introduced in **API level 21**. In addition to the elements available in **ActionBar**, Toolbar also allows placing other views inside it.

Now we'll create an application that demonstrates how the navigation bar works. The activity code is located in the Applicatio34 folder. In the layout, we'll place a view representing the **Toolbar**.

```
<?xml version="1.0" encoding="utf-8"?>
<LinearLayout
 xmlns:android="http://schemas.android.com/apk/res/android"
    xmlns:tools="http://schemas.android.com/tools"
    android:layout_width="match_parent"
    android:layout_height="match_parent"
    android:orientation="vertical"
    tools:context=".MainActivity">

    <androidx.appcompat.widget.Toolbar
        android:id="@+id/toolbar"
        android:layout_width="match_parent"
        android:layout_height="wrap_content"
        android:background="@color/lightblue" />
</LinearLayout>
```

Listing 5.189 Layout Code for Adding a Toolbar

As you can see, the **Toolbar** is added to the application just like a regular **view.** In the **colors.xml** file, we created a new color that will be used in the application.

```
<?xml version="1.0" encoding="utf-8"?>
<resources>
    <color name="black">#FF000000</color>
    <color name="white">#FFFFFFFF</color>
    <color name="lightblue">#418CE1</color>
</resources>
```

Listing 5.190 colors.xml File with New Color Definition

After launching, the application will look as follows:

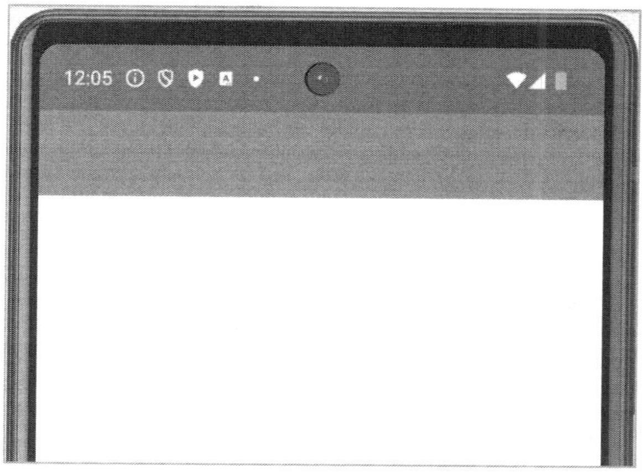

Figure 5.118 Application with Toolbar

In the window, we see a **blue bar** - this is the **Toolbar**. The next step is to add the application name to it. This can be done in the **MainActivity.java** file.

```
public class MainActivity extends AppCompatActivity {

    @Override
    protected void onCreate( Bundle savedInstanceState )
{
        super.onCreate(savedInstanceState);
        setContentView(R.layout.activity_main);
        Toolbar toolbar = (Toolbar)
findViewById(R.id.toolbar);
        setSupportActionBar(toolbar);
    }
}
```

Listing 5.191 Activity Code for Adding a Toolbar

In the **onCreate** method, we create a **Toolbar** object and assign it to the corresponding view from the layout file. The **setSupportActionBar** method ensures the proper functioning of the **Toolbar**. After launching the application, the app title will appear on the **Toolbar**. The application code with the title can be found in the folder named **Application34a**.

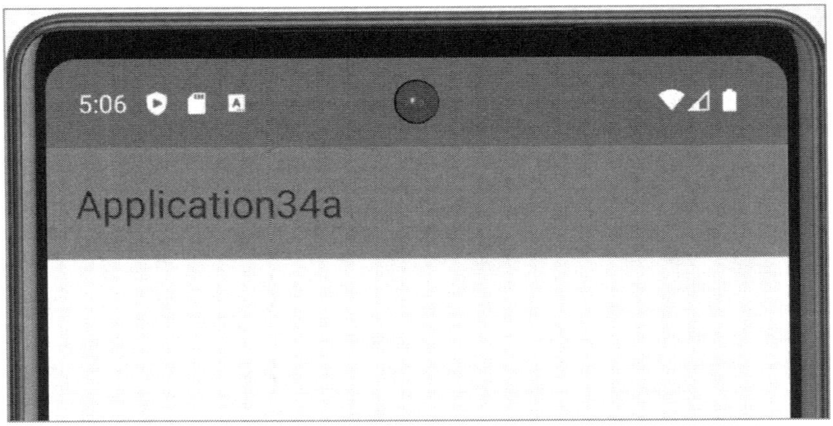

Figure 5.119 Application Title Displayed on the Toolbar

5.18.2 Creating a Menu

As the name suggests, the **Toolbar** has a specific purpose. You can place elements on it that help operate the application. One of the most important advantages of the **Toolbar** is the ability to create a simple menu.

We'll now create a new application where we'll use the code from the previous task and then modify it. The application code is located in the folder named **Application34b**.

We'll start with a menu containing links to other parts of the application. The first step is to create a new resource file named **menu**, where we'll define the items and appearance of the application menu. In the project tree, right - click on the **res** branch. From the context menu, choose **New** and then **New Resource File.** In the **File name** field, enter **main_menu,** and set the **Resource type** to menu. A new folder named **menu** will appear in the directory tree, containing the new resource file **main_menu.xml**.

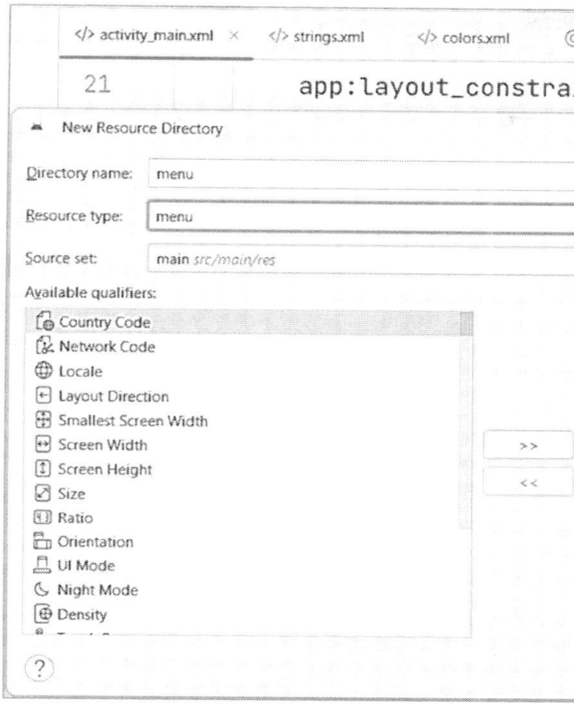

Figure 5.120 Creating the Menu Directory

In the **menu** file, we place the items that will appear on our **Toolbar**. The file code will look like the example below:

```
<?xml version="1.0" encoding="utf-8"?>
<menu
xmlns:android="http://schemas.android.com/apk/res/android"
    xmlns:app="http://schemas.android.com/apk/res-auto">
    <item android:id="@+id/menu1"
        android:title="@string/f1"
        android:orderInCategory="1"
        app:showAsAction="never" />
    <item android:id="@+id/menu2"
        android:title="@string/f2"
        android:orderInCategory="2"
        app:showAsAction="never" />
    <item android:id="@+id/menu3"
        android:title="@string/f3"
        android:orderInCategory="3"
        app:showAsAction="never" />
</menu>
```

Listing 5.192 Main_menu.xml File Code

Each item element creates a single entry in the **menu**.The **android:title** attribute assigns a title to each item, which will be displayed in the app menu. The **android:orderInCategory** attribute determines the display order of items in the menu – items with lower values appear first. The **app:showAsAction** attribute defines how the item is displayed. In the example, the value **"never"** means the item will be hidden (collapsed) in the overflow menu. Other options for this attribute include:

- **ifRoom** – displays the item on the toolbar only if there is enough space; otherwise, it goes into the overflow menu.
- **withText** – displays both the icon and the title from the title attribute.
- **always** – always displays the item on the toolbar.

The created menu must be connected to the rest of the application files. We'll do this in the **MainActivity.java** file.

```
public class MainActivity extends AppCompatActivity {
    @Override
    protected void onCreate(Bundle savedInstanceState) {
        super.onCreate(savedInstanceState);
        setContentView(R.layout.activity_main);
        Toolbar toolbar = findViewById(R.id.toolbar);
        setSupportActionBar(toolbar);
    }

    @Override
    public boolean onCreateOptionsMenu(Menu menu) {
        getMenuInflater().inflate(R.menu.main_menu, menu);
        return super.onCreateOptionsMenu(menu);
    }
}
```

Listing 5.193 Activity File Defining Menu Handling

In the main class, we add a new **method** of type **boolean** called **onCreateOptionsMenu**. We create a menu **instance** using **getMenuInflater** and return the list of menu items. After launching the application, its appearance is shown in the illustration below.

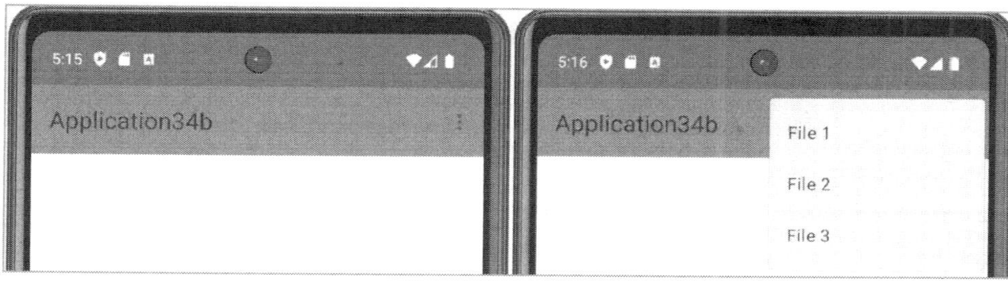

Figure 5.121 Dropdown Menu on the Toolbar – Collapsed (Left Side), Expanded (Right Side)

A menu icon (three dots) has appeared on the toolbar. Clicking it will reveal the menu options. If you change the value of the app:showAsAction attribute in the **main_menu.xml** file to **"always",** the application will look slightly different.

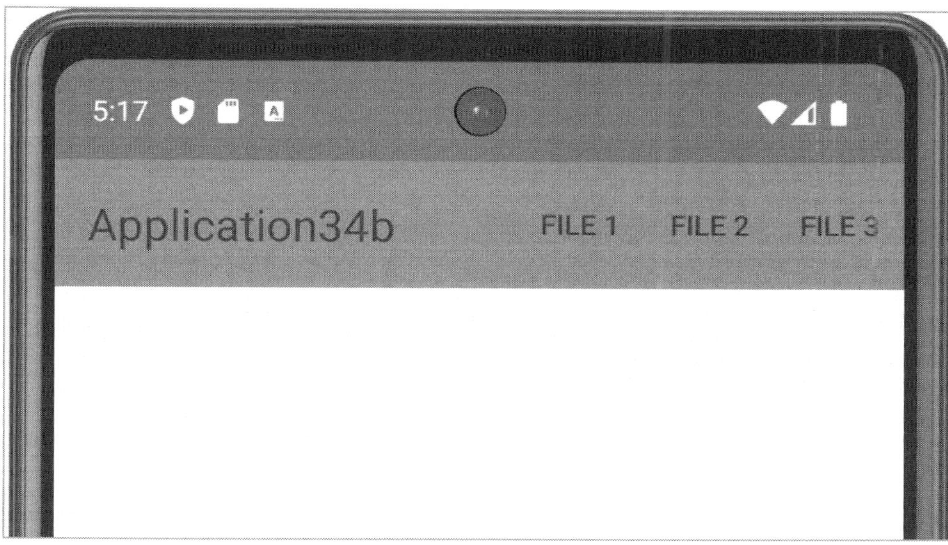

Figure 5.122 Action Buttons Visible on the Toolbar

5.18.3 Creating Navigation – Back Button

We will now add an extra **action button** to our application, whose purpose will be to return to the main activity. We'll start by creating a **second activity**.

The next step is to edit the **manifest file**. We need to specify which activity is the parent. Considering the structure of the application, **MainActivity.java** will be at the top of the hierarchy, and this annotation must be added to the **AndroidManifest.xml** file. In the manifest file, locate the section responsible for the second activity **Menu2.java**.

```
<activity
    android:name=".Menu2"
    android:exported="false"/>
```

Listing 5.194 Manifest File Fragment

At this point, you need to include information that **MainActivity** is the **parent activity.**

```
<activity
    android:name=".Menu2"
    android:exported="false"
    android:parentActivityName=".MainActivity"/>
```

Listing 5.195 Manifest File Fragment with Activity Hierarchy Set

We modify the main activity code by adding a new method named **onOptionsItemSelected**, which will respond to menu button presses. The code for this method is shown below:

```
public boolean onOptionsItemSelected(MenuItem item) {
    if (item.getItemId() == R.id.menu1) {
        Intent intent = new Intent(this, Menu2.class);
        startActivity(intent);
        return true;
    }
```

Listing 5.196 Definition of the onOptionsItemSelected Method

The method retrieves the **id** of the selected **item** and uses it in an if statement. When the menu button is clicked, an **intent** is triggered that navigates to the **Menu2.java** activity. In this part of the application, an action is defined for the **FILE1** button. Completing the code for the remaining buttons should not be a problem; feel free to finish the method on your own. In the second activity, we create an "**Up**" navigation button.

```
Toolbar toolbar = (Toolbar) findViewById(R.id.toolbar);
 setSupportActionBar(toolbar);
 ActionBar actionBar = getSupportActionBar();
 actionBar.setDisplayHomeAsUpEnabled(true);
```

Listing 5.197 Creating a Toolbar Object and Adding Functionality

This code is placed inside the **onCreate** method. The first two lines are familiar. They reference the layout file and specifically the **Toolbar** element placed there. The last two lines create an **ActionBar** object and enable the "**Up**" navigation button. Now, when the application is launched and the **Menu1** button is pressed, you'll be taken to the **second activity**. There, a back **arrow icon** will appear on the **Toolbar**. Clicking it will return you to the main activity.

Figure 5.123 Application Window with Visible Back Icon

Full Code of the Main Activity – **MainActivity.java**:

```
package example.app34b;

import androidx.appcompat.app.AppCompatActivity;
import androidx.appcompat.widget.Toolbar;
import android.content.Intent;
import android.os.Bundle;
import android.view.Menu;
import android.view.MenuItem;

public class MainActivity extends AppCompatActivity {
    @Override
    protected void onCreate(Bundle savedInstanceState) {
        super.onCreate(savedInstanceState);
        setContentView(R.layout.activity_main);
        Toolbar toolbar = findViewById(R.id.toolbar);
        setSupportActionBar(toolbar);
    }

    @Override
    public boolean onCreateOptionsMenu(Menu menu) {
        getMenuInflater().inflate(R.menu.main_menu, menu);
        return super.onCreateOptionsMenu(menu);
    }
    @Override
    public boolean onOptionsItemSelected(MenuItem item) {
        if (item.getItemId() == R.id.menu1) {
            Intent intent = new Intent(this, Menu2.class);
            startActivity(intent);
            return true;
        }
        return super.onOptionsItemSelected(item);
    }
}
```

Listing 5.198 Main Activity Code

Menu2.java Activity Code:

```
package example.app34b;

import androidx.appcompat.app.ActionBar;
import androidx.appcompat.app.AppCompatActivity;
import androidx.appcompat.widget.Toolbar;
import android.os.Bundle;
public class Menu2 extends AppCompatActivity {

    @Override
    protected void onCreate(Bundle savedInstanceState) {
        super.onCreate(savedInstanceState);
        setContentView(R.layout.activity_menu2);
        Toolbar toolbar = findViewById(R.id.toolbar);
        setSupportActionBar(toolbar);
        ActionBar actionBar = getSupportActionBar();
        actionBar.setDisplayHomeAsUpEnabled(true);

    }
}
```

Listing 5.199 Code for the First Menu Option Activity

5.18.4 Creating Custom Icons

The **Toolbar** allows you to display custom icons on the bar instead of text labels. You can use icons that you've designed yourself as small images. These should be placed in the **drawable** directory. Alternatively, you can use icon libraries available online. A large collection can be found at: **https://fonts.google.com/icons?icon.set=Material+Symbols**

Downloaded images should also be placed in the **drawable** directory. In the next example, we'll use the ready - made application from **Application34a**. The full application code is located in the folder **Application34c.** In this example, we'll replace the text labels of menu items with icons. The code for the main_gmenu.xml file will look like the example below:

```
<?xml version="1.0" encoding="utf-8"?>
<menu
xmlns:android="http://schemas.android.com/apk/res/android"
xmlns:app="http://schemas.android.com/apk/res-auto">

    <item android:id="@+id/menu1"
        android:title="File1"
        android:orderInCategory="2"
        app:showAsAction="always"
        android:icon="@drawable/p1"/>

    <item android:id="@+id/menu2"
        android:title="File2"
        android:orderInCategory="3"
        app:showAsAction="always"
        android:icon="@drawable/p2"/>

    <item android:id="@+id/menu3"
        android:title="File3"
        android:orderInCategory="4"
        app:showAsAction="always"
        android:icon="@drawable/p3"/>
</menu>
```

Listing 5.200 Layout Code with References to Icon Images

Each item has an additional line with the attribute **android:icon**, which references the **drawable** directory and the appropriate **image file**. After launching, the application will look like the illustration below.

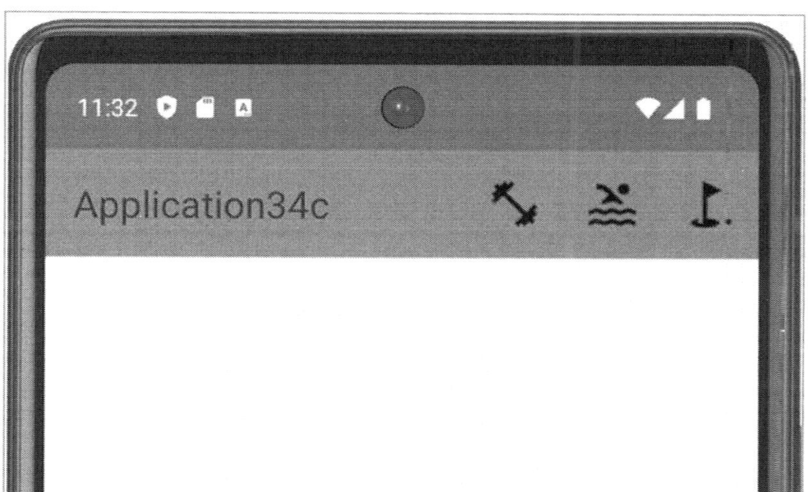

Figure 5.124 Toolbar with Icon Buttons

5.18.5 Changing the Toolbar Position

The **Toolbar** is treated like any other view. This means we can move it around the application screen and change its default position. In the next exercise, we will move the **Toolbar to the bottom of the application**.

You can find the application code in the folder **Application34d**. The simplest way to achieve this is by using a **RelativeLayout** instead of a regular **LinearLayout**. The changes will be made in the **activity_main.xml** file. The first step is to switch the layout type. Then, in the settings of the view **android.support.v7.widget.Toolbar**, add a line that positions the view at the bottom of the layout **androidx.appcompat.widget.Toolbar**. This will place the **Toolbar** at the bottom of the window.

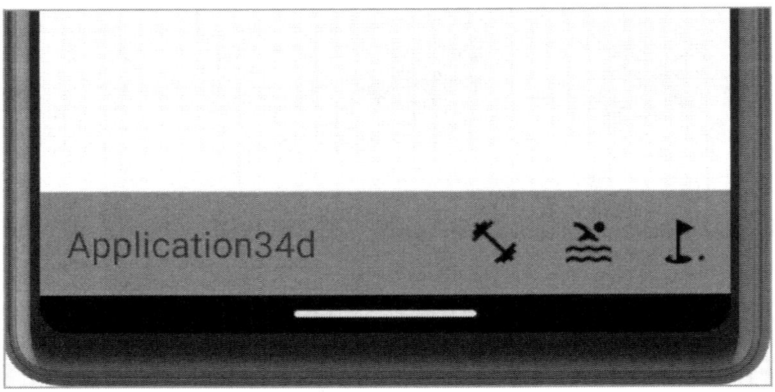

Figure 5.125 Toolbar Positioned at the Bottom of the Application

5.18.6 Slide - Out Menu – Navigation Drawer

You can find the application code and resources needed to create it in the folder named **Application35**.

In the next application, we will create a so - called **navigation drawer**. It will be a kind of list that slides out using the menu button (commonly known as the hamburger menu), allowing the user to choose from several options.

We will use the same images that were used when creating the **CardView**, and we'll build a simple cookbook app. Since the application will be based on fragments, the next step will be to create four fragments named after different salads:

- **FCaprese** – Caprese salad;
- **FShrimps** – Shrimp salad;
- **FFruit** – Fruit salad;
- **FEgg** – Egg salad;

Each **fragment** will have its own **layout file**. The layout files will be automatically created when each fragment is generated. To create a **new fragment**, click on the package name in the **Java directory** within the project tree. This process was covered in the chapter about **fragments.** If you need a reminder on how to do it, go back a few pages. Now it's time to complete the created **fragments**. We'll start with the layout file for the **FCaprese** fragment, named **fragment_fcaprese.xml**.

We'll use a traditional **LinearLayout**. Inside it, we'll place:

- A **TextView** to display the name of the salad
- An **ImageView** to show the salad image
- **Another TextView** to list the ingredients needed to prepare the salad.

Code of the fragment_caprese.xml file:

```
<?xml version="1.0" encoding="utf-8"?>
<LinearLayout
xmlns:android="http://schemas.android.com/apk/res/android"
    xmlns:tools="http://schemas.android.com/tools"
    android:layout_width="match_parent"
    android:layout_height="match_parent"
    android:orientation="vertical"
    tools:context=".FCaprese">

    <!-- TODO: Update blank fragment layout -->
    <TextView
        android:layout_width="wrap_content"
        android:layout_height="wrap_content"
        android:text="Caprese salad"
        android:textSize="15pt"/>
    <ImageView
        android:layout_width="wrap_content"
        android:layout_height="wrap_content"
        android:src="@drawable/caprese"/>
    <TextView
        android:layout_width="wrap_content"
        android:layout_height="wrap_content"
        android:text="Ingredients:\n -mozarella \n-tomato
        \n-fresh basil \n-olive oil"
        android:textSize="10pt"/>
</LinearLayout>
```

Listing 5.201 Layout Code for fragment_caprese.xml

The layout files for the other salad fragments will look very similar. You only need to change the salad name in the **TextView**, the image name in the **ImageView,** and the list of ingredients. In the activity files, we include the following code for the **FCaprese.java** activity:

```
package example.app35;

import android.os.Bundle;
import android.view.LayoutInflater;
import android.view.View;
import android.view.ViewGroup;
import androidx.fragment.app.Fragment;

public class FCaprese extends Fragment {
    @Override
    public View onCreateView(LayoutInflater inflater,
ViewGroup container,
    Bundle savedInstanceState) {
        return inflater.inflate(R.layout.fragment_caprese,
container, false);
    }
}
```

Listing 5.202 Activity file for the FCaprese.java fragment

The remaining activity files: **FEgg.java, FShrimps.java, and FFruit.java**, will have similar code. You only need to change the name of the **main class** and the **layout file** name.

We are creating a **ToolBar.** We'll create it in a separate file to make it easier to add to other parts of the program. We create a new resource file and name it **toolbar.xml**. Its code is shown below:

```
<?xml version="1.0" encoding="utf-8"?>
<androidx.appcompat.widget.Toolbar
  android:id='@+id/toolbar'
  xmlns:android="http://schemas.android.com/apk/res/android"
  android:layout_width="match_parent"
  android:layout_height="?attr/actionBarSize"
  android:background="#D57EBF"
  android:theme="@style/ThemeOverlay.AppCompat.Dark.ActionBar"
/>
```

Listing 5.203 toolbar.xml file

We change the default application style in the **manifest file**. The new style will be named **Menu**, and this name will be entered in the **AndroidManifest.xml** file.

```
<application
    android:allowBackup="true"

android:dataExtractionRules="@xml/data_extraction_rules"
    android:fullBackupContent="@xml/backup_rules"
    android:icon="@mipmap/ic_launcher"
    android:label="@string/app_name"
    android:roundIcon="@mipmap/ic_launcher_round"
    android:supportsRtl="true"
    android:theme="@style/Menu"
    tools:targetApi="31">
```

Listing 5.204 Fragment of the manifest file

The added style is edited in the **styles.xml** file. This file should be located in the **values directory**. If it's not there yet, you need to create it. The completed file should be supplemented with the following code:

```
<?xml version="1.0" encoding="utf-8"?>
<resources>

<style name="Menu"
parent="Theme.AppCompat.Light.NoActionBar">

<item name="colorPrimary">@color/menu1</item>
<item name="colorPrimaryDark">@color/menu2</item>
<item name="colorAccent">@color/menu3</item>

</style>
<style name="Menu.menu1">
<item name="android:textSize">12pt</item>
</style>
</resources>
```

Listing 5.205 Definition of the theme that creates the menu

The colors used in the style need to be defined in the **colors.xml file**. The application uses selected colors, but they can be changed according to your preferences.

```
<?xml version="1.0" encoding="utf-8"?>
<resources>
    <color name="black">#FF000000</color>
    <color name="white">#FFFFFFFF</color>
    <color name="menu1">#EA0C63</color>
    <color name="menu2">#EC75A3</color>
    <color name="menu3">#EAC3D2</color>
</resources>
```

Listing 5.206 colors.xml file

Now it’s time to create the **menu file**. This will be a resource file named **menu.xml**, which we’ll create in the **menu subdirectory**. The file will contain four item options. Each of them will represent **one field** on the card.

```
<?xml version="1.0" encoding="utf-8"?>
<menu
xmlns:android="http://schemas.android.com/apk/res/android">

    <item
        android:id="@+id/Caprese"
        android:title="Caprese"
        android:checked="true" />
    <item
        android:id="@+id/Egg"
        android:title="Egg" />
    <item
        android:id="@+id/Shrimp"
        android:title="Shrimp" />
    <item
        android:id="@+id/Fruit"
        android:title="Fruit" />

</menu>
```

Listing 5.207 menu.xml file

We will add a button to the **ToolBar** that allows the menu to be opened. First, we create an object of the **Toolbar** class and create a reference to the **view** from the layout file.

```
Toolbar toolbar = findViewById(R.id.toolbar);
```

Listing 5.208 Reference to the ToolBar

We create another object. This time it's a **drawer object** from the **DrawerLayout** class, and we create a reference to the **drawer_layout** element located in the **activity_mail.xml** layout file.

```
DrawerLayout drawer = findViewById(R.id.drawer_layout);
```

Listing 5.209 Creating the DrawerLayout object

The **ActionBarDrawerToggle** instruction will create a so - called hamburger menu in our application – an icon consisting of three horizontal lines, which when clicked will display the side menu.

The **constructor of this class** takes five parameters:

- **Context** – refers to the class in which we are creating the menu;
- DrawerLayout layout – drawer;
- Toolbar bar – toolbar;
- **String** displayed when opening the menu – R.string.Open;
- **String** displayed when closing the menu – R.string.Close;

```
ActionBarDrawerToggle toggle =
 new ActionBarDrawerToggle(this, drawer, toolbar,
R.string.Open, R.string.Close);
```

Listing 5.210 Creating the ActionBarDrawerToggle object

Both strings have been defined in the **strings.xml** file. Their declarations look as follows:

```
<string name="Open">Open Menu</string>
<string name="Close">Close Menu</string>
```

Listing 5.211 Definition of strings in the strings.xml file

The function **drawer.addDrawerListener(toggle)** adds the toggle to the layout. The final function defined in the code fragment synchronizes the behavior of the icon – the hamburger menu.

```
drawer.addDrawerListener(toggle);
        toggle.syncState();
```

Listing 5.212 Synchronizing the hamburger menu behavior

All that remains is to define the action for pressing the button, which is shown in the code below:

```
implements
NavigationView.OnNavigationItemSelectedListener {
```

Listing 5.213 Defining the button press action

We place it in the main class of the **MainActivity.java** file. It is responsible for handling the application's response when the user clicks on a menu option. Meanwhile, the following two lines are placed inside the **onCreate** method:

```
NavigationView navigationView = (NavigationView)
findViewById(R.id.nav_view);
navigationView.setNavigationItemSelectedListener(this);
```

Listing 5.214 Creating a listener object

Its task is to notify the application when the user clicks a selected option. The next step is to define a class that, in response to the click, will open the desired fragment.

```
public boolean onNavigationItemSelected (MenuItem item){
    int id = item.getItemId();
    Fragment fragment;
    switch (id) {
        case R.id.Egg:
            fragment = new FEgg();
            break;
        case R.id.Shrimp:
            fragment = new FShrimp();
            break;
        case R.id.Fruit:
            fragment = new FFruit();
            break;
        default:
            fragment = new FCaprese();
    }
  FragmentTransaction ft =
getSupportFragmentManager().beginTransaction();
    ft.replace(R.id.content_frame, fragment);
    ft.commit();
    DrawerLayout drawer = findViewById(R.id.drawer_layout);
    drawer.closeDrawer(GravityCompat.START);
    return true;
}
```

Listing 5.215 Definition of the onNavigationItemSelected class

The **onNavigationItemSelected** class takes **one parameter** - our menu. First, three objects are created:

- **id** – an integer that retrieves the ID of the selected item from the **menu.xml** file;
- **fragment** – an object of type Fragment, responsible for launching the appropriate fragment file;
- **a simple switch statement** – based on the retrieved item ID, it launches the corresponding fragment file.

If no option is selected, the default fragment will be the first item on the list - in this case, the FCaprese fragment. The complete code of the **MainActivity.java** activity looks as follows:

```
package example.app35;

import androidx.appcompat.app.ActionBarDrawerToggle;
import androidx.appcompat.app.AppCompatActivity;
import androidx.appcompat.widget.Toolbar;
import androidx.core.view.GravityCompat;
import androidx.drawerlayout.widget.DrawerLayout;
import androidx.fragment.app.Fragment;
import androidx.fragment.app.FragmentTransaction;
import android.annotation.SuppressLint;
import android.os.Bundle;
import android.view.MenuItem;
import com.google.android.material.navigation.NavigationView;

public class MainActivity extends AppCompatActivity
        implements
NavigationView.OnNavigationItemSelectedListener {
    @Override
    protected void onCreate (Bundle savedInstanceState){
        super.onCreate(savedInstanceState);
        setContentView(R.layout.activity_main);
        Toolbar toolbar = findViewById(R.id.toolbar);
        setSupportActionBar(toolbar);
 DrawerLayout drawer = findViewById(R.id.drawer_layout);
 ActionBarDrawerToggle toggle =
    new ActionBarDrawerToggle(this,
                        drawer,
                        toolbar,
                        R.string.Open,
                        R.string.Close);
        drawer.addDrawerListener(toggle);
        toggle.syncState();
NavigationView navigationView =
findViewById(R.id.nav_view);
navigationView.setNavigationItemSelectedListener(this);
        Fragment fragment = new FCaprese();
        FragmentTransaction ft =
getSupportFragmentManager().beginTransaction();
        ft.add(R.id.content_frame, fragment);
        ft.commit();
    }

    @SuppressLint("NonConstantResourceId")
    @Override
 public boolean onNavigationItemSelected (MenuItem item){
        int id = item.getItemId();
        Fragment fragment;
        switch (id) {
            case R.id.Egg:
                fragment = new FEgg();
                break;
            case R.id.Shrimp:
                fragment = new FShrimp();
                break;
            case R.id.Fruit:
                fragment = new FFruit();
                break;
            default:
                fragment = new FCaprese();
        }
FragmentTransaction ft =
getSupportFragmentManager().beginTransaction();
        ft.replace(R.id.content_frame, fragment);
        ft.commit();
DrawerLayout drawer = findViewById(R.id.drawer_layout);
drawer.closeDrawer(GravityCompat.START);
        return true;
    }
}
```

Listing 5.216 Main activity code

The result of the application's operation is shown in the illustration.

Figure 5.126 Aplication 35

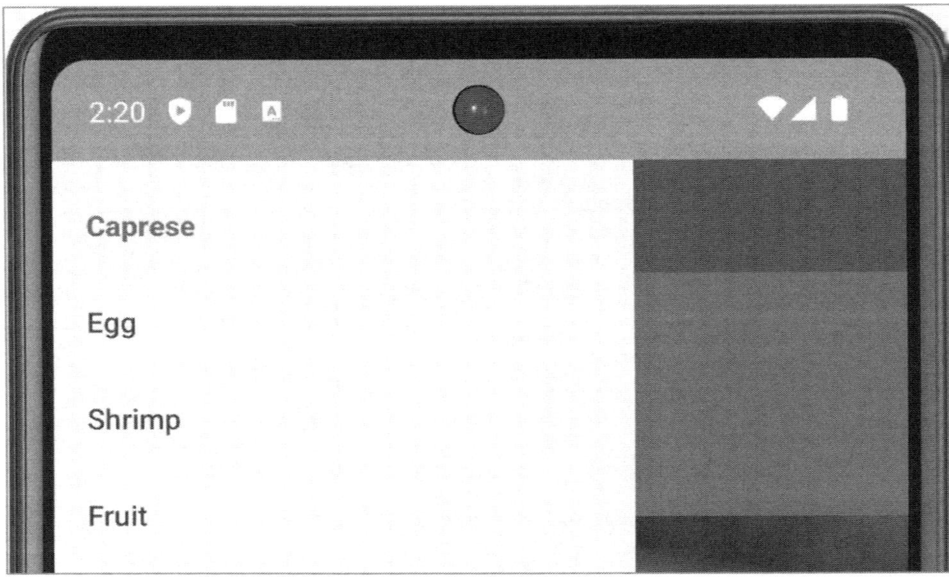

Figure 5.1267 Navigation Drawer – Expanded Version

5.19 Calendar and Clock – DataPicker and TimePicker Classes

5.19.1 Inserting a Calendar

The application code is located in a folder named **Application36.**

Date and time are important elements of an application. In the following example, we will demonstrate how to insert a calendar into an app. The calendar is added using the **CalendarView** component. The layout code with the calendar view will look as follows:

```
<?xml version="1.0" encoding="utf  - 8"?>
<LinearLayout
xmlns:android="http://schemas.android.com/apk/res/androi
d"
    android:id="@+id/LinearLayout1"
    android:layout_width="match_parent"
    android:layout_height="match_parent"
    android:orientation="vertical">
    <CalendarView
        android:id="@+id/cal1"
        android:layout_width="wrap_content"
        android:layout_height="0dp"
        android:layout_weight="1" />
</LinearLayout>
```

```
<?xml version="1.0" encoding="utf-8"?>
<LinearLayout
xmlns:android="http://schemas.android.com/apk/res/android"
    android:id="@+id/LinearLayout1"
    android:layout_width="match_parent"
    android:layout_height="match_parent"
    android:orientation="vertical">
    <CalendarView
        android:id="@+id/cal1"
        android:layout_width="wrap_content"
        android:layout_height="0dp"
        android:layout_weight="1" />
</LinearLayout>
```

Listing 5.217 Layout with CalendarView

A simple calendar in the application will look like the illustration shown below:

Figure 5.1278 Calendar in the Application

The **CalendarView** component has several interesting attributes that can change its appearance. As shown in the illustration above, the first day of the week in the calendar is Sunday. Setting the attribute **android:firstDayOfWeek** to the value **2** will change the first day of the week to Monday.

Another useful attribute is **android:dateTextAppearance**, which changes the font size. It offers the following options:

- @android:style/TextAppearance.Large – sets a large font size;
- @android:style/TextAppearance.Small – sets a small font size;
- @android:style/TextAppearance.Medium – sets a medium font size;

- **@android:style/TextAppearance.Large.Inverse** – sets a large font size and inverts the colors.

It's worth trying out a few of these options.

5.19.2 Inserting a Clock

Android allows you to insert a digital clock. The **TextClock** view will be helpful here. The code that inserts this widget will look as follows: The application code is located in a folder named **Application37**.

```
<?xml version="1.0" encoding="utf-8" ?>
<LinearLayout

xmlns:android="http://schemas.android.com/apk/res/android"
    android:id="@+id/LinearLayout1"
    android:layout_width="match_parent"
    android:layout_height="match_parent"
    android:orientation="vertical">
    <TextClock
        android:id="@+id/clock1"
        android:layout_width="wrap_content"
        android:layout_height="wrap_content"
        android:layout_gravity="center"
        android:textSize="20pt"
        android:format24Hour="HH:mm:ss"/>
</LinearLayout>
```

Listing 5.218 Layout with a TextClock view

When the application is launched, the clock will look like this:

Figure 5.129 Application displaying time in 12 - hour format

First, we focus on the appearance of the clock. By default, it is set to the **12 - hour format.** However, we usually use the **24 - hour format**. Let's try to 'fix' our clock. In the layout file, within the TextClock view, we add an additional attribute:

```
android:format24Hour="HH:mm:ss"
```

Listing 5.219 Setting the clock display format

We indicate that we want our clock to use the 24 - hour format and to display seconds alongside hours and minutes. Changes also need to be made in the activity file. The activity code will look as follows:

```
package example.app37;
import androidx.appcompat.app.AppCompatActivity;
import android.os.Bundle;
import android.widget.TextClock;
public class MainActivity extends AppCompatActivity {
    TextClock clock1;
    @Override
    protected void onCreate(Bundle savedInstanceState) {
        super.onCreate(savedInstanceState);
        setContentView(R.layout.activity_main);
        this.clock1 = this.findViewById(R.id.clock1);
        this.clock1.setFormat12Hour(null);
        clock1.setTimeZone("Europe/Warsaw");
    }
}
```

Listing 5.220 Full activity code

We create an object of the **TextClock** class named clock1. In the onCreate method, we create a reference to this object, linking it to the TextClock view defined in the layout file. Then, we disable the 12 - hour format display by setting the setFormat12Hour method to null. After making these changes in the code, the clock will look as follows:

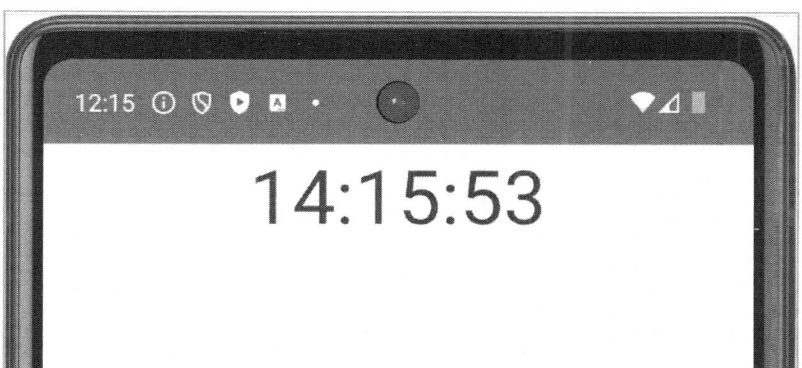

Figure 5.130 Application displaying time in 24 - hour format

We can see the format has changed. The time is now displayed in 24 - hour notation. In addition to hours and minutes, seconds are also visible.

There is one more detail we need to take care of setting the time zone. One line of code needs to be added to the activity code:

```
clock1.setTimeZone("Europe/Warsaw");
```

Listing 5.221 Setting the time zone

We set the time zone to European time in Warsaw. The clock application is now ready.

5.19.3 Retrieving the date

The user of the application has the ability to retrieve the date and time and pass them, for example, to a database or another part of the application. Two classes will help us with this:

- **DatePicker** – which allows the user to select a date;
- **TimePicker** – which allows the user to select a time.

We will now create an application called **DatePicker**, which will retrieve the date from the user. The application code is located in a folder named **Application38**. The layout of the application will resemble the one shown below:

```
<?xml version="1.0" encoding="utf-8"?>
<LinearLayout
xmlns:android="http://schemas.android.com/apk/res/android"
    xmlns:tools="http://schemas.android.com/tools"
    android:layout_width="match_parent"
    android:layout_height="match_parent"
    android:orientation="vertical">
    <DatePicker
        android:id="@+id/getDate"
        android:layout_width="wrap_content"
        android:layout_height="wrap_content"
        android:firstDayOfWeek="2"
        android:layout_gravity="center"/>
    <Button
        android:id="@+id/Button"
        android:layout_width="wrap_content"
        android:layout_height="wrap_content"
        android:text="Get Date"
        android:onClick="getDate"/>
    <TextView
        android:id="@+id/text1"
        android:layout_width="match_parent"
        android:layout_height="wrap_content"
        android:text="Show the data"
        android:textSize="30dp"/>
</LinearLayout>
```

Listing 5.222 Layout file with the DatePicker element

When the application is launched, it will display a calendar – similar to the exercise with the **CalendarView** widget. With **DatePicker**, we also have the option to display the date selection field in the form of a spinner. In the layout code, we make the following changes:

```
<DatePicker
    android:id="@+id/getDate"
    android:layout_width="wrap_content"
    android:layout_height="wrap_content"
    android:firstDayOfWeek="2"
    android:layout_gravity="center"/>
```

Listing 5.223 Definition of the DatePicker widget

We set the attribute **android:datePickerMode** to Spinner, and disable the calendar view by setting **calendarViewShown** to **false**. When the application is launched, the widget will look like this:

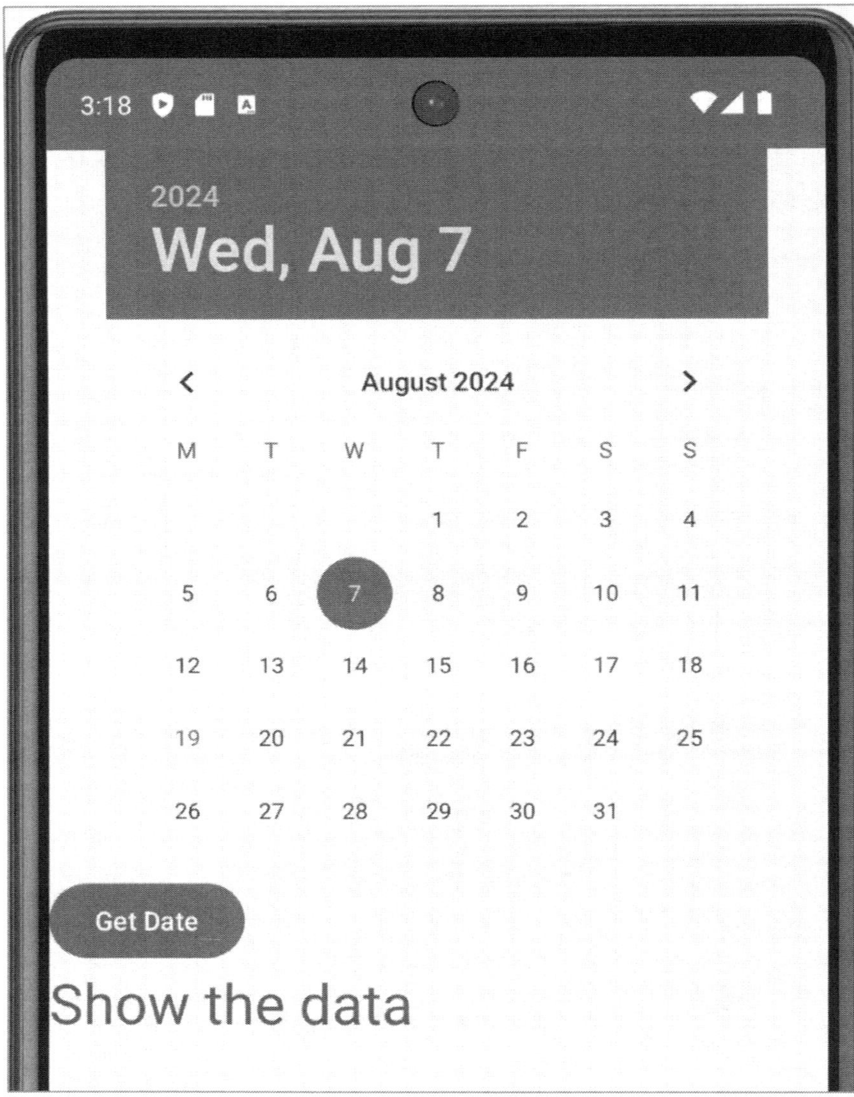

Rysunek 5.131 DatePicker – a tool for setting the date. Version: spinner

We will now create an application that retrieves data from the calendar. We create a **linear layout** in which we place the following widgets: **DatePicker, Button** and **TextView**.

```
<?xml version="1.0" encoding="utf-8"?>
<LinearLayout
xmlns:android="http://schemas.android.com/apk/res/android"
    android:layout_width="match_parent"
    android:layout_height="match_parent"
    android:orientation="vertical">
    <DatePicker
        android:id="@+id/getDate"
        android:layout_width="wrap_content"
        android:layout_height="wrap_content"
        android:firstDayOfWeek="2"
        android:layout_gravity="center"/>
    <Button
        android:id="@+id/Button"
        android:layout_width="wrap_content"
        android:layout_height="wrap_content"
        android:text="Get Date"
        android:onClick="getDate"/>
    <TextView
        android:id="@+id/text1"
        android:layout_width="match_parent"
        android:layout_height="wrap_content"
        android:text="Show the data"
        android:textSize="30dp"/>

</LinearLayout>
```

Listing 5.224 Linear layout with a DatePicker view

For this layout, we now create the corresponding activity.

```
package example.app38;
import androidx.appcompat.app.AppCompatActivity;
import android.os.Bundle;
import android.widget.DatePicker;
import android.widget.TextView;
import android.view.View;

public class MainActivity extends AppCompatActivity {
    TextView textView1;
    DatePicker datePicker;
    @Override
    public void onCreate(Bundle savedInstanceState) {
        super.onCreate(savedInstanceState);
        setContentView(R.layout.activity_main);
        textView1=findViewById(R.id.text1);
        datePicker=findViewById(R.id.getDate);
    }
public void getDate(View view){
        int d=datePicker.getDayOfMonth();
        int m=datePicker.getMonth();
        int y=datePicker.getYear();
textView1.setText("Day: "+d+"\nMonth: "+m+ "\nYear: " +y);
    }
}
```

Listing 5.225 MainActivity.java activity code

We create two objects: one of type **TextView** , and one of type **DatePicker.** We will use them in the next part of the code.

```
TextView textView1;
DatePicker datePicker;
```

Listing 5.226 Creating TextView and DatePicker objects

In the **onCreate** method, we retrieve references to the **DatePicker** and **TextView** views defined in the layout file and assign them to the previously created variables.

```
textView1=findViewById(R.id.text1);
datePicker=findViewById(R.id.getDate);
```

Listing 5.227 Creating references to objects

The next task will be to define the **Download** class, which will be triggered when the button is clicked. In Java, instead of creating a separate class, it's common to define an inner class or use an anonymous class or a lambda expression. Here's an example of how this can be done:

```
    int d=datePicker.getDayOfMonth();
    int m=datePicker.getMonth();
    int y=datePicker.getYear();
textView1.setText("Day: "+d +"\nMonth: "+m+ "\nYear: "+y);
```

Listing 5.228 Creating variables to store data retrieved from the calendar

In this class, we create three **variables** of type **int** and assign them **values** retrieved from the **calendar**. We use three date - related functions:

- **getYear** – retrieves the selected year;
- **getDayOfMonth** – retrieves the selected day of the month;
- **getMonth** – retrieves the month number.

Next, the retrieved data is used to create a string that will be displayed in the **TextView** field. It's worth noting the **\n** character, which moves the text to the next line. After launching the application, selecting the current date, and pressing the button, the app will return the following information:

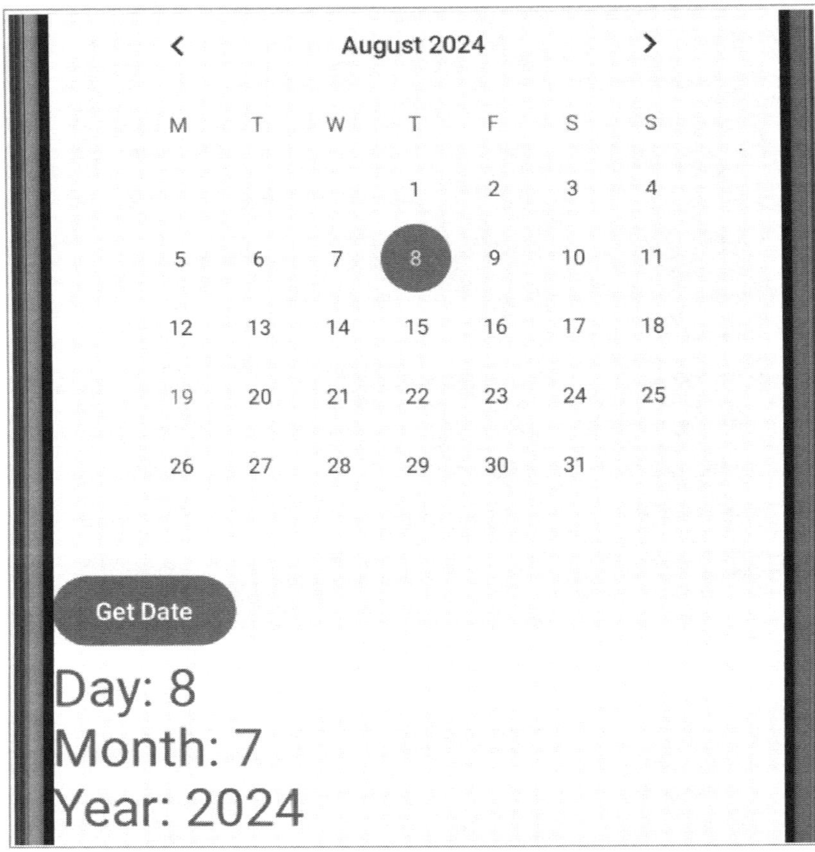

Figure 5.128 An application that retrieves the date from the calendar

However, we can see that something isn't quite right. The year and day are correct. The issue lies with the month number. The months are arranged in an array. The first month, January, occupies the first position in this array, while the current month, November, is in the eleventh position.The problem stems from how the array is structured.

We must remember that arrays are zero - indexed. So January is at position 0, and November is at position 10. Therefore, we need to add one simple operation. Before displaying the month number (i.e., the variable m), we need to increase it by 1. So we add the following line to the program code:

```
m=m+1;
```

Listing 5.229 Zmiana wartości zmiennej m

5.19.4 Retrieving time – TimePicker

The application code is located in a folder named **Application39**. To retrieve the time, we will use the **TimePicker** component. We'll start by presenting it in its simplest form by inserting it as a **view** into the **layout** file.

TimePicker, like **DatePicker**, can take two different forms. The first resembles a clock, where the time is set by moving the hands. The second form is similar to **DatePicker** with the Spinner setting.

The following code inserts both forms into the application for comparison.

```
<?xml version="1.0" encoding="utf-8"?>
<LinearLayout
    xmlns:android="http://schemas.android.com/apk/res/android"
    xmlns:tools="http://schemas.android.com/tools"
    android:id="@+id/LinearLayout1"
    android:layout_width="match_parent"
    android:layout_height="match_parent"
    android:orientation="vertical">
    <TimePicker
        android:layout_width="wrap_content"
        android:layout_height="wrap_content"
        android:id="@+id/timePicker2"
        android:layout_gravity="center"
        android:timePickerMode="clock"/>
    <TimePicker
        android:layout_width="wrap_content"
        android:layout_height="wrap_content"
        android:id="@+id/timePicker"
        android:layout_gravity="center"
        android:timePickerMode="spinner"/>

</LinearLayout>
```

Listing 5.230 Linear layout with TimePicker view

Figure 5.129 TimePicker – clock - style version (at the top), and spinner - style version (at the bottom)

For practice, we'll use the clock with hands – the one with the attribute **android:timePickerMode** set to **clock**. Next, we move to the main activity file. There, in the **onCreate** method, we add code that sets both clocks to 24 - hour format.

```
time = findViewById(R.id.clock1);
time.setIs24HourView(true);
```

Listing 5.231 Creating a reference to the TimePicker element

The next task will be to retrieve the time from the clock. First, let's prepare the layout file, which will be similar to the one from the previous task. It will contain a **TimePicker** element, a **Button,** and a **TextView**. In the **MainActivity.java** file, we place the following code:

```
package example.app39;

import androidx.appcompat.app.AppCompatActivity;
import android.annotation.SuppressLint;
import android.os.Bundle;
import android.widget.TextView;
import android.widget.TimePicker;
import android.view.View;

public class MainActivity extends AppCompatActivity {
    TimePicker time;
    TextView textView1;
    @Override
    protected void onCreate(Bundle savedInstanceState) {
        super.onCreate(savedInstanceState);
        setContentView(R.layout.activity_main);
        textView1 = findViewById(R.id.text1);
        time = findViewById(R.id.clock1);
        time.setIs24HourView(true);
    }
    @SuppressLint("SetTextI18n")
    public void getTime(View view) {
        int hour, minute;
        hour = time.getHour();
        minute = time.getMinute();
    textView1.setText("Selected time "+ hour +":"+ minute);
    }
}
```

Listing 5.232 Main activity code

We create two variables: one of type **TimePicker** named **time,** and one of type **TextView** named **textView1**. In the onCreate method, we create references to these objects.

The **Download** class will be triggered when the **Button** is clicked. This will retrieve the hour and minute using two methods: **getHour** and **getMinute**. Then, the retrieved time will be displayed in the **textView1** view.

Figure 5.130 An application that retrieves time using the clock icon

If we look closely at the application above the **Button**, we can notice a keyboard icon. This is a built - in mechanism included in the **TimePicker** view when using the **Clock** mode. When we tap the icon, a form appears that allows us to manually enter the desired time.

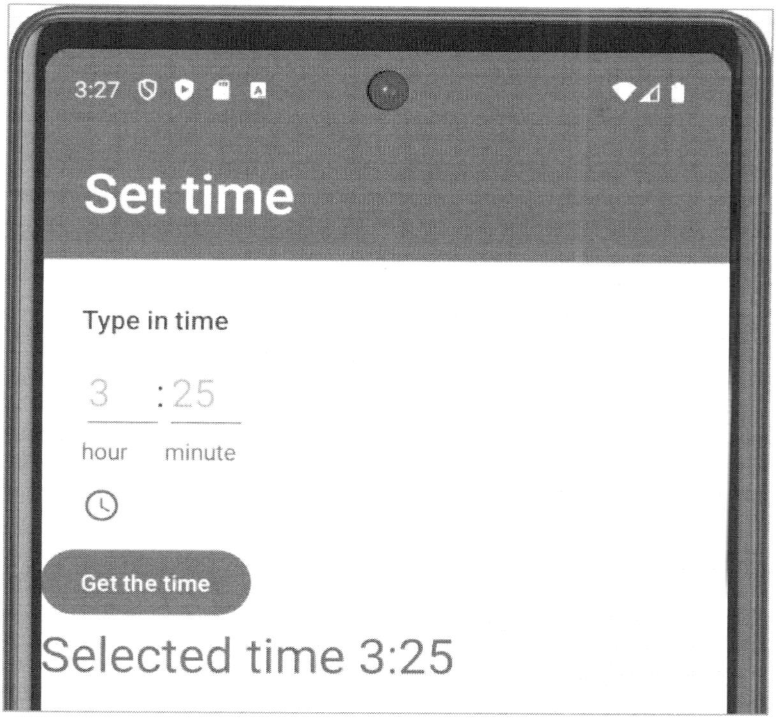

Figure 5.131 An application that retrieves time using a form

Pressing the clock icon switches the view back.

5.20 Storing data in the application

5.20.1 Saving user preferences

Every advanced application we use frequently has certain persistent settings. An example of such an app could be an email client - an application for receiving and sending email messages. Persistent settings might include, for example, the default sender address (when using more than one account in the app) or the email signature.

To define such persistent saved settings, we can use **User Preferences**, which in **Android Studio** are handled using the **SharedPreferences** class. We'll create a simple application with a layout consisting of: one **Checkbox** field, one **EditText** field, and a **Button**. The full application code is located in a folder named **Application40**.

```
<LinearLayout
xmlns:android="http://schemas.android.com/apk/res/android"
    android:layout_width="match_parent"
    android:layout_height="match_parent"
    android:orientation="vertical" >

    <CheckBox
        android:layout_width="wrap_content"
        android:layout_height="wrap_content"
        android:text="@string/regulations"
        android:id="@+id/regulations"/>

    <EditText
        android:id="@+id/text1"
        android:layout_width="match_parent"
        android:layout_height="wrap_content" />

    <Button
        android:id="@+id/button"
        android:text="Save"
        android:layout_width="match_parent"
        android:layout_height="wrap_content"
        android:onClick="onClick"/>
</LinearLayout>
```

Listing 5.233 Layout code – activity_main.xml

In the activity file, we create a preference:

```
SharedPreferences appPrefs =
getPreferences(MODE_PRIVATE);
```

Listing 5.234 Using the getPreferences method

The **getPreferences** method retrieves the user's settings and stores them in the **appPrefs** object. The argument **MODE_PRIVATE** ensures that the saved settings are kept only within the application, so the data does not leak outside. Next, we retrieve the settings of the layout elements so they can be remembered.

```
String text = appPrefs.getString("text", "");
EditText editText = findViewById(R.id.text1);
editText.setText(text);

boolean check = appPrefs.getBoolean("checkBox", false);
CheckBox checkBox = findViewById(R.id.regulations);
checkBox.setChecked(check);
```

Listing 5.235 Saving retrieved user preferences

Here, we use two methods: **getString**, which retrieves the text entered in the **EditText** field and **getBoolean**, which retrieves the value from the **CheckBox** field. Of course, the checkbox can have two states: **checked** or unchecked. We also use two methods: **setText** and **setChecked**, which, after retrieving the data, save the settings in the application. The next step is to define the **onClick** method.

```
public void onClick(View view) {
     SharedPreferences sharedPreferences =
getPreferences(MODE_PRIVATE);
     SharedPreferences.Editor prefsEditor =
sharedPreferences.edit();
     EditText editText = findViewById(R.id.text1);
     String text2 = editText.getText().toString();
     prefsEditor.putString("text", text2);
     CheckBox checkBox = findViewById(R.id.regulations);
     boolean cb = checkBox.isChecked();
     prefsEditor.putBoolean("checkBox", cb);
     prefsEditor.apply();
}
```

Listing 5.236 Saving retrieved user preferences

We retrieve the created settings (**preferences**). Next, we get the text entered in the **EditText** field. The **putString** method saves the text to the **preferences** file. We follow a similar process for the **CheckBox** field. Here, we use the **putBoolean** method, which saves the state of the **checkbox** - whether it is checked or unchecked. The **apply** method confirms and commits the changes.

Now we run the application. We check the **CheckBox** and enter some text into the **EditText** field. After pressing the **Button**, the selected fields will be saved. We can verify the application's behavior by restarting it. The checkbox will remain checked, and the text field will contain the previously entered text.

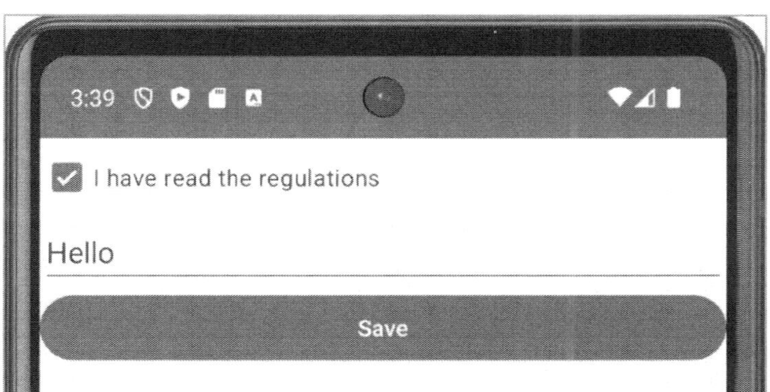

Figure 5.1326 Form collecting preference

The complete **MainActivity.java** file looks as follows:

```
package example.app40;
import androidx.appcompat.app.AppCompatActivity;
import android.content.SharedPreferences;
import android.os.Bundle;
import android.view.View;
import android.widget.CheckBox;
import android.widget.EditText;

public class MainActivity extends AppCompatActivity {
    @Override
    protected void onCreate(Bundle savedInstanceState) {
        super.onCreate(savedInstanceState);
        setContentView(R.layout.activity_main);
SharedPreferences appPrefs = getPreferences(MODE_PRIVATE);
        String text = appPrefs.getString("text", "");
        EditText editText = findViewById(R.id.text1);
        editText.setText(text);
boolean check = appPrefs.getBoolean("checkBox", false);
        CheckBox checkBox = findViewById(R.id.regulations);
        checkBox.setChecked(check);
    }
    public void onClick(View view) {
SharedPreferences sharedPreferences =
getPreferences(MODE_PRIVATE);
SharedPreferences.Editor prefsEditor =
sharedPreferences.edit();
        EditText editText = findViewById(R.id.text1);
        String text2 = editText.getText().toString();
        prefsEditor.putString("text", text2);
        CheckBox checkBox = findViewById(R.id.regulations);
        boolean cb = checkBox.isChecked();
        prefsEditor.putBoolean("checkBox", cb);
        prefsEditor.apply();
    }
}
```

Listing 5.237 MainActivity.java Main Activity Code

5.20.2 Retrieving and saving data using files.

Data in the application can be retrieved from a file located in the app's resources. We also have the option to save such data to a file. The first version of the program will save data to a file. The application code is located in a directory named **Application41**. We create a simple **LinearLayout** layout containing: an **EditText** field from which we will retrieve the text to be sent, and a **Button.**

```
<?xml version="1.0" encoding="utf-8"?>
<LinearLayout

xmlns:android="http://schemas.android.com/apk/res/android"
    xmlns:app="http://schemas.android.com/apk/res-auto"
    xmlns:tools="http://schemas.android.com/tools"
    android:layout_width="match_parent"
    android:layout_height="match_parent"
    tools:context=".MainActivity"
    android:orientation="vertical">

    <EditText
        android:id="@+id/text"
        android:layout_width="wrap_content"
        android:layout_height="wrap_content"
        android:hint="Write the text here"
        android:textSize="15pt"/>
    <Button
        android:layout_width="wrap_content"
        android:layout_height="wrap_content"
        android:text="Save text"
        android:onClick="save"/>

</LinearLayout>
```

Listing 5.238 Layout file with a form for data input

In the activity file, we create an **EditText** object, and in the **onCreate** method, we retrieve a **reference** to it from the **layout** file.

```
EditText editText;
@Override
protected void onCreate(Bundle savedInstanceState) {
    super.onCreate(savedInstanceState);
    setContentView(R.layout.activity_main);
    editText = findViewById(R.id.text);
```

Listing 5.239 Creating a reference to the text field

The most important part of the code will be located in the **Save** function, which will be triggered when the **Button** is pressed.

```
String text1 = editText.getText().toString();
```

Listing 5.240 Creating a text variable

We create a variable of type **String** and assign to it the text retrieved from the **EditText** field.

```
try {
FileOutputStream file = openFileOutput("file.txt",
MODE_PRIVATE);
 OutputStreamWriter stream = new OutputStreamWriter(file);
     stream.write(text1);
     stream.close();
     editText.setText("");
}
```

Listing 5.241 Try block

Next, in the **try** block, we open our text file. We use the **FileOutputStream** class, which creates an output stream. The **openFileOutput** method takes two parameters: the first is the name of the file where we will save the data. If a file with the given name does not exist, it will be created. The second parameter is the so - called **open mode**. The mode used in the example, **MODE_PRIVATE**, will cause previously saved data in the file to be deleted. There is also another mode, **MODE_APPEND**, which will append new data to an existing file.

Using an object of the **OutputStreamWriter** class, we create a stream that writes data. The write method saves the data to the file, and **close** closes the stream after the operation is complete. Finally, the **setText** method of the **EditText** object replaces the user - entered text with an empty string (i.e., clears the field). We still need to define the exception.

```
catch (IOException exc ){
exc.printStackTrace();
}
```

Listing 5.242 Defining the exception

If any errors occur while opening the file or writing data to it, the exception will display an error code.

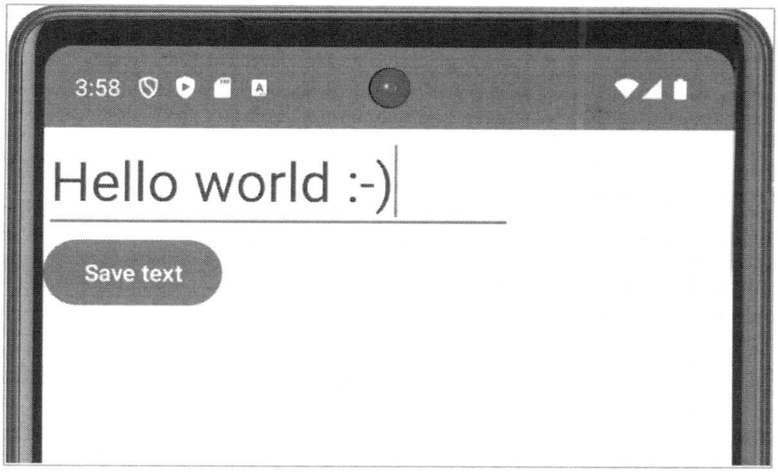

Figure 5.1337 Form for saving text to a file

If we successfully launched the application and saved data to it, it would be a good idea to check whether the entered text is actually present in the file. Locating the correct file is not that simple. We'll start by opening the **Device File Explorer** tab. On the left side of the editor, we find the icon with **three dots**. Click it and from the context menu, select the option: **Device Explorer**.

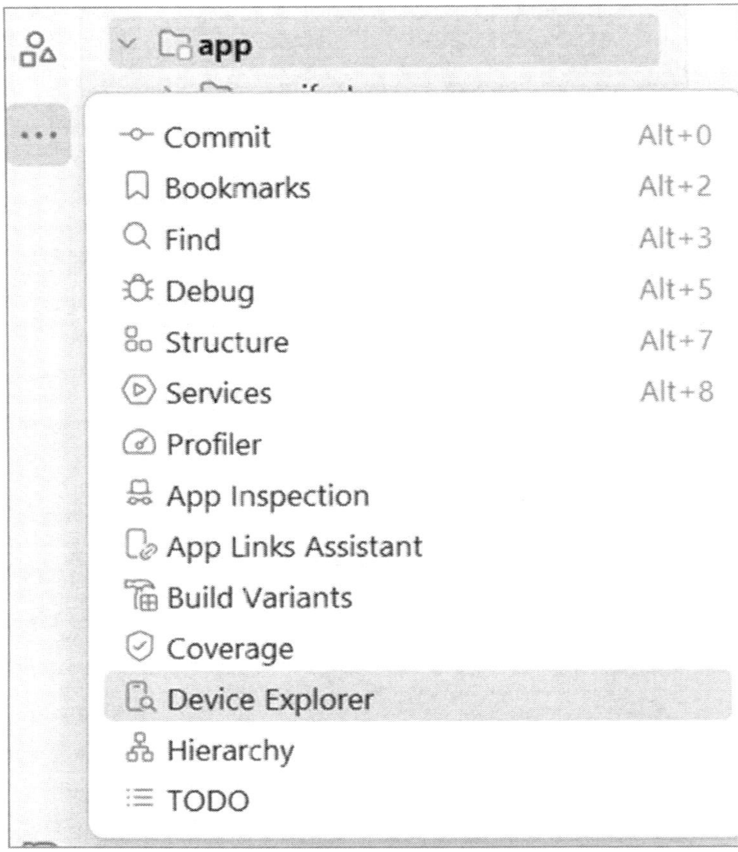

Figure 5.1348 Menu used to open the Device Explorer tool

After clicking it, a button will appear on the right side that allows you to open the file explorer.

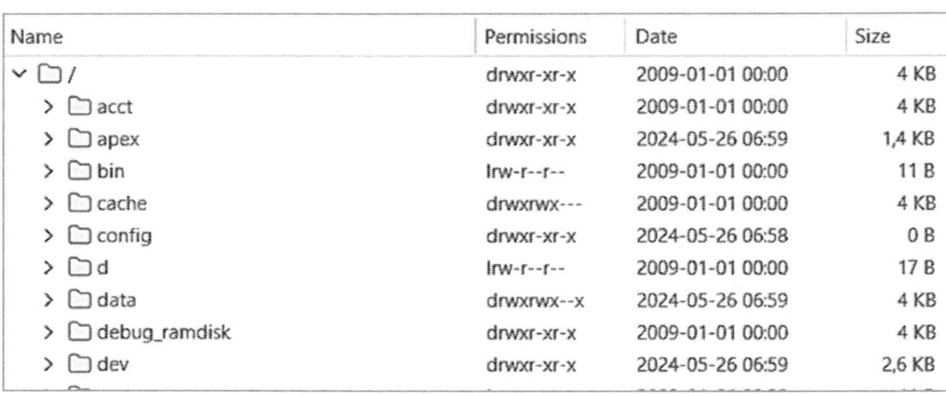

Name	Permissions	Date	Size
/	drwxr-xr-x	2009-01-01 00:00	4 KB
acct	drwxr-xr-x	2009-01-01 00:00	4 KB
apex	drwxr-xr-x	2024-05-26 06:59	1,4 KB
bin	lrw-r--r--	2009-01-01 00:00	11 B
cache	drwxrwx---	2009-01-01 00:00	4 KB
config	drwxr-xr-x	2024-05-26 06:58	0 B
d	lrw-r--r--	2009-01-01 00:00	17 B
data	drwxrwx--x	2024-05-26 06:59	4 KB
debug_ramdisk	drwxr-xr-x	2009-01-01 00:00	4 KB
dev	drwxr-xr-x	2024-05-26 06:59	2,6 KB

Figure 5.1359 Device Explorer – File explorer for application contents

This tab will display a list of files that were created by Android Studio during runtime. It contains data from all created applications. If different emulators were used during testing, each version is also saved.

We begin searching for files by expanding the Data branch, and then expanding the next folder with the same name. In the internal directory, we look for the name of our application. Its name will start with the **package** name. The application created in this exercise will therefore be named **example.nr41.Application41**. Inside the folder with the correct name, there is a subfolder called **Files**. After expanding it, we will find our text file.

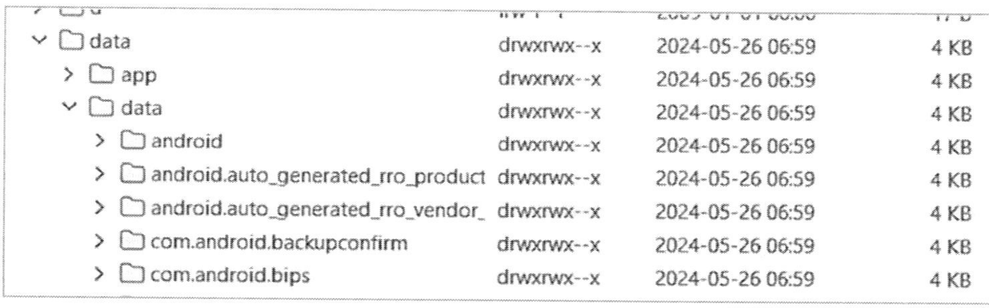

Figure 5.136 Data directory

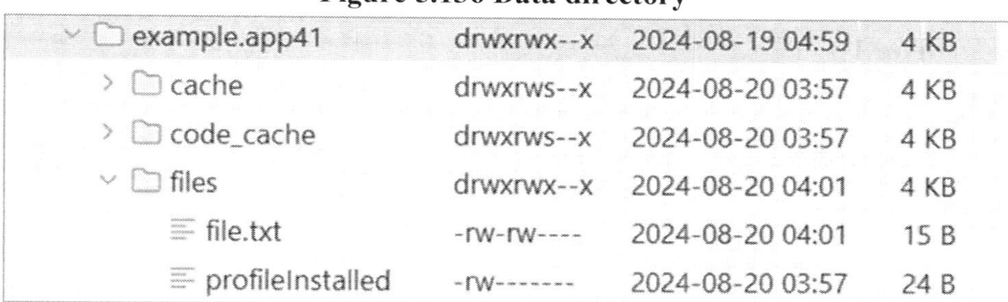

Figure 5.137 File with saved data visible in the file explorer

Just click on it, and a tab will appear in the application window displaying the text. You can easily read its contents.

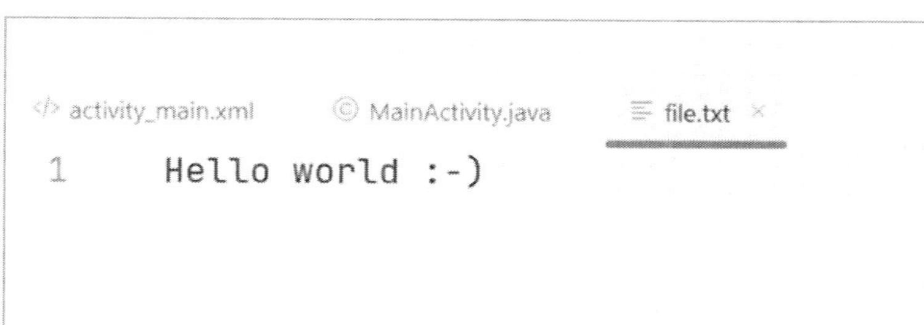

Figure 5.138 Opened file in the application window

If we want to open the file on the computer's disk, simply right - click in the code area and select **Open in Explorer** from the context menu.

5.20.3 Reading data from the file

We will add another button to our application's layout. Its purpose will be to read data from the file and display it in the application. The application code is located in the directory **Application41a**. In the activity file, we add a class called **Read**, which will be triggered when the button is pressed.

```
public void read(View view){
    try
    {
  FileInputStream file2 = openFileInput("file2.txt");
  InputStreamReader stream = new InputStreamReader(file2);
  BufferedReader reader = new BufferedReader(stream);
  StringBuilder text2 = new StringBuilder();
    String line;
  while ((line = reader.readLine()) != null) {
            text2.append(line).append("\n");
        }
        reader.close();
        editText.setText(text2.toString());
    }
    catch (IOException ex) {
        ex.printStackTrace();
    }
}
```

Listing 5.243 Definition of the Read Method

We create another **stream,** this time to open a file for reading. In the **openFileInput** method **attribute**, we provide the name of the file whose contents we want to read. Since we want to read the information we previously saved in the file **file1.txt**, we specify its name.

The **BufferedReader** class is responsible for reading the contents of the file. It uses a special buffer to temporarily store the data being read. An object of the **StringBuilder** class will construct a string from the retrieved data. The data is in binary form, and the class's task is to convert it back into a readable string.

The **while** loop will continue executing until it encounters an empty line, which will happen when we reach the end of the file. Upon encountering a newline character, the program will start displaying the retrieved text from a new line.

We close the **stream** using the **close** method, and the retrieved text is placed in an **EditText** field. This class also includes a **catch** section, which will be triggered in case of issues with data retrieval and will then display an error. The application's behavior after launching will look like in the illustration below:

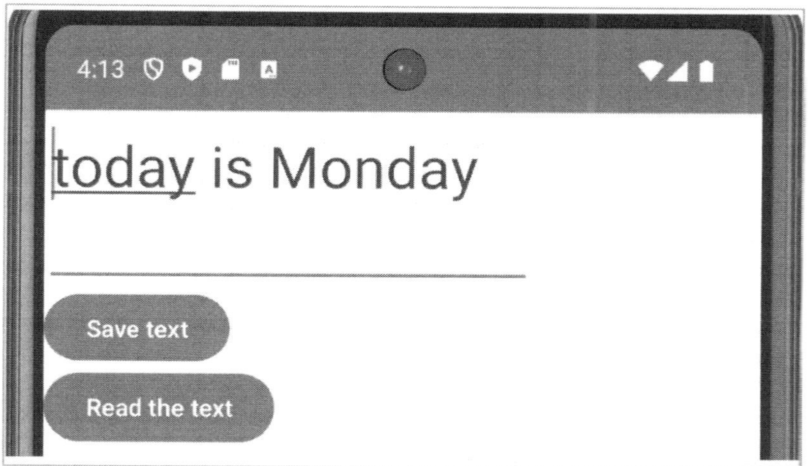

Figure 5.139 Application for Retrieving and Displaying Data to and from a File

The full code of the **MainActivity.java** file is as follows:

```
package example.app41a;

import androidx.appcompat.app.AppCompatActivity;
import android.os.Bundle;
import android.view.View;
import android.widget.EditText;
import java.io.BufferedReader;
import java.io.FileInputStream;
import java.io.FileOutputStream;
import java.io.IOException;
import java.io.InputStreamReader;
import java.io.OutputStreamWriter;

public class MainActivity extends AppCompatActivity {
    EditText editText;
    @Override
    protected void onCreate(Bundle savedInstanceState) {
        super.onCreate(savedInstanceState);
        setContentView(R.layout.activity_main);
        editText = findViewById(R.id.text1);
    }
    public void read(View view){
        try
        {
  FileInputStream file2 = openFileInput("file2.txt");
  InputStreamReader stream = new InputStreamReader(file2);
  BufferedReader reader = new BufferedReader(stream);
  StringBuilder text2 = new StringBuilder();
            String line;
            while ((line = reader.readLine()) != null) {
                text2.append(line).append("\n");
            }
            reader.close();
            editText.setText(text2.toString());
        }
        catch (IOException ex) {
            ex.printStackTrace();
        }
    }
    public void save(View view){
        String text3 = editText.getText().toString();
        try {
    FileOutputStream file = openFileOutput("file2.txt",
MODE_PRIVATE);
 OutputStreamWriter stream = new OutputStreamWriter(file);
            stream.write(text3);
            stream.close();
            editText.setText("");
        }
        catch (IOException exc){
            exc.printStackTrace();
        }
    }
}
```

Listing 5.244 MainActivity.java file

5.21 SQLite Databases

5.21.1 Creating a Simple Database

Retrieving and saving data using text files is a straightforward operation. However, in applications, a better solution is to store information in databases. An ideal choice for mobile applications is using **SQLite**. It is, in a way, a simplified version of the popular **MySQL** and is operated with similar commands. The application code is located in a folder named **Application42**.

In this exercise, we will use a simple database designed to store information about students. In relational databases, tables are used to organize information. Before we start programming, we need to prepare a table with the data we want to store in the database. As mentioned at the beginning, the database will store information about students. The table we will use will look as follows:

Id	FirstName	Last Name	Class
1	John	Smith	1PT
2	Thomas	Jones	2PT
3	Elisabeth	Green	3PT

Table 5.4 Data Table Used in the Database

We will begin creating the application by preparing the layout file. It will contain a **TextView** field, which will be used to display the contents of the database.

```
<?xml version="1.0" encoding="utf-8"?>
<LinearLayout

xmlns:android="http://schemas.android.com/apk/res/android"
    xmlns:app="http://schemas.android.com/apk/res-auto"
    xmlns:tools="http://schemas.android.com/tools"
    android:layout_width="match_parent"
    android:layout_height="match_parent"
    android:orientation="vertical"
    tools:context=".MainActivity">
    <TextView
        android:id="@+id/t1"
        android:layout_width="wrap_content"
        android:layout_height="wrap_content"
        android:text="@string/t1"
        android:textSize="12pt"
        android:textColor="@color/black"/>

</LinearLayout>
```

Listing 5.245 Layout File: main_activity.xml

The next step is to create a class named Assistant.java. This class will be responsible for handling the database.

```
public class Assistant extends SQLiteOpenHelper
```

Listing 5.246 Declaration of the Assistant Class Inheriting from SQLiteOpenHelper

The **Assistant** class will inherit from the **SQLiteOpenHelper** class. This class is responsible for managing and editing databases. To function properly, it requires a **constructor**, which we create in the following way:

```
public Assistant(Context context){
    super(context, "school.db", null, 1);
}
```

Listing 5.247 Constructor of the Assistant Class

Using the constructor, we will pass four parameters: the context, the name of the database, information about the so - called cursor, and the database version number.

Database handling also requires **two additional methods** to ensure proper functionality. The first one is **onCreate**, in which we will create the table. In our application, the **onCreate** method will look as follows:

```
public void onCreate(SQLiteDatabase db1) {
    db1.execSQL("CREATE TABLE STUDENT (id INTEGER PRIMARY
KEY AUTOINCREMENT, "+ "NAME text," + "LAST_NAME text, " +
"CLASS text);");
}
```

Listing 5.248 Creating the STUDENT Table

The argument of the **onCreate** method will be the name of the database. The **execSQL** method allows us to execute SQL statements. We create a table named student, which contains four columns, as defined in the table we prepared earlier. You can notice that the SQL command used to create the table is very similar to the syntax used in MySQL.

We create four columns:

- Id
- First Name
- Last Name
- Class

The **id** column will be of type INTEGER. Additionally, it will serve as the primary key, as indicated by **PRIMARY KEY**. The **AUTOINCREMENT** function ensures that each new record in the table will be assigned the next sequential number starting from **1**.

The remaining columns are of type TEXT, which allows us to enter data in text format. The next method we need to create is **onUpgrade**. This method will be useful when we need to replace one database with another, for example, after editing the data. The method takes three arguments: the **name of the database,** the **version number of the new database** and the **version number of the current database.**

```
public void onUpgrade(SQLiteDatabase db1, int new1, int
old1) {

}
```

Listing 5.249 Declaration of the onUpgrade Method

At this stage, all the essential components of the Assistant class are ready. The remaining classes are created with a specific database in mind and are not always required. The **school** database will need a few additional **classes** to handle its operations. The first of these will be the **add** class. Its purpose is to add records to the database.

```
public void add(String name, String last_name, String
class1)
{
    SQLiteDatabase db1 = getWritableDatabase();
    ContentValues data = new ContentValues();
    data.put("name", name);
    data.put("last_name", last_name);
    data.put("class", class1);
    db1.insertOrThrow("STUDENT", null, data);
}
```

Listing 5.250 Definition of the add Method

The class takes three parameters of type **String,** as we will be passing records in **text** format. These parameters are: **first name, last name** and **class** . They correspond to the **column names** in the database table. The method **getWritableDatabase** is used to open the database and allows for editing. We assign this method to the object **bd1**, which represents our database.

An object of the **ContentValues** class will store the values passed to the method. The **put** method is used to pass **key** - value pairs to the database, where the key is the **column** name and the value is the data (similar to passing intents).

The final method, **insertOrThrow,** will insert the data into the **Student** table.

To display the contents of the database, we will need a class called **writeAll**. This class will be based on an **object** of the **Cursor** class. A cursor is a type of pointer that indicates selected parts of the database. It also allows navigation through the database elements.

```
public Cursor write_all()
{
    SQLiteDatabase db1 = getReadableDatabase();
    return db1.rawQuery("SELECT * from STUDENT ", null);
}
```

Listing 5.251 Definition of the writeAll Method

We create an **SQLiteDatabase** object and use **getReadableDatabase** to open the database in read - only mode. The **getReadableDatabase** method differs from **getWritableDatabase** in that it allows only reading data, without the ability to modify it. Next, we create a **Cursor** object and use the **rawQuery** method to execute a query on the database. This is a standard **MySQL** query that retrieves all data from the **STUDENT** table. The cursor will fetch and store the retrieved data.

Finally, we return the cursor object, which contains the results of the query. At this point, the **Assistant** class is fully ready to operate. Its complete code looks as follows:

```
package example.app42;
import android.content.ContentValues;
import android.content.Context;
import android.database.Cursor;
import android.database.sqlite.SQLiteDatabase;
import android.database.sqlite.SQLiteOpenHelper;

public class Assistant extends SQLiteOpenHelper {
     public Assistant(Context context){
          super(context, "school.db", null, 1);
     }

     @Override
     public void onCreate(SQLiteDatabase db1) {
          db1.execSQL("CREATE TABLE STUDENT (id INTEGER
PRIMARY KEY AUTOINCREMENT, "+ "NAME text," + "LAST_NAME
text, " + "CLASS text);");
     }
     @Override
     public void onUpgrade(SQLiteDatabase db1, int new1, int
old1) {

     }
     public void add(String name, String last_name, String
class1)
     {
          SQLiteDatabase db1 = getWritableDatabase();
          ContentValues data = new ContentValues();
          data.put("name",name);
          data.put("last_name",last_name);
          data.put("class", class1);
          db1.insertOrThrow("STUDENT",null,data);
     }
     public Cursor write_all()
     {
        SQLiteDatabase db1 = getReadableDatabase();
        return db1.rawQuery("SELECT * from STUDENT ", null);
     }
}
```

Listing 5.252 Code of the Assistant Class

Now it's time to edit **MainActivity.java**. We will start by creating two objects. The first one, named **assistant**, will be an instance of the **Assistant** class and will be used to manage the database. The second object, of the **Cursor** class, will be named **k**.

```
Assistant assistant = new Assistant(this);
Cursor c;
```

Listing 5.253 Creating an Instance of the Assistant Class

We create a simple class that will populate the database table.

```
public void addData()
{
    assistant.add("John","Smith","1PT");
    assistant.add("Thomas","Jones","2PT");
    assistant.add("Elisabeth","Green","3PT");
}
```

Listing 5.254 Definition of the addData Method

This method will add new records to the database. It uses the assistant object and the previously defined add method. You can observe that each record includes only three fields: **first name, last name**, and **class**. The contents of the **ID** column are added automatically, since this field is defined with AUTOINCREMENT. The values in this column will be filled with consecutive numbers. Next, we move on to the **onCreate** method, where we obtain a **reference** to the **TextView** field, which will be used to display data from the database.

```
TextView text = findViewById(R.id.t1);
```

Listing 5.255 Reference to the TextView View

We launch the **addData** method:

```
addData();
```

Listing 5.256 Calling the addData Method

Ana also wrtieAll:

```
c = assistant.write_all();
```

Listing 5.257 Calling the writeAll Method

As mentioned earlier, a **cursor** is a type of pointer. When data is retrieved using the writeAll method, the cursor is positioned at the first retrieved element. To allow the display method to show all the necessary data, we need to properly move the cursor. For this purpose, we will use a simple **while** loop.

```
while(c.moveToNext())
{
    int id=c.getInt(0);
    String imie = c.getString(1);
    String nazwisko = c.getString(2);
    String klasa = c.getString(3);
    text.setText(text.getText()+"\n " + id + ". " + imie +
" "+ nazwisko +   " " +klasa );
}
```

Listing 5.258 Loop for Reading and Displaying All Records from the Database

The loop **condition** depends on the **moveToNext method**, which handles cursor movement. The **loop** will continue to run until it reaches the last element. The **moveToNext** method, as the name suggests, moves the cursor to the next element. If the cursor can no longer move forward, it means it has reached the last element, and the loop will terminate.

There are three other methods for handling cursors:

- **moveToFirst()** – moves the cursor to the first element
- **moveToLast()** – moves the cursor to the last element
- **moveToPrevious()** – moves the cursor one element backward, to the previous item

Once the loop starts, a kind of **data array** is formed. The cursor will move between elements and retrieve data, which will then be stored in prepared variables. In the final line, we create a string using the **setText** method and place it in the **TextView** view. Finally, the database should be closed, and we will use the following code for that:

```
c.close();
```

Listing 5.259 Closing the Cursor

The complete **MainActivity.java** activity will look as follows:

```
package example.app42;

import androidx.appcompat.app.AppCompatActivity;
import android.annotation.SuppressLint;
import android.os.Bundle;
import android.database.Cursor;
import android.widget.TextView;

public class MainActivity extends AppCompatActivity {
    Assistant assistant = new Assistant(this);
    Cursor c;
    public void addData()
    {
        assistant.add("John","Smith","1PT");
        assistant.add("Thomas","Jones","2PT");
        assistant.add("Elisabeth","Green","3PT");
    }
    @SuppressLint("SetTextI18n")
    @Override
    protected void onCreate(Bundle savedInstanceState) {
        super.onCreate(savedInstanceState);
        setContentView(R.layout.activity_main);
        TextView text = findViewById(R.id.t1);
        addData();
        c = assistant.write_all();

        while(c.moveToNext())
        {
            int id=c.getInt(0);
            String imie = c.getString(1);
            String nazwisko = c.getString(2);
            String klasa = c.getString(3);
            text.setText(text.getText()+"\n " + id + ". " +
imie + " "+ nazwisko +  " " +klasa );
        }
        c.close();
    }
}
```

Listing 5.260 MainActivity.java Activity File

After launching the application, we see the contents of the database displayed.

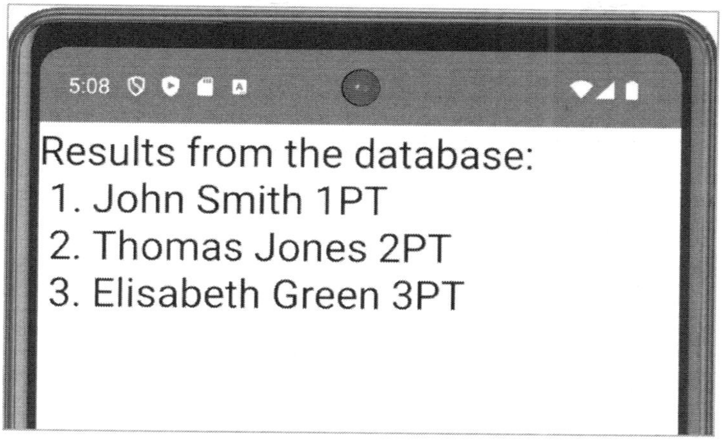

Figure 5.140 Displayed Information Stored in the Database

A problem arises when we relaunch the application. Data is added to the database every time the app is started. As a result, after reopening the application, we receive the following data from the database.

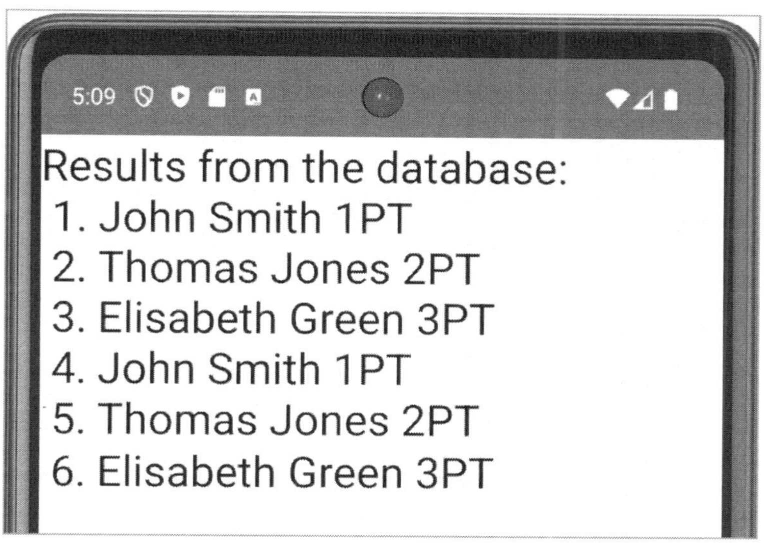

Figure 5.141 Displayed Information Stored in the Database After Reopening the Application

Now imagine a situation where the application is launched 100, 1000, or even more times. That's why it's important to ensure that the app inserts data into the database only when it is empty. The program will count the number of records and insert data only if the database is empty. In the **Assistant** class, we create another method to handle this logic.

You can find the following solution in the application named **Application42a**.

```
public int count()
{
    SQLiteDatabase db1 = getReadableDatabase();
    String counter = "SELECT count(*) FROM STUDENT";
    Cursor c2 = db1.rawQuery(counter, null);
    c2.moveToFirst();
    int quantity = c2.getInt(0);
    return quantity;
}
```

Listing 5.261 Definition of the count Method

We open the database in read - only mode. We create a variable named **meter,** which will send an appropriate **query** to the database. The **query** is designed to count the number of **records** currently stored in the database. The **result** is then passed to a **cursor**, and from there to a variable named **quantity**. This variable will be used in the main activity. We then slightly modify the **addData** function:

```
public void addData() {
    int quantity2 =  assistant.count();
    if (quantity2 == 0) {
        assistant.add("John", "Smith", "1PT");
        assistant.add("Thomas", "Jones", "2PT");
        assistant.add("Elisabeth", "Green", "3PT");
    }
}
```

Listing 5.262 Definition of the addData Method

We retrieve the data returned by the **count** method and assign it to a variable named **quantity2**. The name of this variable is intentionally different to emphasize that it is not the same as the one used in the **Assistant** class. Before inserting data into the database, a **conditional statement** checks whether any records already exist. If the database already contains data, the method will not execute. As a result, even after launching the application multiple times, the database will display the same data as it did the first time.

5.21.2 Adding Data Using a Form

Databases are a practical tool for storing and processing data in an application, especially one that collects large amounts of information. Until now, we've used a database that was initialized automatically when the app started. However, a database should also allow for editing and adding data based on the user's needs.

In the next exercise, we will use the Student database. This time, however, we will add data using a simple form. The application code is located in the folder named **Application42b**.

In the layout file of the new application, we create a form consisting of three **EditText** fields. Using this form, we will add student information to the database: **First Name**, **Last Name**, and **Class**. To confirm the entered data, we will need a **Button.** The layout code will look as follows:

```
<?xml version="1.0" encoding="utf-8"?>
<LinearLayout

xmlns:android="http://schemas.android.com/apk/res/android"
    xmlns:app="http://schemas.android.com/apk/res-auto"
    xmlns:tools="http://schemas.android.com/tools"
    android:layout_width="match_parent"
    android:layout_height="match_parent"
    android:orientation="vertical"
    tools:context=".MainActivity">

    <EditText
        android:id="@+id/name"
        android:layout_width="match_parent"
        android:layout_height="wrap_content"
        android:hint="@string/hint1"
        android:inputType="textCapSentences"/>
    <EditText
        android:id="@+id/lastName"
        android:layout_width="match_parent"
        android:layout_height="wrap_content"
        android:hint="@string/hint2"
        android:inputType="textCapSentences"
        />
    <EditText
        android:id="@+id/cl1"
        android:layout_width="match_parent"
        android:layout_height="wrap_content"
        android:hint="@string/hint3"
        android:inputType="textCapSentences"/>
    <Button
        android:layout_width="wrap_content"
        android:layout_height="wrap_content"
        android:text="@string/btn1"
        android:onClick="add"/>
</LinearLayout>
```

Listing 5.263 Code for the data - fetching system to the database

In the database, we'll need a class called **Assistant**. We create it in exactly the same way as in the previous example. Since the data will be added to the database externally, we can omit the **calculate** method in this class. Now, in the **Main Activity** file, we create a class that will retrieve data from the **EditText** fields and then send it to the database. This will be the **Add** class, which is linked to a button and will be triggered when the user presses the button. The code for the class will look like the one in the next listing. First, we create **references** to the **EditText** fields: first name, last name, and class.

```
public void add(View view) {
    EditText nm = findViewById(R.id.name);
    EditText ln = findViewById(R.id.lastName);
    EditText cl = findViewById(R.id.cl1);
```

Listing 5.264 Definition of the add method

Using the **getText** method, we retrieve the text entered by the user in the appropriate field. The **toString** method converts the entered data into a **String**. The retrieved strings are then assigned to the corresponding variables.

```
String nm2 = nm.getText().toString();
String ln2 = ln.getText().toString();
String cl2 = cl.getText().toString();
```

Listing 5.265 Creating string variables

We will pass the information to the database using an **intent**. Therefore, we create an object of the **Intent** class and send the data to a new **activity**, which we will call **SecondActivity**.

```
Intent newIntent = new Intent(this, SecondActivity.class);
```

Listing 5.266 Creating the intent

The **putExtra** method, used three times – once for each string – will send the data to the second activity. The final step is to launch the intent.

```
newIntent.putExtra("name", nm2);
newIntent.putExtra("last_name", ln2);
newIntent.putExtra("class", cl2);
startActivity(newIntent);
```

Listing 5.267 Data passed via intents

To receive the information from the intent, we will create the previously mentioned class: **SecondActivity.java**. The layout file for the second activity, named **activity_second_activity.xml**, will contain a single **TextView** view, which we will use to display the contents of the database. In the **SecondActivity** class, we will retrieve the data from the intent:

```
Bundle bundle = getIntent().getExtras();
```

Listing 5.268 Creating a Bundle object

We retrieve the strings via the intent:

```
TextView text1 = findViewById(R.id.t2);
String name = bundle.getString("name");
String lastName = bundle.getString("last_name");
String class2 = bundle.getString("class");
ast.add(name, lastName, class2);
```

Listing 5.269 Retrieving data with the intent

Using the **add** method, we place the information into the database, and then display the entire contents of the database on the screen. Below is the code for the **SecondActivity** class.

```
package example.app42b;

import androidx.appcompat.app.AppCompatActivity;

import android.annotation.SuppressLint;
import android.database.Cursor;
import android.os.Bundle;
import android.widget.TextView;
public class SecondActivity extends AppCompatActivity {
    Assistant ast = new Assistant(this);
    @SuppressLint("SetTextI18n")
    @Override
    protected void onCreate(Bundle savedInstanceState) {
        super.onCreate(savedInstanceState);
        setContentView(R.layout.activity_second);
        Bundle bundle = getIntent().getExtras();
        TextView text1 = findViewById(R.id.t2);
        String name = bundle.getString("name");
        String lastName = bundle.getString("last_name");
        String class2 = bundle.getString("class");
        ast.add(name, lastName, class2);
        Cursor k = ast.write_all();
        while (k.moveToNext()) {
            int id = k.getInt(0);
            String nm2 = k.getString(1);
            String ln2 = k.getString(2);
            String cl2 = k.getString(3);
 text1.setText(text1.getText() + "\n" + id + ". " + nm2 + "
" + ln2 + " " + cl2);
        }
    }
}
```

Listing 5.270 Code of the second activity

5.21.3 Separating the operations of adding and displaying data in the database

Displaying data from the database every time can be time - consuming and often unnecessary. Therefore, it's a good idea to separate these two operations and create one class for data entry and another for data display. We will do this in the next exercise. The application code is located in a folder named **Application42c**. We are creating a new application, which will initially consist of the following classes: **Assistant** and **MainActivity**, as well as the layout file **activity_main.xml**. In the **activity_main.xml** layout file, we will place a **TextView** with a message encouraging the user to use the database, and two Button elements – "**Enter Data**" and "**Display Data**". Code of the **activity_main.xml** file:

```
<?xml version="1.0" encoding="utf-8"?>
<LinearLayout

xmlns:android="http://schemas.android.com/apk/res/android"
    xmlns:tools="http://schemas.android.com/tools"
    android:layout_width="match_parent"
    android:layout_height="match_parent"
    android:orientation="vertical"
    tools:context=".MainActivity">

    <TextView
        android:id="@+id/name"
        android:layout_width="wrap_content"
        android:layout_height="wrap_content"
        android:text="@string/t2"
        android:textColor="@color/darkblue"
        android:layout_gravity="center_horizontal"
        android:textSize="25sp"/>
    <Button
        android:layout_width="wrap_content"
        android:layout_height="wrap_content"
        android:text="@string/button1"
        android:layout_marginTop="10dp"
        android:textSize="25sp"
        android:layout_gravity="center_horizontal"
        android:onClick="enter"/>
    <Button
        android:layout_width="wrap_content"
        android:layout_height="wrap_content"
        android:text="@string/button2"
        android:textSize="25sp"
        android:layout_gravity="center_horizontal"
        android:onClick="write"/>
</LinearLayout>
```

Listing 5.271 Layout code for activity_main.xml

Two methods, **enter** and **display**, have been linked to the **Button** elements. These methods will be defined in the main activity file, **MainActivity.java**. The activity code is as follows:

```
package example.app42c;

import androidx.appcompat.app.AppCompatActivity;
import android.content.Intent;
import android.os.Bundle;
import android.view.View;

public class MainActivity extends AppCompatActivity {
    @Override
    protected void onCreate(Bundle savedInstanceState) {
        super.onCreate(savedInstanceState);
        setContentView(R.layout.activity_main);
    }
    public void enter(View view) {
        startActivity(new Intent(this, EnterData.class));
    }
    public void write(View view) {
        startActivity(new Intent(this, WriteData.class));
    }
}
```

Listing 5.272 Main Activity Code

Both the **enter** and **display** methods launch an intent to the appropriate class. The first one is used to enter data into the database, and the second to display it on the app screen. Clicking the **Enter Data** button will launch a form used for entering data. This will start the **EnterData** class, which will resemble the class from the previous exercise. The only difference is that we will skip the automatic data display. The layout file associated with this activity will contain three **EditText** field – for entering data – and a button. The full code of this layout will look as follows:

```
<?xml version="1.0" encoding="utf-8"?>
<LinearLayout
xmlns:android="http://schemas.android.com/apk/res/android"
    xmlns:tools="http://schemas.android.com/tools"
    android:layout_width="match_parent"
    android:layout_height="match_parent"
    android:orientation="vertical"
    tools:context=".EnterData">
    <EditText
        android:id="@+id/name"
        android:layout_width="match_parent"
        android:layout_height="wrap_content"
        android:hint="@string/hint1"
        android:inputType="textCapSentences" />
    <EditText
        android:id="@+id/lastName"
        android:layout_width="match_parent"
        android:layout_height="wrap_content"
        android:hint="@string/hint2"
        android:inputType="textCapSentences"/>
    <EditText
        android:id="@+id/cl"
        android:layout_width="match_parent"
        android:layout_height="wrap_content"
        android:hint="@string/hint3"
        android:inputType="textCapSentences"/>
    <Button
        android:layout_width="wrap_content"
        android:layout_height="wrap_content"
        android:layout_marginTop="10dp"
        android:textSize="25sp"
        android:layout_gravity="center_horizontal"
        android:text="@string/button1"
        android:onClick="enter"/>
</LinearLayout>
```

Listing 5.273 Code of the data entry form activity

The **add** method will insert the data into the database. Below is the full code of the activity **EnterData.java**:

```
package example.app42c;

import androidx.appcompat.app.AppCompatActivity;
import android.content.Intent;
import android.os.Bundle;
import android.view.View;
import android.widget.EditText;

public class EnterData extends AppCompatActivity {

    @Override
    protected void onCreate(Bundle savedInstanceState) {
        super.onCreate(savedInstanceState);
        setContentView(R.layout.activity_enter_data);
    }
    public void enter(View view) {
        EditText nm = findViewById(R.id.name);
        EditText ln = findViewById(R.id.lastName);
        EditText cl = findViewById(R.id.cl);
        String nm2 = nm.getText().toString();
        String ln2 = ln.getText().toString();
        String cl2 = cl.getText().toString();
        Intent newIntent = new Intent(this, Add.class);
        newIntent.putExtra("name", nm2);
        newIntent.putExtra("lastName", ln2);
        newIntent.putExtra("class", cl2);
        startActivity(newIntent);
    }
}
```

Listing 5.274 Code of the EnterData activity

Clicking the **EnterData** button after filling out the form will trigger an **intent** that passes the data collected from the **form** to the next **activity**. In the **AddToDatabase** activity file, the information received from the **EnterData** class via the form is inserted into the database. This works exactly the same way as in the previous exercise. The code for the **AddToDatabase.java** activity is shown in the following listing:

```
package example.app42c;

import android.os.Bundle;
import androidx.activity.EdgeToEdge;
import androidx.appcompat.app.AppCompatActivity;
import androidx.core.graphics.Insets;
import androidx.core.view.ViewCompat;
import androidx.core.view.WindowInsetsCompat;
import androidx.appcompat.app.AppCompatActivity;
import android.content.Intent;
import android.os.Bundle;
import android.view.View;

public class Add extends AppCompatActivity {
    Assistant assistant = new Assistant(this);
    @Override
    protected void onCreate(Bundle savedInstanceState) {
        super.onCreate(savedInstanceState);
        setContentView(R.layout.activity_add);
        Bundle bundle = getIntent().getExtras();
        String nm = bundle.getString("name");
        String ln = bundle.getString("lastName");
        String cl = bundle.getString("class");
        assistant.add(nm, ln, cl);
    }
    public void write(View view) {
        startActivity(new Intent(this, WriteData.class));
    }
    public void enter(View view) {
        startActivity(new Intent(this, EnterData.class));
    }
}
```

Listing 5.275 AddToDatabase.java Activity

This class contains two **Button** elements, which function identically to those in the main activity file – **MainActivity.java**. The first button allows the user to display data from the database, while the second reopens the data entry form from the **EnterData.java** file. The layout file **activity_add_to_database.xml** is structured as follows:

```
<?xml version="1.0" encoding="utf-8"?>
<LinearLayout

xmlns:android="http://schemas.android.com/apk/res/android"
    xmlns:tools="http://schemas.android.com/tools"
    android:layout_width="match_parent"
    android:layout_height="match_parent"
    android:orientation="vertical"
    tools:context=".Add">
    <TextView
        android:id="@+id/t1"
        android:layout_width="match_parent"
        android:layout_height="wrap_content"
        android:textSize="25sp"
        android:layout_gravity="center_horizontal"
        android:text="@string/t1"/>
    <Button
        android:layout_width="wrap_content"
        android:layout_height="wrap_content"
        android:layout_marginTop="10dp"
        android:textSize="25sp"
        android:layout_gravity="center_horizontal"
        android:text="@string/button2"
        android:onClick="write"/>
    <Button
        android:layout_width="wrap_content"
        android:layout_height="wrap_content"
        android:text="@string/button1"
        android:layout_marginTop="10dp"
        android:textSize="25sp"
        android:layout_gravity="center_horizontal"
        android:onClick="enter"/>
</LinearLayout>
```

Listing 5.276 Layout code for activity_add_to_database.xml

There is one last **class** left to discuss. It is launched when we want to display the data stored in the database. The code for the **DisplayData.java** activity is as follows:

```
package example.app42c;

import androidx.appcompat.app.AppCompatActivity;
import android.annotation.SuppressLint;
import android.content.Intent;
import android.database.Cursor;
import android.os.Bundle;
import android.view.View;
import android.widget.TextView;

public class WriteData extends AppCompatActivity {
    Assistant asistant = new Assistant(this);
    @SuppressLint("SetTextI18n")
    @Override
    protected void onCreate(Bundle savedInstanceState) {
        super.onCreate(savedInstanceState);
        setContentView(R.layout.activity_write_data);
        TextView tekst = findViewById(R.id.t1);
        Cursor c = asistant.write_all();
        while (c.moveToNext()) {
            int id = c.getInt(0);
            String name2 = c.getString(1);
            String last_name2 = c.getString(2);
            String class2 = c.getString(3);
tekst.setText(tekst.getText() + "\n" + id + ". " + name2 +
" " + last_name2 + " " + class2);
        }
    }
    public void enter(View view) {
        startActivity(new Intent(this, EnterData.class));
    }
    public void back(View view) {
  startActivity(new Intent(this, MainActivity.class));
    }
}
```

Listing 5.277 DisplayData Activity

In this class, we use the exact same **loop** as in the previous exercise. Its purpose is to retrieve data from the database – line by line – using a cursor. The retrieved information is then converted into a string using **setText**. After displaying the data, a button appears that allows the user to return to the form and enter another person into the database. To ensure the application works correctly, we will also need the **strings.xml** file.

```
<resources>
    <string name="app_name">Application42c</string>
    <string name="button1">Enter the data</string>
    <string name="button2">Write the data</string>
    <string name="button3">Enter another person</string>
    <string name="button4">Back to start</string>
    <string name="hint1">Enter name</string>
    <string name="hint2">Enter last name</string>
    <string name="hint3">Enter class</string>
    <string name="t1">The data has been added to the
database</string>
<string name="t2">- - - - - Welcome in the database - - - -
\n- - - - - What do you want to do? - - - - -</string>
</resources>
```

Listing 5.278 Strings.xml file

The example discussed is highly simplified. It was presented to illustrate how the database mechanism works. The individual classes and database operations could be moved into a simple menu such as a **navigation drawer**. This would make the database more functional and certainly more professional in appearance. Additionally, search and filter forms could be added to the database to enhance its usability.

5.22 Displaying the application on devices with different screen sizes

Mobile applications are currently very popular. We have dozens of them installed on our smartphones. However, phones are not the only devices that allow app installation.

Applications can also be installed and run on tablets. As we know, these devices have much larger screens than mobile phones, which allows for better layout possibilities.

Mobile apps can be developed simultaneously for both smaller and larger screens. The next application will demonstrate the simplest way to achieve this. The application code and the resources needed to create it are located in a folder named **Application43**.

Let's start by installing the appropriate emulator. In addition to the smartphone emulator already available, we need to install an emulator that simulates a tablet. The installation of a new virtual device was discussed in previous chapters.

Once we have the appropriate emulator, we can begin testing our applications on a device with a larger display. We'll start by creating a simple layout that includes several views.

```
<?xml version="1.0" encoding="utf-8"?>
<LinearLayout

xmlns:android="http://schemas.android.com/apk/res/android"
    xmlns:tools="http://schemas.android.com/tools"
    android:layout_width="wrap_content"
    android:layout_height="wrap_content"
    android:orientation="vertical"
    tools:context=".MainActivity">
    <TextView
        android:layout_width="wrap_content"
        android:layout_height="wrap_content"
        android:text="@string/t1"
        android:textSize="30sp"/>
    <ImageView
        android:layout_width="wrap_content"
        android:layout_height="300dp"
        android:scaleType="center"
        android:id="@+id/pic1"
        android:src="@drawable/pic1"/>
    <ImageView
        android:layout_width="wrap_content"
        android:layout_height="300dp"
        android:scaleType="center"
        android:id="@+id/pic2"
        android:src="@drawable/pic2"/>
    <Button
        android:layout_width="wrap_content"
        android:layout_height="wrap_content"
        android:text="@string/btn"/>
</LinearLayout>
```

Listing 5.279 Layout code for activity_main.xml

In the layout, we create:

- A **TextView** with text displayed using a font size of 30sp
- **Two ImageView widgets**, each with a width set to wrap_content and height set to 300dp
- A simple Button

When the application is launched on a smartphone, it looks as follows:

Figure 5.142 Layout as seen on a smartphone device

When we run the application on a larger device, it will appear as illustrated in the image below.

Figure 5.143 Layout on a larger device: Tablet

On a large device, the application looks essentially the same as it does on a smaller one. The elements are arranged in the same layout and do not look very good. There is a lot of unused space in the app that could be better utilized. To create a different layout for larger screens, we need to redefine the **main_activity.xml** file. However, before we begin, we must add an additional layout file specifically for large devices. In the app's resources, we create an additional directory and name it **layout-large**.

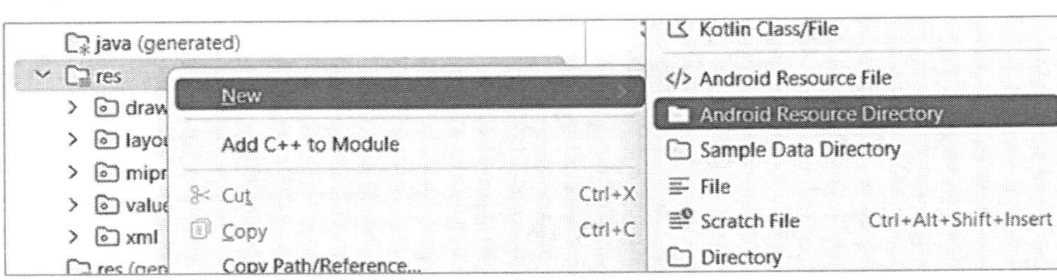

Figure 5.144 Creating a new directory

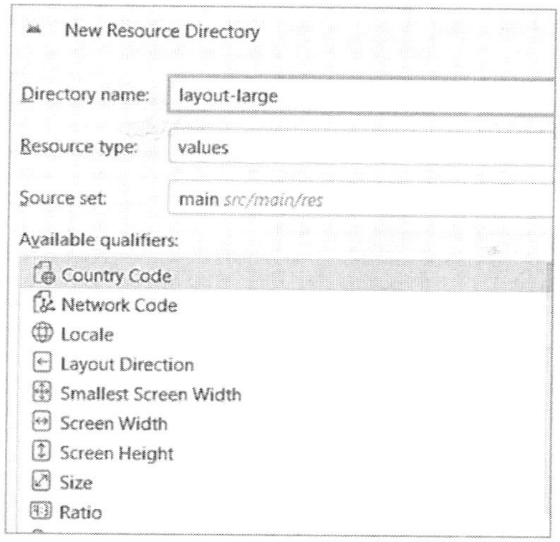

Figure 5.145 Creating the layout-large directory to store layouts for devices with larger screens.

After creating the directory, it may not be immediately visible in the application tree. To view it, go to the **Project** tab.

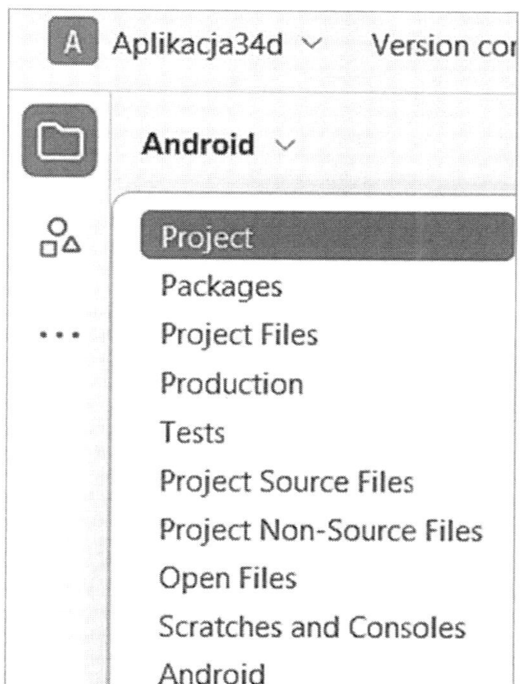

Figure 5.146: Project tab in the project tree

Expand the following branches in order: **app** → **src** → **main** →→ **res**. At this point, you should see the newly created directory. The folder will appear empty, as indicated by the absence of an arrow to expand it.

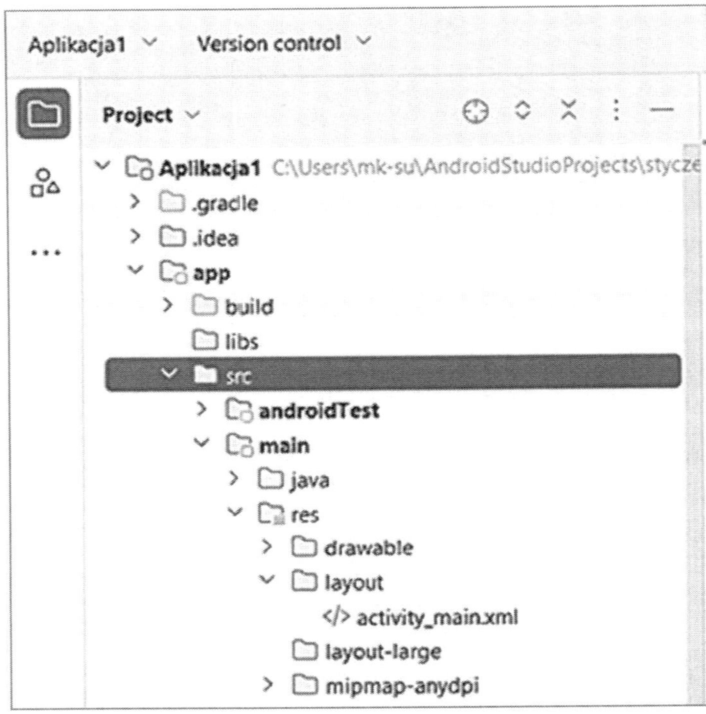

Figure 5.147 The layout-large directory visible in the project tree

In this directory, we place a copy of the **activity_main.xml** file from the **layout** folder. Now, both files will be available in the application tree.

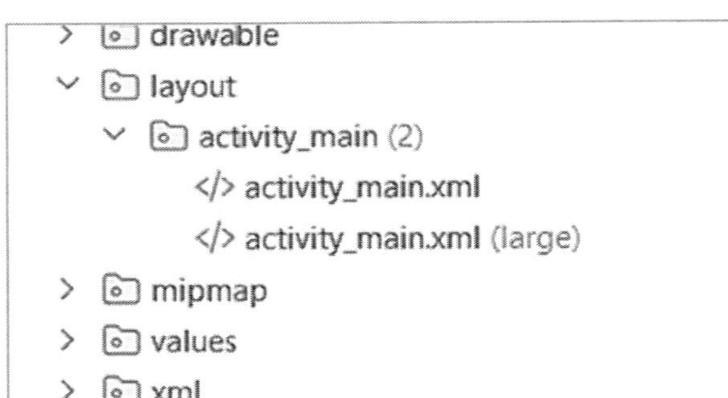

Figure 5.148: Files activity_main.xml and activity_main.xml with the large option in the project tree

After opening the file, we see that it is the same as before, and when launched on a tablet, nothing changes. The layout file can be freely edited and adapted to better suit a large screen.

When we look at the tabs in the project, we can clearly see which **activity_main.xml** file defines the layout for smaller screens and which one is used for larger screens.

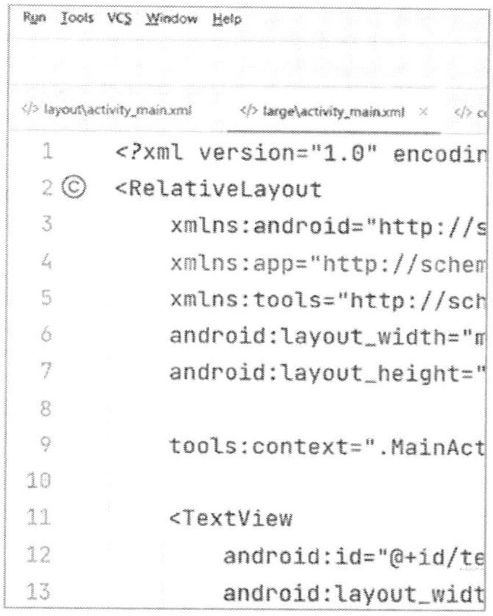

Figure 5.149: Files activity_main.xml and activity_main.xml (large version) as tabs in the project

To start, we'll change the font size of the text to **50sp** and set the text color to **red**. Then, we'll run the application and check whether the changes have taken effect.

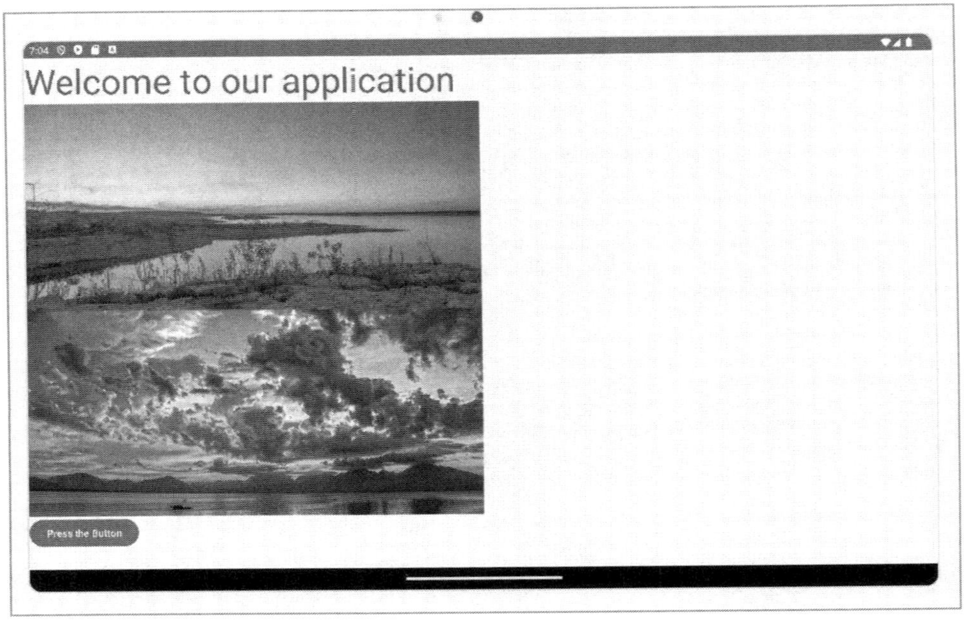

Figure 5.150 Application on a large screen after modifying parameters in the activity_main.xml file (large version)

As shown in the illustration, the font color and size have changed. In the version of the app running on a smartphone, the **TextView** settings remain the same as before. We edit the **activity_main.xml** file for large screens. The layout code will look as follows:

```
<?xml version="1.0" encoding="utf-8"?>
<RelativeLayout
 xmlns:android="http://schemas.android.com/apk/res/android"
    xmlns:app="http://schemas.android.com/apk/res-auto"
    xmlns:tools="http://schemas.android.com/tools"
    android:layout_width="match_parent"
    android:layout_height="match_parent"
    tools:context=".MainActivity">

    <TextView
        android:id="@+id/t1"
        android:layout_width="wrap_content"
        android:layout_height="wrap_content"
        android:layout_centerHorizontal="true"
        android:text="@string/t1"
        android:layout_alignParentTop="true"
        android:textColor="@color/red"
        android:textSize="50sp"/>
    <ImageView
        android:layout_marginTop="100dp"
        android:layout_width="wrap_content"
        android:layout_height="wrap_content"
        android:id="@+id/pic1"
        android:src="@drawable/pic1"
        android:layout_below="@id/t1"
        android:layout_alignParentTop="true"/>
    <ImageView
        android:layout_marginTop="100dp"
        android:layout_width="wrap_content"
        android:layout_height="wrap_content"
        android:layout_centerHorizontal="true"
        android:layout_toRightOf="@id/pic1"
        android:id="@+id/pic2"
        android:src="@drawable/pic2"/>
    <Button
        android:layout_width="wrap_content"
        android:layout_height="wrap_content"
        android:text="@string/btn"
        android:textSize="35dp"
        android:layout_alignParentBottom="true"/>
</RelativeLayout>
```

Listing 5.280 Code of the activity_main.xml/large layout

After the changes are made, the application will look as follows:

Figure 5.151 Application with a modified layout designed for devices with larger screens

5.23 Preparing the application for publication on the Google Play Store

Once our application is ready, we have the opportunity to share it with others. For applications intended for phones running the Android operating system, the appropriate place is the **Google Play Store.**

Before we can submit the application for publication, we need to prepare it properly. The application should be optimized accordingly. We remove unused **classes** and **methods** from the code. It's also important for the code to be properly compressed. Tools available on the market, such as **R8** or **ProGuard**, can help with this. We set appropriate access permissions so that users cannot, for example, excessively modify the database structure.

Next, we handle all multimedia files. In the case of images, we need to ensure appropriate sizes. It's worth testing the application's performance on various screen sizes.

The application should look flawless on every device it runs on. It's also worth checking its performance across different API levels. Music and video files should be properly compressed. The application should be as lightweight as possible, meaning the **code should be optimized**.

When publishing the app, you need to include a description. It's a good idea to be prepared and have the publication text ready at the time of release. Once all the above steps are completed and the application is ready to be shared with internet users, you need to prepare the appropriate installation file.

Android Studio allows you to generate a signed **APK** or **bundle** file. As for the format choice, **APK** is considered outdated, and the best solution is to create a **bundle** file. To generate the appropriate file, go to the **Build** tab and select **Generate Signed Bundle / APK**.

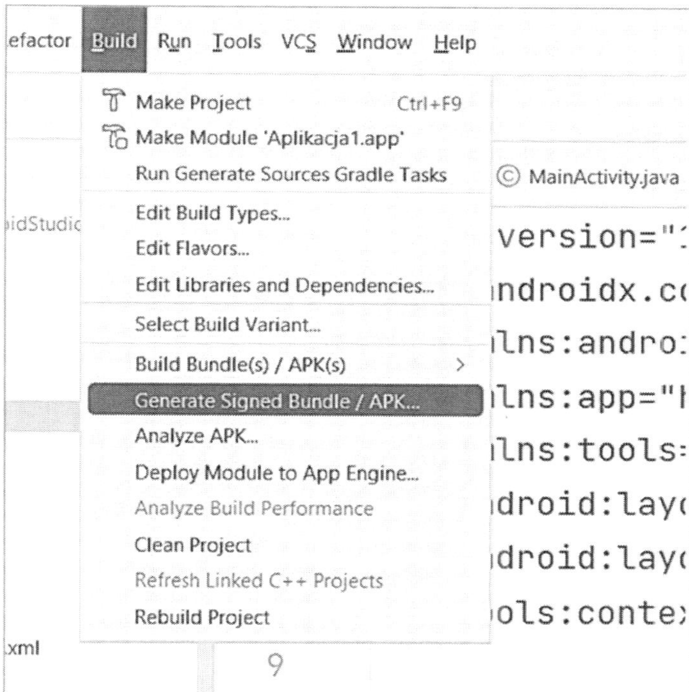

Figure 5.1526 Generating a Bundle File

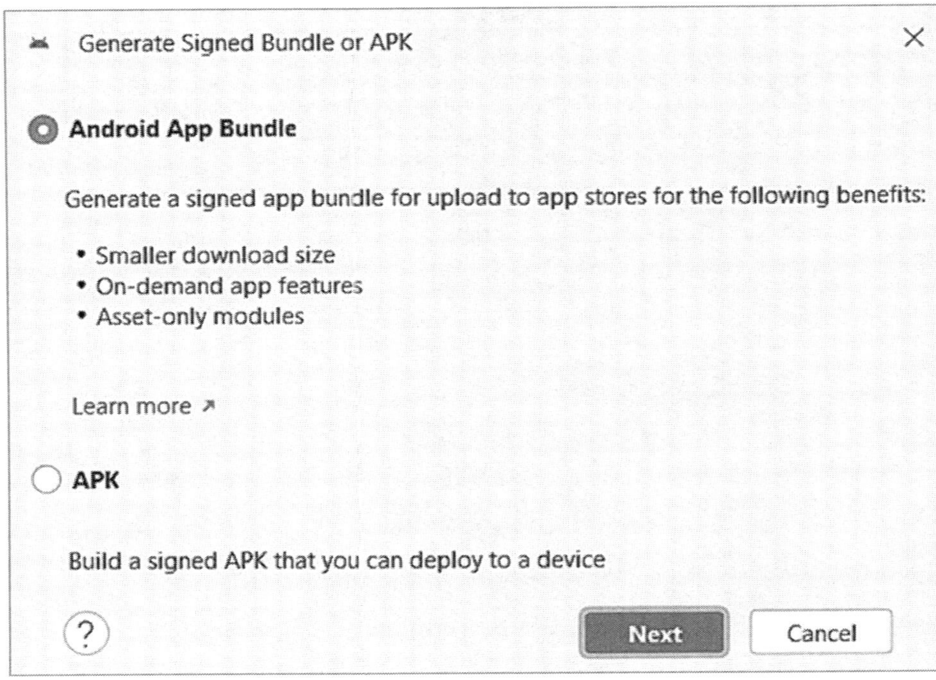

Figure 5.1537 Generating a Signature for the Bundle File

In the window that appears, select the **Android App Bundle** option and click **Next**. In the next step, you need to create a so-called **key**. Click **Create New** and proceed to the next window.

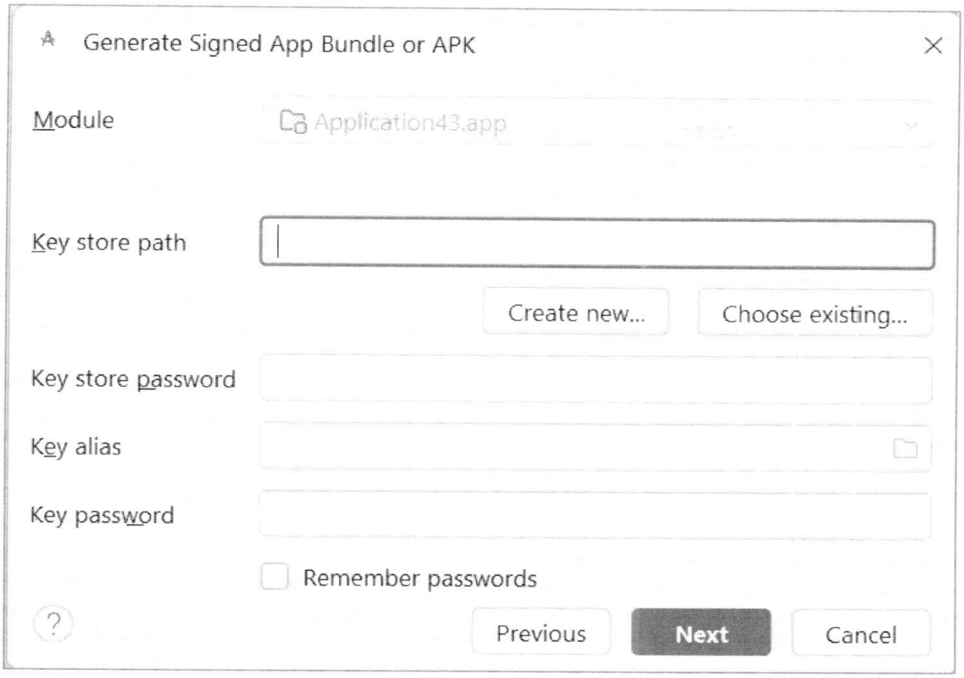

Figure 5.1548 Generating a Signature for the Bundle File – Form

Figure 5.1559 Creating a Key

Key store path – choose the directory where the key will be stored. Click the **Folder** icon. A new window will appear.

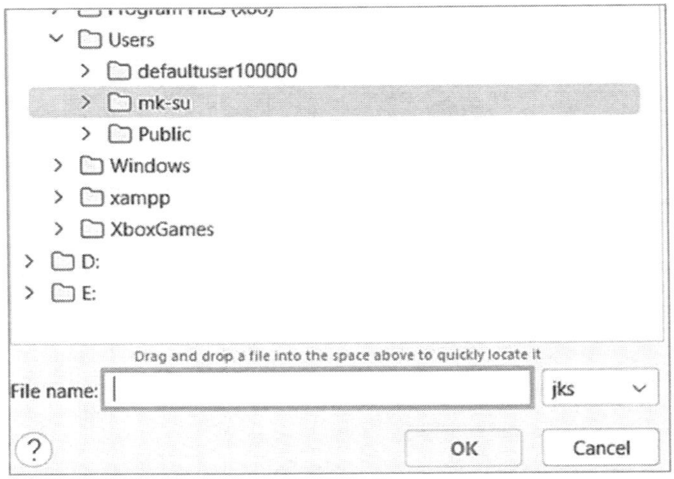

Figure 5.156 Directory Selection Window for Storing the Generated Key

Choose the **directory** where the **key** will be stored. At the bottom of the form, enter the name of the key, e.g., **key1**. After clicking **OK**, you'll return to the previous window and continue filling it out. **Password** – create a password, and in the **Confirm** field, repeat it. Enter the same password in the fields under the **Key** section.

Next, you need to fill in the developer's information: First and Last Name – your full name. Organizational Unit – your department or unit. Organization – your company or organization. City or Locality – your city. State or Province – your region (e.g., voivodeship). Country Code – your country code.

After filling in all the fields, click **OK.** You'll return to the first window, where you click **Next**. Choose the **folder** where the application file should be saved. Then select between the **debug** and **release** variant.

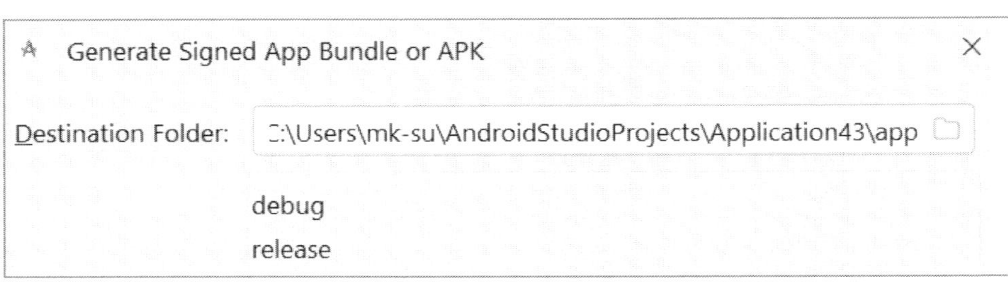

Figure 5.161 Build Variants Selection Window

If you want the application to be published on the **Play Store,** select the **release** option. Click the **Create** button.

Gradle will start building the file. Wait until the Gradle Build process is complete. A confirmation message will appear on the screen. In the window that pops up, click **Locate**. This will open the application directory where you'll find the installation file.

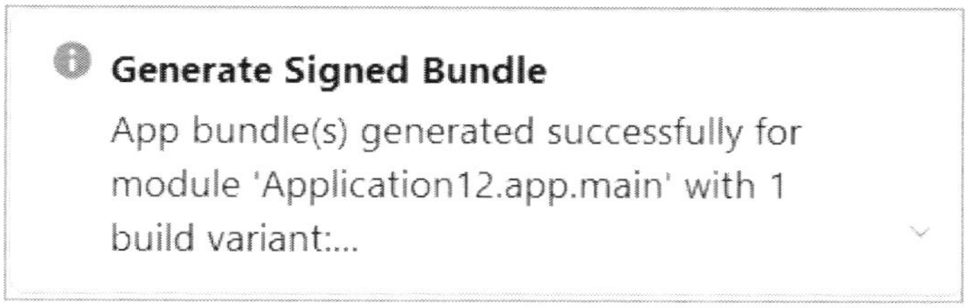

Figure 5.1572 Confirmation of Bundle File Creation

Figure 5.1583 Release Directory on the Computer's Disk

The file is located in the **release** directory.

Figure 5.1594 Bundle File on the Computer's Disk

To publish the application, you still need to create a developer account on **Google Play.** The cost of creating the account is **$25**. This is a one - time fee for setting up an account under which you can publish an unlimited number of applications.